A New Era in Focus Group Research

Rosaline S. Barbour • David L. Morgan
Editors

A New Era in Focus Group Research

Challenges, Innovation and Practice

Editors
Rosaline S. Barbour
WELS
The Open University
Milton Keynes, UK

David L. Morgan
Portland State University
Portland, USA

ISBN 978-1-137-58613-1   ISBN 978-1-137-58614-8 (eBook)
DOI 10.1057/978-1-137-58614-8

Library of Congress Control Number: 2017951104

© The Editor(s) (if applicable) and The Author(s) 2017
The author(s) has/have asserted their right(s) to be identified as the author(s) of this work in accordance with the Copyright, Designs and Patents Act 1988.
This work is subject to copyright. All rights are solely and exclusively licensed by the Publisher, whether the whole or part of the material is concerned, specifically the rights of translation, reprinting, reuse of illustrations, recitation, broadcasting, reproduction on microfilms or in any other physical way, and transmission or information storage and retrieval, electronic adaptation, computer software, or by similar or dissimilar methodology now known or hereafter developed.
The use of general descriptive names, registered names, trademarks, service marks, etc. in this publication does not imply, even in the absence of a specific statement, that such names are exempt from the relevant protective laws and regulations and therefore free for general use.
The publisher, the authors and the editors are safe to assume that the advice and information in this book are believed to be true and accurate at the date of publication. Neither the publisher nor the authors or the editors give a warranty, express or implied, with respect to the material contained herein or for any errors or omissions that may have been made. The publisher remains neutral with regard to jurisdictional claims in published maps and institutional affiliations.

Cover illustration © Tom Merton/Getty

Printed on acid-free paper

This Palgrave Macmillan imprint is published by Springer Nature
The registered company is Macmillan Publishers Ltd.
The registered company address is: The Campus, 4 Crinan Street, London, N1 9XW, United Kingdom

For Mike and Alasdair
&
For Susan

Contents

1. Setting the Scene for a New Era of Focus Group Research 1
   Rosaline S. Barbour

Section I Using Focus Groups in New Settings

2. Outsiders on the Inside: Focus Group Research with Elite Youth Footballers 17
   Chris Platts and Andy Smith

3. Reflections on Outsourcing and Applying for Funding 35
   Laurence Kohn and Wendy Christiaens

4. Cross-Cultural Focus Group Discussions 59
   Monique M. Hennink

5. Exploring Sex, HIV and 'Sensitive' Space(s) Among Sexual and Gender Minority Young Adults in Thailand 83
   Peter A. Newman, Suchon Tepjan and Clara Rubincam

Section II Capitalizing on Focus Groups in Mixed Methods Contexts

6 Use of Focus Groups in Developing Behavioural mHealth Interventions: A Critical Review   109
Helen Eborall and Katie Morton

7 The Use of Focus Groups in Programme Evaluation: Experience Based on the Project P.A.T.H.S. in a Chinese Context   129
Daniel T. L. Shek

8 Focus Groups in Triangulation Contexts   155
Sabine Caillaud and Uwe Flick

9 Hybrid Focus Groups as a Means to Investigate Practical Reasoning, Learning Processes and Indigenous Activities   179
Ana Prades, Josep Espluga and Tom Horlick-Jones

Section III Innovations in Focus Group Facilitation

10 The Use of Video Recording in Longitudinal Focus Group Research   207
Claire Thompson, Daniel J Lewis and Stephanie J C Taylor

11 Best Practices for Synchronous Online Focus Groups   227
Bojana Lobe

12 Performance-Based Focus Groups   251
Jennifer Wooten

13 Collective Production of Discourse: An Approach Based on the Qualitative School of Madrid   277
Jorge Ruiz Ruiz

Section IV   Theoretical Developments

14   A Kaleidoscope of Voices: Using Focus Groups
     in a Study of Rural Adolescent Girls   303
     Erin E. Seaton

15   Bringing Socio-Narratology and Visual Methods
     to Focus Group Research   325
     Cassandra Phoenix, Noreen Orr and Meridith Griffin

16   Focus Groups as Anticipatory Methodology:
     A Contribution from Science and Technology
     Studies Towards Socially Resilient Governance   343
     Phil Macnaghten

17   Using Focus Groups to Study the Process of (de)
     Politicization   365
     Sophie Duchesne

18   Practice Theoretically Inspired Focus Groups:
     Socially Recognizable Performativity?   389
     Bente Halkier

19   Conclusions: A Call for Further Innovations
     in Focus Groups   411
     David L. Morgan

Index   421

List of Figures

Fig. 4.1	Framework for conducting cross-cultural focus group research	64
Fig. 6.1	Exemplar messages used in the pre-testing phase of the PROPELS development	121
Fig. 8.1	Social representations of ecology	165
Fig. 9.1	Research design in the 'railway safety' case study	182
Fig. 9.2	Research design for the 'social perception on fusion energy' case study	184
Fig. 9.3	Policy issues and meetings of the whole PACHELBEL project	188
Fig. 9.4	STAVE process in Metafpercom project	191
Fig. 9.5	Example of questions used to develop a 'narrative' about a socially controversial issue based on metaphors	192
Fig. 9.6	The structure of the STAVE citizen process	194
Fig. 10.1	Slides from the reflexive video tool. A series of clips of participant interactions and utterances followed each of these slides. We used each of these clusters of themed clips to prompt discussion and reflection	219

List of Tables

Table 3.1	Description of six projects using focus groups in KCE studies (2010–2015)	41
Table 3.2	Complementarity between academic and non-academic teams	51
Table 7.1	Details of focus groups with programme participants and implementers	134
Table 7.2	Topic/question guide for focus groups	137
Table 7.3	Categorization of programme descriptors used by focus group participants	142
Table 7.4	Metaphors used by focus group participants to describe the programme	144
Table 7.5	Categorization of responses on the perceived benefits for programme participants	145
Table 7.6	Reliability of coding across years	147
Table 7.7	A summary of the major evaluation findings of the Project P.A.T.H.S.	149
Table 11.1	Comparison of various online groups according to social context cues	239

1

Setting the Scene for a New Era of Focus Group Research

Rosaline S. Barbour

Introduction

The appearance of this edited collection testifies to the ascendance of focus groups as an established method and to the variety of usages involved. No longer do social science researchers struggle to justify their choice of focus groups to ethics committees, collaborators or funding bodies, as the method has now undeniably entered the mainstream. However, with this new – and sometimes hard-won – acceptability come particular challenges: some of these are new, as researchers bring focus groups to bear in a new disciplinary context or when they use them to explore a fresh research topic; others are perennial, although some of the contributors to this volume suggest fresh approaches to addressing these. Many of the more creative developments that have occurred have not, so far, reached the wider audience they deserve.

R.S. Barbour (✉)
WELS, The Open University, Milton Keynes, UK
e-mail: rose.barbour@open.ac.uk

© The Author(s) 2017
R.S. Barbour, D.L. Morgan (eds.), *A New Era in Focus Group Research*, DOI 10.1057/978-1-137-58614-8_1

This book aims to redress the balance, by showcasing new usages and developments in focus group research across a range of substantive topic areas, disciplines, cultural, and theoretical contexts. It also aims to illuminate the challenges and possibilities involved in designing, carrying out, analyzing, and utilizing focus group research, recognizing the tensions between different research traditions, disciplinary emphases, funding climates, cultural and political constraints, and the ever-changing policy backdrop.

This collection seeks to cover a broad spectrum of focus group usages and associated challenges, together with their potential benefits. Drawing out differences – and, sometimes, instructive parallels – it spans focus group research in the disparate fields of sports science; health services research; sexual health; education; youth work; and political science. It explores issues including public opinion, environmental issues, sustainability and climate change. Orientations range from more traditional usages (e.g. in order to gauge participants' views) to approaches that take a more participatory – even politicized – approach to the collective production of discourse. Thus, it encompasses focus group research ranging from applied to more theoretically focused applications, macro- and micro-approaches, and, importantly, the embedding of focus groups in mixed methods designs. Some of the work showcased here involves stand-alone focus group studies, while other researchers have used focus groups alongside other methods – whether qualitative or quantitative. While some focus group teams are closely aligned along disciplinary and theoretical lines, others involve inter-disciplinary collaborations. Not surprisingly, these different situations give rise to varying opportunities for innovation – both in relation to enhancing data generation and informing data analysis.

Rather than presenting a consensus statement, the collection, in line with the reflective and reflexive potential of focus groups, themselves, seeks to highlight and debate differences of opinion and practice between contributors, thus laying the ground for future developments and further innovation.

Outline of the Book

The contributions are divided into four sections:

Section I – Using Focus Groups in New Settings
Section II – Capitalizing on Focus Groups in Mixed Methods Contexts
Section III – Innovations in Focus Group Facilitation
Section IV – Theoretical Developments

Researchers new to focus groups, or those seeking to use focus groups in uncharted topic areas, are likely to benefit from a close reading of the chapters in **Section I**, while, for more seasoned focus group researchers, these contributions may serve mainly as a concise reminder of the issues they need to address in setting up fresh projects. **Section II** is concerned with focus group research within mixed methods designs. It offers guidance for both novice and experienced focus group researchers, who may find themselves tasked with working with a new set of collaborators with different assumptions, expectations and working practices. Many funding bodies currently emphasize the importance of mixed methods and inter-disciplinary collaborations, rendering such insights relevant for increasing numbers of researchers. **Section III** (on innovations in facilitation) and **Section IV** (on theoretical developments) aim to showcase 'state-of-the-art' focus group applications and are likely to be of most immediate interest to those already conversant with, and enthused by, focus group research. However, novice researchers may also benefit from dipping into these chapters and extracting some ideas useful for their own projects, while reserving a repeat, but more nuanced, reading for a later stage in their focus group career.

Section I – Using Focus Groups in New Settings

This section begins with **Platts & Smith** (Chapter 2) reflecting on their experience of using focus groups – a relatively new method in the field of sports science – in order to study the closed world of professional football. They outline some of the logistical challenges they faced and the ever-present need to negotiate power relationships; not just with regard to gaining access, but as something they had to address throughout the whole research process. Opting to use pre-existing – or pre-acquainted (Bloor et al. 2001) – groups, the researchers were able to elicit data that illuminated the processes of interaction and negotiation between young players, as they engaged in 'face work' through 'focused encounters' which afforded a unique window on their co-construction of meaning.

Much of the discussion that has, to date, taken place surrounding the use of focus groups has privileged the project-specific detail – whether this relates to technical/procedural aspects or to theoretical approaches to interpreting/analyzing data. However, it is also important to consider the broader context in which focus group research is carried out – including the funding climate. **Kohn & Christiaens** (Chapter 3) provide insights into the world of commissioning, drawing on real world examples of qualitative research, that has used focus groups, when responding to calls from a government agency. They critically examine their experience with six projects, in order to tease out the strengths and weaknesses of academic teams as compared with private sector research teams. While methodological skills are not sufficient in order to deliver a successful project, private sector teams tend to be more flexible and better equipped to produce work within tight timescales. Although academic teams generally produce work of a high scientific quality, they view their work for specific research calls as an opportunity to further their own interests and agenda and are less likely to write succinct reports that are tailored to address commissioners' requirements. These are issues that are not usually discussed within academic circles, perhaps due to the fierce competition for research grants. However, some important lessons for focus group researchers can be drawn from this chapter.

Using focus groups in cross-cultural research is the topic of the next contribution from **Hennink** (Chapter 4), who offers advice on delivering such projects while satisfying the often-competing demands of flexibility, cultural sensitivity and rigour. She argues that, although there are overarching theoretical principles that govern focus group research, field application can – and, indeed, should – vary from project to project. Hennink stresses the importance of remaining alert, throughout the process, to cultural norms and values and the need to cultivate a willingness on the part of the researcher/research team to adapt their research design and approach to generating data, in order to ensure that it is relevant, acceptable, and appropriate for the groups involved in the study. This chapter raises specific issues relevant to cross-cultural applications, but also highlights some perennial challenges involved in designing focus group studies, generating and analyzing data, while engaging meaningfully with participants in, and audiences for, our research.

Some focus group applications may give rise to specific constellations of challenges, as research designs are developed and implemented in the complexity that characterizes the social world. **Newman, Tepjan & Rubincam** (Chapter 5) reflect on the multiple challenges that they faced in their mixed methods study of a sensitive topic (the introduction of a rectal application with the purpose of reducing risk of HIV) with 'hard-to-reach' participants (men who have sex with men (MSMs)) in the cross-cultural context of Thailand – a Buddhist country, where focus groups were originally viewed suspiciously by the funding body. While insider knowledge and collaboration with trusted community-based organizations were key components for successful recruitment, the authors acknowledge that professionals occupy a very different subject position to that of research participants, and that more egalitarian relationships require a considerable amount of work. The researchers had to be flexible throughout, relying particularly on their facilitation skills, to encourage and also to temper disclosure in focus group sessions. This project also provides an exemplar of the use of focus group data in order to inform domains for use in a survey and to guide decisions with regard to a choice experiment – both challenging tasks for qualitative researchers.

Section II – Capitalizing on Focus Groups in Mixed Methods Contexts

This next section develops the theme of mixed methods applications. Focus groups have been embraced, in particular, by health services researchers and medical sociologists (Barbour 2007; 2017 in press).

Given recent funding developments and priorities, many such researchers now find themselves working as part of multi-disciplinary teams, comprising medical researchers from various specialties and a wide variety of health professionals (such as nurses, dieticians and physiotherapists), as well as health psychologists, economists and statisticians, engaged in work under the broad remit of complex interventions. **Eborall & Morton** (Chapter 6) report on their focus group work as part of an mHealth (i.e. using mobile technology) project for people with pre-diabetes. Qualitative methods are a well-accepted aspect of such work, with a range of guidelines available, including those that are overtly user-centred. The Medical Research Council (MRC) framework envisages the process as involving a cycle, comprising development, feasibility testing, implementation and evaluation. However, focus groups are most frequently used in the development phase (where they can, of course, be valuable in generating possible solutions). Eborall & Morton argue that such mixed methods research may not be using focus groups to their full potential, since they could, for example, afford useful insights if carried out prior to writing grant proposals and could also contribute meaningfully to ongoing review and modification of interventions. This mirrors, to a degree, the history of mixed methods research more generally, with qualitative methods – and particularly focus groups -often being confined to the initial phase; whereas more imaginative approaches could yield dividends (Barbour 1999).

Shek (Chapter 7) provides an account of his use of focus groups within the field of youth development programme evaluation. This involved a longitudinal, 5-year study, which looked at the experience, not just of programme recipients, but also that of programme implementers. It was also unusual in that it employed random sampling in order to convene a large number of focus groups. This led to the somewhat more controversial step of translating qualitative data in order to render it amenable to quantitative analysis – and it is this aspect that leads Shek to describe this as a mixed methods study. Also of note is the role of metaphors (more commonly used in in-depth small-scale qualitative studies) in illuminating responses to the programme.

Critically examining the practice of triangulation, **Caillaud & Flick** (Chapter 8) stress the importance of taking a reflexive approach to research design and recommend that researchers take account of the particular properties of focus groups, when seeking to combine these with other methods. They illustrate how combining focus groups with one-to-one interviews provided new insights that would otherwise not have surfaced. These involved, respectively, highlighting the normative function of knowledge about climate change, and the ways in which ecological practices were legitimated in public and in private. Thus, rather than seeking to achieve corroboration, different methods provide parallel – and potentially valuable – insights (Barbour 2014a). This constitutes an analytic resource rather than a problem – as Morgan (1993) argues: '... if research finds differences between the results from individual and group interviews, then the methodological goal should be to understand the *sources* of these differences' (1993, p. 232; my emphasis).

Prades, Espluga & Horlick-Jones (Chapter 9) are also enthusiastic about the capacity of focus groups to afford privileged access to features of social life that are otherwise hard to capture. They used re-convened focus groups to uncover patterns of practical reasoning of lay citizens with regard to diverse topics (genetically modified crops; railway safety decision-making; fusion energy) and also included policymakers in order to shed light on how they draw on knowledge and to make linkages between policymaking and everyday worlds. Crucially, the reflective spaces between re-convened focus groups allowed participants to further develop their ideas and enabled researchers to develop fresh, responsive materials, such as a simulated newspaper article and an oral mapping exercise.

Rather than adopting a 'one-size fits-all' template, all of the authors writing here acknowledge the importance of 'translating' focus groups in order to meet the needs of a specific project (Morgan and Bottoroff 2010). This also means that researchers have to 'think on their feet', constantly reviewing the research design and remaining amenable to tweaking this should the need arise.

Section III – Innovations in Focus Group Facilitation

'Thinking on their feet' in this way, the researchers whose work is represented in this section have all sought to use innovative methods in order to elicit focus group data. In the context of a study of neighbourhood regeneration in the wake of the London 2012 Olympic Games, **Thompson, Lewis & Taylor** (Chapter 10) used visual methods longitudinally within a participatory framework, in order to explore the unfolding perceptions of secondary school-aged children. In common with Prades et al., they wanted to involve their research participants as producers of knowledge. This formed part of a much larger study, but the researchers were, nevertheless, able to be flexible with regard to choosing their methodological approach, which led them to adopt visual methods in a spirit of experimentation and risk-taking. The gambit of setting up a room as a mock television studio proved to be popular with children and elicited impassioned and opinionated narratives. The longitudinal design allowed for repeat sessions, using clips from the original filming in order to encourage reflection, commentary on past narratives, and the creation of new and potentially more complex accounts.

Lobe (Chapter 11) outlines the possibilities afforded by synchronous online focus groups, comparing their advantages and disadvantages with face-to-face and asynchronous online focus groups. Issues such as the lack of social context cues and the limits of online video are highlighted, but Lobe argues that, amongst the advantages, is the greater scope for sample selection and, hence, coverage of various constituencies. She reflects on the skills that moderators and participants require and advocates using smaller groups than would generally be the case for face-to-face focus groups. This chapter also provides advice on technical specifications and requirements and considers, in depth, the ethical issues raised by synchronous focus groups, while acknowledging that many such issues are also present with regard to more conventional focus group formats.

Performativity is taken to a new level by **Wooten** (Chapter 12) who advocates using performance-based focus groups (PBFGs), involving physical engagement of participants' bodies. Focusing on the experience of non-native teachers of Spanish in US schools, these theatrical exercises and the incorporation of the body throughout the process of data generation afforded insights into the goals and desires of teachers. This innovative focus group format produced findings that could not have readily been gleaned using other, more conventional, methods of elicitation/facilitation. Of particular note is the role of the facilitator, or 'Joker', described here as being someone who questions, or 'problematizes' (Barbour 2007, 2017, in press) – which is also an approach that is of potential value in other settings. In the context of PBFG exercises, moreover, Wooten points out that this can be empowering for participants.

Ruiz (Chapter 13) is overtly concerned with the collective production of discourse and draws on the work of the Qualitative School of Madrid – to date little known outside the context of Spanish/Latin-American social researchers. He outlines the conditions for successful production of group discourse and is careful to distinguish this from the attempt to research agreement or consensus. Although this may be the outcome of discussion groups, Ruiz unpicks such apparent agreement, emphasizing that this can be relative, tacit or implicit, and highlights the importance of the facilitator's skills in provoking, encouraging, questioning, and analyzing collective discourse.

Section IV – Theoretical Developments

Contributors to this section demonstrate the added value of theoretically informed focus group usage and make a case for embedding such insights into practice in more traditional fields. Thus, they offer valuable suggestions as to how to address that gap between theory and practice, which is frequently bemoaned by commentators on both sides of the applied-theoretical divide.

Seaton (Chapter 14) also highlights the potentially transformative power of communal narratives of identity, elicited via focus group discussions. In this case, focus groups allowed rural adolescent girls, living in a tight-knit community, whose voices had previously been muted, to explore and consolidate their identities. Rather than viewing identity as the property of an individual, Seaton's work is underpinned by a relational framework and she examines the ways in which narrative identities were crafted and negotiated as a communal activity.

Again, using focus groups to elicit narratives, **Phoenix, Orr & Griffin** (Chapter 15) advocate a combination of visual methods and the underpinning framework afforded by socio-narrative/'socio-narratology' (Frank 2010). The empirical research on which this contribution is based looked at the perceptions of UK-based physically active older adults taking part in focus groups convened to cover different stages across the lifecourse. It critically examines the work done by stories – conveyed through visual stimuli, involving photography and film – on the collaborative production of discourse through 'narratives at work', imbued with stereotypes, contradictions, and reflexive commentaries.

Macnaghten (Chapter 16) demonstrates vividly the potential of focus groups as an 'anticipatory method', which, if used at an early stage in the consultation process, can make a significant contribution to public policy, affording valuable insights into the processes through which opinions are constructed, expressed and, subsequently, hardened into attitudes. Drawing on the experience of a range of projects, relating to new science and technology (agricultural biotechnology; climate geoengineering; fracking); and lay ethical engagement, this chapter also serves as an object lesson in taking on board many of the recommendations made by other contributors to this collection. Macnaghten and collaborators have, throughout all these projects, employed thoughtful approaches to sampling (based on prior knowledge, e.g. of participants' habits, practical interests and investment in the future – in terms of lifecourse stage). They have also developed responsive materials, recognizing the salience of how information and issues are 'framed' (Vliegenthart and van Zooten 2011), and have sought to use this as a resource, presenting participants with accounts, apparently offered by various interested parties - with different agendas. Along the way, this chapter also highlights illuminating cross-cultural comparisons. Focusing on discourses invoked, created, and challenged by participants (Barbour 2014b), in order to identify counter-narratives, the analysis

1 Setting the Scene for a New Era of Focus Group Research 11

identified, amongst other things, the conditionality of public acceptance - thereby making a convincing case for the use of focus groups as a form of 'upstream public engagement'.

Public engagement is also the focus for **Duchesne** (Chapter 17), but here the topic is de-politicization. In common with Macnaghten, this research sought to elicit responses from people who were not necessarily already conversant with the issues under discussion. In order to avoid the risk of exposing participants' lack of interest or of steering talk in a particular direction, Duchesne and colleagues chose not to disclose the central topic of their research, as, indeed, did Macnaghten. Instead, the focus groups were convened around the broader topic of European integration, which blurred the focus on the absence of politicization and which also avoided the difficulties inherent in seeking to address a negative concept. Again, this project necessitated some 'thinking on their feet' on the part of researchers, who opted for small groups and sampled to allow for comparison between participants in different countries, having varying social positions and levels of political activism. Their approach to generating data was developed afresh, using some of the principles of non-directive interviewing (but adapted to a group context) and data were elicited using a card exercise, with sessions being video-recorded.

Halkier (Chapter 18) revisits here the debate regarding the relative importance of content and form in relation to analyzing focus group data. She poses the question as to the extent to which patterns of expression produced in focus groups are culturally and socially recognizable in everyday life. At one end of the continuum are those who focus on the content of data, in order to argue that patterns uncovered in focus groups are, indeed, generalizable and, at the other end, are those who emphasize the uniquely situational character of exchanges that occur in such settings. Drawing on a practice theoretical perspective, Halkier contends that everyday life consists of a mixture of tacit and explicit elements and that it also involves performativity. Illustrating her argument with excerpts from her own work on contested food habits, she concludes that it is possible to occupy a middle position: that is, it is possible to use focus groups in order to identify patterns with regard to reasoning and behaviour, while, at the same time, acknowledging that these are situationally negotiated. Halkier then offers three strategies which should ensure that, while responses are actively constructed in the group setting, discussions are grounded in the everyday worlds of participants. These involve utilizing existing social networks; using common, even ubiquitous items as stimulus materials (in her case everyday food items); and including relevant media representations. While such choices are explicitly outlined by Halkier (and referred to by Duchesne and Macnaghten), such reasoning can be seen to implicitly underlie much of the practice that focus group researchers report – both in this volume and elsewhere.

The final chapter, from **David Morgan** (Chapter 19), makes a plea for further innovation in focus groups. He highlights the use of reconvened focus groups and suggests that these can be valuable, especially when researchers are investigating a topic to which participants have previously given little thought, and where discussion might develop as knowledge and engagement increase. Focus group researchers are also urged to consider convening very small or very large focus groups, both of which offer intriguing, but very different, possibilities. Re-examining the case for homogeneous focus groups, Morgan outlines some of the advantages afforded by heterogeneity, but stresses the importance for moderators of drawing out 'common ground' in order to facilitate discussion. Finally, he makes a plea – to which some contributors to this volume have already paid attention – for flexibility in research design. There is, then, considerable scope for further development, as focus groups continue to offer exciting possibilities and to pose new and engaging challenges. We look forward to seeing how future cohorts of focus group researchers employ and shape the method.

References

Barbour, R.S. (1999) 'The case for combining qualitative and quantitative approaches in health services research'. *Journal of Health Services Research and Policy*, 4(1): 39–43.
Barbour, R. (2007) *Doing Focus Groups*. London: Sage.
Barbour, R. (2007; 2017 2nd ed. in press) *Doing Focus Groups*. London: Sage.
Barbour, R. (2014a) *Introducing Qualitative Research; A Student's Guide* (2nd ed.). London: Sage.

Barbour, R.S. (2014b) 'Analyzing focus groups', In U. Flick (ed.), *The SAGE Handbook of Qualitative Data Analysis*. London: Sage, pp. 313–26.
Bloor, M., Frankland, J., Thomas, M., and Robson, K. (2001) *Focus Groups in Social Research*. London: Sage.
Frank, A.W. (2010) *Letting Stories Breathe: A Socio-Narratology*. Chicago: The University of Chicago Press.
Morgan, D.L. (1993) 'Future directions in focus group research', In D.L. Morgan (ed.), *Successful Focus Groups: Advancing the State of the Art*. Thousand Oaks, CA: Sage, pp. 225–44.
Morgan, D.L., and Bottoroff, J.L. (2010) 'Advancing our craft: Focus group methods and practice'. *Qualitative Health Research*, 20(5): 579–81.
Vliegenthart, R., and van Zooten, L. (2011) 'Power to the frame: Bringng sociology back to frame analysis'. *European Journal of Communication*, 26 (2): 101–15.

Rosaline S. Barbour is Emerita Professor at the Open University, UK, where she was previously Professor of Health and Social Care. A medical sociologist, Rose has carried out research across a range of substantive topics, including reproductive health care, HIV/AIDS, obesity and professional practice in social work, primary care and nursing. Her work is located at the intersection of the social and the clinical and is informed by a commitment to using and developing rigorous qualitative methods. She has been running qualitative research workshops for nearly 30 years, and, since retiring, has set up a company to offer bespoke workshops and training sessions (www.barbourworkshops.com). She has published widely in a range of health and social care and methodology journals and has contributed numerous book chapters. Rose co-edited *Developing Focus Groups: Politics, Theory and Practice* (1999) and is the author of *Doing Focus Groups* (2007; with 2nd edition in press); and *Introducing Qualitative Research: A Student's Guide* (2nd ed. 2014) – all published by Sage.

Section I

Using Focus Groups in New Settings

2

Outsiders on the Inside: Focus Group Research with Elite Youth Footballers

Chris Platts and Andy Smith

Introduction

For a global sport that receives significant social and cultural attention and invites much comment from fans, media, current and former players, and many other interested commentators, professional football (soccer) remains a largely under-researched area academically (Roderick 2006). Of the studies that do exist, many have investigated the provision of sports science support to players and several aspects of the clinical management of conditions which may limit performance (e.g. pain and injury). These investigations have most often been conducted by researchers with an interest in disciplines such as exercise physiology, psychology, biomechanics, coaching, nutrition

---

C. Platts
Sheffield Hallam University, Sheffield, UK
e-mail: c.platts@shu.ac.uk

A. Smith (✉)
Edge Hill University, Ormskirk, UK
e-mail: Andy.Smith@edgehill.ac.uk

© The Author(s) 2017
R.S. Barbour, D.L. Morgan (Eds.), *A New Era in Focus Group Research*, DOI 10.1057/978-1-137-58614-8_2

and strength and conditioning. Much less common are sociological investigations of players' experiences of working in professional football. Indeed, as Roderick and Gibbons (2015) have noted, accounts of the everyday realities of working in sports such as professional football are frequently absent from dominant portrayals of workers' lives, one consequence of which is the continued production of often one-sided, overly romanticized and glorified media-led presentations of the apparent luxuries of pursuing a career in professional football. Among other things, such one-sided views of professional players' lives are based upon a series of ideological assumptions which suggest that 'athletes must always strive to win and be successful, and that they must love their work and treat it as a privilege; they must realize, and not squander, their "God given" talents' (Roderick and Gibbons 2015: 153–54). This is especially true of younger players who seek to pursue a career in football and whose workplaces can be violent, highly authoritarian, insecure and untrustworthy underpinned by an almost constant fear of failure and punishment (Kelly and Waddington 2006; Roderick 2006).

Professional football is, thus, a notoriously difficult context for researchers to access, especially when studies investigate welfare-related issues that may produce findings which are politically uncomfortable and which may question the appropriateness of everyday practice. Brackenridge (2007), for example, noted that 'professional football clubs are often close-knit, very traditional, male-dominated environments characterized by "authoritarian leadership" and an 'almost collusive secrecy and suspicion of "outsiders"' (2007: 67). Reflecting upon the findings of research on the management of pain and injury in English professional football, Waddington (2014) also recalled the steps that were necessary in order to assure players of the anonymity of their interview responses – especially in environments where the revelation of 'insider' information to 'outsiders' is rarely welcome. Other studies of the working lives of current and former professional players (e.g. Roderick 2006, 2013), as well as aspiring young players[1] seeking entry into the apparently lucrative world of professional football

---

[1] Over the past 30 years or so, young footballers have been referred to using a range of labels including 'youth team players', 'scholars' and 'apprentices'. For ease of presentation, we shall refer to them here as 'players'.

(e.g. Parker 1996, 2000), have similarly identified the dilemmas and difficulties encountered by researchers undertaking sociological investigations in the generally closed social world of professional football.

These introductory remarks outline the context in which we conducted the research on which this chapter is based and which was, to our knowledge, the largest study of its kind since the publication in the mid-1990s of Parker's seminal ethnographic study of players' lives (Parker 1995, 1996, 2000). Our study involved the use of focus groups and a four-part self-completion questionnaire to investigate the working lives of 303 young elite male footballers (aged 16–18) who at the time (2008) worked in 21 professional football academies in England and Wales (Platts 2012). The questionnaires – which were conducted immediately preceding the focus groups – generated data on the types of activities players engaged in during their daily work, the amount of time they spent doing them and with whom they did them. Since young footballers are part of complex networks of social relations, focus groups were also used to identify patterns of behaviour which were not peculiar to a single individual player, but which were shared, to a greater or lesser degree, by groups of players who shared common situations. In this regard, focus groups – rather than individual interviews – were used to help replicate the collective social contexts in which players formed their impressions of their everyday experiences and illuminate processes of interaction and negotiation between them in their workplaces. In this chapter, we draw upon our experiences of conducting focus groups to examine: (i) how we negotiated access to our sample of clubs and players; (ii) how we elicited data from focus group participants, with a particular emphasis on encouraging them to share and compare experience as part of our concern with studying the co-construction of meaning; (iii) the implications of focus groups for players; and (iv) some of the disciplinary advantages conferred by focus groups held with players in the workplace.

Negotiating Access to Clubs and Players

Given the general distrust of the media, suspicion of outsiders (such as academic researchers) seeking to investigate workplace practices, and a reluctance to grant public access into highly privatized working environments, we anticipated, from the outset, many difficulties. These related to negotiating access into what are traditionally closed social worlds and in being able to speak with young players who – while not as high status as first team players – were, nevertheless, club employees over whom influential figures had significant control. There was also a possibility that, if granted access to club premises, we might encounter first team players and other high profile figures (such as managers and coaches) making our presence potentially problematic for insiders.

In the initial planning of our focus groups and the broader study of which they were a part, we spent a considerable amount of time reflecting upon some key questions. For example, would clubs want to be involved in the study? If they were, would key gatekeepers (e.g. Academy Directors/Managers, managers and coaches) allow the researchers to be left alone with the players? Would players be released for up to 2 hours to participate in the study? How could we convince the clubs that the research would be conducted ethically and that it would be of benefit to them and their players? How could we allay any suspicions they would have of us, as outsiders, whom they have never met personally? And how would we be able to convince them of the merits of our work, relative to the many other requests they receive from researchers, so that we could meet our objectives?

Heads of Academies occupied a significant position of power and, while they might have been willing to facilitate our research, they were also able to prevent us gaining access to clubs and conducting the study as we intended. Our initial strategy towards negotiating access to clubs and players – via the Academy Manager – thus sought to operate within, rather than work against, the rather unequal, largely hierarchical, structures of power and relational constraints that characterize the workplace of professional football (Brackenridge 2007; Parker 1996; Roderick 2006). As will become clear, this strategy worked well and proved an important first step in securing access to our focus group participants.

Altogether 21 clubs agreed to participate in our research. Despite the clubs' desire to take part in the research, it was not uncommon, however, to find that, upon contacting them by phone, they had not read the research brief, were rather unclear about what they had signed up to, or were rather vague regarding the time commitments being requested (especially for the focus groups). While partly frustrating, this process enabled us to better understand some of the more pragmatic reasons why clubs had provisionally agreed to participate in the study – reasons which we may have otherwise missed and which proved helpful in recruiting others clubs to the study. In particular, some gatekeepers explained that agreeing to participate would enable them to use our visit and the tasks (i.e. focus groups and other methods) we were proposing as part of Continuing Professional Development for staff, or as evidence for the education qualifications players were expected to undertake while pursuing their football career. Interestingly, given our focus on player education and welfare, none of the clubs explicitly stated the potential benefits of our research for them, and their players, as being amongst the reasons for granting us insider access to conduct our research! We shall return to the implications of this apparent insignificance of player education and welfare for our research later.

Eliciting Data

Context, Settings and 'Getting Onside'

Given the anticipatory anxiety we felt prior to negotiating access to clubs, we were also mindful of the possibility that previous (perceived and real) misrepresentations of clubs and players might have further fostered emotional hostility towards us once we were 'on-site' inside clubs. In practice, however, when we began planning the logistical matters of our research, the majority of clubs were accommodating both of us and the requests we made of them. In the main, the Head of Academies, Education and Welfare Officers and coaches whom we met ensured the research could take place by, amongst other things, altering schedules, providing access to rooms and equipment, and most important of all leaving us alone with the players to conduct our focus groups and other methods.

In total, 41 focus groups were conducted with between four and ten players at each of the 21 clubs. For the most part, two focus groups were held in each club: one with a group of first year players (aged 16 and 17) and one with players in the second year of their scholarship (aged 17 or 18).[2] In this regard, our sample of players – overall and in each focus group – was relatively homogenous, had experienced some 'particular concrete situation' (i.e., were seeking to secure a professional football contract) (Merton and Kendall 1946: 541), and, unlike many focus groups, consisted of 'groups in the sociological sense of having a common identity or continuing unity, shared norms, and goals' (Merton 1987: 555). The construction of our groups of participants in this way was intended to help encourage discussion about a range of topics and stimulate interaction amongst group members while discussions were taking place (Morgan 2010, 2012). It also enabled us to examine the different experiences recalled by players at varying stages in their careers as aspiring professionals, within and between clubs across the respective football leagues.

As Stewart and Shamdasani (2015: 97) have noted, the focus group research situation is 'a complex interaction of the purpose of the research, the composition of the group, and the physical setting in which the group takes place'. In our research, we were clear about its purpose, had a large measure of success in securing the appropriate composition of the intended sample, but had relatively little control over the physical setting in which to conduct the research, especially the focus groups. Given the importance of maximizing continuity in the social settings of focus group discussions, we ideally wanted to conduct them in similar settings across clubs. This, however, proved impossible and we were required to be completely flexible – and above all agreeable – when accepting the locations in which to hold the discussions with players. Some focus groups were held at the club's home ground, others at their training ground. In both settings, the availability of space varied considerably and so the focus groups were held in changing rooms, canteens, classrooms, boardrooms, hospitality lounges and a physiotherapy room. We were also required to be flexible with the timing of our

---

[2] Although it was intended that two focus groups would be held at each club, in two clubs (1 Championship; 1 League Two) players in their first year were unavailable to participate in the study, and in one Premier League club the unusually high number of players meant that three focus groups were organized over two separate visits to the club.

discussions with players for, in many clubs, it was often the case that the pre-agreed time for the research was changed upon our arrival for reasons outside of our control and sometimes that of the club gatekeeper. At one club, the players were detained at the training ground by the first-team coach for an extra 3 hours as (a somewhat curious) punishment for the club's first team losing the previous day. Another club forgot the research team were visiting on the agreed date and the research had to be rescheduled, while in other instances, players would arrive late having been delayed for various reasons, including the need to complete work associated with the payment of fines, undertaking extra training, completing first-team duties and sometimes simply socializing!

Once these logistical challenges had been overcome, each focus group lasted for between 45 and 60 minutes and was conducted following the completion of the questionnaire. The focus groups took place without the presence of anyone else at the club and were conducted by the lead author (who acted as the facilitator) and a moderator (the second author, who acted as a scribe and managed the recording of each session) who introduced themselves on first-name terms. The focus groups were audio-recorded with the permission of the clubs and players themselves. Players were reminded that anything they disclosed during the focus group was completely anonymous and were told that the audio recording could be stopped at any time should they desire. This was particularly important for some players who sought reassurance that their answers would not be revealed to coaches and other club staff since they felt the disclosure of potentially sensitive, or controversial, matters could undermine their chances of securing a professional contract. The researchers sought, therefore, to convince the players to 'buy in' to the research and to persuade them that it was worth engaging with the focus group without fear of things 'getting back' to others in the club, a concern which is common in many players' recollections about their daily work in a professional football club (Kelly and Waddington 2006; Roderick 2006, 2013; Roderick et al. 2000).

To reassure players of the anonymity of their responses, two main strategies were adopted to maximize the researcher's familiarity with them. First, the researchers emphasized to the group members that, having never had the opportunity to be a player themselves, they were interested in finding out from their perspective the realities of being a youth team player in the professional workplace. Second, having formed the view that players had few people in the respective academies who were willing to listen to what they had to say, the researcher positioned themselves as someone to whom they could freely express their views without the fear of being judged or chastised (Barbour 2008; Morgan 1997; Stewart and Shamdasani 2015). In retrospect, this was one of the most important operational features of the focus groups since many of the players had a number of personal and collective concerns they wished to talk about, but rarely had the chance to discuss them with club staff for fear of being perceived as complaining, as being ungrateful, and above all as someone who was unlikely to cope with the demands of being a professional footballer. The focus groups thus appeared to provide players with a forum for getting things 'off their chest' and their enthusiasm towards the group discussion increased when they realized that they were permitted to discuss whatever they wanted without fear of what they said being disclosed to authority figures in the club. This was particularly significant not only because some of the focus groups were conducted in rather public spaces, but also because 'what participants tell the researcher is inherently shared with other group participants as well' (Morgan 1997: 32) and this can raise concerns about the invasion of privacy and limit the range of topics discussed (Morgan 1997). In our experience, we did not appear to encounter many difficulties in encouraging players to discuss sensitive topics (though we cannot, of course, be certain about what was not disclosed), and to ensure this continued throughout the research we made every attempt to convince players that neither of the researchers were in positions of authority within the game of football, that the research was being undertaken by a university and that it was not in any way associated with their club or any other organization associated with the game.

Given the focus groups were held with pre-existing groups, we also sought to emphasize to players the importance of group confidentiality. In particular, before the focus groups began and, where necessary, during the discussions (e.g. when exploring issues including contractual concerns, home sickness, personal relations), players were reminded of the importance of not disclosing the experiences their peers recalled outside of the group. While players appeared to recognize the importance of such group confidentiality during the time they spent with us, we cannot be sure that they disclosed anything about what was said after we had left the club. Nor can we be certain that some players deliberately withheld information during the focus groups out of fear that others might subsequently reveal sensitive information to their peers or significant others (e.g. managers and coaches). Nonetheless, as Roderick (2006: 7) observed in relation to his study of professional players, it was clearly important to reassure players that 'their comments, whether positive or negative, would not be traceable to them. If they had not received this type of assurance they may not have responded to questions so unguardedly'.

Sharing, Comparing and the Co-Construction of Meaning

As Morgan (2006) has noted, sharing and comparing thoughts, experiences and action is an essential feature of focus group interactions and it is this which constituted the basis of much of our discussions with players. In particular, we set out to maximize players' engagement in interactive discussion because:

> When the participants are mutually interested in the discussion, their conversation often takes the form of sharing and comparing thoughts about the topic. That is, they share their experiences and thoughts, while also comparing their own contributions to what others have said. This process of sharing and comparing is especially useful for hearing and understanding a range of responses on a research topic. The best focus groups thus not only provide data on *what* the participants think but also explicit insights into *why* they think the way they do. (Morgan 2006: 123; emphases in the original)

The questions we asked players were thus oriented towards developing co-construction of meaning through sharing and comparing their experiences as a 'basic interactive process that establishes ... [an] ongoing connection' (Morgan 2012: 165) between the content of what they say and what was just said. To encourage initial interaction and discussion among players, the focus groups opened with a series of questions intended to stimulate players' willingness to share experiences that 'connect to the previous remark by adding similar content to that remark' (Morgan 2012: 165). This was most usually achieved through a dynamic period of questioning about everyday life at their club, which incorporated discussions about what constituted a typical working day, their reflections upon their life as a young footballer, and the jobs they were expected to undertake whilst at their club. These were among the areas where we anticipated many of the similarities in participants' experiences to be identifiable, not least because they were likely to have experienced similar club-based practices in relation to training, preparing for games and engaging in other (often rather routinized) activities, such as undertaking jobs and pursuing education.

Following the opening emphasis on sharing experiences, we anticipated our line of questioning to elicit greater degrees of comparing; that is to say, we anticipated a greater propensity for players to differentiate elements of the topic being discussed by identifying variations in the content of what they say and the previous remark (Morgan 2012). This was particularly true when players were asked about their relationships with others inside (e.g. club management and teammates) and outside (e.g. friends and family) the club, the expectations players had of these significant others, and their experiences of education and other welfare-related matters (Platts 2012).

In these sections of the focus groups, it was possible to identify a number of similarities and differences in what players said via the sharing and comparing of experience. For example, as in other studies (e.g. Parker 1996, 2000), players frequently commented upon how they invariably placed much greater emphasis on gaining a professional contract than any form of compulsory educational qualification, since there was universal agreement that 'getting an education' was at best to be employed as a 'back-up plan' should they not 'make it' in realizing their dream as a professional footballer. In this regard, players explained how being seen to pay too much attention to the educational component of their time in club meant they were almost always at risk of being stigmatized or discredited (Goffman 1963) by the more central members of their social networks (especially coaches and managers) (Platts 2012). It was clear, however, that while education was regarded as a second priority behind playing professional football by players, not all of them viewed education in the same way. Indeed, through the comparing of experience, there appeared among players at three broad groups (Platts 2012). For one (small) group, further and higher education was of interest and an aspiration should they not pursue a career in the game. For example, when asked about what they might do if they failed to secure a professional contract, players at one club said:

Jon: Yeah, I think about it every day ...
Dave: Yeah, I just looked at unis and that.
Callum: To be fair, you are smart as though.
Daniel: Look for a contract first then uni.
Steven: America.
James: Yeah, America.
Dave: I like the sound of America.
Steven: I have had quite a few offers through the post from universities in America.

Another group, which constituted the largest number of players, included those who were prepared to go along with the expectation of undertaking an educational qualification and wished to avoid failing, but who conveyed rather irreverent attitudes towards the benefits of education. As one group of players recalled:

Billy: Well [education] it's ok if you wanna do something in sports if you don't get a contract, say like a physio or something like that. I don't know, but if you don't then it's hard to go there and put effort in if you know what I mean? ...
Phil: If you don't want to go to university or something like that, I think it's hard to get motivated to do it.
Billy: I mean, most boys would just rather come here and play football 5 days a week, and play on the weekend and not do the college I think.
Ian: Yeah, yeah.
Billy: But, to be honest, if they'd made us do something like business, I don't think half of us would wanna turn up ...

Jack: But for the people who don't wanna go to college, at least it's something that they know of a little bit isn't it?

A third group of players failed to see the value of education, said they would not have attended further education had they not pursued a career in football and had no clear aspirations for what they would do after their time in the sport had ended. Commenting on their experience of education, one group of players said:

Shane: Shit.
Fabio: Boring …
Tommy: College is just shit and boring
Fabio: Boring, it is literally the worst college ever …
Tommy: It's like we've done school already.
Shane: The facilities are crap in there [college].

Implications for Participants

Notwithstanding the benefits of encouraging the co-creation of meaning through the development of sharing and comparing of experience amongst players, it was clear that some participants appeared 'uncomfortable in presenting their views publically' (Roulston 2010: 40), especially when those views may have been unpopular (e.g. expressing an interest in education) or controversial (e.g. revealing an allegiance to a particular member of club staff or teammate) by other group members. Thus, while it might be claimed that the information players provided in our focus groups could have been different if they were interviewed individually, this does not mean that they were 'necessarily providing untruthful information' (Roulston 2010: 38). Rather, the experiences players recalled were inevitably the social products of group interaction (Morgan 2010, 2012) in which players may have moderated their answers in line with acceptable group norms and the interactive discussions of which they were a part. As we noted earlier, while the players already knew one another and brought 'pre-established relationships to the interaction' (Roulston 2010: 39), it was impossible to determine precisely the impact these had on their inclination to share and compare their experience through the variety of impression management techniques (Goffman 1963) adopted in our focus groups. Indeed, it is almost inevitable that 'participants are likely to orient to others within the group according to existing relationships' (Roulston 2010: 39), and will often 'enact particular identities occupied outside the group and position their perspectives in particular ways for other members of the group'. That our focus groups provided the opportunity for players to engage in 'face work' (Goffman 1959) during these 'focused encounters' (Goffman 1961) was, however, arguably one of the key advantages of using focus groups to help illuminate processes of interaction and negotiation between players.

The encouragement of sharing and comparing of meaningful experience by players also enabled us to identify how participants implicitly co-constructed and defined 'the research topic by what they include[d] within the boundaries of their discussion' (Morgan 2012: 167). This was particularly true in relation to the experiences players recalled of their relationships with managers and coaches who, because of their position as powerful authority figures in the workplace, were not to be questioned by players. This generally discouraged players from discussing sensitive matters with these significant others in the day-to-day conditions of work. As the next section indicates, the focus groups, in contrast, provided a relatively safe context in which to discuss the effects of these relationships on players' personal and professional lives.

Disciplinary Advantages Conferred by Focus Groups

As successive studies have shown, players are socialized from a young age into accepting the hierarchical and unequal power ratios which exist between them, senior professionals, coaches and above all the manager (Parker 1996; Roderick 2006; Roderick et al. 2000), which generally discourages them from questioning the practices to which they are subject. Such situations can often generate a climate of distrust and fear between players and authority figures which can, among other things, discourage players from help-seeking whether for performance or personal reasons (Roderick 2006; Roderick and Gibbons 2015). Our sample of players were similar in this respect and it was clear from the focus group interactions that many of them viewed authority figures such as coaches, managers and those responsible for education with a strong degree of suspicion and mistrust. This came to impact negatively on the confidence with which players felt able to discuss sensitive issues with club management, since they feared that these matters would 'get back' (Roderick 2006; Roderick et al. 2000) to others inside the club. Players thus repeatedly explained that they had little confidence in authority figures to manage confidentially the disclosure of private or sensitive information. As researchers, we were therefore faced with the need to consistently reassure the focus group participants that anything they said would 'not get back' (a phrase we used repeatedly given its subcultural significance in professional football) to coaches and managers. In offering this reassurance, we emphasized to players our desire for them to make public – to us as research outsiders – their experiences of the closed social worlds they inhabited so that we could better understand their work situations and experiences.

It quickly became clear to us that engaging in our research, and especially the focus group discussions, was the first opportunity many of them had been given to talk as openly as possible about their grievances, frustrations and their worries without the fear of a coach or other member of staff using the information 'against them' (Platts 2012). It was thus not unusual for the focus groups to conclude with the players thanking us for our interest in their real lives, rather than being simply preoccupied with their performances on the field. In two cases, the players even applauded when the focus group was over, such was their enjoyment of being able to 'get things off their chest'!

Adopting such an empathetic approach to studying players' experiences – in their eyes at least – enabled us to engage them in the focus of our enquiries relatively straight forwardly. However, as useful as this approach was in helping players to disclose individual and collective experience about sensitive topics (e.g. the pressure of living away from home, being expected to play when hurt or injured, the uncertainty of their future), it simultaneously generated significant constraints on us to balance that empathy with a critical degree of detachment from what players said.

Conclusion

In this chapter, we have been centrally concerned with outlining some of our experiences of conducting focus groups with what can be a hard-to-reach sample of participants (young elite male footballers), working in a hard-to-access workplace (professional football clubs), for the purposes of academic research. It became clear during the course of our research, however, that the subject matter – education and welfare of elite young footballers – was perceived by clubs as somehow less important, less intrusive and less sensitive than other investigations in the sport and exercise sciences (e.g. talent identification, players' physical performance, nutrition). In this regard, since the topic of our research did not require us to 'take time away from the pitch' and was by comparison with the performance of players in training and matches perceived (by authority figures) as relatively insignificant, we were able to undertake our research in just under one-quarter of all English football league clubs. That we did not wish to speak with professional players also almost certainly helped our participant recruitment; in this respect, our research was not perceived as a threat to the 'real business' of the football club because it did not focus on professional players, but on those who have not yet 'made it' and whose experiences may be perceived as less newsworthy. On reflection, our proposed research methods (including focus groups) did not seem to confer significant advantages or disadvantages on the likelihood of us being able to undertake our research. Instead, it relied upon us: (i) overcoming our status as outsiders; (ii) undertaking research which can be accommodated within the practical and organizational priorities of clubs; (iii) investigating topics which were often regarded as being less important to the core business of football academies, namely, producing players for the first team; and (iv) of course, with all probability, a healthy piece of good luck!

The selection of focus groups (rather than other methods such as semi-structured interviews) did, however, have numerous advantages for us. On a practical level, speaking with players in groups, rather than as individuals, appeared more organizationally convenient for clubs and enabled us to engage hard-to-reach participants in our research. The loosely structured and relaxed approach we adopted to the conduct of the focus groups also appeared to facilitate positive interaction between group members and between them and ourselves. In doing so, focus groups enabled participants to discuss, challenge and modify their recollections and experiences, thus maximizing the possibility of us obtaining more realistic accounts of how players thought and acted in the workplace. Theoretically, the emphasis placed on encouraging players to focus on their daily interactions enabled us to shed sociological light on such things as: (i) the interdependence between the personal and professional lives of players; (ii) the complex social relations in which players are entangled with many other people inside and outside of the workplace; (iii) how the closed social world of professional football constrains players (and significant others) to think and act in particular ways; and (iv) how relatively closed work spaces (such as professional football, but also other occupations including the armed services) are characterized by particularly strong modes and cultures of occupational socialization which can be investigated through the analysis of group norms, experiences and interactions shared with focus group researchers.

References

Barbour, R. (2008) *Doing Focus Groups*. London: Sage.
Brackenridge, C. (2007) 'Researching the football family', In C. Brackenridge, A. Pitchford, K. Russell and G. Nutt (eds.), *Child Welfare in Football: An Exploration of Children's Welfare in the Modern Game*. London: Routledge, pp. 56–68.
Goffman, E. (1959) *The Presentation of Self in Everyday Life*. London: Penguin.
Goffman, E. (1961) *Asylums*. London: Penguin.
Goffman, E. (1963) *Stigma: Notes on the Management of Spoiled Identity*. Houndsworth: Penguin.
Kelly, S., and Waddington, I. (2006) 'Abuse, intimidation and violence as aspects of managerial control in professional soccer in Britain and Ireland'. *International Review for the Sociology of Sport*, 41(2): 147–64.
Merton, R.K. (1987) 'Focussed interviews and focus groups: Continuities and discontinuities'. *Public Opinion Quarterly*, 51(4): 550–66.

Merton, R.K., and Kendall, P.L. (1946) 'The focussed interview'. *American Journal of Sociology*, 51(6): 541–57.

Morgan, D. (1997) *Focus Groups as Qualitative Research* (2nd ed.). Thousand Oaks, CA: Sage.

Morgan, D.L. (2006) 'Focus group', In V. Jupp (ed.), *The Sage Dictionary of Social Research Methods*. Thousand Oaks, CA: Sage, pp. 121–23.

Morgan, D.L. (2010) 'Reconsidering the role of interaction in analysing and reporting focus groups'. *Qualitative Health Research*, 20(5): 718–22.

Morgan, D.L. (2012) 'Focus groups and social interaction', In J.F. Gubrium, J.A. Holstein, A.B. Marvasti and K.D. McKinney (eds.), *The Sage Handbook of Interview Research: The Complexity of the Craft* (2nd ed.). Thousand Oaks, CA: Sage, pp. 161–76.

Parker, A. (1995) '"Great expectations": Grimness or glamour? The football apprentice in the 1990s'. *The Sports Historian*, 15(1): 107–28.

Parker, A. (1996) *Chasing the 'big-time': Football apprenticeship in the 1990s*. Unpublished Ph.D. Thesis. Warwick: University of Warwick.

Parker, A. (2000) 'Training for glory, schooling for failure: English professional football, traineeship and education provision'. *Journal of Education and Work*, 13(1): 61–76.

Platts, C. (2012) *Education and Welfare in Professional Football Academies and Centres of Excellence: A Sociological Study*. Unpublished Ph.D. Thesis. Chester: University of Chester.

Roderick, M. (2006) *The Work of Professional Football. A Labour of Love?* London: Routledge.

Roderick, M. (2013) 'From identification to dis-identification: Case studies of job loss in professional football'. *Qualitative Research in Sport, Exercise and Health*, 6(2): 143–60.

Roderick, M., and Gibbons, B. (2015) '"To thine own self be true": Sports work, mental illness and the problem of authenticity', In J. Baker, P. Safai and J. Fraser-Thomas (eds.), *Health and Elite Sport: Is High Performance Sport a Healthy Pursuit?* London: Routledge.

Roderick, M., Waddington, I., and Parker, G. (2000) 'Playing hurt: Managing injuries in English professional football'. *International Review for the Sociology of Sport*, 35(2): 165–80.

Roulston, J. (2010) *Effective Interviewing*. London: Sage.

Stewart, D., and Shamdasani, P. (2015) *Focus Groups: Theory and Practice* (3rd ed.). London: Sage.

Waddington, I. (2014) 'Researching the world of professional football', In A. Smith and I. Waddington (eds.), *Doing Real World Research in Sports Studies*. London: Routledge, pp. 11–25.

Chris Platts is a Senior Lecturer at Sheffield Hallam University, UK, where he teaches on various aspects of sport development, sport coaching and sport business management. He was awarded a PhD from the University of Chester for his research into education and welfare in professional football academies – one of the largest academic studies of young players to have been carried out. His works are in a range of peer-reviewed journals.

Andy Smith is Professor of Sport and Physical Activity at Edge Hill University, UK. His research interests centre on the sociology of sport, physical activity and health, with particular reference to youth, mental health and wellbeing. He is a co-editor of several books, including *Doing Real World Research in Sports Studies* (2014), and most recently, *The Routledge Handbook of Youth Sport* (2016). Co-authored books include *An Introduction to Drugs in Sport* (2009); *Disability, Sport and Society* (2009) and *Sport Policy and Development* (2010). His work has been published widely in sports studies and sociology of sports journals. Current research includes projects related to mental health and wellbeing in community and elite sport. Andy Smith is also a member of Edge Hill's Institute for Public Policy and Professional Practice.

3

Reflections on Outsourcing and Applying for Funding

Laurence Kohn and Wendy Christiaens

Introduction

Focus groups have a lot to offer to those studying health care and health services (Pope and Mays 2006), since they can furnish in-depth information about patients' and health care providers' needs, wishes, experiences and fears regarding health care (Barbour 2000).

The Belgian Health Care Knowledge Centre (KCE) is a publicly funded institution that has the mission to inform policymakers on decisions relating to health care and health insurance, basing this on scientific analysis and research. When formulating appropriate recommendations, researchers working at KCE are aware that focus groups could significantly strengthen this capacity. Indeed, recommendations have to be tailored to the needs of care seekers and providers both by taking into account the context of the research

---

L. Kohn (✉) · W. Christiaens
Belgian Health Care Knowledge Centre, Kruidtuinlaan 55, Brussels, 1000 Belgium
e-mail: Laurence.Kohn@kce.fgov.be; Wendy.Christiaens@kce.fgov.be

questions and by involving the stakeholders at different steps of the research projects (Piérart et al. 2012). This is the reason that we regularly use focus groups in our studies. However, because of a lack of human resources within KCE, we are obliged to assign this work to external research teams.

When a study utilizes qualitative research methods, including focus groups, both academic and non-academic research teams – that is, private companies or consultants, commercial agencies or research consultancies – have the opportunity to tender. In our experience, these two types of researchers respond to the mission in somewhat different ways.

In order to clearly identify and seek to explain the differences in these two approaches, we propose to critically examine the strengths and the weaknesses of each, drawing on our experience with six different projects, selected to cover a range of relevant research topics/briefs.

This chapter will focus on comparing the approaches to focus groups taken by academic and non-academic research teams. We will characterize these types of research teams, looking at the advantages and disadvantages of each. In what follows, more specifically we will assess (i) the capacity of academic and non-academic teams to carry out focus groups in an institutional context of policy-oriented research in health care – that is, the kind of expertise they propose in reply to a call for tender; (ii) their skills with regard to working in several languages (as this is important for carrying out and analyzing focus groups at national level in a multilingual country such as Belgium; (iii) the proposed cost; (iv) their scientific approach; (v) their capacity to recruit participants; and (vi) their analysis and reporting skills.

We will also address more practical aspects such as whether, and how, the two types kinds of team collaborate, whether within a consortium (when there is one), or with the funding institution. The issue of respect for deadlines will also be covered.

On the one hand, our analysis seeks to clarify what to expect from different types of teams, allowing KCE and other commissioning agencies, to determine how best to optimize the experience of outsourcing qualitative data collection. This should, in turn, enable interested bodies to make an informed choice of research team, depending on the aims and focus of the research in question. On the other hand, researchers from academic or non-academic teams could learn from having their potential weaknesses and strengths identified and could, perhaps, adapt their working practices in order to comply more closely with the needs of the funders.

KCE in the Field of Health Care Research

KCE is a governmental institution. The KCE's role is to identify and shed light on the best possible solutions, in the context of an accessible, high-quality health care system, with due regard for growing demand and budgetary constraint. KCE is, however, not involved in decision-making or implementation processes per se (Belgian Health Care Knowledge Centre 2011).

Scientific studies that are carried out at KCE are assigned to the following activity domains: Good Clinical Practice (guidelines); Health Technology Assessment or Health Services Research.

Research topics are selected after an annual call for proposals. These can be submitted by any private person, or organization, institution with an interest in health care and its delivery – including the policymakers themselves. Studies will enter the KCE's annual programme after a selection process, which assesses whether the identified topic matches a governmental research priority. All of the proposals are then classified according to their feasibility; the availability of data (if applicable); and an estimation of the workload involved. Studies are also expected to have an impact on future health care policy. KCE will thus respond to precise questions formulated by the initiator and the commissioned studies are, therefore, very tightly focused.

Generally, once they are launched, KCE studies are carried out by internal researchers, often in collaboration with external scientific teams. Internal researchers employed at KCE are recruited for their high level of expertise in scientific research – particularly medical and paramedical researchers specializing in health services research, social scientists and health economists. Most of them have previously worked (or may still be working) in universities, as researchers or lecturers. For example, the authors of this chapter are both social scientists, with a PhD, one in sociology and the other in Public Health. We have both formerly been employed in academia, as researchers in public health and sociology of health and illness, and as lecturers.

External teams are selected by a KCE jury, that is, generally one KCE manager, the principal investigator and KCE experts are involved, in two steps for each study by means of a public tender.

The first step in the selection process consists of identifying a maximum of three candidates from the total number of applicants (usually involving up to 7 research teams). At this stage, the selection is based only on the description of the teams (presented according to a specified format) and the Curricula Vitae of the team members (presented according to a standard template). More precisely, the following selection criteria are used by the KCE committee to differentiate between candidates:

1. Scientific reputation: In general, have the research teams established a good scientific reputation? (Particular attention will be given to the track record with regard to publications in highly rated international journals.)
2. Specific skills: Can the team demonstrate specific competencies in the research field as specified in the tender? Do the researchers in the team have adequate experience of using the techniques required/proposed for this research? Does the team (or individual members in case of a new consortium) have recent publications related to the subject? Has the team previously shown an interest in this field of research? Ability to work in both French and Dutch is also taken into consideration.
3. Multi-disciplinary composition of the team: In general, for a tender focusing on qualitative health service research, a psychological or

social scientific and (para)medical profile is sought, depending on the topic of the research.
4. Networks: Is the team in contact with, or is it used to working with, Belgian scientific institutions; with foreign research teams; or with health care institutions and health care professionals? (N.B. This is interesting and raises the question as to whether this leads to a situation where tenders are awarded to 'the usual suspects'?

The second step culminates in the award of the contract. Selected candidates are next invited to submit a full research proposal based on a short description of the project written by KCE researchers. This short description presents information on the initiator of the project, a pre-assessment of the literature, research questions, a tentative methodology, expected deliverables and a tentative timetable. In order to discriminate between proposals, the KCE panel will invite one or two external experts – selected because of their expertise on the relevant topic and/or the methodology – to join the jury. At this stage, criteria used to make the decision as to who is going to carry out the study are:

1. Relevance of the proposed methodology: Does the project proposal demonstrate a good grasp of the subject? Does the approach to the research suggest that it will be carried out in the best possible way and within the designated timescale?
2. Suggestions for improving KCE's pre project form: Are there any variations or modifications suggested with regard to the methodology described in KCE's pre-project form? Do these suggestions improve the chance of achieving the proposed goals within the same deadline?
3. Cost: Does the budget they propose deviate from what KCE has foreseen? A slightly higher cost is permissible, but should be justified by, for example, offering methodological choices that differ from those proposed by the KCE researchers. A comparison of the budget proposed by the different teams could help the panel to discriminate between applicants.

4. Availability and skills of the researchers assigned to the project: Which researchers will actually be involved? What is their level of competence in the field of research? Do they have other responsibilities during the project's timespan? If so, which ones? And how will they combine such activities with this project? What are their contractual obligations with regard to their institution?

Once the team is selected, the methodology and final design and timetable are decided in collaboration with the external team during a kick-off meeting.

Description of the Data

We identified KCE projects conducted in the last 5 years, which used focus groups as one of their methods, and which were subcontracted to an external team. Six projects were identified, three that were conducted by academic teams and three by private companies. These are briefly presented in Table 3.1.

We retrieved all documents used in project management, ranging from the call for tender to the final report and recommendations, including the proposal submitted by the external team, the final contract, and the minutes of the debriefing meeting.

After familiarization with the data, we identified topics pertinent to our focus. We then designed a template to allow us to extract information, in order to describe and systematically compare each project. Topics covered by the template include the tender specification; description of the expertise available in the selected team (based on Curricula Vitae) and its proposal, the final contract specifications, the final report content and the information retrieved from the debriefing process, systematically done at the end of a project. In addition, we interviewed project leaders or the researcher responsible for the supervision of the qualitative part of the study which consisted of using focus groups. This allowed us to get more insight into the process, the facilitators and barriers to effective collaboration and production of the report. Afterwards, these

Table 3.1 Description of six projects using focus groups in KCE studies (2010–2015)

Project title	Publication year	Specific research question	Type of subcontractor	Duration of the qualitative part
Reduction of the treatment gap for alcohol use disorders in Belgium (Mistiaen et al. 2016)	2016	What are the barriers and facilitating factors to identify the persons with problematic alcohol use, assess their problems and initiate treatment?	Academic consortium	4 months
Comprehensive geriatric care in hospitals: the role of inpatient geriatric consultation teams (Deschodt et al. 2015)	2015	To perform a SWOT-analysis of the current practice of internal geriatric liaison teams	Non-academic team	3 months
The organization of Health care for undocumented migrants in Belgium? (Roberfroid et al., 2015)	2015	What are the SWOTs of the current procedure for allowing undocumented migrants an access to health care in Belgium?	Academic consortium	4 months
Informed choice on breast cancer screening: messages to support informed decision (Kohn et al. 2014)	2014	What are the expectations and needs of Belgian women regarding information required to decide if they would participate in breast screening or not? What are the preferences regarding different forms of information provision?	Non-academic consortium	3 months

(continued)

Table 3.1 (continued)

Project title	Publication year	Specific research question	Type of subcontractor	Duration of the qualitative part
Caring for mothers and newborns after uncomplicated delivery: towards integrated postnatal care (Benahmed et al. 2014)	2014	What are the barriers and motivations for a short hospital stay with follow up at home after an uncomplicated delivery	Academic team	6 months
Organization of aftercare for patients with severe burn injuries (Christiaens et al. 2013)	2013	What are the specific problems for patients with severe burn injuries during after care and what are the unmet care needs (if any)?	Non-academic team	4 months

findings were discussed and were used to formulate hypotheses that should be tested in another context or in a larger sample of studies.

Comparison of the Strengths and Weaknesses of Academic Teams versus Non-Academic Teams: The Selection Process for Conducting Research Using Focus Groups

Expertise in the Field and Scientific Reputation

Interviews suggested that the most important deciding factor for academic teams is the topic for study. Academic teams who submit an application tend to already be expert in the field, have a large network and are usually familiar with the context. In consequence, they are interested in a limited number of KCE tenders, with applications being submitted often only on one or two occasions throughout the course of their (individual and team) career. Researchers belonging to academic teams mostly have a strong scientific reputation, which is obviously very valuable for KCE projects, in order to increase the quality of the report. In conclusion, academic teams are very attractive applicants for research projects, because of their expertise and their renown, and the potential to lend scientific rigour to the report and robustness to the recommendations.

Non-academic teams, in contrast, tend to be more generalist in focus. They, most frequently, have expertise in the health (care) sector in general and in specific research approaches – such as conducting focus groups. Although most also have prior experience in particular domains within the broad field of study, it is unusual for them to have developed specific expertise within one particular niche. In consequence, they are not usually motivated to apply because of the identified topic and are, thus, in a position to apply for a much broader range of projects than are academic teams. They rarely demonstrate scientific renown, but offer, instead, a guarantee that they will deliver the project in a timely manner, while respecting agreed quality standards.

Capacity to Work in Several Languages

Doing research in Belgium raises language issues. Indeed, a total of three official languages is represented in administrative communities: the French-speaking one in the South of the country, the Dutch-speaking community in the North and the smaller German-speaking constituency in the East. Moreover, health (care) organizations sometimes differ, both in terms of policy and practice, from one region to another (e.g. in prevention policies, mental health etc.). In addition, there are cultural differences between the North and the South of the country. It is, therefore, very important to collect data in all languages – mainly in French and Dutch, the German often being, somewhat unfortunately, omitted, because of limited resources. In consequence, the particular linguistic situation in Belgium adds a further selection criterion in terms of identifying the external team best-suited to conduct focus groups. Indeed, teams conducting focus groups are expected to be entirely bilingual, to be able to both collect and analyze the data in both languages, as well as being capable of discussing the results in both languages, regardless of which language is employed for data collection and data analysis. Researchers have to either be completely bilingual or able to work equally easily in Dutch or in French. In addition, as KCE reports are written in English, they have to be able to present their results in English.

All these linguistic skills are not easy to find in a specific pre-existing team, whether this is an academic one or not. Candidates will, therefore, often have to find solutions to this requirement. They may propose the formation of a consortium, or they may engage a specific qualified freelance researcher, in order to compensate for the missing language skills in their initial team. In order to meet this criterion on linguistic skills, teams are often obliged to collaborate with other researchers and they are not always used to doing so.

Non-academic teams regularly collaborate with *ad hoc* freelance researchers or with another research team – although often only for a short period of time. In our experience, such collaborations, within the private sector, do not give rise to particular problems that are relevant to conducting focus groups. However, academic teams appear to experience more difficulties with regard to engaging one person for a short/specific mission. Overall, it is difficult for them, at the point of making their application to KCE, to already be in a position to guarantee the availability of such an identified individual to work intensively on the project, in the event of the contract being awarded. Academic teams, therefore, tend to build a temporary consortium – for example, with two different university teams making a joint proposal. Such consortia bundle expert knowledge, hence reducing the need for hiring additional personnel.

Cost

During the selection procedure, the price is also taken into account and the tender stipulates an estimation of the budget foreseen for the study. Private companies are often more expensive than academic teams. The former usually cost their services at a price per day that is higher than the estimated budget. Included in their costings are overheads covering time for meetings, travel costs, transcription costs, etc. Academic teams are, generally, less expensive – at least at the outset of the process. They often do not estimate practical costs in their offer, such as travel to meetings. They also may be able to offer more, because they may already have data they are able to reuse or draw on in the project. Academic teams tend to offer more and for less money than do non-academic teams. At first sight, this seems to be advantageous for KCE. However, as only a part of the estimated cost is allocated to the researchers, the rest consisting of overheads for the university, this apparently beneficial deal may, in the end, cost KCE more, because the proposed budget was, in effect, not realistic.

In conclusion, when opting for an academic team the funder risks being obliged to reduce its expectations or to allocate an additional budget, in order to ensure that the aims of the project are met.

Conducting Research Using Focus Groups

Scientific Approach – Skills to Develop the Methodology and the Data Collection Tools

Selected academic teams undeniably possess methodological skills. They generally work within a valid conceptual framework and they have mastery of data collection techniques. Although selected non-academic teams may be skilled in conducting focus groups, they often require expert methodological support. They do not necessarily refer to a theoretical framework, and when they do, they often recycle the same framework over successive projects.

In terms of data collection skills, both types of team are expert in moderation with very diverse publics. However, our experience shows that academic teams are more often reluctant to work with a very detailed protocol, or with a pre-determined interview guide. They may argue that they do not need such a tightly formatted tool because of their expertise in the field and in the art of moderation. Non-academic teams are more willing to follow our processes (with regard to using pre-defined guidelines) but they also need more support – unless they take time to make the subject tangible (for example, carrying out site visits, developing preparatory informal contacts, producing a literature review.) In particular, they need support for the development of the interview guide because of their generalist approach. However, once the interview guide has been developed, they use it systematically.

Recruitment Capacity

KCE is required to produce reports within a timeframe of 1 year. When using qualitative research techniques, 1 year is often quite a short period of time. Teams have, thus, to be very effective, in order to recruit participants to focus groups; to organize and conduct these; to analyze the data; and to produce the report. Throughout the six studies selected for our analysis, three types of participants were involved: people from the general population or patients in general (women between 40 and

70 years for breast cancer screening, mothers), specific patients (ex-alcoholic patients) or practitioners and stakeholders (burn care centres, geriatric liaison teams, migrants).

When focus group recruitment seeks to target the general public, private companies have greater facilities at their disposal, allowing them to efficiently recruit and organize meetings. Some of them have pre-existing panels of individuals ready to participate in studies, and they tend to have logistical and administrative support, offices etc. When health care practitioners are targeted, they also have access to a range of networks that can prove useful. However, in situations which require research teams to target participants with a specific profile, private companies generally need support (from KCE researchers) in order to identify a relevant sampling pool.

Academic teams generally have readier access to specific potential participants: they know the network, are likely to have previous good experience of such collaborations, and can, in consequence, more easily find participants. Nevertheless, they have to put more energy into the organization of focus groups, since, lacking focussed administrative support, academic researchers often have to do this time-consuming task themselves.

Analysis and Reporting Skills

Both types of teams are likely to possess the skills required for analyzing focus group data, but the way in which they do it will depend on the expertise of the researcher(s) assigned to carry out the analysis. We have had good experiences with both types of teams, but have also found that, with some projects, we have needed to have more of an input than anticipated – in relation to the work of both academic and non-academic teams. In the case of collaboration with an academic team, if the researcher is junior, s/he has not always received adequate research training and may not be well-supported by her/his supervisor. In such cases, KCE has had to compensate for such shortcomings, in order to help the academic team to meet the deadlines. For non-academic teams, we have sometimes had no option but to select a team with scant analysis skills, simply because there were no applicants with superior expertise.

Although it is not always necessary, teams – both academic and non-academic – generally have some expertise in using software for the analysis of qualitative data. However, in terms of depth of analysis of focus group data, the difficulties we encountered with academic teams related to the difficulty they experienced in terms of staying focused on the definitive research questions posed by the commissioners. Such teams tend to be very exhaustive, or expansive, in that they tend to go in many directions for analysis; and to be very accurate and detailed in their description at the level of interpretation. We attribute this to their interest in the topic, to their degree of expertise and specialization – sometimes in another area related to the subject of the research – and, perhaps, also because they are used to working with longer time schedules.

Non-academic teams tend to require a little more incentive to persuade them to go deeper in the analysis and to attempt to be more accurate. This is also true for the writing of the final report. At KCE, we try to limit the number of pages, in order to give clear messages to interested parties, who often do not have time to read and process longer reports. Academic teams seem to experience greater difficulty in limiting their written production and are often reluctant to renounce deeper interrogation with regard to some aspects of their findings. Non-academic teams, in contrast, generally respect and comply with restrictions on the allocated number of pages.

The Collaboration Process

Collaboration Within a Consortium

As we mentioned, teams are often obliged to create a consortium in order to be able to collect and analyze data relating to a bi-lingual population. In addition, in such circumstances, collaboration between the consortium and KCE researchers is more difficult. We identified two main reasons for this.

First of all, collaboration with an academic consortium appears to be difficult for practical reasons, especially because of the availability that this requires. Designing a joint protocol, making decisions, carrying out the analysis collaboratively etc., all involve demands to meet. These meetings need to identify and utilize common time, in order to work and require travel time, in addition. Indeed, time appears as a real issue for academic teams: researchers working in academic teams are also engaged in a range of other academic responsibilities, such as lecturing, supervision, evaluation and administration, and are, therefore, bound to the academic calendar and holidays. Because of their busy agenda and their generally less flexible priorities, academic researchers are less available in general, and less able, in particular, to schedule working meetings, which may need to be set up on an *ad hoc* basis. Also, generally speaking, teams are often geographically removed from each other, perhaps with one in the North of the country, the other in the South, making significant demands in terms of travel.

Second, collaboration between academic teams means, by definition, collaboration between highly qualified experts. This type of collaboration can be extremely rich but can also be very demanding. Indeed, it may happen that academic researchers do not totally agree on the theoretical framework or methodological approaches and this, inevitably, eats into the project timetable. Research team members also need to agree on series of intermediate drafts, before submission to the funder. Depending on the views of the researchers, their expertise, readiness to use other frameworks or processes, ensuing discussions could be difficult and likely to increase the total workload of the teams.

In conclusion, when a consortium proposes to work together for the first time – particularly in case of academic teams – the funder should be aware of the risk that the collaboration process will be difficult and that this collaboration will offer no in-built guarantee of delivery.

Work in Collaboration with Researchers from the Funding Institution

KCE subcontract the part of the research that involves using focus groups because of lack of time and human resources – not because of lack of in-house expertise. It is, therefore, anticipated that the research will involve collaborative work with many exchanges, discussion and close follow up by the KCE researchers – and this is made explicit to research teams. Moreover,

KCE processes include an external validation, requiring transparent and systematic data collection. Each step in the research process has to be accurately documented, allowing validators to assess the scientific feature of the final report. For those three projects carried out with academic teams, this type of collaboration could be experienced by them as being difficult. Our experience, and our ensuing hypothesis, is that, the KCE experts may have no legitimacy in academic researchers' eyes, in relation to stating their point of view or stipulating requirements for the work.

Another explanation is that academic teams may not be used to working in collaboration with this particular funding institution. Other public funders in Belgium are not so closely involved in the research as is KCE. These, however, are not centres of knowledge, do not have their own internal scientific experts, as it is the case in KCE, and are entirely dependent on the input of academic teams in order to access specific essential expertise. While other public institutions subcontract the work, they can generally be expected not to intervene in the methodology or in the research process. The KCE (established in 2002) is rather new to the public funding arena and has its own, somewhat different, approach to collaboration. Although we stipulate that the work will be 'collaborative', this is not always perceived in the same way by all parties involved; with our approach being perceived by some as intrusive or as implying a lack of confidence in teams' skills and expertise.

Such a problem was not identified with regard to working with non-academic teams. They are, probably by definition, more client-oriented with regard to their approach to collaboration and expect detailed ongoing communication and discussion with funders

Respect for Deadlines

Because of their limited availability and multiple academic tasks, academic teams are often frustrated by time constraints. In addition, academic researchers do not find it so easy to be involved on an *ad hoc* basis, where they need to respond rapidly. Non-academic teams seem to be more used to working on a short-term and flexible basis. They appear to find it easier either to recruit collaborators to do the work, or to secure the commitment of a specific collaborator. This impacts favourably on their ability to meet deadlines, at least with reference to the studies we examined for this exercise.

How Can the Differences Between Academic and Non-Academic Teams be Explained?

From this detailed comparison of six KCE focus group based research projects, we were able to explore the ways in which the type of team – academic versus non-academic – affects the course, management and output of the project. Overall, it seems that academic and non-academic teams show complementary characteristics. This complementarity allows for outsourcing institutions to choose a team appropriate to the particular project needs. We summarized the main characteristics in Table 3.2.

Table 3.2 Complementarity between academic and non-academic teams

	Academic	Non-academic
Profile	Specialised	Generalist
	Theoretical approach	Pragmatic approach
	Own research agenda	Client-oriented
Price	Cheaper	More expensive
Work rhythm	Less flexible	More flexible
	Often delayed deliverables	Deliverables on time
Recruitment	Strong in the recruitment of specific topic related profiles	Strong in recruitment within the general public or easily accessible groups
Preparation of the focus groups	Strong in interview guide design	Need input for interview guide design
Experience of the researchers	Work delegated to junior researchers	Senior researchers
Analysis	Strong competences in analysing data in depth	Often descriptive analyses of the data
	Difficulties to stay focused on the research question	No problem to stay focused
Reporting	Produce a longer report	Concise reports

What Are the Issues for Academic Teams?

Publications in highly ranked international peer-reviewed journals are the main indicator of the scientific reputation of academic teams. Academic researchers, therefore, search for opportunities, including additional funding, to increase their expertise and knowledge, but also their scientific reputation and visibility. Carrying out research for a third party, such as KCE, can, in theory, satisfy both objectives.

However, in order to get the most out of the collaboration, researchers need guarantees that the final (KCE) reports (and all derived products) are compatible with their own research agenda and that the research conforms to the highest scientific standards. Also, academic teams can seldom completely free up their diaries for a certain period of time to allow them to work exclusively on KCE projects. Therefore, KCE demands inevitably compete with what is already quite a full academic agenda. The expectations of KCE and the contracting academic teams, hence, diverge to some extent – especially in terms of work flexibility and short time delays.

What Are the Issues for Non-Academic Teams?

Private companies have a commercial reputation to defend with regard to their ability to provide appropriate client-centred services. Their clients have to be satisfied and, in consequence, likely to contract again with the company in the future. They tend to focus on customer satisfaction, rather than scientific excellence, which would oblige them to shift to another, more academic, frame of reference. Moreover, for them, the shorter the projects are, the more projects they can carry out within a certain time frame. Thus, short timescales are likely to be viewed as an advantage.

At the end of a research project, we perceive greater frustration in the academic teams compared to non-academic teams. Our hypothesis is that academic researchers, because they have expertise on the topic, expect to satisfy KCE demands with little effort, because it is in line with their expertise and core business. They may expect the KCE project in which they engage to fit very closely with their ongoing (and previous) research work, meaning that the KCE contract can be viewed as a source of additional income for little extra effort.

Academic teams could legitimately consider that they have sufficient expertise, material and networks to enable them to seamlessly engage with the project in hand, exploiting already available resources and knowledge. In the end, however, KCE turns out to be a very exigent funder, requiring availability, responsiveness, short time delays, and, overall, very accurate answers to very specific questions – all things that academic teams may not be expecting to be asked to provide.

Nevertheless, KCE reports offer academic teams an appreciative audience, visibility to the general public and within the sector. Indeed, the public availability of the report and its announcement (often with repercussions) in the press ensure wide diffusion of the results. Moreover, recommendations are directly addressed to policymakers through their representation on the KCE board of directors, affording academic researchers the ear of policymakers, which is something they do not automatically enjoy in their more academic research pursuits. KCE gathers representatives of all stakeholders in Belgian health care policy, including patients. The involvement of the board of directors in the selection of the topics and their presence throughout – including in the final step before the publication of the report – guarantee that the results will, at least, be adapted to their expectations, and, in the best case, that it will lead to concrete decisions and possibly change. KCE reports are very demanding but can, thus, make a direct impact – something that is increasingly valued by academic teams working in public health field and, indeed, their home institutions and other funding bodies.

Limitations of Our Findings and Analysis

This review aimed to compare researchers from academic or non-academic teams to highlight their respective potential weaknesses and strengths in relation to designing, carrying out and analyzing focus groups. To this end, we examined the six most recent projects carried out in our institution, that included focus groups data collection. The teams that have conducted these projects were selected following a standard process. Our reflections are thus confined to those six selected teams, who were seen as offering the best proposal for the best price, and do not, therefore, take into account the rejected proposals.

The first obvious limitation relates to our position with regard to the context of the analysis. We, the authors, are both social scientists, coming from academia where we have worked for several years. Neither of us has experience of carrying out research while employed by private companies. We are, thus, more familiar with the academic context than the non-academic one. In addition, we based our analysis on six cases of reports published in the institution in which we work. In all except one of these report's at least one of us was involved.

A second limitation relates to our personal involvement in five out of the six selected reports, where we were part of the collaboration with the external teams. The difficulties we met could be partly related to our own way of working with these teams rather than signalling systemic issues characteristic of the commissioning and tendering process.

Third, in a similar vein, it is impossible to compare the final output of the academic vs. non-academic teams. Qualitative outsourced KCE research involves, as already mentioned, a collaboration characterized by many interventions from our side: the teams base their proposals on a preliminary protocol written by KCE researchers (including sampling and scheduling); it is recommended that the teams follow KCE process guidelines; the data collection tools and the analytical framework are both constructed in collaboration with KCE researchers; and the final text of the report is revised by KCE researchers. We, therefore, based our comparison on our experience of the process rather than on the outputs.

Fourth, our material relates to the Belgian context, which has somewhat unusual requirements with regard to language skills and we are, therefore, not confident that what we have described here will apply in all other contexts.

Finally, we acknowledge that the non-academic teams that were involved in carrying out these projects were all located in the Dutch-speaking part of Belgium. It may, therefore, be possible that the way they work is influenced by this particular cultural context. In conclusion, therefore, as already mentioned, our hypotheses should be tested in other contexts or in a larger sample of studies.

Conclusions and Recommendations

We carried out here a comparison of two types of research teams, based on our experience of working within one government-funded agency. Several aspects are not specific to 'focus groups' per se and could be applied to qualitative methods in general. Indeed, in order to generate and analyze focus group data, you need expertise in qualitative research and skills in research design. Next to the methodological aspect, the main features that distinguished between academic researchers and non-academic teams were, first, linked to their expert knowledge on the topic. Methodological skills are not, in themselves, sufficient to carry a research project successfully from A to Z. In this respect, while academic teams have a great advantage, as compared to the non-academic ones, they tend to find it difficult to stay focused on the research question posed by the initiator and to adapt themselves to the specific requirements of applied research within the policy domain.

However, when we consider the more practical aspects, non-academic teams seem to be more efficient: they are more available, can devote more time to the organizational and administrative aspects and have more facilities to draw on in convening and carrying out focus groups, etc. They can also dedicate more time to the research in general, and, in consequence, are more reliable with respect to meeting deadlines. We suspect that these differences are ultimately related to the differing focus of non-academic and academic teams – that is, a client-oriented one vs. a more scientific one. In terms of moderation skills, we did not notice any difference.

Academic and non-academic teams are, in fact, rather different with regard to their specific strengths. This is not surprising, since they start from a different *raison d'être*. Academic teams have their own research agenda within a well-defined field of interest. They mostly design research projects to reflect and further explore this agenda and search for funding to finance them in this endeavour. Occasionally, they tender for a project in response to a call by an institution such as the KCE, if the research goals appear to largely coincide with their own research agenda and field of expertise. In other words, they submit proposals for those projects which they view as touching upon their core business and about which they are passionate. Consequently, the end product needs to be of high (scientific) quality in order to reaffirm their expert position in the field. Private companies do not have their own research agenda; rather, they offer a package of skills, techniques, methods and approaches with which they are familiar and which they believe will enable them to get the job done, efficiently and, thus, affirming their competitive position in a market share. They do not assume the role of experts in a particular field, but, rather, the role of consultants aiming at customer satisfaction. The deliverables need to be of high quality in order to keep the customer satisfied, and thus be a potential partner for future assignments.

In sum, our review allows us to formulate recommendations to all teams to optimize the chance to be selected and for all parties involved to facilitate and even improve the collaboration process.

Academic teams should be prepared to free the agreed time in order to be able to respect the deadline. They should also be aware that collaboration with KCE researchers takes time and requires flexibility not just in terms of agendas, but also in terms of attitude (less theoretic, more pragmatic). The funding aims, indeed, to develop concrete (policy) recommendations, and does not offer additional financing for fundamental research or 'Research' in general. Greater awareness of these points could lead to better and more satisfactory collaboration and, in the future, perhaps, less reluctance on the part of academic teams, in particular, to apply for funding. In addition, academic teams should give particular consideration as to exactly what they are offering in return for the requested funding. Non-academic teams could include a topic expert in their team – preferably with a scientific research background – in order to increase their credibility and efficiency.

Finally, funders should be aware that, if they contract with academic teams, they can expect to have more input in order to help them to stay focused, to respect deadlines, and to help them to distinguish between what is 'nice to know' and what we 'need to know' – that is, to be able to appreciate a policy – rather than a purely academic-agenda. It is important that funders are able to take advantage of the particular expertise of academic teams, and that they can ensure appropriate recognition in the final report and further publications. Private teams will require more in the way of scientific advice and input from funding bodies, while academic teams could improve their contribution through seeking to achieve more fluent collaboration, more 'on time' deliverables and through devoting less attention to theoretical discussions.

References

Barbour, Rosaline. S. (2000) 'The role of qualitative research in broadening the "evidence base" for clinical practice'. *Journal of Evaluation in Clinical Practice*, 6(2): 155–63.

Belgian Health Care Knowledge Centre (2011) 'About the KCE', (https://kce.fgov.be/about-kce).

Benahmed, N., Devos, C., San Miguel, L., Vinck, I., Vankelst, L., Lauwerier, E., Verschueren, M., Obyn, C., Paulus, D., and Christiaens, W. (2014) 'Caring for mothers and newborns after uncomplicated delivery: Towards integrated postnatal care', *KCE Reports*, 232; Brussels: Belgian Health Care Knowledge Centre (KCE).

Christiaens, W., Van de Walle, E., Devresse, S., Van Halewyck, D., Dubois, C., Benahmed, N., Desomer, A., Van De Sande, S., Van Loey, N., Peulus, D., and Van den Heede, K. (2013) 'Organisation of aftercare for patients with severe burn injuries', *KCE Reports*, 209; Brussels: Belgian Health Care Knowledge Centre (KCE).

Deschodt, Mieke, Claes, V., Van Grootven, B., Milisen, K., Boland, B., Flamaing, J., Denis, A., Daue, F., Mergaert, L., Devos, C., Mistiaen, P., and Van den Heede K. (2015) 'Comprehensive geriatric care in hospitals: The role of inpatient geriatric consultation teams', *KCE Reports*, 245; Brussels: Belgian Health Care Knowledge Centre (KCE).

Kohn, L., Mambourg, F., Robays, J., Albertijn, M., Janssens, S., Hoefnagels, K., Ronsmans, M., and Jonckheer, P. (2014) 'Informed choice on breast cancer screening: Messages to support informed decision', *KCE Reports*, 216; Brussels: Belgian Health Care Knowledge Centre (KCE).

Mistiaen, P., Kohn, L., Mambourg, F., Ketterer, F., Tiedke, C., Lambrechts, M-C, Vanmeerbeek, M., Godderis, L., Eyssen, M., and Paulus, D. (2016) 'Reduction of the treatment gap for problematic alcohol use in Belgium', *KCE Reports*, 258; Brussels: Belgian Health Care Knowledge Centre (KCE).

Piérart, J., Léonard, C., Chalon, P., Daue, F., and Mertens, R. (2012) 'Stakeholder Involvement in KCE working processes', *KCE Reports*, 174; Brussels: Belgian Health Care Knowledge Centre (KCE).

Pope, Catherine., and Mays, Nicholas (eds.) (2006) *Qualitative Research in Health Care* (3rd ed.). Oxford: Blackwell Publishing/BMJ Books.

Roberfroid, D., Dauvrin, M., Keygnaert, I., Desomer, A., Kerstens, B., Camberlin, C., Gysen, J., Lorant, V., and Derluyn, I. (2015) 'What health care for undocumented migrants in Belgium ?', *KCE Reports*, 257; Brussels: Belgian Health Care Knowledge Centre (KCE).

Laurence Kohn trained in social sciences and public heath at the Université Libre de Bruxelles (ULB). Her PhD thesis used both qualitative and quantitative methods. Between 2004 and 2015, she taught qualitative methods at the School of Public health in ULB and, since 2016, at the Université Catholique de Louvain (UCL). She has been employed as an expert in Health Service Research and Qualitative Inquiry at the Belgian Health Care Knowledge Centre (KCE) since 2004. During this time, she has researched or supervised nearly 20 studies covering Health Services Research; Good Clinical Practice; and Health Technology Assessment; providing methodological expertise.

Wendy Christiaens is a sociologist with a special interest in sociology of health and illness, qualitative research, complexity and systems thinking. She received her PhD from Ghent University, where she lectured courses such as Introduction to sociology, Family and living arrangements and Medical sociology during her post-doctoral years. Since 2011, she is employed by the Belgian Health Care Knowledge Centre (KCE) as an expert in health services research and qualitative methods. This has involved her in carrying out research into a wide variety of public health topics, including aftercare for severely burned patients, postnatal care, child abuse and prostate cancer.

# 4

Cross-Cultural Focus Group Discussions

Monique M. Hennink

Introduction

Conducting focus group discussions across cultures poses specific challenges for researchers. It requires flexibility, cultural sensitivity, maintaining methodological rigour and additional time and resources. Navigating these challenges can involve a steep cultural learning curve for researchers and requires a research team equipped to balance cultural sensitivity with methodological rigor. Using focus groups in cross-cultural research does not necessitate a new methodological approach, since the core principles remain the same. It does pose a challenge in applying the principles of focus group research while embracing the cultural norms of a given research context – which requires flexibility in the application of some methodological tasks. Cross-cultural focus group research is becoming increasingly common with this method being used

M.M. Hennink (✉)
Hubert Department of Global Health, Rollins School of Public Health,
Emory University, Atlanta Georgia, USA
e-mail: mhennin@emory.edu

in an ever-widening range of study contexts. This chapter identifies the methodological principles that remain constant despite the study setting and research tasks where flexibility is needed in cross-cultural focus group research. These issues are described for three stages of research: study design, data collection and data analysis.

Cross-Cultural Focus Group Discussions

Cross-cultural research, as described in this chapter, refers both to international research conducted outside of a researcher's own country and to domestic research conducted within a researcher's country but with a sub-group of the population who have a different language or cultural background to that of the researcher. Therefore, cross-cultural research encompasses both U.S. researchers conducting a study in Bolivia and U.S. researchers conducting a study in the U.S. amongst Indian migrants. Both these scenarios pose similar challenges in that researchers are working with study populations that have a different social, cultural or linguistic background and require the adaptation of certain methodological tasks when using focus group discussions. In cross-cultural studies, researchers are working in a cultural context different from their own. This requires obtaining a degree of *cultural knowledge* about the study population, to become aware of both explicit issues (e.g. languages spoken) and implicit issues (e.g. cultural norms or styles of communication) that may impact the research process. It also involves developing *cultural sensitivity* in order to effectively adapt components of the research methodology to reflect the cultural context of the study. Cultural sensitivity involves becoming familiar with the cultural norms of the study population, assessing how these may intersect with research tasks and adapting these tasks to ensure they are culturally appropriate for the research setting. Cultural sensitivity, thus, involves a willingness for tacit learning and flexibility to notice issues and adapt research tasks throughout the study. This may require a steep cultural learning curve for the research team and continued attention to cultural adaptations throughout the entire research process. While some cultural norms are clearly apparent to outsiders – particularly language differences – other cultural practices and preferences are less discernable and require guidance from 'cultural brokers'. Cultural brokers are individuals familiar with the cultural context of the research who can advise the study team on culturally appropriate strategies to meet research objectives. This is critical to ensure that the research does not cause offense or harm to study participants and to collect culturally relevant and valid data. Cultural brokers are invaluable for cross-cultural research, often becoming critical members of the field team.

Focus group discussions are particularly well-suited to cross-cultural research and their use in these contexts has increased significantly over the past decade. It is perhaps the group context of data collection that makes the method so well suited to cross-cultural research, in at least two respects. First, the group nature of data collection makes focus groups well suited for exploratory research (Hennink 2008b). A group of participants can quickly identify a wide range of issues and perspectives on the study topic, with a single group discussion generating almost three quarters of the issues as in-depth interviews with the same number of people (Fern 1982). This is particularly valuable in cross-cultural research, where the issues and cultural perspectives are often unknown. Using focus groups for exploratory research is also valuable for mixed methods research – for example, where focus groups are used to develop culturally appropriate questions on a survey instrument that reflect terminology and cultural concepts of the study population, or for designing interventions and social campaigns that reflect the cultural preferences of the target community. Using focus groups as the formative component in mixed methods research thereby improves the validity of the quantitative instrument or intervention by focusing on culturally relevant issues and reflecting terminology that is understood by the study population.

Second, the group context of data collection makes focus groups highly effective for identifying community views and social norms, which is particularly important in cross-cultural research. The discussion element of focus groups is effective for capturing community perspectives on the research issues. 'Focus group discussions are able to produce "collective narratives" on the research issues that go beyond individual perspectives to generate a group perspective on the issues discussed, which produces a different type and level of data from that gained in individual interviews' (Hennink 2014: 3). These collective narratives result from participants' discussion and debate in a group setting and often reflect core community or cultural perspectives on the research issues. The group environment is also very effective in identifying and validating social norms. A group of participants can collectively describe, explain and validate typical beliefs and behaviours in the community as well as nuances and variations in these (Morgan 1997 cited in Hesse-Biber 2006). The group environment also allows for social moderation of views, whereby extreme views or atypical behaviours are tempered by the group, so that social or cultural norms are identified and acknowledged by the group (Morgan 1997; Patton 1990) and, thus, made explicit for the researchers.

There has been a significant increase in focus group research over recent decades, such that focus groups have become a 'standard' research tool (Wilkinson 2011; Morgan et al. 2008). Their increased use stems from 'a greater diversity of disciplines embracing focus group discussions, the exposure of focus group methods to traditionally quantitative disciplines, and the application of focus group research to an increasingly diverse range of study settings' (Hennink 2008b: 210). One aspect of these changes has been the increased use of focus groups in cross-cultural research in a broad range of disciplines (e.g. social sciences, epidemiology, medical research, public health, political science, business studies), and amongst different types of organizations (e.g. academic, non-governmental, social marketing, government agencies).

Although there is now a greater diversity of researchers, research settings and institutions using focus group discussions than in the past, there is little guidance in the methodological literature on cross-cultural applications of the method. Most textbooks assume that researchers share the same language and culture as their study participants and do not discuss issues in using focus groups in cross-cultural settings, notable exceptions include Hennink (2014, 2008a, 2008b, 2007) and Liamputtong (2010). One area that does not receive adequate attention is the *extent* to which methodological adjustments are needed when using focus groups in cross-cultural research. Although, it can be assumed that some flexibility is needed, it is not clear which aspects of the method are typically adjusted in cross-cultural research and, perhaps more importantly, what remains constant despite the study context. A basic guideline that will be reiterated in this chapter is that the theoretical principles underlying the method remain constant to ensure methodological rigour, but the field application of these principles may need adaptation for different cultural settings. 'Good quality focus group research, regardless of the context in which it is conducted, should reflect certain theoretical principles and be based on informed methodological decisions. Too often methodological rigour is overtaken by the management of fieldwork challenges' (Hennink, 2007: xvi). Thus, the challenge for researchers is to balance methodological rigour with cultural sensitivity in designing and implementing cross-cultural focus group research.

Framework for Cross-Cultural Flexibility

The framework for this chapter is shown in Fig. 4.1, which depicts three stages of research – study design, data collection and data analysis – and some of the challenges in the cross-cultural application of focus groups in each stage. In the centre are core principles that remain constant despite the study context. This chapter highlights issues at each stage of research that require flexibility in cross-cultural focus group research, while noting areas that remain the same despite the study context. The intention is not to describe all issues exhaustively but provide broad guidance in delineating underlying principles from field tasks that require flexibility and cultural sensitivity. Several case studies highlight these issues in specific studies.

The application of focus group discussions is guided by the principles of the interpretive paradigm that underlies all qualitative research. These principles (shown in Fig. 4.1) still guide methodological tasks in cross-cultural focus group research despite the differing study context. As a method of qualitative research, focus group discussions seek to uncover the *emic perspective* of study participants. The design of the discussion

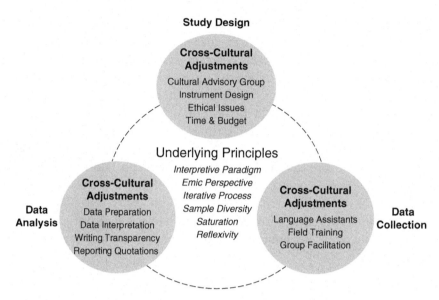

Fig. 4.1 Framework for conducting cross-cultural focus group research

guide, the roles of the moderator and selection of study participants all contribute to gaining the emic perspective, and this goal remains when focus groups are used in cross-cultural research. The *sample size* also reflects the principles of the interpretive paradigm, whereby the goal is to seek diversity of issues and participants in order to provide a comprehensive and nuanced understanding of the research issues. This goal necessitates a purposive sample that is iteratively refined as data collection progresses. The principle of *saturation* also remains applicable to gauge when the sample is adequate, by assessing whether a diverse and relevant range of issues have been identified, understood and validated. The use of *reflexivity* remains important to manage potential subjectivity in the research process and study team. These principles underlie the design of focus group research and remain relevant when applying the method in cross-cultural settings. These principles apply to all stages of the research and are thus depicted in the centre of Fig. 4.1, as they underlie tasks undertaken in study design, data collection and data analysis.

Study Design Issues

Several aspects of study design require attention in cross-cultural focus group research: the composition of the research team, design of the discussion guide, ethical approvals and the time and budget needed for the study, as described below.

Cultural Advisory Group

When researchers do not share the same cultural background as study participants, it is beneficial to establish a cultural advisory group for the study. This advisory group comprises members of the study community who act as 'cultural brokers' between the research team and the study population. The cultural advisory group can guide the study team on cultural norms to ensure cultural sensitivity in the research process, which not only protects the study participants from harm but also improves the quality of data collected.

A cultural advisory group may take several forms. First, the study team may include members who are familiar with the cultural context of the study or the study population. These members are invaluable cultural experts who guide the study team on: adapting the research tasks to the cultural context of the study, assessing the cultural appropriateness of field strategies, effective language and communication strategies, and cultural protocols to follow. A second strategy to maintain cultural sensitivity is to develop an external community advisory committee, typically comprising community members who hold key roles in their community, such as religious leaders, educators, health officials or service providers. Their community role provides a strong platform from which to advise on culturally appropriate strategies for accessing the community, seeking local permissions, recruiting participants, venues for data collection and language and communication issues. The community advisory committee may convene at critical points in the research process to provide advice on specific issues. For example, at the outset of a study to gauge community interest in the study topic, during data collection to guide fieldwork strategies or during data analysis to assist in cultural interpretation of study findings. A community advisory committee is an effective option for cross-cultural studies in a researcher's own country since the advisory committee can easily be convened as needed (see e.g. Case Study 4.1 and 4.2). A third strategy, for international research, involves identifying in-country collaborators who may become part of the study team or form a separate advisory group. In-country collaborators fulfil the same tasks as described earlier to provide advice on cultural sensitivity to the study team. They have the added advantage of being located in the study country itself so can also assist with fieldwork logistics prior to the arrival of the research team.

Instrument Design and Translation

The discussion guide is the instrument used to collect data in a focus group discussion. The basic design principles of a focus group discussion guide remain relevant for cross-cultural research. These include the *funnel structure* of the guide in which questions flow from broad to specific; the *number of questions* on the guide; the *introduction statement* covering ethics and group conduct; the *question structure* that includes warm-up, key and closing questions. The principles of question design also remain present, for example, designing *open and non-leading* questions, minimizing *dichotomous* questions, phrasing questions to *promote discussion*, using *less personal* phrasing of questions due to the group context and *using probes* to gain depth (see Krueger and Casey 2015; Hennink 2014; Barbour 2007). The main areas of divergence in designing a discussion guide for cross-cultural focus group research relate to the language and translation of the guide, designing culturally appropriate and culturally relevant questions and using appropriate questioning strategies.

Questions on the discussion guide need to be both culturally appropriate and culturally relevant to the study context. Each question should be reviewed for *cultural appropriateness* to ensure that the wording of the question will not cause discomfort to participants and are suitable to discuss in a group. Some questions may seem innocuous to researchers not familiar with the cultural context of the study but may be unacceptable to ask participants from that culture. Questions also need to be *culturally relevant*. For example, asking questions to women about economic decision-making in cultures where women do not control finances would be irrelevant. Culturally appropriate and culturally relevant questions are both ethical and more likely to generate valid data. In addition, the questioning strategy needs to be culturally acceptable. In some cultures, asking pregnant women to discuss potential health issues during pregnancy is seen as jeopardizing their pregnancy and thus an inappropriate questioning strategy. In other cultures, participants have difficulty responding to hypothetical questions or scenarios, thus these questioning strategies would not be culturally appropriate. There will undoubtedly be differences from one study to the next on what is viewed as a culturally inappropriate question, which underscores the value of establishing a cultural advisory group for the study.

In cross-cultural focus groups, the discussion guide is typically translated into the language(s) of study participants. A translated discussion guide enables the use of appropriate colloquial language that contributes to rapport development but also ensures that questions are understood by participants as intended, thereby increasing data validity (Hennink 2014, 2007). A key decision involves identifying the most appropriate language(s) in which to translate the discussion guide. The discussion guide should also reflect colloquial language, which may be achieved by using the cultural advisory group described previously, employing bi-lingual community members to translate the guide or including instrument translation as part of the field training process. It is important to identify common phrases and relevant cultural references that effectively capture the meaning of each question rather than using a translation service which may reflect more formal wording and reduce rapport with participants (Hennink 2007). It is critical to pilot test a translated instrument to ensure that questions are phrased appropriately, understood as intended and elicit the type data needed.

Ethical Issues

Conducting ethical research is critical in all studies. However, approaches to achieve this may differ in cross-cultural research, particularly with regards to seeking ethical approval and ensuring informed consent. Research studies are typically approved by an ethical review board in a researcher's own institution and, for international research, may also require ethical approval in the study country. Navigating ethical approval in the study country can be challenging and time consuming and may benefit from guidance of in-country collaborators. In addition to formal ethical approvals, it is often customary in some social contexts to seek informal permission from community leaders. This involves meeting community leaders to describe the study purpose, benefits and outcomes, which can significantly improve rapport with the study community and provide a potential source of assistance with field tasks.

Using culturally relevant means to seek informed consent from study participants is an area that needs particular attention in cross-cultural research. First, the mode of communication used in seeking informed consent needs to be tailored to the study community, in particular by translating documents into the language of study participants or by obtaining oral consent in contexts where participants may be illiterate in their own language or feel uncomfortable to sign formal consent documents. Second, seeking individual consent can be challenging in settings where behaviours are controlled by others, such as community leaders, employers or husbands who may authorize individuals to participate in the study. Researchers are obliged to ensure that consent is gained from individual participants themselves and to protect them from potential harm if they decline participation. Third, incentives offered for participation should not be coercive such that participants might choose to undergo some risks to be involved in the study. This is particularly important where research is conducted in resource poor settings.

Time and Budget

Conducting cross-cultural focus group research may require additional tasks that lead to longer fieldwork time and require additional resources. Additional tasks may include: seeking in-country ethical approval and community permissions, translating informed consent documents, translating the discussion guide and training of bi-lingual field assistants. Cross-cultural research also necessitates longer time for data analysis due to the need to translate the recordings of each group discussion into the researchers' language. These additional tasks extend the fieldwork time, require additional field staff and resources, all of which need to be added to the study proposal and budget when planning cross-cultural focus group research.

Case Study 4.1
Focus Group Discussions in the Refugee Community in Atlanta, USA.
We used focus group discussions for a community needs assessment amongst refugee families. Although the focus group format was ideal, implementing cross-cultural focus group discussions posed several challenges. Our first challenge was to build trust and effectively communicate with the community to recruit participants. Common recruitment strategies such as using flyers, phone calls and print or online advertisements posed a range of challenges due to plurality of languages spoken, resource constraints (i.e. no access to phones, computers), illiteracy and accessing multiple cultural groups of refugees. Instead, we asked respected community leaders to recruit participants face-to-face which overcame logistical difficulties and built trust and credibility for the research. Focus group discussions were also held in culturally appropriate and familiar places, such as churches and community centers.
The refugee community comprise residents from a wide variety of countries who speak different languages and have variable English language fluency. This posed challenges for group composition and identifying a unifying language for the group discussions. For logistical reasons, groups were stratified by language, including English, rather than other demographic characteristics that would normally be used (e.g. age and gender). This allowed those not comfortable speaking English to participate and speak their own language. Although this led to a greater number of groups than stratifying by demographic characteristics, it reinforced community trust in the research and led to higher-quality data.
Focus groups had to be moderated well to ensure methodological rigor yet also allow participants to express themselves in their own language. To meet both these needs, group discussions were co-facilitated by an experienced moderator and a community member with language and cultural expertise. This approach provided expertise in focus group facilitation while also providing the flexibility for participants to express themselves and seek clarification in English or their native language. It also allowed cultural knowledge to be shared in real time, enabling facilitators to probe more deeply on cultural issues during the discussion.

Carolyn Kulb, MPH.
Independent Research Consultant

Data Collection Issues

The principles of qualitative data collection remain applicable in cross-cultural focus group research. These include using an *iterative process*, whereby data collection is refined as the study progresses; employing *purposive recruitment* of participants; using *saturation* to assess an adequate sample size; and practicing *reflexivity* to assess potential influences on the data collection. In addition, the procedures for conducting focus group discussions also remain in place for cross-cultural focus groups. For example, following guidelines for group size and composition, using circular seating to promote discussion, developing rapport with participants, applying moderation techniques to foster a discussion and managing group dynamics. Although there may be some adjustments in different settings, overall these principles and procedures are still followed in cross-cultural focus group research. The areas where the most adjustments are needed relate to language and communication issues, which influence the composition and training of the field team, and moderation of the group discussion, as discussed next.

Language Assistants

In conducting cross-cultural focus group research, issues of language and communication inevitably arise. Language and communication are critical for qualitative research, since language represents data, and communication the process through which data are generated. Language provides a window to understand culture, through the words, expressions and phrases used by participants and the cultural meanings that are embedded in these. Thus language helps to understand human behaviour and social processes in different cultural settings (Hennink 2008a, Winchatz 2006; Safran 2004). In cross-cultural studies, researchers often do not share the same language and/or culture of study participants and therefore need to recruit language assistants. Language assistants become important members of the field team who fulfil several roles: as focus group facilitators, transcribers of the discussion and translators of written transcripts. Researchers also rely on language assistants as 'cultural brokers' who not only collect data for the study but also interpret these data when they translate discussions into written transcripts. Dialogue holds meaning, thus participants' words, expressions and their manner of communication all convey underlying cultural meanings that need to be understood and captured in the translated transcripts. The quality of these cultural interpretations, and thus data quality itself, is highly dependent on language assistants' cultural knowledge. 'Cultural insiders have the additional advantage over outsiders because they have facility with the language and culture that allows them access to the cultural community, which can be extremely difficult to gain even by sensitive and knowledgeable outsiders' (Birman 2005: 172). The contribution of language assistants, therefore, goes beyond simply collecting data but also in shaping the meaning of these data which is central to qualitative research. When recruiting language assistants their language proficiency alone may be insufficient without also having familiarity with the cultural context of study participants (Denzin and Lincoln 2008; Hennink 2008a; Tsai et al. 2004; Temple and Edwards 2002; Madriz 2000). Therefore, it is important to recruit language assistants familiar with *both* the language and culture of study participants to not only communicate effectively with participants but also to interpret data accurately and convey the cultural meaning of participants' words (see e.g. Case Study 4.3).

Language assistants thus become an invaluable part of the field team in cross-cultural focus group research. In selecting language assistants, a range of characteristics are considered. Fluency in the language of study participants is a clear criterion; however, bi-lingual fluency is also critical to communicate effectively with the study team and bi-lingual literacy is also needed to produce valid translations of written transcripts. Demographic characteristics are important to enable matching of moderators to the age and gender of participant in each focus group. A further consideration is whether language assistants are from the same community as study participants. Language assistants familiar to study participants may increase the group rapport by making participants feel at ease, but conversely their familiarity may inhibit the contribution of focus group participants due to concerns of confidentiality. Participants may also omit to discuss issues with which they assume the moderator is familiar, because they come from the same community, leading to less detailed data. One strategy is to select language assistants from the local area but not from within the study communities themselves, thereby gaining the needed language skills and cultural knowledge but reducing issues caused by their familiarity to participants. The ideal combination of characteristics of language assistants will likely differ for each study and be influenced by logistical considerations.

Field Training

Training a field team is essential to maintain methodological rigor and conduct ethical research. In cross-cultural research, language assistants are likely to be involved in a range of field tasks, so their inclusion in the training is critical. Language assistants are primarily selected for their language skills and may be community members, thus not familiar with scientific research. They may also have little exposure to qualitative research or focus group discussion methodology in particular and require guidance in developing skills such as building rapport, group facilitation, impartial moderation and managing group dynamics. The focus and content of training sessions may therefore need to be tailored to suit the experience level of language assistants. Language assistants also play a lead role in facilitating the group discussions by asking questions, probing for detail, listening to the discussion and formulating follow-up questions. To effectively guide a discussion and produce useable data, language assistants also need to fully understand the research questions and the overall goals of the study. This will enable them to make quick decisions during the discussion on whether or not to probe on certain topics raised as they relate to the study objectives. The field training session also provides opportunities for two-way exchange, whereby researchers impart methodological knowledge and skills while language assistants can provide important cultural information to guide data collection. Translation of the research instruments may also become a part of the field training sessions, again necessitating the inclusion of language assistants.

In qualitative research, it is understood that the characteristics, perspectives, culture and opinions of the researcher influence the research process and resulting data (Temple 2002; Alibhai-Brown 2000). An interviewer's 'social location' in the world influences how they hear, interpret and respond to the views and experiences of study participants (Temple and Edwards 2002) and thus how they conduct an interview itself. Language assistants, like researchers, bring their own perspectives and background characteristics to the research process that shape the data generated (Hennink 2008a). In addition, they further shape data when transcribing and translating the recorded interview into the language of the researchers. Translators need to listen to the words of study participants, interpret the meaning of words, phrases, proverbs or tone, and reflect the equivalent meaning in the translated text (Green and Thorogood 2004). This process requires a significant amount of interpretation (Culley et al. 2007; Larkin 2007; Maynard-Tucker 2000) and a high degree of cultural fluency in both the source and target languages to both understand inherent cultural meanings and convey these in the translated transcript. Therefore, translators are not simply neutral conduits of information in cross-cultural research but play an active role in shaping the meaning of the data produced. Given that language assistants 'become active producers of knowledge who add an additional layer of subjective understanding to the data' (Hennink 2008a: 26), it is important to encourage reflexivity amongst language assistants as part of the field training sessions. Practicing reflexivity may involve encouraging self-reflection amongst the field team, to become aware of their own personal, social or cultural perspectives about the research issues, considering their attitudes towards the study population, and reflecting on how this may influence their role in collecting, interpreting or transcribing data. For further guidance on reflexivity amongst language assistants see Hennink 2007, 2008a.

Common components of field training for cross-cultural focus group research may include the following:

- Background of study (research problem, study design and goals)
- Research ethics
- Principles of qualitative research

- Procedures of focus group discussions
- Roles of the field team
- Practicing team reflexivity
- Review of research instrument(s)
- Translation of instrument(s)
- Transcription and translation protocols
- Skills training (recruitment, moderation, note-taking)
- Field practice sessions

Focus Group Facilitation

Facilitating a focus group discussion requires a range of skills to build trust and rapport with participants, encourage interaction, conduct impartial moderation, maintain flexibility on discussion topics, probe for depth and detail and manage group dynamics. Many of the strategies for achieving these goals remain the same when conducting cross-cultural research. The main challenge in facilitating cross-cultural focus groups lies in bridging language differences between researchers and study participants to conduct an effective discussion.

Cross-cultural focus groups are often conducted in the language of study participants. It may seem logical to conduct the discussion through an interpreter to bridge the language divide between researchers and participants. However, facilitating a discussion through an interpreter significantly impairs a free-flowing dialogue, influences group dynamics and takes considerably longer. A more effective strategy is to train a bi-lingual moderator, who can foster a natural discussion and generate higher quality data, as they are familiar with cultural norms and cues for communication that can aid in conducting the discussion in a culturally appropriate way. In some cross-cultural studies, there may be multiple languages spoken that require alternative strategies (see Case Study 4.1). Where study participants speak a range of languages or regional dialects, there sometimes exists a *lingua franca* or 'official language' that is used for communication between the different regions. Not all participants may be fluent or confident in the *lingua franca*, but this may be the best option in some study contexts (see Hennink 2007 for more on this). Another strategy is to use a team moderation approach, whereby one moderator is fluent in the main language of the discussion and the second in the regional language. This enables participants to express themselves in either the *lingua franca* or their regional language, with moderators providing simultaneous translation for each other and for participants. This can aid in maintaining the flow of the discussion and enable free expression amongst participant. See Case Study 4.1 shown earlier as an example.

Case Study 4.2

Focus Group Discussions amongst the South Asian Community in USA
The South Asian Health and Prevention Education (SHAPE) study aimed to assess the feasibility of promoting lifestyle change to prevent diabetes among South Asians in the U.S. Since little is known about the lifestyle behaviours and preferences of this community around diabetes prevention, formative focus group discussions were used to inform the intervention design. Three unique aspects were implemented due to the cross-cultural nature of the study.
First, we formed a community advisory board comprised of influential members of the local South Asian community (e.g. South Asian physicians, researchers, and community leaders). The advisory group met quarterly and were instrumental in guiding the study team on tailoring the study to cultural norms, promoting the study in the community and providing logistical assistance in implementing the discussion groups. Some advisory board members were very engaged in the study, working directly with community organizations to recruit participants or arranging venues for discussions.
Second, since all participants were fluent in English, we were able to use non-South Asians moderators who were 'outsiders' to the cultural norm of study participants. This strategy encouraged participants to provide more detailed descriptions of their behaviours and experiences than if they perceived the moderator to be a cultural insider who would 'know how things are done.' Using outsider moderators can be challenging if not implemented carefully. We believed that using outsiders was effective in our study because: the topic of discussion was not sensitive; moderators were experienced in collecting qualitative data as outsiders so they focused on building rapport with participants before and during the early parts of the discussions; and it was stressed to participants that the programme was being designed for their needs and preferences so their honest feedback was vital.
Third, an important tool for building rapport with study participants was holding group discussions in Indian restaurants. Food plays a central role in

> South Asian culture and is a key part of most social functions. Holding group discussions at popular Indian restaurants increased participation and helped participants to feel more comfortable. We noticed that the entire tone of the discussion became more open and relaxed because the event reflected a typical social gathering in their community, leading to a more lively and informative discussion.
>
> **Mary Beth Weber, Ph.D., MPH.**
> **Emory Global Diabetes Research Center**
> **Hubert Department of Global Health, Emory University**

Data Analysis Issues

Most adjustments to cross-cultural focus group research are made in the study design and data collection stages rather than in data analysis. Data analysis is guided by the analytic approach selected which provides the principles and procedures to follow, for example, grounded theory or narrative analysis. Data from cross-cultural focus group research require attention to data preparation, data interpretation and presentation of findings.

Many approaches to qualitative data analysis require a written transcript. In cross-cultural research, data will often need to be translated into the language of the research team; however, if analysts are fluent in language of the discussion it is beneficial to analyze data in the original language to maintain the richness of participants' expressions and cultural meanings (Twinn 1997). With this approach, translation is only needed when using quotations from data in a research report. More often data need to be translated, which requires a process of *meaning* translation from the original expressions into equivalent phrases in the target language. This process involves not only fluidity between languages but also sensitivity to the cultural meanings underlying certain expressions, so that these are not lost in the translated transcript. A significant level of interpretation is needed to achieve meaning equivalence between two languages, therefore translators need familiarity with both the language *and* culture of study participants (see Case Study 4.3). It can be useful to retain certain phrases in their original language in a translated transcript, particularly where they represent specific cultural concepts, with a brief translation in brackets, for example, *purdah* (the practice of gender segregation). This ensures that important cultural references are retained in translated transcripts (Hennink 2007). It is also important to check the accuracy of translated data in cross-cultural research to manage potentially subjective interpretations of data during translation.

Qualitative data analysis involves interpretation, which can be subjective. This is typically managed in qualitative data analysis by practicing reflexivity, whereby researchers' become aware of their potentially subjective interpretation of data. In cross-cultural research there exists an additional layer of cultural interpretation, whereby researchers may project assumptions and expectations of their own culture onto data from another cultural context, thereby adding further layer of subjective interpretation to data. Due to the multiple layers of interpretation in cross-cultural research, strategies to balance subjectivity are needed. It is therefore important to practice reflexivity with the research team, by reviewing emerging findings and their interpretation and checking that these are well grounded in the data itself rather than reflecting researcher's expectations about the culture or community studied. A cultural advisory group can be particularly useful for checking the validity of cross-cultural interpretation of issues during data analysis. Esposito (2001) and Twinn (1997) describe several approaches that may enhance validity of translated data, for example, using several translators, using back-translation of transcripts, bi-lingual peer review of recordings against transcripts, and member-checking interpretations with participants.

In writing and presenting cross-cultural qualitative research, a range of issues need consideration. Transparency is needed in describing the study methods, particularly how language, cultural and communication challenges were managed, the role of language assistants in data generation, the process of translation of transcripts, how reflexivity was used, and how cross-cultural interpretation of data was validated. Including these details reflects the cross-cultural nature of the study and demonstrates researchers' attention to validity. When writing the study results it is necessary to describe the cultural context of issues discussed and to maintain particular words in their original language that capture specific cultural concepts. It is also common to include quotations from participants as examples of issues described in the results. When including quotations from cross-cultural research, it should be remembered that quotations are a product of participants' actual words *and* the linguistic fluency of the translator. Therefore, translated quotations that are presented in broken English or with poor grammar may not be an accurate reflection of participants' own ability to articulate themselves, but reflect the English language skills of a translator. Researchers, therefore, have an ethical responsibility to accurately reflect participant's words *and* their manner of communication when presenting quotations, to avoid shedding negative light on a study population.

> **Case Study 4.3**
>
> **Focus Group Discussions Amongst Widowed/Divorced Women in Ethiopia.** Widowed/divorced women are extremely impoverished and marginalized in Ethiopia, and their sexuality seen as threatening by the wider community. We used focus group discussions to explore community perceptions of widowed/divorced women and their access to family planning services. This was a culturally sensitive topic and the cross-cultural nature of the study presented several challenges. The expertise of local collaborators was vital since we were from a different cultural background and speak a different language from our study participants.
> *Cross-Cultural Translation.* Working cross-culturally required careful translation of the discussion guide, beyond phrasing questions from one language to another. It involved knowing how to ask context-appropriate questions, how to raise sensitive topics, and how to select phrases to reflect certain ideas. NGO programme staff (who also facilitated groups) translated the discussion guide as they had both cultural knowledge and English language fluency to capture the meaning of our questions in the Oromifa language. Translation involved lengthy discussions about the most appropriate phrases to use in Oromifa. The translation process was also beneficial for programme staff to become familiar with the questions and their intention, which was useful when they later facilitated the group discussions.
> *Cross-Cultural Training.* Language barriers again provided a challenge during field training sessions. While the training was conducted in English, the practice sessions were conducted in Oromifa, therefore it was difficult for me to gauge how well the team were applying qualitative research skills. Once data collection began I noticed from transcripts that facilitators were not probing effectively. For example, if a

participant said 'it is forbidden for widows to use family planning,' the facilitator would not ask 'why' or probe deeper. Perhaps facilitators felt it was culturally inappropriate to challenge speakers or ask more about sensitive topics. Given this experience, I realized that piloting the discussion and reviewing issues prior to data collection is critical in cross-cultural research.

Cross-Cultural Interpretation. Collaborating with programme staff was particularly beneficial during data analysis to provide cultural context to the issues raised. We would have missed or misinterpreted several issues without the cultural knowledge of our local collaborators. For example, widowed/divorced women described no longer receiving '*gusa*' from their community, which translates as 'help'. To an outsider the meaning appears simple, but the cultural practice of '*gusa*' requires more understanding. Receiving '*gusa*' is an important social tradition in Ethiopia. Individuals in need can '*beg gusa*' from others to receive support, with the understanding that some form of reciprocity would follow at a later time. Understanding this gives much greater meaning to widowed/divorced women's experience of being denied '*gusa*' from their community.

Anna Newton-Levinson, MPH
PhD Student, Behaviour Sciences and Health Education, Emory University

Conclusion

Using focus group discussions in cross-cultural research requires some adjustments throughout the research process. During study design, consider including cultural advisors on the study team, designing a culturally appropriate discussion guide, seeking additional ethical approvals and adding time and resources for additional tasks. During data collection, language and communication issues arise that require language assistants to conduct, transcribe and translate the discussions, and ensure cultural sensitivity during fieldwork. During data analysis, attention is needed in translating transcripts, cultural interpretation of data and in presenting quotations. While all these tasks require flexibility and cultural sensitivity, the underlying principles of focus group research remain relevant to ensure methodological rigor and data validity.

References

Alibhai-Brown, Y. (2000). *Who Do We Think We Are? Imagining the New Britain.* London: Penguin.

Barbour, R. (2007). *Doing Focus Groups.* The SAGE Qualitative Research Kit. London: Sage Publications.

Birman, D. (2005). Ethical Issues in Research with Immigrants and Refugees. In J. Trimble and C. Fisher (eds.), *Handbook of Ethical Research with Ethnocultural Populations and Communities* (pp. 155–177). Thousand Oaks, CA: Sage Publications.

Culley, L., Hudson, N., and Rapport, F. (2007). Using Focus Groups with Minority Ethnic Communities: Researching Infertility in British South Asian Communities. *Qualitative Health Research,* 17(1), 102–112.

Denzin, N., and Lincoln, Y. (eds.) (2008). *Collecting and Interpreting Qualitative Materials* (3rd ed.). Thousand Oaks, CA: Sage Publications.

Esposito, E. (2001). From Meaning to Meaning. The Influence of Translation Techniques on Non-English Focus Group Research. *Qualitative Health Research,* 11(14), 568–579.

Fern, E. (1982). The Use of Focus Groups for Idea Generation: The Effects of Group Size, Acquaintanceship, and Moderator on Response Quality and Quality. *Journal of Marketing Research,* 19, 1–13.

Green, J., and Thorogood, N. (2004). *Qualitative Methods for Health Research.* London: Sage Publications.

Hennink, M. (2007). *International Focus Group Research: A Handbook for the Health and Social Sciences.* Cambridge: Cambridge University Press.

Hennink, M. (2008a). Language and Communication in Cross-Cultural Qualitative Research. In Liamputtong (ed.), *Doing Cross-Cultural Research: Ethical and Methodological Perspectives.* Springer Publications.

Hennink, M. (2008b). *Emergent Issues in International Focus Group Discussions.* In Hesse-Biber & Leavy (eds.), *Handbook of Emergent Methods.* New York: The Guildford Press.

Hennink, M. (2014). *Understanding Qualitative Research: Focus Group Discussions.* New York: Oxford University Press.

Hesse-Biber, S., and Leavy, P. (2006). *The Practice of Qualitative Research.* Thousand Oaks: CA: Sage Publications.

Krueger, R., and Casey, M. (2015). *Focus Groups: A Practical Guide for Applied Research* (5th ed.). Thousand Oaks, CA: Sage.

Larkin, P. (2007). Multilingual Translation Issues in Qualitative Research: Reflections on a Metaphorical Process. *Qualitative Health Research*, 17(4), 468–476.
Liamputtong, P. (2010). *Performing Cross Cultural Qualitative Research*. New York: Cambridge University Press.
Madriz, E. (2000). Focus Groups in Feminist Research. In N. Denzin and Y. Lincoln (eds.), *Handbook of Qualitative Research*. Thousand Oaks, CA: Sage Publications.
Maynard-Tucker, G. (2000). Conducting Focus Groups in Developing Countries: Skill Training for Bi-lingual Facilitators. *Qualitative Health Research*, 10(3), 396–410.
Morgan, D. (1997). Focus Groups as Qualitative Research. Second Edition. Qualitative Research Methods Series, Volume 16, Thousand Oaks, CA: Sage Publications.
Morgan, D., Fellows, C., and Guevara, H. (2008). Emergent Approaches to Focus Group Research. In Hesse-Biber & Leavy (eds.), *Handbook of Emergent Methods*. New York: The Guildford Press.
Patton, M. (1990). *Qualitative Evaluation and Research Methods* (2nd ed.). Newbury Park, CA: Sage Publications.
Safran, W. (2004). The Political Aspects of Language. *Nationalism and Ethnic Politics*, 10(1), 1–14.
Temple, B. (2002). Crossed Wires: Interpreters, Translators, and Bilingual Workers in Cross-Language Research. *Qualitative Health Research*, 12(6), 844–854.
Temple, B., and Edwards, R. (2002). Interpreters/Translators and Cross-Language Research: Reflexivity and Border Crossings. *International Journal of Qualitative Methods*, 1(2). Article 1. Retrieved April 20, 2017 from http://www.uaberta.ca/~ijqm/
Tsai, J., Choe, J., Lim, J., Acorda, E., Chan, N., Taylor, V., and Tu, S. (2004). Developing Culturally Competent Health Knowledge: Issues of Data Analysis of Cross-cultural, Cross-language Qualitative Research. *International Journal of Qualitative Methods*, 3(4). Article 2. Retrieved April 20, 2017 from https://ualberta.ca/~iiqm/backissues/3_4/html/tsai/html
Twinn, S. (1997). An Exploratory Study Examining the Influence of Translation on the Validity and Reliability of Qualitative Data in Nursing Research. *Journal of Advanced Nursing*, 26, 418–423.

Wilkinson, S. (2011). Analyzing Focus Group Data. In D. Silverman (ed.), *Qualitative Research* (3rd ed., pp. 168–186). London: Sage Publications.

Winchatz, M. (2006). Fieldworker or Foreigner? Ethnographic Interviewing in Non-native Languages. *Field Methods*, 1(18), 83–97.

Monique M. Hennink, PhD, is an Associate Professor in Hubert Department of Global Health in Rollins School of Public Health at Emory University in Atlanta, USA. She is author of several textbooks on qualitative research, including: *Focus Group Discussions: Understanding Qualitative Research* (Oxford University Press 2014); *International Focus Group Research* (Cambridge University Press, 2007) and *Qualitative Research Methods* (2011 with Inge Hutter and Ajay Bailey). She has been using, teaching and publishing qualitative and mixed methods research for over 20 years, and conducted over 50 training workshops on qualitative research for social scientists and public health professionals worldwide (see http://tinyurl.com/rsph-qr). She has extensive experience in the cross-cultural application of qualitative research. Her research focuses on understanding social, cultural and contextual influences on public health behaviour in order to develop effective health interventions. Her work focuses primarily on sexual and reproductive health, sanitation behaviour, chronic disease management and women's empowerment.

5

Exploring Sex, HIV and 'Sensitive' Space(s) Among Sexual and Gender Minority Young Adults in Thailand

Peter A. Newman, Suchon Tepjan
and Clara Rubincam

Introduction

New prevention technologies for HIV are poised to transform the epidemic. The scaling-up of HIV testing and treatment has contributed to dramatically slowing the epidemic in many countries where antiretroviral therapy (ART) is broadly accessible. ART serves both to improve the health of people living with HIV and to prevent onward transmission of the virus. Recently, pre-exposure prophylaxis (PrEP), based on the prophylactic use of antiretroviral medications ('a pill a day'), has

---

P.A. Newman (✉) · C. Rubincam
Faculty of Social Work, University of Toronto Factor-Inwentash,
Toronto, Canada
e-mail: p.newman@utoronto.ca; c.c.rubincam@gmail.com

S. Tepjan
VOICES-Thailand foundation, Chiang Mai, Thailand
e-mail: t.suchon@voices-th.com

© The Author(s) 2017
R.S. Barbour, D.L. Morgan (Eds.), *A New Era in Focus Group Research*, DOI 10.1057/978-1-137-58614-8_5

been demonstrated to be highly effective in reducing risk of HIV acquisition among several key populations, including gay and bisexual men (GBM) (McCormack et al. 2015; Molina et al. 2015). Other HIV prevention technologies, including rectal microbicides and HIV vaccines, are at various stages in the research pipeline.

Despite these biomedical advances, the AIDS epidemic continues largely unabated in many countries and populations. This is generally a result of social-structural conditions that constrain the effectiveness of behavioural risk reduction, limit access and adherence to HIV prevention and treatment, and produce ubiquitous stigma among key populations most vulnerable to HIV. In the context of enduring social-structural and behavioural challenges to controlling the epidemic, the effective responses to HIV require not only basic science research and randomized controlled trials of new biomedical technologies, but also social science research, including qualitative investigations, in order to address crucial questions in relation to which sociology, psychology and anthropology might more aptly be termed the 'basic' sciences (Woolf 2008). To this end, we aimed to explore and provide an understanding of acceptability and preferences for rectal microbicides – a new HIV prevention technology in development, among young gay and bisexual men (GBM) and transgender women (TGW) in Thailand.

Context

The incidence of new HIV infections among GBM in Bangkok is among the highest in the world (Van Griensven et al. 2013). Given that, among sexual behaviours, unprotected receptive anal intercourse has the highest risk of HIV acquisition (Vittinghoff et al. 1999), the introduction of an effective topical product to reduce the risk of HIV through anal sex would be a tremendous asset to HIV prevention. Rectal microbicides – topical products designed to be applied to the rectal mucosa to prevent or significantly reduce the risk of HIV acquisition – are currently in development, with encouraging results from early clinical trials (McGowan et al. 2013, 2015). Nevertheless, several recent studies reveal that, despite the promise of investigational vaginal microbicide products, lack of adherence in large-scale clinical trials rendered them largely inefficacious (Marrazzo et al. 2015; Rees et al. 2015). A host of social-structural factors were identified, particularly in several developing countries, as likely contributing factors in relation to women not using the products as intended (van der Straten et al. 2014). Rather than awaiting expensive, resource-intensive large-scale clinical trials to reveal social and behavioural challenges that undermine the efficacy of rectal microbicides, we aimed to explore, with individuals from key populations for whom new HIV prevention technologies are most sorely needed, their concerns and preferences for a future rectal microbicide. Since existing studies of rectal microbicide acceptability had been conducted predominantly in the USA (Carballo-Diéguez et al. 2007, 2008), and with clinical trials planned in Thailand, we implemented research with GBM and TGW in two Thai cities.

Building on our past research on other HIV prevention technologies, and in order to advance research methodology as well as substantive knowledge in the field, a transdisciplinary collaboration was forged among researchers with expertise in social work, social psychology, economics, public health and information technology. In earlier discussions with economists who specialize in choice analysis, we were excited to discover that while we used different terminology, we agreed strongly in principle on the importance of exploratory qualitative research as being foundational to the assessment of user choices and priorities. Thus, we used a sequential mixed methods design, involving focus groups, a pilot survey, and then a full survey, including a discrete choice experiment. The present chapter focuses on the first, qualitative, research stage using focus groups, and the application and integration of focus group results with subsequent quantitative stages.

Proposed Data Collection Methods and Grant Reviewer Critiques

The project of exploring individuals' concerns and preferences about the use of a topical rectal product to prevent HIV infection, a highly stigmatized disease, in the context of their own sexual behaviours, arguably constitutes a 'sensitive' area of research. Pursuing such research in a culture other than one's own – more so an Asian country depicted as valuing privacy and being especially conscientious in face-to-face encounters and public disclosures around sexual practices – might be deemed highly sensitive. Accordingly, we could understand grant reviewers' and research ethics boards' concerns in our proposing to conduct focus groups to explore acceptability and preferences for future rectal microbicides among young GBM and TGW in Thailand. Granting agencies found the project interesting, but reviewers conversant with HIV and sexual health research criticized the methods as being untenable, citing concerns about confidentiality and comfort levels of participants.

There is a history in HIV prevention and sexual health research with young people that uses focus groups to explore perceptions of risk, safety, and to develop tailored educational approaches for diverse youth (Crowe 2003; Hoppe et al. 2004; O'Brien 1993), including in other cultures (de Oliveira 2011; Munodawafa et al. 1995). However, in the revised grant proposal, we opted to de-emphasize focus groups by describing them as a back-up, if feasible, to individual interviews, while, personally, remaining convinced of the superiority of focus groups for our investigation.

In a previous study on acceptability of future HIV vaccines in Thailand, we had conducted qualitative, in-depth individual interviews. In that case, a researcher from the Thai Ministry of Public Health – otherwise supportive of the project – advised that Thais would be unlikely to speak out in a public/group setting in general, and even less so about sex and HIV. Given my lesser cultural familiarity and research experience in Thailand at that time, I wholly accepted this advice. Interestingly, in implementing this past study, several of the young GBM and TGW (18–24 years old), some of whom were sex workers, asked if they could be interviewed with a friend/s rather than individually. Both a community-based organization (CBO) staff person, and my Thai research assistant, explained that these individuals were interested in participating but were nervous about the individual research interview and would feel more comfortable being interviewed together. These dual and group interviews proved to be highly informative; we offered participants questions individually, but they took the initiative to interact with their peers – at times agreeing, at times gently disagreeing, at times laughing aloud – in recounting experiences around sexual partners and condom use, and the role of HIV and sexual stigma in attitudes towards future HIV vaccines.

Without doubt our gay affirmative, sex-positive and non-judgmental approach, and participants' ability to read the interviewers as gay, along with the familiarity of the CBO setting, facilitated candour and openness. As feminist scholars have discussed, focus groups help to shift power away from the researcher to the participants, in contrast to individual interviews, by giving participants greater control over their level of engagement and disclosure, enabling them to guide the direction of the discussion, and also through the increased ratio of participants to researchers in contrast to a one-to-one interview (de Oliveira 2011; Farquhar and Das 1999). In our case, we believed that individual interviews introduced an inevitable power dynamic, further influenced by sociocultural norms. Although the interviewer was another gay Thai, he was a few years older and identified by participants as a 'researcher' – to be looked up to and obeyed, similar to Thai cultural dynamics with healthcare providers. Thus, for the proposed study, we believed the focus group method would help to interrupt a bilateral hierarchical relationship and disrupt some of the power dynamics that might thwart comfort and openness.

The Study

Our research team collaborated with CBOs in two cities serving young GBM and TGW to conduct recruitment and host the groups – in an environment experienced as safe and supportive. Between them, the two CBOs provided services for over 1,000 clients, including youth and young adult GBM and TGW who engaged in sex work, college students and working people.

Given the objectives of the study, participant eligibility criteria were: self-identifying as a GBM or TGW, aged 18–30 years and fluent in Thai. Based on our experience with the population, including in other settings, and other focus group research on sexuality (de Oliveira 2011;

Tufford et al. 2012), we segmented focus groups by age (18–24 years; 25–30 years) and sexual/gender identity (gay/bisexual men; transgender women) among participants recruited from similar sociocultural contexts in order to mitigate power dynamics and encourage comfort and candour. By design, including the use of venue-based sampling in CBOs (Newman et al. 2012a) participants were somewhat familiar with one another as CBO clients or members – many as casual or occasional clients, some closer as roommates or CBO volunteers. Although some investigators have described ongoing social contact outside the research as potentially constraining discussion in focus groups – and this may be the case for certain topics and contexts – in this case we believed it would support discussion and facilitate constructive disclosure of relevant feelings and preferences more so than individual interviews (Farquhar and Das 1999; Frith 2000).

We used a semi-structured topic guide to explore factors that might influence acceptability of future rectal microbicides. The guide was based on the limited past research on rectal microbicides largely conducted in the USA (Carballo-Diéguez et al. 2007, 2008; McGowan 2011) and our previous mixed methods HIV prevention research in Thailand (Newman et al. 2010; Newman et al. 2012b), which we aimed to expand on by applying a social ecological lens (Bronfenbrenner 1979; Stokols 1996). We used questions and probes to elicit rectal microbicide preferences and possible contexts of rectal microbicide acceptability at individual, interpersonal and social-structural levels (Newman et al. 2013).

Each focus group was led by a co-facilitator from the CBO (reflecting the organizations' approach to education and empowerment), in addition to the Thai facilitator from the research team. The facilitators began each group by eliciting awareness and understanding of rectal microbicides, and emphasizing that the products were hypothetical and not yet available. We then provided a definition of rectal microbicide to ensure participants were addressing the intended product. The topic guide was created in English, translated into Thai, back-translated into English and revised in the Thai language. The topic guide was then revised in an iterative process to reflect new data and questions that emerged in subsequent focus groups (Charmaz 2006; Schutt 2004).

Sample questions and probes included: What features of the rectal microbicide would make you more or less likely to use it? Probes: formulation (gel, cream, suppository, other), colour, smell, etc., (In what ways) might your relationship or the partner you are having sex with influence your use of rectal microbicides? Probes: ability to conceal use, partner type, etc. Are there possible social or community concerns that might influence you or your friends' use of a rectal microbicide? Probes: prescription requirement, stigma, etc. All participants completed an anonymous, two-page socio-demographic questionnaire.

Data Analysis

All focus groups were digitally recorded, transcribed verbatim in the Thai language, and then translated into English. We retained certain Thai terms that could not be readily translated into English or for which significant aspects of their meaning might be lost in translation.

We analyzed focus group data using a variety of approaches. First, we conducted thematic analysis, with two team members independently reviewing selected transcripts, and met as a team to construct a codebook, which we applied in coding all transcripts. Differences in coding were resolved by group consensus.

Rather than using a traditional qualitative software analysis package, we worked with a programmer to create a customized database in Microsoft Access. The database reflected our codebook, and like other qualitative software allowed entry of new codes that arose inductively. We then used axial coding to relate themes and categories to one another (Strauss and Corbin 1998).

In addition to thematic analysis, the Access database enabled us to apply content analysis by calculating theme frequencies by focus group. Subsequent to thematic analysis, we ran customized word/theme searches and counts to identify the frequency of each theme (i.e. product, individual, interpersonal, social-structural) and sub-theme (i.e. product efficacy, side effects, formulation, etc.) overall and by focus group. This facilitated our identification of patterns in the data with respect to differences between focus groups and by age and gender identity/sexual orientation of participants. We used data source triangulation (across focus groups) and methodological triangulation (thematic and content analysis) to enhance the validity of the findings (Lincoln and Guba 1985; Mays and Pope 2000).

Findings and Reflections

We conducted five focus groups, with a total of 37 participants, most of whom self-identified as gay, with others identifying as bisexual or TGW.

We present findings and reflections in three sections that reflect major challenges and opportunities in our research process: (1) *Cross-cultural issues* – considerations of using the focus group method to explore sexual behaviour and HIV prevention with young sexual and gender minority populations in a different culture; (2) *'Sensitive' topics* – critical perspectives on research in domains and populations deemed 'sensitive', including ethical and practical considerations with regard to recruitment and implementation of the focus groups, and the elicitation of participant experiences and perspectives; and, (3) *Mixed methods* – incorporating focus groups in the larger research design, and connections between qualitative and quantitative data. The study results in full are described elsewhere (Newman et al. 2013, 2016).

Cross-Cultural Issues

Thai culture is characterized by a collectivist orientation and Buddhist tradition. The Buddhist tenet of *krengjai* – a pre-eminent value on maintaining interpersonal harmony and avoiding confrontation (Bechtel and Apakupakul 1999; Newman et al. 2012b) – which permeates Thai society, might be expected to render focus groups non-viable, particularly for research on potentially taboo topics, such as sex and HIV. However, rather than hindering the research process, focus groups proved an ideal vehicle, enabling us to gain in-depth understanding of acceptability and preferences for future rectal microbicides within interpersonal and sociocultural contexts; knowing only the ostensible preferences would have given us little in the way of understanding the motivations and decision-making that informed particular priorities and choices.

5 Exploring Sex, HIV and 'Sensitive' Space(s)

An example that illustrates the role of Thai culture, and the benefits of the focus group method in eliciting the cultural context of rectal microbicide acceptability, emerged in the following interchange, in which participants position challenges in product usage in a relational context. By contrast, the limited social science research on rectal microbicides to date has emphasized individual choices and behaviours much more so than interpersonal concerns.

P1: It's about trusting. There might be a fight. Think about this if the microbicide has a smell and we f–k somebody else, then we come back with that smell . . . . Oh my God!

P2: Talking about this . . . supposing we have an affair, despite the fact that we don't know each other before; the thing is who knows . . . ? One or the the other might have HIV. We can't see this with our eyes, so we must use the microbicide. But if that partner doesn't accept it . . . , we don't have to have sex. It's risky.

P3: Safety first. I think they might not deny our using it, because they might not trust us either.

P2: Some guys might say, 'don't you trust me?' But if it relates to our health, we must think of safety first.

P4: But in this case, sex partners may have judgments about us, right?

P5: The others will think that these people (who use the microbicide) are safe.

P2: I think it's a good idea . . . they will think that we take good care of ourselves.

P6: They will probably use it with us.

Herein, personal safety and HIV risk, concerns that in other sociocultural contexts might be largely positioned at the individual level, are discussed and synthesized in a relational framework. Strongly evident alongside motivations to protect oneself are considerations of the impact of using a rectal microbicide on sexual partners' perceptions and judgments of the user, and its effect on relationships. Furthermore, beyond a dichotomous approach – for instance, pitting personal safety versus risking others' judgments, or individual HIV risk versus relational discord – participants can be understood as collectively navigating an understanding in which interpersonal agreement and mutual benefit converge to support rectal microbicide use. Both the focus group process and content contribute to this interpretation, which is itself a product of cross-cultural and transdisciplinary collaboration on the research team.

Even with successful implementation of the focus groups and evocation of sociocultural concerns, the principal investigator (PAN) has no illusions that he could have accomplished this project on his own, as an outsider to Thai culture. High-level collaborations with Thai public health officials and researchers, insiders to Thai culture, would have similarly been unlikely to achieve our aims. Two characteristics of our study team and our approach proved essential. First, our project was highly collaborative and community-based, involving prolonged engagement with Thai co-investigators and research staff – with whom we could comfortably discuss challenges and differing or ambiguous interpretations – and enduring community partnerships with CBOs (with intimate familiarity and trusting relationships with participants). The present project was undertaken in the context of a five-plus year collaboration with Thai CBO leaders and outreach staff, which encompassed other research projects, and knowledge translation and exchange, including debriefings, consultations, and community reports in Thai.

A second essential aspect of the project relates to the facilitators' training, skills, language and identity. The primary facilitator was from a region of Northern Thailand in which both 'official' Thai and local dialect are commonly spoken. He began each group in official Thai language, but then calibrated his level of language and use of dialect to the language used in the group, also attending to within group differences to ensure everyone understood the language and vocabulary. In focus group implementation, one group was conducted largely in dialect, two in official Thai language, and two in Thai but with language to accommodate the lower educational status of some group members. Beyond language *per se*, the identity of the facilitator and co-facilitator as young gay men, and a TGW co-facilitator in the TGW group, coupled with their fluency and comfort with the sexual vernacular of participants (Frith 2000) was likely a vital component of successful elicitation of frank views and conversation about sex, anal sex, sex work, etc.

It is important to note that focus groups, much as other domains of life, often suffer from a heterosexist bias that both truncates open discussion and limits interpretation of findings – in addition to stigmatizing participants (Braun 2000). In fact, such bias remains apparent in academic textbooks on focus group methods – for example, Stewart and Shamdasani (2015) offer generalizations about gender dynamics in how women and men behave in 'same-sex' and 'mixed-sex' groups that completely elide considerations of sexual orientation and gender identity. The facilitators in our study were well-versed in sex-positive and gay-affirmative communications, as well as being privy to certain vernaculars about sexual roles and practices commonly used among sexual minority youth in Thailand; lack of familiarity with such terminology would likely be seen as confirmation of 'outsider' status that, in this case, would limit discussion and disclosure.

Conducting research on apparently sensitive topics such as HIV risk and sexual behaviour using focus group methodology may have seemed, at the outset, to be ill-advised; more so for a study led by a non-Thai academic based at a North American research institution. Yet, the use of focus groups proved successful in eliciting rich, in-depth insights into user acceptability and preferences for rectal microbicides that reflected the sociocultural context.

'Sensitive' Topics

Although research on topics deemed 'sensitive' has traditionally been the provenance of individual interviews, we experienced distinct benefits of the focus group method with young Thai GBM and TGW. It is important to address, even before data collection, crucial considerations about sampling, recruitment and the ethical conduct of research with marginalized populations. In our case, these were amplified by multifaceted stigma – around sexuality, gender non-conformity, and HIV – and the criminalization of sex work. Although, 'hard-to-reach' is a term often used as if it applies to the population in question, this may be better understood as a function of who is carrying out the research and the process of engagement. Our access to populations of young GBM and TGW was mediated by trusting collaborations with established CBOs that provided safe spaces for these communities and who enabled us to invite their clients to participate.

Within this community-based process, beyond satisfying requirements for Research Ethics Board approvals, we remained strongly attuned to practices that supported voluntary participation, privacy and confidentiality. In addition to staff ethics trainings, ongoing supervision and debriefing, we explicitly communicated with CBO leaders, staff persons and potential participants that we valued ensuring the voluntary nature of participation more so than recruitment numbers. We also understood the quality of our data as directly contingent on mitigating perceived coercion on the part of populations of youth and young adults who routinely experience hierarchy and power dynamics in their everyday lives – by virtue of social-structural contexts of sexual stigma and criminalization of sex work, and even within the context of HIV prevention and sexual health – such that their perspectives and narratives about sex and HIV are generally under the surveillance of counsellors and older adults. The latter includes a received orthodoxy about safer sex (i.e. 'use a condom every time'), which may limit frank discussions and encourage socially desirable responses.

As described in research on sexual health with female adolescents (de Oliveira 2011) and lesbian adults (Farquhar and Das 1999), focus groups may be instrumental in shifting the terms of engagement from one that merely recapitulates existing hierarchies – through the interviewer/research-participant dyad of individual interviews – by ceding power to enable participants more control in determining the narrative. We understood voluntary participation and confidentiality (i.e. only nicknames were used; no names or contact information was shared with the research team) as foundational to supporting this dynamic – more so in a context in which public health authorities have been known to conduct HIV surveillance, including HIV testing, among young GBM and TGW in the gay entertainment industry without individual consent and with the risk of losing one's employment if one refuses testing.

Within our focus groups, participant narratives reveal a good degree of comfort in the discussion of what might otherwise be considered intimate (and regulated) details of sexual practices, condom use, numbers of partners, and sex work. Conversations about product formulation, for instance, illustrate participants' comfort in a group setting discussing what may be thought of as sensitive topics. They also show the utility of focus groups in eliciting differing views among participants, and the reasoning and context (Morse 1994) for those perspectives. Participants explained, 'In my opinion I think it would be nice if it is made in gel form because normally we have sex every day and we need to use a gel-based lubricant' (FG4); and 'make it in gel form because gay people have already got gel for lubricant' (FG1). Some participants indicated alternative preferences: 'like a suppository, I feel like it can go deeper and I feel safer' (FG3); and, 'if it's in suppository form nobody will insert it before having sex' (FG4). In addition to particular preferences, and the reasoning behind them, these responses reveal comfort in discussing sexual practices and frequency of sex, as well as differences in product preferences.

During discussion of other product characteristics, such as pericoital versus daily use, key insights emerged from the perspectives of those involved in sex work: 'It would be nice if it is one-day long because we don't have sex only one time ... we have it two or three times per day' (FG4). This spontaneous discussion of engaging in sex work testifies to the ability of the focus group format to encourage openness.

The importance of our skilled focus group facilitators emerges in their striking a careful balance between, on the one hand, asking highly personal questions of individual participants – potentially threatening and uncomfortable, more so in Thai culture – and, on the other hand, avoiding or averting certain topics or discussions presuming no one would want to disclose (de Oliveira 2011; Kitzinger and Farquhar 1999). Particularly in sex and HIV research among marginalized populations, the latter may model shame, confer stigma, and truncate an otherwise illuminating discussion; the sensitivities revealed, however, may be more indicative of the researcher's rather than participants' subjectivities and discomfort. Participants, through spontaneous discussion and disclosure, collaborate with researchers or even take the lead in setting boundaries about what may and may not be deemed overly sensitive in the group (de Oliveira 2011). The facilitator also allowed participants to joke and laugh as acceptable forms of self-expression, and tension-releasing mechanisms, and did not avoid the topics raised (Farquhar and Das 1999).

An illustrative interchange occurred in the TGW group. The facilitator, a young gay man, was initially caught off-guard when upon one participant's offering information that inadvertently revealed specifics of her stage in the process of gender reassignment, other participants jokingly attacked, 'Oh my god, you don't have a [vagina]! Everyone has a [vagina] nowadays.' The group as a whole was laughing, including the ostensible target. The facilitator withheld his own possible laughter, not wanting to contribute to any targeting or shaming of the participant; but he did not truncate discussion, which quickly evolved into preferences for the colour of a microbicide: 'I want a gel to have glitter....'

Another example emerged from a younger GBM group in a participant's seemingly defensive statement in terms of his preferences for a rectal microbicide: 'I don't know; I'm a top. I can't speak for a bottom.' For one, from this and other related statements, the facilitator discerned that disclosure of one's primary sexual role, as '*rub*' (bottom) rather than '*rook*' (top) or '*boat*' (both top and bottom), was often more sensitive than discussion of body parts, sexual practices or condom use. Again, in this case, the facilitator did not intervene, as some might; rather, other group members appropriately responded that the individual could speak about using a rectal microbicide with his partner or boyfriend. This provided a perfect entrée for others to speak about various rectal microbicide attributes, while reserving the option of disclosing or not one's own sexual role, again demonstrating participants' active involvement in setting boundaries for the group and navigating group discussion.

One challenge in discussion of topics that may be deemed sensitive, and for which we did note some evidence, is that of 'overdisclosure' – a result of 'a certain thrill in the open discussion of taboo topics' (Morgan 1998; Morgan and Krueger 1993: 7). This may result in participants' compromising their own privacy, including in response to other participants' disclosures, perhaps later regretting overly candid revelations, which presents an ethical concern (Morgan 1998). Others have described the importance of viewing focus groups as sites where participants 'perform' and refine their identities in front of one another (Brannen and Pattmen 2005); in our study, instances of overdisclosure occurred when participants sought to assert their confidence in their sexual identities, outdoing each other in using profane language and in describing details of past sexual encounters. An example occurred in the TGW group, which seemed at least as motivated by wanting to 'one-up' other participants in asserting who was the most 'authentic' TGW as in broaching taboo topics. This particular instance took place subsequent to the earlier reported back-and-forth about having or not a vagina. Lest we be accused of the same overdisclosure, suffice it to say that the preference for a glittery microbicide was revealed in graphic detail. However, we also note this dynamic occurred earlier in the group process and subsided, perhaps owing in part to the facilitator and the TGW co-facilitator's successful navigation, and that this was a group in which many participants were quite familiar with one another. Finally, as discussed by Morgan (1998), the potential downsides of overdisclosure may in fact be more pronounced in groups of strangers (with perhaps a false sense of security that theirs is a one-time encounter) than in groups with ongoing relationships among participants.

In fact, this TGW focus group was also one of the most information-rich and productive, leading to substantial methodological and substantive input to the mixed methods project. Similar to what is deemed 'sensitive', 'overdisclosure' is also subjective, no doubt importantly determined by participants' feelings and experience. In our case, given the particular CBO setting and activities, and the participants and their intimate familiarity with the sexual vernacular, the most emotional reaction may have been for the facilitator, who nevertheless maintained a reflexive stance and appropriately enabled continued discussion of highly relevant material.

The rich discussions in our focus groups appear to challenge presumptions that might lead researchers to mechanistically argue against focus groups as a preferred method for research on sex and HIV as 'sensitive' topics. Rather, our findings and the process of the groups demonstrate several benefits of focus groups in sex and HIV research, as others have noted (Farquhar and Das 1999; Frith 2000). These included revealing new and unanticipated findings (O'Brien 1993), illustrating participants' varied language and vocabulary (Frith 2000; O'Brien 1993), and providing a context for understanding participant preferences (Morse 1994). Our findings further suggest that the group dynamic supported appropriate disclosure and expression of shared experiences around sex, sexuality and HIV (de Oliveira 2011; Farquhar and Das 1999; Morgan and Krueger 1993), and diverse perspectives including agreement and disagreement about rectal microbicide preferences, behavioural risks, and the possible impact of rectal microbicides on condom use and on sex work.

Focus Groups in Mixed Methods Research

Our use of focus groups prior to the commencement of our quantitative phase of research brought several significant benefits. Findings from the qualitative study were used to: (1) generate new hypotheses and guide decisions about sampling for the survey, (2) select which product attributes to assess in quantitative (Bayesian) analysis of rectal microbicide preferences, (3) select relevant domains for the survey questionnaire, and (4) integrate with quantitative results, as well as to refine the language in the questionnaire.

First, several themes in the qualitative analysis suggested possible differences – in structural concerns about cost, and interpersonal concerns about loss of sex work clients, among both GBM and TGW, and individual concerns among TGW in which ability to attract men may function as affirmation of one's female gender identity. A TGW participant indicated risks of disclosure of rectal microbicide use with 'straight guys': 'Talking about straight guys, not gay guys, they will not be able to accept this. They won't know; they may think that you have AIDS' (FG3). These issues generated new hypotheses (Kitzinger and Barbour 1999) indicating to us the importance of designing the sampling and recruitment strategy for the survey to include a sufficient proportion of TGW. This would allow statistical power to determine any significant differences in rectal microbicide preferences between GBM and TGW, and between those who did and did not engage in sex work (Newman et al. 2016).

Second, the qualitative findings guided our team's decisions about which rectal microbicide attributes to include in the choice experiment featured in the pilot and full surveys. The choice experiment involved the sequential presentation of sets of five cards on a tablet screen, each of which described a multi-attribute product – for example, this rectal microbicide has 50% efficacy, no side effects, gel formulation, etc. Participants then choose their favourite and least favourite product from among the set of five cards by dragging and dropping their chosen cards into the appropriate boxes ('Best' and 'Worst') situated on either side of the tablet screen above the card set – much like a game of computer solitaire. This 'best' and 'worst' selection is done in two rounds for each set of five cards (the second round with the three remaining cards), with the one remaining card identified by default as the third-ranked choice among the five cards. As one cannot include an infinite array of product features in assessing user preferences, lest the choice experiment become impossible for participants to execute, one needs to make highly consequential decisions beforehand about which features are most important to model in quantitative analysis. Based on evidence from the focus groups, we chose to include, for example, whether a prescription would be required or not, and to exclude colour of the microbicide, which emerged as a topic of conversation but without the level of impact of having to get a doctor's prescription.

A related connection between the qualitative and quantitative stages is in our use of focus groups to provide evidence to support Bayesian analysis. Rather than assuming an open field of possible choices absent any prior knowledge – in this case of rectal microbicide preferences – characteristic of traditional statistical analysis, we purposefully used qualitative methods to provide what the expert economists on our team referred to as 'informed priors.' Focus group results guided our choices of which attributes to include in the pilot survey; in turn, pilot survey ($n = 24$) results were used to calculate the statistical weights used to model rectal microbicide priorities in quantitative analysis of the full survey ($n = 408$). This resulted in the first published data of its kind on a matter of considerable practical importance for HIV prevention, that is, evidence to quantify preferences for rectal microbicides and to support the mitigation of challenges in product usage for young GBM and TGW, including sex workers, among those at highest risk for HIV globally (Newman et al. 2016).

Third, the utility of focus groups in providing evidence to select domains for inclusion in the survey emerged in the importance of stigma as a challenge to future rectal microbicide use. Rectal microbicides were described as potentially signifying HIV infection and being 'dirty': 'it's like a sign on our forehead' (FG5). Prescription requirements and hospital access were invoked as exacerbating concerns about stigma. Upon reflection, this topic – of being judged, viewed as 'dirty' – appeared more challenging for participants to address than details of intimate sexual practices or sex work. Consequently, we added measures of stigma to the full survey instrument. In fact, stigma was associated with lower rectal microbicide acceptability and lower likelihood of having been HIV tested (Logie et al. 2016) – a crucial measure for HIV prevention, corroborated by qualitative and quantitative findings.

Fourth, and critically important, focus group results provided a context for understanding and interpreting the quantitative data. This included, for example, how participants approached and framed considerations of what would be considered reasonable cost for a microbicide. Understandably, several participants gauged cost in reference to condoms, the existing product. Another context for evaluating cost emerged in discussions among TGW sex workers, particularly those with lower incomes: 'We earn a few hundred [Thai *baht*; ~ \$9.00 USD] a day and then we have to spend more for having sex?' (FG3); and 'They have to think of low-income TGs too ... a onetime-use pack should cost like 5 *baht*' (~ \$0.15 USD) (FG3). This provided another indication, borne out in later quantitative modelling, of differences between young GBM and TGW, and sex workers and non-sex workers, with regard to rectal microbicide acceptability (Newman et al. 2016). In particular, although all participants indicated sensitivity to cost, sex workers' choices revealed more constraints due to potential costs of a rectal microbicide.

Finally, using focus groups prior to the commencement of our survey data collection enabled us to refine our research questions and language to better reflect the preferred wording and the vernaculars of participants in Thai (Frith 2000; O'Brien 1993).

Conclusion

Overall, focus groups proved highly instrumental to our research objectives of exploring acceptability and preferences for future rectal microbicides in the context of individual, interpersonal and social-structural influences among young GBM and TGW, including sex workers, in Thailand. An important qualification in interpreting our findings, along the lines of critically engaging with the sociocultural context, is that we purposively recruited young GBM and TGW who were in contact with CBOs that provided sexual health and HIV prevention services, including for those working in the gay entertainment industry; these participants do not represent, nor are they meant to represent, all sexual and gender minority Thai youth – some of whom may have been very uncomfortable in these groups, some without any sexual experience. Our aim was to engage youth for whom new HIV prevention technologies are most sorely needed and whose opinions, much like in high-income countries, are sometimes last to be solicited.

Furthermore, just as we describe the evaluation of what constitutes 'sensitive' topics and what research is appropriate for focus group methods as subjective, so too 'culture' involves numerous subjectivities. Our Thai research advisors had in mind our best interests for what would result in research success, and certainly imparted helpful insights; but they occupied a very different subject position from our Thai research participants. Thai officials' perceptions of sensitive topics and evaluation of what young GBM and TGW would feel comfortable discussing in a group may have been closer to the perspectives of our North American grant reviewers than to those of our participants. While it is important to respect, acknowledge and negotiate culture, this is, clearly, not monolithic. An essential component of the success of our mixed methods project was the ongoing relationships with Thai co-investigators, research assistants, and CBOs, who were well-placed to advise on appropriate, respectful approaches to the research topic, and to critically evaluate received wisdom about our study populations and methods.

In conclusion, the focus group process and findings were crucial in providing depth and rich context for understanding rectal microbicide preferences, and differences in preferences, across subgroups of GBM and TGW, as well as gendered sociocultural dynamics. These sociocultural and structural factors may ultimately determine the success of rectal microbicides and other new biomedical prevention technologies in ending the AIDS epidemic.

References

Braun, V. (2000) 'Heterosexism in focus group research: Collusion and challenge'. *Feminism & Psychology*, 10(1): 133–140.
Bechtel, G. A., & Apakupakul, N. (1999) 'AIDS in southern Thailand: Stories of krengjai and social connections'. *Journal of Advanced Nursing*, 29(2): 471–475.
Brannen, J., & Pattmen, R. (2005) 'Work-family matters in the workplace: The use of focus groups in a study of a UK social services department'. *Qualitative Research*, 5(4): 523–542.
Bronfenbrenner, U. (1979) *The Ecology of Human Development*. Cambridge, MA: Harvard University Press.
Carballo-Diéguez, A., Exner, T., Dolezal, C., Pickard, R., Lin, P., & Mayer, K. H. (2007). 'Rectal microbicide acceptability: Results of a volume escalation trial'. *Sexually Transmitted Diseases*, 34(4): 224–229.
Carballo-Diéguez, A., Dolezal, C., Bauermeister, J. A., O'Brien, W., Ventuneac, A., & Mayer, K. (2008) 'Preference for gel over suppository as delivery vehicle for a rectal microbicide: Results of a randomized, crossover acceptability trial among men who have sex with men'. *Sexually Transmitted Diseases*, 84(6): 483–487.
Charmaz, K. (2006) *Constructing Grounded Theory: A Practical Guide Through Gualitative Analysis*. Thousand Oaks, CA: Sage.
Crowe, T. V. (2003) 'Using focus groups to create culturally appropriate HIV prevention material for the deaf community'. *Qualitative Social Work*, 2(3): 289–308.
de Oliveira, D. L. (2011) 'The use of focus groups to investigate sensitive topics: An example taken from research on adolescent girls' perceptions about sexual risks'. *Ciência & Saúde Coletiva*, 16(7): 3093–3102.
Farquhar, C., & Das, R. (1999) 'Are focus groups suitable for "sensitive" topics?', In R. Barbour and J. Kitzinger (eds.), *Developing Focus Group Research: Politics, Theory and Practice*. London: Sage, pp. 47–63.
Frith, H. (2000) 'Focusing on sex: Using focus groups in sex research'. *Sexualities*, 3(3): 275–297.

Hoppe, M. J., Graham, L., Wilsdon, A., Wells, E. A., Nahom, D., & Morrison, D. M. (2004) 'Teens speak out about HIV/AIDS: Focus group discussions about risk and decision-making'. *Journal of Adolescent Health*, 35 (4): 345e27–e35.

Kitzinger, J., & Barbour, R. S. (1999) 'Introduction: The challenge and promise of focus groups', In R. S. Barbour & J. Kitzinger (eds.), *Developing Focus Group Research: Politics, Theory and Practice*. London: Sage, pp. 1–20.

Kitzinger, J., & Farquhar, C. (1999) 'The analytical potential of "sensitive moments" in focus group discussions', In R. S. Barbour & J. Kitizinger (eds.), *Developing Focus Group Research: Politics, Theory and Practice*. London: Sage, pp. 156–172.

Lincoln, Y., & Guba, E. (1985) *Naturalistic Inquiry*. Newbury Park, CA: Sage.

Logie, C. H., Newman, P. A., Weaver, J., Roungprakhon, S., & Tepjan, S. (2016) 'HIV-related stigma and HIV prevention uptake among young men who have sex with men and transgender women in Thailand'. *AIDS Patient Care & STDs*, 30(2): 92–100.

Marrazzo, J. M., Ramjee, G., Richardson, B. A., Gomez, K., Mgodi, N., Nair, G., et al. (2015) 'Tenofovir-based preexposure prophylaxis for HIV infection among African women'. *New England Journal of Medicine*, 372(6): 509–518.

Mays, N., & Pope, C. (2000) 'Qualitative research in health care: Assessing quality in qualitative research'. *British Medical Journal*, 320(7226): 50–52.

McCormack, S., Dunn, D. T., Desai, M., Dolling, D. I., Gafos, M., Gilson, R., et al. (2015) 'Pre-exposure prophylaxis to prevent the acquisition of HIV-1 infection (PROUD): Effectiveness results from the pilot phase of a pragmatic open-label randomised trial'. *Lancet*, 387(10013): 53–60.

McGowan, I. (2011) 'Rectal microbicides: Can we make them and will people use them?' *AIDS and Behavior*, 15(Suppl. 1): S66–S71.

McGowan, I., Hoesley, C., Cranston, R. D., Andrew, P., Janocko, L., Dai, J. Y., et al. (2013) 'A phase 1 randomized, double blind, placebo controlled rectal safety and acceptability study of tenofovir 1% gel (MTN-007)'. *PLoS One*, 8(4): e60147.

McGowan, I., Cranston, R. D., Duffill, K., Siegel, A., Engstrom, J. C., Nikiforov, A., et al. (2015) 'A phase 1 randomized, open label, rectal safety, acceptability, pharmacokinetic, and pharmacodynamic study of three formulations of tenofovir 1% gel (the CHARM-01 Study)'. *PLoS One*, 10(5): e0125363.

Molina, J. M., Capitant, C., Spire, B., Pialoux, G., Cotte, L., Charreau, I., et al. (2015) 'On-demand pre-exposure prophylaxis in men at high risk for HIV-1 infection'. *New England Journal of Medicine*, 373: 2237–2246.
Morgan, D. L. (1998) 'The focus group guidebook', In D. L. Morgan & R. A. Krueger (eds.), *The Focus Group Kit*. Thousand Oaks, CA: Sage.
Morgan, D. L., & Krueger, R. A. (1993) 'When to use focus groups and why', In D. L. Morgan (ed.), *Successful Focus Groups: Advancing the State of the Art*. Newbury Park, CA: Sage, pp. 3–19.
Morse, J. M. (1994). *Critical Issues in Qualitative Research Methods*. London: Sage.
Munodawafa, D., Gwede, C., & Mubayira C. (1995) 'Using focus groups to develop HIV education among adolescent females in Zimbabwe'. *Health Promotion International*, 10(2): 85–92.
Newman, P. A., Roungprakhon, S., Tepjan, S., & Yim, S. (2010) 'Preventive HIV vaccine acceptability and behavioral risk compensation among high-risk men who have sex with men and transgenders in Thailand'. *Vaccine*, 28(4): 958–964.
Newman, P. A., Lee, S. J., Roungprakhon, S., & Tepjan, S. (2012a) 'Demographic and behavioral correlates of HIV risk among men and transgender women recruited from gay entertainment venues and community-based organizations in Thailand: Implications for HIV prevention'. *Prevention Science*, 13(5): 483–492.
Newman, P. A., Roungprakhon, S., Tepjan, S., Yim, S., & Walisser, R. (2012b) 'A social vaccine? Social and structural contexts of HIV vaccine acceptability among most-at-risk populations in Thailand'. *Global Public Health*, 7(9): 1009–1014.
Newman, P. A., Roungprakhon, S., & Tepjan, T. (2013) 'A social ecology of rectal microbicide acceptability among young men who have sex with men and transgender women in Thailand'. *Journal of the International AIDS Society*, 16(1): 18476.
Newman, P. A., Cameron, M. P., Roungprakhon, S., Tepjan, S., & Scarpa, R. (2016) 'Acceptability and preferences for hypothetical rectal microbicides among a community sample of young men who have sex with men and transgender women in Thailand: A discrete choice experiment'. *AIDS and Behavior*, 20(11): 2588–2601.
O'Brien, K. (1993) 'Using focus groups to develop health surveys: An example from research on social relationships and AIDS-preventive behaviour'. *Health Education Quarterly*, 20(3): 361–372.

Rees, H., Delany-Moretlwe, S. A., Lombard, C., Baron, D., Panchia, R., Myer, L., et al. (2015) 'FACTS 001 Phase III Trial of pericoital tenofovir 1% gel for HIV prevention in women', Abstract presented at the 2015 *Conference on Retroviruses and Opportunistic Infections (CROI)*, Seattle, USA.

Schutt, R. K. (2004). *Investigating the Social World: The Process and Practice of Research* (4th ed.). Newbury Park, CA: Sage.

Stewart, D. W., & Shamdasani, P. N. (2015) 'Group dynamics and focus group research', In D. W. Stewart & P. N. Shamdasani (eds.), *Focus Groups: Theory and Practice* (3rd ed.). London: Sage, pp. 17–38.

Stokols, D. (1996) 'Translating social ecological theory into guidelines for community health promotion'. *American Journal of Health Promotion*, 10(4): 282–298.

Strauss, A. L., & Corbin, J. M. (1998) *Basics of Qualitative Research: Techniques and Procedures for Developing Grounded Theory* (4th ed.). Thousand Oaks, CA: Sage.

Tufford, L., Newman, P. A., Brennan, D. J., Craig, S. L., & Woodford, M. R. (2012) 'Conducting research with lesbian, gay and bisexual populations: Navigating research ethics board reviews'. *Journal of Gay & Lesbian Social Services*, 24(3): 221–240.

van der Straten, A., Stadler, J., Luecke, E., Laborde, N., Hartmann, M., Montgomery, E. T., et al. (2014) 'Perspectives on use of oral and vaginal antiretrovirals for HIV prevention: The VOICE-C qualitative study in Johannesburg, South Africa'. *Journal of the International AIDS Society*, 17 (3 Suppl 2): 19146.

Van Griensven, F., Thienkrua, W., McNicholl, J., Wimonsate W., Chaikummao, S., Chonwattana, W., et al. (2013) 'Evidence of an explosive epidemic of HIV infection in a cohort of men who have sex with men in Bangkok, Thailand'. *AIDS*, 27(5): 825–832.

Vittinghoff, E., Douglas, J., Judson, F., McKirnan, D., MacQueen, K., & Buchbinder, S. P. (1999) 'Per-contact risk of human immunodeficiency virus transmission between male sexual partners'. *American Journal of Epidemiology*, 150(3): 306–311.

Woolf, S. H. (2008) 'The meaning of translational research and why it matters'. *Journal of the American Medical Association*, 299(2): 211–213.

Peter A. Newman is Professor, University of Toronto Factor-Inwentash Faculty of Social Work, and Canada Research Chair in Health and Social Justice. He has received substantial external funding for his transdisciplinary, mixed methods research programme on social-structural and behavioural challenges of new HIV prevention technologies, and community engagement in biomedical HIV prevention trials, with a focus on vulnerable populations in resource-limited settings. As principal investigator of the Canadian Institutes of Health Research (CIHR) Team in Social and Behavioral Research on HIV Vaccines, he is engaged in ongoing research and training collaborations with investigators in Canada, India, South Africa and Thailand. His work also focuses on promoting health and human rights for sexual and gender minority populations. He has authored or co-authored more than 120 peer-reviewed publications. His work on HIV vaccine acceptability has been widely profiled in venues including *Nature Medicine, American Association for the Advancement of Science*, and the media.

Suchon Tepjan is Research Manager of VOICES-Thailand foundation, a non-profit organization focused on HIV prevention and healthcare access for vulnerable populations in Thailand. His BA in English Linguistics was awarded by Chiang Mai University. He has coordinated several research projects focused on HIV prevention and acceptability of new prevention technologies among sexual and gender minorities, and other vulnerable populations in Thailand, India and South Africa.

Clara Rubincam is a postdoctoral fellow with Peter A. Newman and a member of the CIHR Team in Social and Behavioral Research on HIV Vaccines, at the Factor-Inwentash Faculty of Social Work, University of Toronto. Her current research focuses on HIV vaccine acceptability and uptake, as well as pediatric vaccine acceptability. She completed her PhD in Social Policy at the London School of Economics in 2013.

Section II

Capitalizing on Focus Groups in Mixed Methods Contexts

6

Use of Focus Groups in Developing Behavioural mHealth Interventions: A Critical Review

Helen Eborall and Katie Morton

Introduction

The contribution of qualitative research to the development and evaluation of complex health-related behaviour change interventions is now widely accepted. Within the field of digital health interventions (including 'mhealth'), qualitative methods with target groups are often used in the initial stages of development. This chapter specifically explores the use of *focus groups* to facilitate this process.

We first provide a brief introduction to 'mHealth' and to a range of frameworks that exist for developing complex interventions (in general) including those that guide the development of mHealth interventions specifically.

H. Eborall (✉)
Department of Health Sciences, University of Leicester, University Road, Leicester, LE1 7RH UK
e-mail: hce3@leicester.ac.uk

K. Morton
Innovia Technology Limited, St Andrew's House, St Andrew's Road, Cambridge, CB4 1DL UK

© The Author(s) 2017
R.S. Barbour, D.L. Morgan (eds.), *A New Era in Focus Group Research*, DOI 10.1057/978-1-137-58614-8_6

We then provide a range of examples from the literature of where focus groups have been used in different stages of the development process, ranging from formative research to pre-testing to implementation and evaluation. Throughout the chapter, we provide a more detailed example from our own work – the 'PROPELS' study (full title: *The Promotion of Physical activity through structured education with different levels of ongoing support for those with pre-diabetes: randomised controlled trial in a diverse multi-ethnic community*) – for which we developed an mHealth intervention for promoting and maintaining physical activity behaviour change. We conclude with a brief discussion that critically reflects on the use of focus groups and provides a number of recommendations to researchers seeking to adopt this approach.

mHealth

Over that last decade, the promotion of behaviour change via mobile health (mHealth) has attracted widespread interest within the fields of behavioural science, healthcare and public health. mHealth is broadly defined as 'medical and public health practice supported by mobile devices, such as mobile phones, patient monitoring devices, personal digital assistants, and other wireless devices' (WHO 2011).

mHealth-assisted interventions have the potential to improve health by (a) reducing unhealthy behaviours in the population (e.g. help people to reduce alcohol consumption or stop smoking), (b) increasing healthy behaviours (e.g. help people to increase physical activity or promote attendance at screening programmes), (c) facilitating self-management of long-term conditions (e.g. stress management), (d) improving healthcare professional effectiveness or adherence to guidelines (e.g. promoting good hygiene and treatment selection).

Frameworks for the Development of mHealth Interventions

mHealth interventions are complex and often target multiple behaviour change techniques (Michie et al. 2013). Robust development of mHealth interventions draws on relevant behaviour change theory and uses rigorous (qualitative) methods incorporating user engagement (Morton et al. 2015). The development and testing of mHealth interventions usually go hand in hand, in a highly iterative process; a number of guidelines and frameworks are available to guide researchers through the process.

The Medical Research Council's Framework for developing and evaluating complex interventions to improve health (i.e. interventions that are not exclusively mHealth focused) (Craig et al. 2008) outlines a cycle of development, feasibility testing, implementation and evaluation. It emphasizes the need for early development work and identification of implementation issues prior to evaluation. The use of qualitative methods in this process is widely accepted (Moore et al. 2014); however, the MRC framework does not specify how qualitative methods can (or should) be best embedded in the *development* phase.

Other frameworks have been created specifically to guide the development of mHealth interventions; these clearly emphasize the involvement of the target population within the development phase. The mHealth development framework (Whittaker et al. 2012) outlines a series of iterative steps: (1) conceptualization (decide on the theory and evidence to underpin and inform the intervention and translate into behaviour change techniques and practical methods); (2) formative research (explore and understand the target population and context in relation to the target behaviour and use and acceptability of technological vehicle); (3) pre-testing (try out elements of the proposed intervention with members of target group); (4) pilot testing (try out proposed intervention in the format in which it is to be delivered); and, (5) qualitative research for intervention refinement (explore experiences of the intervention in use). This framework places a strong emphasis on concurrent and sequential quantitative and qualitative research with the target population.

Other models emphasize a 'user-centred' approach; indeed this terminology has proliferated in the recent research literature in the area (see, e.g. the Journal of Medical Internet Research). For example, the Information Systems Research (ISR) framework (Hevner 2007) specifies the importance of user-centred methods to identify users' mHealth needs, preferences (e.g. in terms of mobile app design), and barriers and facilitators to uptake and sustained use of a technology (Schnall et al. 2016). Similarly, other models refer to a 'person-centred' approach. One such example (Yardley et al. 2015) places emphasis on continued user involvement from the initial concept formulation through to implementation. Not only is this approach concerned with acceptability, usability and satisfaction, but also centres on developing a deep understanding of the psychosocial context of users and their views of the behavioural elements of the intervention.

In sum, regardless of which underpinning framework or model is used to guide the development and implementation of an mHealth intervention for behaviour change, the inclusion of target population groups and/or stakeholders is integral to designing an intervention that is feasible and acceptable (and in turn, effective). The next section of the chapter considers how focus groups in particular can be used in this process.

Use of Focus Groups Throughout the Development Process

Focus groups can provide a different perspective from other research methods, due in part to the interaction between multiple individuals each bringing their own perspective to discuss the topic of focus. The group setting can encourage reluctant contributors (Morgan 1988; Barbour 2007); this may be particularly relevant when exploring acceptance of an intervention which may represent a new way of using technology – particularly where confidence and familiarity with the technology may have an impact (i.e. in the case of mobile phones in an older population). Further, the group setting can give participants 'permission' to be more honest and critical about a proposed intervention, in comparison to an individual interview where they may feel a pressure to answer in a way that they imagine they researcher is anticipating. The arrangement of participants around a table is ideal for the presentation of visual material – which in the case of intervention development is invaluable for exploring and comparing elements of the proposed intervention.

We argue that in the context of mHealth intervention development, focus groups can be employed in *all* of the stages of the development process, to make a greater contribution that for 'usability' testing alone. For each phase of intervention development, we outline how focus groups have been used – referring to published papers, and drawing from our own research – the PROPELS study (See Box 6.1). In doing this, we critically reflect on the use of focus groups – giving examples of when they have been used well, but also missed opportunities.

> **Box 6.1: Case study – The PROPELS mHealth intervention**
>
> The PROPELS (Promotion Of Physical activity through structured Education with differing Levels of ongoing Support for those at high risk of type 2 diabetes) study is a multisite randomized controlled trial that aims to examine the long-term effectiveness of a group-based structured education programme ('Walking away from Diabetes') that is supplemented by an mHealth (text-messaging) component (Yates et al. 2015).
> To develop the PROPELS mHealth intervention, we used a structured, iterative process involving concurrent and sequential research with the target population – in the form of focus groups, while maintaining a strong focus on integration of theory and evidence. Our framework for intervention development and piloting was informed by the model by Dijkstra and De Vries (1999) for developing computer-generated tailored interventions (to conceptualize the programme) and the mHealth development and evaluation framework by Whittaker et al. (2012). Focus groups were the primary source of data collection to facilitate the development of the PROPELS text-messaging intervention. Full details of the development process and findings have been published (Morton et al. 2015).

Formative Stages of Development

Formative research is research that occurs before a programme or intervention is designed and implemented; sometimes this phase is referred to as the 'pre-intervention' or 'planning' phase. Focus groups have been used in this phase of mHealth development to address a variety of research questions. The most common use of focus groups, within this phase, are to explore and understand the wider context of the target population and behaviour of focus, how the target group engage with their digital devices and their perceptions of the *proposed* mHealth intervention, all of which are crucial to undertake before development of the intervention starts.

As an example, Fjeldsoe and colleagues (2012) adopted the mHealth framework (Whittaker et al. 2012) to develop a physical activity intervention for mums of young children in Australia. Their formative research centred on exploring the perceptions of, and needs for physical activity interventions in this specific target group. Eight focus groups were conducted with mums, who themselves had an age range of 16 to 45 years. The findings from this phase highlighted that walking and water-based activities were the most preferred activities and that the availability of free childcare was their primary perceived need, due to barriers related to attending organized group sessions at allocated times. The authors highlighted that the focus group discussions about flexible modes of providing/receiving support for physical activity, provoked the participants to generate the idea of mobile telephones. The focus group moderator then probed this theme further – which ultimately led to the decision to adopt a short-message service (SMS or 'text-messages') mode of delivery for their intervention (which became known as 'MobileMums') and provoked a further review of the evidence of this delivery mode for behaviour change. Note: this study pre-dated many similar subsequent interventions, hence was somewhat novel at the time. Further conclusions from the formative focus groups included the need for: the SMS content to be tailored to the individual, the establishment of a rapport between the SMS recipient and sender and two-way SMS communication (Fjeldsoe et al. 2012).

Fjeldsoe and colleagues' paper was one of the first to detail the full process of developing and evaluating an mHealth intervention and in doing so they provided a useful exemplar for other researchers. The downside – of the paper covering the full development and evaluation process – is that only limited findings from each stage could be included (e.g. a quotes that referred to the benefits of walking groups and the SMS mode of delivery). Hence, there is little detail relating to both the context mobile phone use in the target population (e.g. how is it used as a tool for social support in this group and/or the specific ways in which this mode could support physical activity). Furthermore, there is insufficient detail for methodologists who are interested in unpicking how and what data the focus group method generated (i.e. through its unique interactive nature).

Other examples that have followed the mHealth development framework (Whittaker et al. 2012) and employed focus groups as the primary method of formative research used the method as a means to exploring participants' experiences and perceptions of previous and/or existing interventions, as well as their perceptions about the additional use of mHealth interventions to the particular intervention in context. Examples include Phaeffli et al's (2012) development of an mHealth cardiac rehabilitation programme and Waterlander et al's (2014) development of an mHealth-assisted weight management programme. The latter involved both focus groups and individual interviews with the target population (people who were overweight and wanting to lose weight) to explore mobile phone usage, positive and negative experiences of previous weight management attempts, acceptability (barriers and benefits) of the proposed mHealth programme, preferences (in terms of style and frequency of messages) and feedback on specific programme components. The findings are reported to have informed the design of the first version of the resulting programme, but the paper does not contain detail on all the topics covered in the topics guide and the data presentation is far from ideal with no indication of the source of each quotation, presumably merging the data generated by the two different methods. This relates to a criticism of many research studies that combine focus groups and interviews – sometimes focus groups appear to be used as a cost-cutting method – that is, akin to a group interview – without treating the data generated by the two methods as fundamentally different (Barbour 2007).

Although other models use different terminology, they often include a phase that is described as similar in terms of stage and aims to the formative phase in the mHealth development model. For example, the ISR model involves cycles, including a user-centred phase, which in the first cycle could be equivalent to the formative phase (see Schnall et al. 2016). Schnall and colleagues (2015) used this model to identify the desired content and features of a mobile app for meeting the healthcare needs of persons living with HIV. Six focus groups were conducted with HIV positive individuals, including one exclusively with women and one with adolescents to explore factors exclusive to these groups and, presumably, capitalize on the benefits of running a focus groups with a homogeneous sample – often typical in researching sensitive topics (Farquhar 1999; Kitzinger and Farquhar 1999).

The authors provide detailed description of the topic guide, data analysis and theoretical underpinnings, along with the strategies used to enhance data quality. The findings provide a detailed account of themes, categorized by theoretical models used to analyze the data, and ultimately prescribe specific features and functions for the resulting intervention (e.g. tools for meeting their healthcare needs including reminders/alerts and lab results tracking, and strategies to bolster social support including chat forums and testimonials). More detail about the differences between the data generated by the different types of groups would have contributed to the discussion about homogeneous and heterogeneous focus group composition. However, in contrast to many mHealth intervention development papers, this provided a detailed account of the evidence that informed the resulting intervention.

PROPELS Case Study: Formative Research

Our approach to developing the PROPELS mHealth intervention was informed by the mHealth intervention development model (Whittaker et al. 2012) and also drew upon Dijkstra and De Vries' (1999) model for developing computer-generated tailored interventions (to inform the conceptualization – i.e. the first phase in Whittaker's model). We first conducted informal observations of the 'Walking Away from Diabetes' group-based education programme for helping people at risk of developing Type 2 diabetes become more physically active (to which the mHealth component was to be added to as a 'follow-on' component) in diverse regions where it has been commissioned, as well as engaging in informal discussions with 'Walking Away' educators. This was to become familiar with the delivery of Walking Away, develop initial ideas about how the mHealth component could supplement the existing programme, understand the cultural and ethnic diversity of our target population and inform the development of topic guides for subsequent focus groups.

Following this, we conducted three focus groups with members of our target population: 15 participants (5 women and 10 men) aged between 39 and 76 years, who had previously attended the Walking Away programme. A flexible topic guide explored participants' experiences of Walking Away (e.g. what was most and least helpful for increasing physical activity and what could be improved to facilitate sustained changes), use of mobile phones in everyday life and the addition of text-messaging follow-on support.

Our analysis was informed by the constant comparative approach; the coding framework reflected two interlinked themes: acceptability of text messaging for physical activity promotion and requirements for the structure and format of the mHealth component. Our findings relating to the latter indicated the need for: (1) two-way interaction (i.e. inputting of step counts and providing immediate feedback about physical activity progress), (2) timely reminders for self-monitoring of physical activity, (3) further consideration of how to overcome perceived barriers to using text messaging (i.e. by providing participants with an overview of the benefits of text messaging for follow-on support at the initial Walking Away session), (4) tailored and personalized text message content (explored further in our next stage of 'pre-testing focus groups'), and (5) additional telephone support to enhance rapport between educator and participant and provide support beyond text messages only (i.e. problem solving and in-depth social support).

We argue that the focus group setting enhanced the generation of the 'needs' of the intervention to be developed in several ways. As discussed earlier, the group setting permitted and encouraged honesty and critique about the proposed intervention type – the use of text-messaging for follow-on support; indeed some participants voiced concern about the method's general appropriateness for their generation or the potential for messages being intrusive and/or impersonal. Further, the setting facilitated an efficient method of moving discussion about concerns and problems into brainstorming about solutions – hence the 'needs' that were generated in situ. We argue that similar explorations in individual interviews would have required more post-hoc analysis in order to do the equivalent work. Finally, it is also worth noting the enjoyment that the participants seemed to have while considering, discussing and critiquing the idea of such an intervention.

A point to consider when planning formative phases of intervention development relates to the level of flexibility in the research protocol and the associated limits on the extent to which a formative phase can shape the resulting intervention. In other words, for most intervention development work that is part of a research programme or trial, funding will be secured based on a proposed intervention in which certain aspects – such as the mode of delivery – will already be detailed in the protocol. In the PROPELS case study, the mode of delivery – text-messaging – had already been determined; the formative research could then inform the format, structure and style, but could not change the mode of delivery. Hence, the formative phase in such development, is often concerned with how to optimize the interventions' feasibility and acceptability, to enhance uptake. Although not always practical, formative focus groups conducted ahead of grant applications could be used to explore different options of mode of delivery. Indeed, it is now common for participant and public involvement (PPI) work to employ focus groups for precisely this purpose; combined with a concurrent literature review, this provides stronger case for selection of a certain type of intervention.

In sum, the use of focus groups in the formative phase of intervention development is a useful approach to investigate (a) the use of mHealth technology (in general) by a particular target group/population, (b) the health behaviours of a target group in relation to the health condition of focus, (c) the general barriers, facilitators and needs in relation to mHealth technology by a target group, and (d) the (general) usability of a specific mHealth technology for a specific purpose. Further, the nature of the group setting can permit and encourage participants to critique intervention proposals if the right atmosphere is created by the moderator, and can facilitate discussion leading to associated needs and solutions.

Pre-testing mHealth Interventions

Focus groups also offer a useful and pragmatic approach to conducting the 'pre-testing' of initial prototypes of mHealth interventions. This is closely related to *usability testing* – evaluating a product or service by testing it with representative users – and while there is debate about the distinctions between the two (e.g. in terms of the aims (Gócza and Kollin 2015), we would argue that, when used to their full potential, focus groups can be used to do test usability and generate discussion that helps to explain and provide insight into this. Of note, focus groups are not the most common method adopted by researchers within the pre-testing or usability testing phases of mhealth development; rather, the majority of development studies opt for interviews (e.g. Fjeldsoe et al. 2012, refs). Within the pre-testing phase, the focus is usually on establishing the target population's preferences in terms of format, style, content and language – for example, of messages – in order to optimize the usefulness and suitability.

Focus groups can be used in a number of ways in the pre-testing phase; their most common function is to inform the adaptation and refinement of a proposed mHealth intervention. For example, Van Mierlo et al's (2014) phased development study aimed to design an mHealth programme to help young adults quit smoking. While not specifically referring to their first phase as pre-testing, the description of methods aligns well with this: they used an existing text-messaging platform for adult smokers and adapted it for young adults (using literature reviews); they then tested the adapted messages for tone and content in four focus groups, and used the findings to refine and adapt the messages further (and then followed this with piloting and so on). Although focus groups were used in just one phase of this study, they had a key role in pre-testing the language and content of the intervention. The paper reports very little from the focus groups; there is no data, rather, a short description of the main themes and subsequent adaptions to the intervention (Van Mierlo et al. 2014).

Revisiting our earlier discussion about the ideal phase at which to make a decision about the mode of delivery, it may sometimes be the case that changes are made about this following pre-testing. For example, in a phased study to develop an mHealth intervention to support post-abortion family planning in Cambodia, which did involve a formative phase (of interviews), the focus groups at the pre-testing phase led to a change in delivery format (from text-messages to voice messages) (Smith et al. 2016) – although the presentation of findings in the paper could have demonstrated more clearly.

PROPELS Case Study: Pre-testing

For the pre-testing phase of the PROPELS intervention development, we conducted four further focus groups with members of the target population (n = 20; ages 52–77). Prior to attending, participants received a pedometer and activity diary via postal mail and were encouraged to record their daily step count every day for 1 week. Participants were asked to bring along their mobile phone to the focus group. The focus groups began with discussion that explored their experiences of wearing the pedometer and recording steps; their diaries and pedometers served as stimulus objects and material to generate discussion. We had also created exemplar text messages based on the findings of the formative phase and literature review. The messages were sent to participants 'live' during the focus group, working through different types of messages – with different participants receiving different messages (see Fig. 6.1 for examples of the messages used). This format enabled us to observe reactions in situ and generate think-aloud style reactions (Fonteyn et al. 1993), and facilitated participants sharing and comparing messages with fellow participants. Furthermore, it provided an insight into the variety in confidence and aptitude levels in mobile phone use in the target population.

The pre-testing focus group findings expanded on the findings from the previous phases of the development by (1) further emphasizing the importance of personalizing and tailoring messages according to key variables (e.g. previous levels of physical activity, mobility issues that limit physical activity, individuals' confidence in increasing physical activity, goal achievement/progress), (2) shaping the content of the messages (i.e. the type of benefits to focus on within the motivational messages), (3) informing the frequency of messages and sequencing of the follow-on support programme, and (4) highlighting the importance of including other activities (e.g. cycling, swimming) to maintain engagement of participants who did other activities than walking alone.

Using focus groups, rather than individual interviews, for the PROPELS pre-testing had the same benefits as those outlined for the formative focus groups – in terms of the nature of the group setting encouraging participation of all – including reluctant participants and permitting critique. Sending text-messages in situ had the added bonus of creating a further enjoyment factor to the discussion, which we argue created an even more relaxed atmosphere for sharing honest views. Furthermore, having each participant receive different exemplar messages on their own phone, and at different times from other participants, capitalized on aspects of group interaction in order to generate useful data: for example, participants

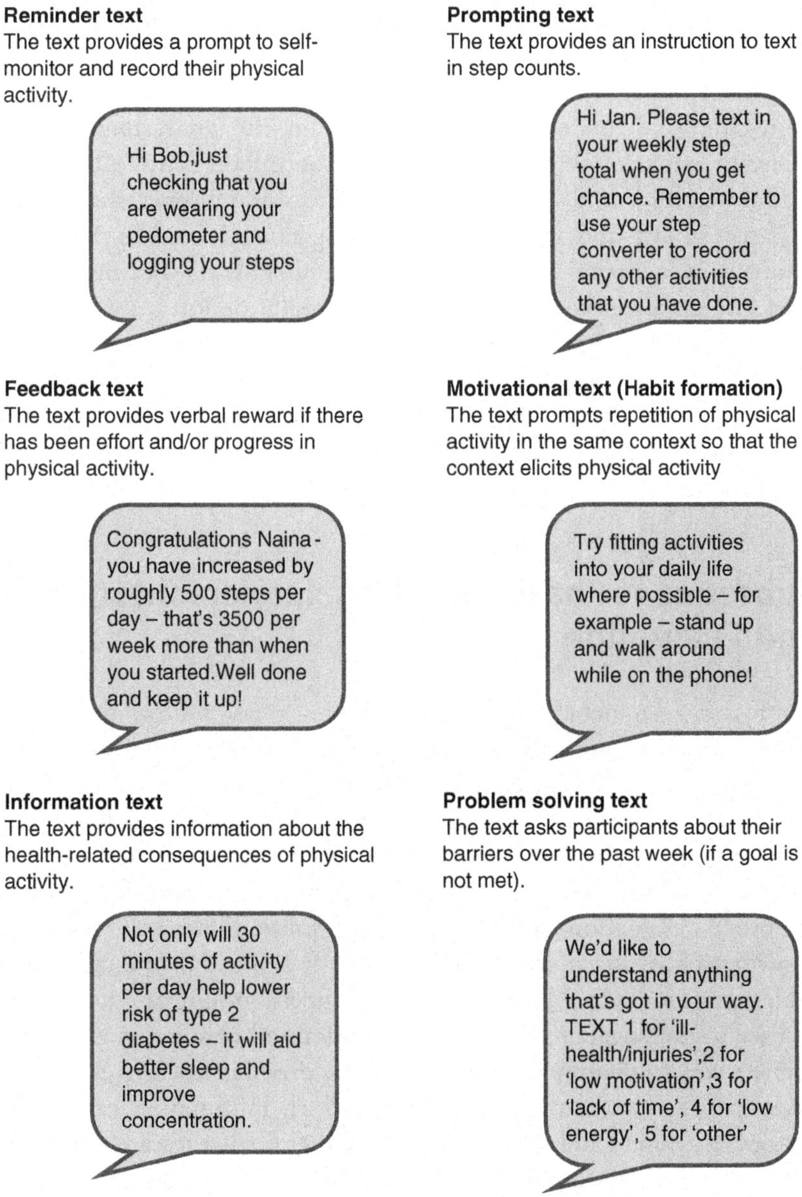

Reminder text
The text provides a prompt to self-monitor and record their physical activity.

> Hi Bob, just checking that you are wearing your pedometer and logging your steps

Prompting text
The text provides an instruction to text in step counts.

> Hi Jan. Please text in your weekly step total when you get chance. Remember to use your step converter to record any other activities that you have done.

Feedback text
The text provides verbal reward if there has been effort and/or progress in physical activity.

> Congratulations Naina - you have increased by roughly 500 steps per day – that's 3500 per week more than when you started. Well done and keep it up!

Motivational text (Habit formation)
The text prompts repetition of physical activity in the same context so that the context elicits physical activity

> Try fitting activities into your daily life where possible – for example – stand up and walk around while on the phone!

Information text
The text provides information about the health-related consequences of physical activity.

> Not only will 30 minutes of activity per day help lower risk of type 2 diabetes – it will aid better sleep and improve concentration.

Problem solving text
The text asks participants about their barriers over the past week (if a goal is not met).

> We'd like to understand anything that's got in your way. TEXT 1 for 'ill-health/injuries', 2 for 'low motivation', 3 for 'lack of time', 4 for 'low energy', 5 for 'other'

Fig. 6.1 Exemplar messages used in the pre-testing phase of the PROPELS development

sharing and comparing of different message type, content and language enabled us to see/hear not only a type of 'think aloud' reaction of the individual participant, but also the wider group.

In sum, the use of focus groups within the pre-testing stage of mHealth intervention development offers an opportunity to undertake usability testing and generate discussion to add deeper insight and explanation over and above usability testing alone. It enables the opportunity to test aspects and/or specific components of the intervention with the target group. It also offers a unique opportunity to gather reactions from target group to the style/format/language/design of aspects of the intervention in situ. In general, however, in publications about mHealth intervention development, there is very little reporting of the focus group data and how the data informed refinements and adaptations.

Subsequent Phases: Piloting, Implementation and Evaluation

In most development frameworks a piloting phase follows pre-testing; this is usually conducted on an individual level, with participants' experiences and perceptions about feasibility and acceptability being sought via one-to-one interview, not focus groups. The MRC framework highlights the continuous and ongoing nature of evaluation of complex interventions (Craig et al. 2008). MRC guidance for conducting process evaluation of complex interventions outlines and reviews the contribution of focus groups to this – both alone and in combination with other methods (Moore et al. 2014). Focus groups can continue to be used to investigate participants' perceptions of usability, as well as any barriers and facilitators to using it (having experienced it over a longer period, than, for example, in piloting). Such information can inform further refinement and development for either further research or implementation and use in clinical practice. However, a review of the literature relating to these phases is beyond the scope of this chapter – as our chosen focus is on development only.

Conclusions

This chapter reflects on the use of focus groups in the development of mHealth interventions; while not presenting a comprehensive review of this literature, it draws upon a number of notable papers to serve as examples in this reflection. Qualitative research methods are now widely used in the development and evaluation of behaviour change interventions – and the sub-field of mHealth is no exception.

While interviews and focus groups can be used for the same purpose – for example, to explore a target population's views and experiences about a potential mHealth intervention – a scope of the literature indicates that focus groups are a particularly popular method to use in the 'formative' (pre-intervention /planning) stage of development. We argue that focus groups can create an atmosphere that permits honesty and critique of a proposed intervention, its format and components, and facilitate useful 'brainstorming' discussions to generate key ideas about needs, preferences and solutions to the problems or barriers raised by participants. In some cases, however, researchers may fall into the trap of using focus groups as group interviews at this stage – that is, not capitalizing on the group setting and interaction to enhance the data generated. On the other hand, the lack of such data being included in publications from such studies may be more due to the need to report the development study as a whole (i.e. all stages) in one publication – and thus insufficient space to provide rich detail.

The use of focus groups in the pre-testing phase of intervention development appears to be less common, with researchers often opting to use individual interviews at this stage. We argue that, in the case of mHealth interventions, focus groups can provide more enhanced data than interviews at this phase. Pre-testing ideally involves people from the target population 'trying out' components of an mHealth intervention, observing their real-time reactions and exploring their views and experiences. While this is feasible to do on an individual basis, the focus group setting provides the added benefits of enabling participants to share and compare – for example, of different format, style and content of text-message in our case study – while maintaining a relaxed group atmosphere that encourages critique (as mentioned re the formative phase).

The broad field of mHealth behaviour change interventions is expanding rapidly, as researchers and intervention developers capitalize on new technology and its ever-changing use in people's daily lives (as evidenced by the Journal of Medical Internet Research recently creating a sister journal dedicated to this – the JMIR mHealth and uHealth). As complex interventions, the incorporation of qualitative research methods into the iterative development, testing and evaluation of mHealth interventions is not only recommended by the MRC framework (Craig et al. 2008), but is crucial for understanding the needs and preferences of the target population. As demonstrated in this chapter, focus groups can play a key part in this – particularly in the formative and pre-testing phases – and, in doing so, can enhance the data generated. Moreover, their use could be expanded further – for example, in increasingly innovative ways to maximize use of the group setting, but also in later phases of the research – in continuous evaluation (by integrating their use in the evaluation stage of a trial) and implementation (as an intervention is rolled out on a wider scale).

References

Barbour, R. (2007) *Doing Focus Groups*. London: Sage.

Craig, P., Dieppe, P., Macintyre, S. et al. (2008) 'Medical Research Council Guidance. "Developing and evaluating complex interventions: The new Medical Research Council guidance"'. *British Medical Journal*, 37: a1655.

Dijkstra, A., and De Vries, H. (1999) 'The development of computer-generated tailored interventions'. *Patient Education and Counseling*, 36(2): 193–203.

Farquhar, C. (with Das, R.) (1999) 'Are focus groups suitable for "sensitive" topics?', In R.S. Barbour and J. Kitzinger (eds.) *Developing Focus Group Research: Politics, Theory and Practice*. London: Sage, pp. 47–63.

Fjeldsoe, B.S., Miller, Y.D., O'Brien, J.L. et al. (2012) 'Iterative development of MobileMums: A physical activity intervention for women with young children'. *International Journal of Behavioral Nutrition and Physical Activity*, 9: 151.

Fonteyn, M., Kuipers, B., and Grobe, S.A. (1993) 'Description of Think Aloud Method and Protocol Analysis'. *Qualitative Health Research*, 3(4): 430–441.
Gócza, Z., and Kollin, Z. (2015) 'UX Myths': http://uxmyths.com/post/1319999199/myth-26-usability-testing-focus-groups.
Hevner, A.R. (2007) 'A three cycle view of design science research'. *Scandinavian Journal of Information Systems*, 19(2): 87–92.
Kitzinger, J., and Farquhar, C. (1999) 'The analytical potential of "sensitive moments" in focus group discussions', In R. Barbour and J. Kitzinger (eds.), *Developing Focus Group Research: Politics, Theory and Practice*. London: Sage, pp. 156–172.
Michie, S., Richardson, M., Johnston, M. et al. (2013) 'The behavior change technique taxonomy (v1) of 93 hierarchically clustered techniques: Building an international consensus for the reporting of behavior change interventions'. *Annals of Behavioral Medicine*, 46(1): 81–95.
Moore, G., Audrey S., Barker, M. et al. (2014) *Process Evaluation of Complex Interventions: Medical Research CouncilGguidance*. London: MRC Population Health Science Research Network.
Morgan, D.L. (1988) *The Focus Group Guidebook* (Focus Group Kit, Book 1). Thousand Oaks, CA: Sage.
Morton, K., Sutton, S., Hardeman, W. et al. (2015) 'A text-messaging and pedometer program to promote physical activity in people at high risk of type 2 diabetes: A development and feasibility study for the PROPELS Trial'. *JMIR mHealth and uHealth*, 3(4): e105.
Pfaeffli, L., Maddison, R., Whittaker, R. et al. (2012) 'A mHealth cardiac rehabilitation exercise intervention: Findings from content development studies'. *BMC Cardiovascular Disor*ders, 12: 36.
Schnall, R., Bakken, S., Rojas, M., Travers, J., and Carballo-Dieguez, A. (2015) 'mHealth technology as a persuasive tool for treatment, care and management of persons living with HIV'. *AIDS and Behavior*, 19: 81–89.
Schnall, R., Rojas, M., Bakken, S. et al. (2016) 'A user-centered model for designing consumer mobile health (mHealth) applications (apps)'. *Journal of Biomedical Informatics*, 60: 243–251.
Smith C., Vannak U., Sokhey L. et al. (2016) 'Mobile technology for improved family planning (MOTIF): The development of a mobile phone-based (mHealth) intervention to support post-abortion family planning (PAFP) in Cambodia'. *Reproductive Health*, 13: 1.

Van Mierlo, T., Fournier, R., Jean-Charles, A. et al. (2014) 'I'll txt u if i have a problem: How the Société Canadienne du Cancer in Quebec applied behavior-change theory, data mining and agile software development to help young adults quit smoking'. *PLoS ONE*, 9: 3.

Waterlander, W., Whittaker, R., McRobbie, H. et al. (2014) 'Development of an evidence-based mhealth weight management program using a formative research process'. *Journal of Medical Internet Research*, 16(7).

Whittaker, R., Merry, S., Dorey, E. et al. (2012) 'A development and evaluation process for mhealth interventions: Examples from New Zealand'. *Journal of Health Communication*, 17(Suppl. 1): 11–21.

World Health Organization (2011) 'mHealth: New Horizons for Health through Mobile Technologies', *Second Global Survey on eHealth Global Observatory for eHealth Series*. 3. World Health Organization, Geneva, Switzerland.

Yardley, L., Morrison, L., Bradbury, K. et al. (2015) 'The person-based approach to intervention development: Application to digital health-related behavior change interventions'. *JMIR*, 17(1): e30.

Yates, T., Griffin, S, Bodicoat, D.H. et al. (2015) 'PRomotion Of Physical activity through structured Education with differing Levels of ongoing Support for people at high risk of type 2 diabetes (PROPELS): Study protocol for a randomized controlled trial'. *Trials*, 16: 289.

Helen Eborall has a BSc in Psychology (University of Warwick), MSc in Health Psychology (University of Surrey), and a PhD in Health Services Research (University of Edinburgh). At the Primary Care Unit, University of Cambridge, she held a post as a Research Psychologist on projects investigating the psychological impact and experience of screening for type 2 diabetes, followed by an ESRC/MRC interdisciplinary postdoctoral fellowship. Helen was appointed as a Lecturer in Social Science applied to Health at the University of Leicester in 2008, where she is based in the Social Science Applied to Healthcare Improvement Research (SAPPHIRE) group and is a longstanding collaborator of the Leicester Diabetes Centre. Her research expertise is in developing and evaluating complex interventions for the prevention and management of long-term conditions, through rigorous methodology, informed by social and behavioural science.

Katie Morton has a BSc in Sports Science and Social Sciences and an MSc in Sport and Exercise Psychology (Loughborough University), and a PhD in Behavioural Medicine (University of British Columbia, Canada). As a postdoctoral Research Associate at the Primary Care Unit, University of Cambridge, Katie worked on a pilot trial to evaluate very brief interventions for physical activity promotion in routine consultations and the PROPELS trial in which she developed a mHealth (text-messaging) intervention for physical activity promotion for individuals at high risk of Type 2 diabetes. She subsequently undertook a Career Development Fellowship, at the Centre for Diet and Activity Research (CEDAR), University of Cambridge, conducting a programme of research to identify and evaluate opportunities within the school environment to improve the distribution of physical activity intensity in adolescents. In 2016, she was appointed as a Consultant in Behavioural Sciences at Innovia Technology. She also retains a long-held visiting Research Fellowship at the Centre for Workplace and Community Health, St. Mary's University, Twickenham.

7

The Use of Focus Groups in Programme Evaluation: Experience Based on the Project P.A.T.H.S. in a Chinese Context

Daniel T. L. Shek

Introduction

In the global context, there is a growing concern about adolescent health. Although adolescents constitute more than a quarter of the world's population (1.8 billion), the health of young people has improved far less than that of the young children in the past five decades

---

D.T.L. Shek (✉)
Department of Applied Social Sciences, The Hong Kong Polytechnic University, Hong Kong, China
Centre for Innovative Programmes for Adolescents and Families, The Hong Kong Polytechnic University, Hong Kong, China
Department of Social Work, East China Normal University, Shanghai, China
Kiang Wu Nursing College of Macau, Macau, China
Division of Adolescent Medicine, Department of Pediatrics, Kentucky Children's Hospital, University of Kentucky College of Medicine, Lexington, Kentucky, United States
e-mail: Daniel.Shek@polyu.edu.hk

© The Author(s) 2017
R.S. Barbour, D.L. Morgan (eds.), *A New Era in Focus Group Research*, DOI 10.1057/978-1-137-58614-8_7

(Sawyer et al. 2012). Adolescent health-compromising and risk behaviour – such as substance abuse, risky sexual behaviour, Internet addiction, violence, school dropout and unemployment – have captured the attention both of the public and policymakers. In response to such adolescent developmental issues, prevention programmes based on prevention science principles have been developed (Catalano et al. 2012). In particular, the school-based prevention programmes 'have shown effects in reducing aggression, crime, alcohol and tobacco use, unwanted pregnancies, sexually transmitted diseases, and mental health symptoms and disorders, and have shown increase in secondary school completion, educational attainment, and income' (Catalano et al. 2012: 1658). In another review of the effectiveness of social and emotional programmes, Durlak et al. (2011) pointed out that students who joined programmes promoting psychosocial competencies in adolescents had better development in many domains, including academic attainment.

One important issue surrounding adolescent prevention and positive youth development programmes relates to programme evaluation. The fundamental question that programme developers should ask is whether the programme achieves its intended outcomes, particularly, whether adolescents thrive after joining the programme. In the mainstream evaluation literature, randomized trials based on the experimental approach are commonly used, and this is regarded as the 'gold standard' to assess programme effects. Several elements characterize this approach, including reliance on standardized procedures, emphasis on objectivity, neutrality of researchers, precise measurement, reliability and validity, use of statistical models, and a focus on representativeness and generalization of the findings (Leung and Shek 2011).

Despite its popularity in the field of evaluation, quantitative evaluation is criticized on several grounds. First, the 'dualist' assumption of the distinction between the 'subject' and 'object' is criticized. For example, social constructivists have argued that the reality is a 'co-created' one. Second, as a social reality is fluid and ever-changing, standardized quantitative methods can, at best, create profiles of responses, but do not account for in-depth subjective experiences of programme participants. Third, the quantitative approach is criticized as being too artificial, relying on procedures in laboratories or standardized items in questionnaires. Finally, while the quantitative approach may provide answers on the outcomes of a programme, it is difficult to understand the processes involved (Leung and Shek 2011).

With reference to the above criticisms, evaluators have argued that qualitative research methods could provide a more holistic picture of programme processes and outcomes. The typical attributes of a qualitative evaluation approach include an emphasis on human experience, a focus on narratives and observations, the uniqueness of cases, and authenticity. While there are different strands of qualitative research, such as ethnographic, interpretive, social constructionist, and grounded theory approaches, qualitative researchers commonly argue against the 'received view' and highlight the importance of a contextual understanding of the meaning of human responses. According to Patton, there are ten characteristics of qualitative research, including naturalistic inquiry (i.e. study in the real worlds and non-artificial settings), inductive analysis (i.e. drawing inferences from individual cases), holistic perspective (i.e. position against reductionism), favouring 'thick' descriptions and in-depth inquiry (i.e. understanding of details), an emphasis on personal contact of the researcher with the informants (i.e. researcher-informant relationship), a belief that reality is fluid and constantly changing, an emphasis on individual uniqueness, a focus on contextual understanding, the maintenance of empathic neutrality (i.e. empathy without personal biases) and flexibility in research design (Patton 1990: 40–41). Hence, instead of using structured questionnaires or structured laboratory procedures, where the evaluators must maintain a distance from programme participants, qualitative research focuses on meaning-making via 'close encounters' with the informants, such as in-depth individual interviews, group interviews (e.g. focus groups), interviewing and naturalistic observations, where evaluators listen to the stories and voices of programme participants.

Although quantitative and qualitative approaches are different, there is a growing trend to combine the two methods to design mixed-methods studies. Based on the tenets of pragmatism, researchers have argued that quantitative and qualitative research can be combined if this increases our understanding of certain phenomena (Creswell 2014; Teddlie and Tashakkori 2009). Greene et al. (1989) suggested five purposes for mixed-methods studies. These include: a) examining the convergence or divergence of results based on different methods (triangulation); b) using different methods to understand the different aspects of a problem (complementarity); c) using a method (quantitative or qualitative) to inform the second method (developmental usage); d) using an alternative approach to illuminate contradictions and inconsistencies (initiation) and e) using either approach to enlarge the breadth of a study (expansion). Greene and Caracelli (1997) outlined the advances, benefits and challenges in mixed-method evaluation.

In the present chapter, we present findings collected via focus groups based on a longitudinal mixed-methods design. Besides the traditional approach of examining the qualitative content, we also 'counted' the qualitative themes to form a quantitative picture about the experiences of the informants. By adopting this research design, we can construct profiles which are particularly useful to answer the question of whether a programme is effective 'on the whole'. In the policy context, having normative profiles as well as unique individual responses will help policymakers to have a more in-depth and holistic understanding of the effectiveness of the programme under evaluation. Furthermore, to have a systematic view of the programme effect over time, we collected data using focus groups over several years.

The Project P.A.T.H.S. in Hong Kong

Shek et al. (2011) highlighted several adolescent developmental problems in Hong Kong that merit the attention of policymakers. Unfortunately, despite the intensification of youth problems in Hong Kong, validated prevention and positive youth development programmes in Hong Kong are almost non-existent (Shek and Sun 2013a, b; Shek and Wu 2016).

To help young people to develop in a holistic manner, The Hong Kong Jockey Club Charities Trust initiated a project entitled 'P.A.T.H.S. to Adulthood: A Jockey Club Youth Enhancement Scheme', referring to **P**ositive **A**dolescent **T**raining through **H**olistic **S**ocial Programmes.

There were five universities involved in this project, with The Hong Kong Polytechnic University as the lead institution. Two tiers of programmes were intrinsic to this project. The Tier 1 Programme was provided to all Secondary 1 to Secondary 3 students (Grade 7 to Grade 9 students, aged around 12 to 15 years old). The Tier 2 Programme was generally provided for students who have greater psychosocial needs. The programmes were based on positive youth development constructs identified in previously successful programmes (Shek and Sun 2013a).

One unique characteristic of the Project P.A.T.H.S. is a systematic, ongoing and in-depth evaluation of the programme. To look at the programme effects from different perspectives, mixed-methods evaluation strategies were used to evaluate the Tier 1 Programme (i.e. triangulation). These included a 5-year longitudinal study, subjective outcome evaluation, process evaluation, interim evaluation, and qualitative evaluation. Besides the 5-year randomized group trial, we used focus groups in different cohorts of students and workers who were randomly selected from the participating schools (Shek 2012; Shek and Sun 2012). In this chapter, the unique features of the focus group evaluation studies employed in this project are presented. Besides, further analyses by integrating the findings based on the focus groups for students and workers were carried out. The integrated findings were further triangulated with evaluation findings collected through other methods.

The Unique Features of Focus Group Evaluation Used in the Project P.A.T.H.S.

Feature 1: Focus Groups Based on the Programme Implementers and Participants

In the Experimental Implementation Phase and Full Implementation Phase, 244 schools participated in the Tier 1 Programme at different times and 28 schools were randomly selected for the focus group study. In each school, we randomly selected students as informants (see Table 7.1).

Table 7.1 Details of focus groups with programme participants and implementers

	2005/2006 (EIP-S1)	2006/2007 (FIP-S1)	2007/2008 (FIP-S2)	2007/2008 (EIP-S3)	2008/2009 (FIP-S3)
Total no. of schools joined PATHS	52	207	196	48	167
(i) 10-h programme	23	95	113	29	104
(ii) 20-h programme	29	112	83	19	63
Total no. of schools joined this study	5[a]	10	10	4	10
(i) 10-h programme	1	2	2	0	3
(ii) 20-h programme	4[b]	8[c]	8[c]	4[c]	7
(a) No. of schools incorporated into formal curriculum	3	4	8	4	7
(b) No. of schools incorporated into form teacher lessons or using other modes	2	6	1	0	4
Average no. of classes per school (range)	5 (5)	4.9 (3–6)	4.9 (3–6)	4.8 (4–6)	4.6 (4–6)
No. of instructor focus groups	5	9	9	3	10
Total no. of instructor respondents	38	61	23	13	42
(i) Teachers	27	54	15	8	34
(ii) Social workers	11	7	8	5	8
Average no. of respondents per group (range)	7.6 (3–12)	6.8 (2–14)	2.6 (1–5)	4.3 (2–8)	4.2 (2–6)
No. of student focus groups	5[d]	10	10	4	N.A.
Total no. of student respondents	43	88	92	29	N.A.
Average no. of respondents per group (range)	8.6 (3–10)	8.8 (4–12)	9.2 (4–11)	7.3 (3–10)	N.A.

Note:
[a]Originally, there were 6 invited schools. Data from 1 school were discarded because the programme implementers had not received training on programme implementation.
[b]1 school could not arrange student focus group.
[c]1 school could not arrange instructor focus group.
[d]11 students in a school were divided into 2 focus groups.
EIP = Experimental Implementation Phase
FIP = Full Implementation Phase

Although random sampling is not commonly used in qualitative research, it was used in the project because it helps to reduce some of the limitations of purposive sampling which cannot minimize chance effects in the subject selection process. In the focus group evaluation studies, we collected data in three areas. First, we invited participants to choose descriptors for the programme and then discussed these in the focus groups. Second, we invited the informants to provide metaphors to represent the programme. Finally, we discussed the perceived benefits of the programme for participants (Shek and Lee 2008; Shek and Sun 2007).

Similarly, focus group studies based on the programme implementers were carried out. First, 39 schools were randomly selected (15 schools for Secondary 1, 10 for Secondary 2, and 14 for Secondary 3). Second, 36 focus groups with 138 teachers and 39 social workers were formed. The characteristics of the schools joining this process evaluation study are presented in Table 7.1. Similar to the student focus groups, we collected data in three areas, including 'descriptors' (i.e. description of the programme by words), 'metaphors' (i.e. things that can represent the programme), and 'benefits' (i.e. how the students look at the benefits of the programme).

In contrast to the common practice that focus groups are formed by the programme participants only, we also convened focus groups with the programme implementers. Shek and Ma (2012) presented several arguments for including the views of the programme implementers. First, programme implementers are legitimate stakeholders with regard to the developed programmes. Second, as programme implementers usually have training in evaluation, their views are likely to be more accurate than those of the clients. Third, a collection of evaluation data from the implementers can help them to reflect on their own conduct. Fourth, evaluation based on implementers can give them a sense of fairness. Fifth, as implementation experiences may vary across different sites, asking for implementers' views is important. Finally, collecting evaluation data from different sources is in line with the principle of triangulation.

Another unique feature of the study is that a fairly large number of focus groups and participants were involved in the studies in this project. Because of the labour-intensive nature of focus group data collection and analyses, small samples are more commonly used (Carlsen and Glenton 2011).

Finally, the schools and informants were randomly selected to join the focus groups. Although there are views suggesting that purposive samples with specific objectives would provide thick data (MacDougall and Fudge 2001) and that homogeneous sampling, maximum variation sampling, and critical case sampling could be used (Morgan 1997), random selection of schools and informants has three advantages. First, by randomly selecting the schools and informants, selection bias can be minimized. Besides, this approach can ensure that informants of different background characteristics can have an equal chance of being selected. Second, random selection can strengthen generalizability of the findings which may not be possible under purposive sampling. Finally, random selection can give more credibility to the findings arising from focus groups.

Feature 2: Focus Groups Guided by the CIPP Evaluation Framework

In the present study, the CIPP model (Stufflebeam 2012) was used for evaluation. This is a management-oriented model, originally proposed by Daniel Stufflebeam, who defined evaluation as 'the process of delineating, obtaining, providing, and applying descriptive and judgmental information about the merit and worth of some object's goals, design, implementation, and outcomes to guide improvement decisions, provide accountability reports, inform institutionalization/dissemination decisions, and improve understanding of the involved phenomena' (Stufflebeam 2012: 34). The term 'CIPP' is an acronym representing an evaluation framework for collecting evaluation data on four levels, including context evaluation, input evaluation, process evaluation, and product evaluation. Within this evaluation framework, an evaluator asks four questions – What are the needs (context evaluation)? What are the strategies (input evaluation)? What happens in the process (process evaluation)? Is it successful (product evaluation)?

The focus group questions for the programme implementers and participants can be seen in Table 7.2. As shown here, some common questions

Table 7.2 Topic/question guide for focus groups

A. Context Evaluation	
Instructor focus group	**Student focus group**
• How much do you know about 'Positive Youth Development Programmes' (e.g. 'Life Skills Education')? What is your overall impression of these programmes? • Have you taught programmes that are similar to the Project P.A.T.H.S. before? • If yes, how effective do you feel they are? • From your perspective, what are the differences between the Project P.A.T.H.S. and other similar programmes? • Do you agree with the vision of the Project P.A.T.H.S.? Why?	N.A.

B. Input Evaluation	
Instructor focus group	**Student focus group**
• What kind of effects do you feel that the implementation of the Project P.A.T.H.S. have on the school's normal operation? • If the school incorporates the Project P.A.T.H.S. curriculum into the normal curriculum (e.g. Life Education, Integrated Humanities, etc.), from your perspective, what are the advantages and disadvantages of this arrangement? • If the school <u>does not</u> incorporate the Project P.A.T.H.S. curriculum into the normal curriculum (e.g. homeroom, extra-curricular activities, etc.), do you feel that this arrangement is successful? • To accommodate the implementation of the Project P.A.T.H.S., did the school make special arrangements? • Do you feel that the principal and administrative staff support the implementation of the Project P.A.T.H.S. at your school? Why or Why not?	N.A.

(*continued*)

Table 7.2 (continued)

B. Input Evaluation	
Instructor focus group	Student focus group
• Do you feel that the training you received is adequate for you to carry out the programme requirements?	

C. Process Evaluation	
Instructor focus group	Student focus group

General Impression of the Programme
- What is your overall impression of the programme? What are your feelings?
- All in all, did you enjoy leading (participating in)* the programme?
- Regarding the programme, what has given you a lasting impression?
- While implementing (participating in)* the programme, did you have any unforgettable experiences?

Comments on the Programme Content
- Regarding the programme, what are the things you like? And what are the things you dislike?
- What are your views on the different units and content of the programme?
- Which units do you like the most? Why?
- Were there any activities that were effective to arouse students' (your)* interest to participate in the programme?

Comments on the Programme Implementation	Comments on the Programme Implementation
• While implementing the programme, did you encounter any difficulties?	• What are your thoughts on the degree or extent of participation of the entire class (all the students)?
• Do you feel that the programme implementation was successful?	• How do you feel about the atmosphere and discipline of the class when the programme was implemented?
• To what degree/extent did you follow the programme curriculum manuals? Why?	• What are the responses of the participating students regarding the programme?
• What are your thoughts on the students' responses to the programme?	**Comments on the Instructors** • What are your views on the instructors who conducted the programme?
N.A.	• Regarding the interactions between the instructors and students, what are your thoughts and feelings?

Table 7.2 (continued)

D. Product Evaluation	
Instructor focus group	**Student focus group**

Evaluation of the General Effectiveness of the Programme
- Do you feel that the programme is beneficial to the development of adolescents?
- Have you noticed any changes in students (yourself)* after their (your)* participation in the programme? If yes, what are the changes? (free elicitation)
- If you noticed changes in students (yourself)*, what do you think are the factors that have caused such changes?
- If you <u>have not</u> noticed changes in students (yourself)*, what do you think are the reasons?
    - Do you think that the programme has helped your development?
    - What have you gained in this programme? (free elicitation)

Evaluation of the Specific Effectiveness of the Programme
- Do you think that the programme can promote students' (your)* self-confidence/ability to face the future?
- Do you think that the programme can enhance students' (your)* abilities in different areas?
    - Do you think that your participation in the programme has affected your school work and grades? Please elaborate your answers.

Optional Questions on Specific Effectiveness of the Programme
- Do you think that the programme can enhance students' (your)* spirituality aspect?
- Do you think that the can promote the students' (your)* bonding with family, teachers and friends?
- Do you think that the programme can cultivate students' (your)*compassion and care for others?
- Do you think that the programme can promote students' (your)* participation and care for the society?
- Do you think that the programme can promote students' (your)* sense of responsibility to the society, family, teachers and peers?

Other Comments
- If you are invited to use three descriptive words to describe the programme, what are the three words that you would use?
- If you are invited to use one incident, object/thing or feeling (e.g. indigestion, enjoyment, child at heart, etc.) to describe the programme, what metaphor will you use to stand for the programme?

(continued)

Table 7.2 (continued)

Instructor focus group	Student focus group
The Programme's Impact on the Instructor • Do you feel you have gained anything by leading this programme? And have you lost anything? • If you have the opportunity in future, do you wish to lead similar programmes again?	N.A.

*The words in brackets are used in student focus groups

on process and products were put to both groups, allowing us to develop triangulated pictures of the experiences of both groups of informants.

Feature 3: Use of Descriptors and Metaphors

Besides asking common questions, the focus group participants were invited to use some descriptors to convey their experience prior to the focus group meeting where they then discussed these descriptors. This arrangement gave participants time to think about the descriptors and group discussion allowed them to socially construct the experiences involved.

In addition, the informants were asked to use metaphor(s) that could be used to stand for the programme. Metaphors allow participants to make use of their imagination, enabling them to work out a less rigid yet articulated account of their experiences. Metaphors can be used as conceptual tools enabling researchers to make sense of the data and provoking new understanding. The attempt to look at words given by the informant is similar to the keyword analysis method proposed by Seale and Charteis-Black (2010). Descriptors such as 'happy', 'relaxing' and 'very positive' given by students and implementers suggest that the programme was well-received by different stakeholders. Similarly, metaphors such as 'street light', 'seeding', 'mirror' and 'sunshine after the rain' also suggest that different stakeholders perceived benefits of the programme.

Feature 4: Combining Quantitative and Qualitative Data

Primarily, focus groups generated qualitative data via the narratives of the research participants. While it is plausible simply to extract themes, forming profiles via counting offers an added advantage in that it provides a picture of the relative importance of the different themes. According to Miles and Huberman (1994), counting is a qualitative research strategy which helps to generate profiles of experiences. In the Project P.A.T.H.S., the narratives were coded and categorized and the frequency of the different themes was described and analyzed (Shek 2012; Shek and Sun 2012). Moreover, description of the narratives can further illuminate the experiences and benefits of the programme to participants. The categories of responses for the descriptors, metaphors and perceived benefits can be seen in Tables 7.3–7.5.

Feature 5: Use of Intra-rater and Inter-rater Reliability Methods

Reliability refers to the consistency of an assessment tool and is frequently seen as a hallmark of positivistic research which is inappropriate for qualitative research. However, many qualitative researchers acknowledge the importance of asking whether the coding and interpretations of members of the research team are consistent (both on an individual and on a team basis), drawing on the principle of dependability. Generally speaking, qualitative researchers ask whether interpretations of the same researcher are stable over time (intra-rater reliability) and whether interpretations are stable across researchers (inter-rater reliability). Reliability findings of the focus groups conducted in this project are presented in Table 7.6.

142 D.T.L. Shek

Table 7.3 Categorization of programme descriptors used by focus group participants

Instructor focus group		Student focus group	
Descriptors	Total (% of total responses)	Descriptors	Total (% of total responses)
Positive responses			
Related to overall satisfaction (e.g. good, satisfied, positive, important, meaningful, worthwhile)	28	Related to overall satisfaction (e.g. good, satisfied, positive, excellent, meaningful, outstanding)	37
Related to programme content (e.g. comprehensive, clear rationale, in-depth, practical, useful, novel, systematic, focused, diversified, all-rounded)	46	Related to programme content (e.g. comprehensive, in-depth, practical, useful, novel, clear, meeting the needs of students)	31
Related to implementation process (e.g. happy, lively, interactive, relaxing, interesting, excited)	42	Related to implementation process (e.g. happy, fun, lively, good atmosphere, relaxed, interesting, excited)	129
Related to effectiveness of the programme (e.g. effective, fruitful, inspiring, have gains, reflective)	31	Related to effectiveness of the programme (e.g. have gains, beneficial, fruitful, applicable to real life, helpful, enlightening)	22
Other positive descriptors	22	Other positive descriptors	18
Subtotal	**169 (62.59%)**	**Subtotal**	**237 (60.93%)**

Category	Count	Category	Count
Negative responses			
Related to overall comments (e.g. painful, harsh, chaotic)	13	Related to overall comments (e.g. Meaningless, unattractive, disappointing)	11
Related to programme content (e.g. superficial, difficult, overlapping)	33	Related to programme content (e.g. senseless, monotonous, empty)	36
Related to programme implementation process (e.g. rush, heavy workload for teachers)	11	Related to programme implementation process (e.g. boring, waste of time, too relaxing)	58
Related to effectiveness of the programme (e.g. useless, could not meet students' needs)	11	Related to effectiveness of the programme (e.g. helpless, useless)	9
Other negative descriptors	8	Other negative descriptors (e.g. troublesome)	6
Subtotal	76 (28.15%)	Subtotal	120 (30.85%)
Neutral responses (e.g. depends on individual, stressful)	19 (7.04%)	Neutral responses (e.g. fair, to be improved)	17 (4.37%)
Undecided nature (e.g. beyond our power to do it)	6 (2.22%)	Undecided nature (e.g. low cost, unlike a class)	15 (3.86%)
Total Count	270 (100%)	Total Count	389 (100%)

Table 7.4 Metaphors used by focus group participants to describe the programme

Instructor focus group			Student focus group		
Nature of responses	Number of responses towards the nature of metaphor	Number of codes derived from the metaphor	Nature of responses	Number of responses towards the nature of metaphor	Number of codes derived from the metaphor
Positive items (%) (e.g. Photographs, Streetlight, Seeding, Cashbox)	40 (55.56%)	65 (50.78%)	**Positive items (%)** (e.g. Mirror, Stair, Rainbow, Sunshine after rain)	109 (57.98%)	158 (65.29%)
Negative items (%) (e.g. Indigestion, Tasteless water, Rowing upstream, Firework)	6 (8.33%)	16 (12.50%)	**Negative items (%)** (e.g. Beat each other, Invisible pen, Disappointment, Talking tactics on paper)	36 (19.15%)	41 (16.94%)
Neutral items (%) (e.g. Bottle-neck, Perceiving the elephant in blind, Durian, Magic box)	26 (36.11%)	47 (36.72%)	**Neutral items (%)** (e.g. Train, Watching movie, Parenting, Medicine)	43 (22.87%)	41 (16.94%)
			Undecided items (%) (e.g. Zip file, White paper)	0	2 (0.83%)
Total Count (%)	72 (100%)	128 (100%)	**Total Count (%)**	188 (100%)	242 (100%)

Table 7.5 Categorization of responses on the perceived benefits for programme participants

Area of Competence	Instructor focus group		Student focus group	
	Subcategory	Total	Subcategory	Total
Societal level	Social responsibility and affairs	2 (0.39%)	Social responsibility and affairs	16 (2.12%)
Familial level	Family relationships	7 (1.35%)	Family relationships	25 (3.32%)
Interpersonal level	General interpersonal competence (e.g. enhanced instructor-student relationship and understanding)	81	General interpersonal competence (e.g. improved relationship with peers/made more friends)	67
	Specific interpersonal competence (e.g. increased ability and willingness to express oneself)	51	Specific interpersonal competence (e.g. improved communication skills and interpersonal relationship)	85
	Subtotal	132 (25.48%)	Subtotal	152 (20.16%)
Personal level	Behavioural competence (e.g. strengthened positive behaviour)	11	Behavioural competence (e.g. promoted presentation skills)	32
	Cognitive competence (e.g. enhanced critical thinking, improved problem-solving skills)	23	Cognitive competence (e.g. enhanced critical thinking, improved problem-solving skills)	45
	Emotional competence	5	Emotional competence	44

(continued)

Table 7.5 (continued)

Area of Competence	Instructor focus group		Student focus group	
	Subcategory	Total	Subcategory	Total
	(e.g. enhanced emotional management)		(e.g. enhanced ability in handling emotions)	
	Moral competence and virtues	10	Moral competence and virtues (e.g. learned to do appropriate things at the right place/right time)	27
	Beliefs in the future	4	Beliefs in the future (e.g. facilitated goal-setting)	21
	Positive self (e.g. enhanced self-confidence, enhanced personal growth)	40	Positive self (e.g. enhanced self-confidence, enhanced personal growth)	87
	Spirituality (e.g. enhanced self-reflection)	35	Spirituality	18
	Resilience	4	Resilience (e.g. learned positive thinking)	21
	General gains (e.g. positive influence)	50	General gains	10
	Subtotal	182 (35.14%)	Subtotal	305 (40.45%)
Other comments	Positive comments (e.g. benefits to instructors, effectiveness in the long run)	81	Positive comments (e.g. benefit to study)	99
	Negative comments (e.g. unhelpful, not much change)	37	Negative comments (e.g. unhelpful)	107

7 The Use of Focus Groups in Programme Evaluation... 147

Table 7.5 (continued)

Area of Competence	Instructor focus group		Student focus group	
	Subcategory	Total	Subcategory	Total
	Neutral comments (e.g. difficult to measure)	64	Neutral comments (e.g. not much change)	35
	Undecided	13	Undecided	15
	Subtotal	195 (37.64%)	Subtotal	256 (33.95%)
	Total Count	**518 (100%)**	**Total Count**	**754 (100%)**

Table 7.6 Reliability of coding across years

	Instructor focus group		Student focus group	
	Average Intra-rater reliability (range)	Average Inter-rater reliability (range)	Average Intra-rater reliability (range)	Average Inter-rater reliability (range)
Agreement towards the nature of descriptors	92% (80%–100%)	88.5% (80%–95%)	96.25% (90%–100%)	94.38% (90%–100%)
Agreement towards the nature of metaphors	89% (80%–100%)	91% (80%–100%)	96.25% (92.5%–100%)	88.75% (85%–95%)
Agreement towards the nature of the perceived benefits of the programme	91.5% (85%–97.5%)	89.5% (85%–92.5%)	98.13% (95%–100%)	95% (90%–97.5%)

Feature 6: Triangulated Picture Based on the Programme Implementers and Participants

The strength of having both programme implementers and programme participants is that we can combine the data to form a comprehensive and holistic picture of programme effectiveness. For the focus groups with programme participants, findings showed that the descriptions and metaphors provided were mainly positive in nature (Shek 2012; Shek and Sun 2012). Similarly, programme implementers also generated positive descriptors for the programme and used positive metaphors. In addition, the workers and students felt that the programme was beneficial to the holistic development of the students (Shek 2012; Shek and Sun 2012). Hence, we can build a triangulated picture based on different stakeholders as well as the similarities and differences in their views. In this study, we saw more similarities than differences in the findings based on different stakeholders.

Feature 7: Triangulated Picture Based on Different Evaluation Methods

In the Project P.A.T.H.S., we used multiple evaluation strategies to evaluate the programme. Roughly speaking, different types of evaluation findings lead to two conclusions. First, different stakeholders generally had positive perceptions of the programme, implementers and benefits of the project. Second, in the randomized controlled trial, students in the experimental group generally performed better than did students in the control group. These two conclusions are shared by the findings using focus group methods (see Table 7.7).

Discussion

There are several strengths in the focus groups conducted for the P.A.T.H.S. Project. First, the related studies were guided by a well-articulated model (CIPP model). Second, the number of focus groups and participants

Table 7.7 A summary of the major evaluation findings of the Project P.A.T.H.S.

Evaluation Strategies	Participants	Major Findings
1. Objective outcome evaluation (one group pretest-posttest design)	■ $N = 546$ in the Experimental Implementation Phase	■ Programme participants showed positive changes based on different indicators
2. Objective outcome evaluation (randomized group trial)	■ Initially 24 experimental schools and 24 control schools ■ Around 3,000 participants in the experimental and control groups	■ Experimental group subjects showed better growth curves compared to control group subjects
3. Subjective outcome evaluation (students)	■ Nine datasets from 2005 to 2009 ($N = $ 200,000+ students)	■ Participants had positive views about the programme, instructors and perceived benefits
4. Subjective outcome evaluation (programme implementers)	■ Nine datasets collected from 2005 to 2009 (around 8,000 participants)	■ Programme implementers had positive views about the programme, instructors and perceived benefits
5. Subjective outcome evaluation: Secondary data analyses based on conclusions of the reports	■ 1,327 reports involving 244 schools	■ Students and implementers had positive perceptions of the programme, instructors, and benefits
6. Interim evaluation	■ Eight datasets collected from 2006 to 2009 (around 380 randomly selected schools)	■ Basically positive evaluation ■ Suggestions for improvement noted
7. Process evaluation	■ 97 teaching units were observed in 62 schools	■ High programme adherence of around 85% ■ Positive programme implementation quality
8. Focus groups based on students	■ 29 focus groups from randomly selected schools	■ Positive descriptors and metaphors noted

(continued)

Table 7.7 (continued)

Evaluation Strategies	Participants	Major Findings
	■ 252 students randomly recruited	■ Generally positive views about the programme
9. Focus groups based on implementers	■ 36 focus groups from randomly selected schools ■ 177 programme implementers randomly recruited	■ Positive descriptors and metaphors noted ■ Suggestions for improvement proposed
10. Student diaries	■ Weekly diaries collected from 1,138 randomly recruited students	■ Overwhelmingly positive stories noted
11. Case study	■ Initially seven cases	■ 5 Ps influencing programme success identified – Programme, people, process, policy and place factors
12. Repertory grid evaluation	■ $N = 104$ randomly selected programme participants	■ Positive changes in self-perceptions after joining the programme

Adapted from Shek and Sun (2013b)

exceeded that usually achieved in qualitative research. In particular, focus groups conducted throughout the years also established the temporal stability of the related findings. Third, besides conversations, descriptors and metaphors were used to generate richer data. This practice is similar to the keyword analyses approach used previously (Seale and Charteis-Black 2010). Fourth, besides analyzing narratives, we also transformed the narrative data into quantitative data (percentages) to enable quantification. Hence, although only qualitative data were collected, we treated the study as a mixed-methods study. Fifth, we included both participants and implementers in our focus group studies. Sixth, the focus group findings are also used to produce a triangulated and holistic picture on the impact of the Project P.A.T.H.S. on programme participants. Finally, we built in both intra-rater and inter-rater reliability measures which enhance the credibility of qualitative findings (Shek et al. 2005).

The present study highlights several strategies in using focus groups to evaluate programmes for service improvement and policy formulation. First, inclusion of both qualitative and quantitative data can help to generate profiles on programme impact. This approach is important because in addition to unique case illustrations based on thick description, normative picture about the experiences of the informants can be generated. One example is that while we can learn from the descriptors and metaphors content, aggregation of the related responses can give an overall picture about the programme effect. Second, using focus groups in both programme participants and implementers can help to provide a more holistic picture about programme effect. Finally, using focus groups over time can create a more stable picture about the programme effect over time. In short, triangulation of focus group data with reference to data types, informants, time, and other evaluation strategies would enhance credibility of the focus group findings which can help improve service and formulate policies.

Acknowledgement The Project P.A.T.H.S. and preparation for this chapter are financially supported by The Hong Kong Jockey Club Charities Trust.

References

Carlsen, B., & Glenton, C. (2011). What about N? A methodological study of sample-size reporting in focus group studies. *BMC Medical Research Methodology, 11*(1), 26–35.

Catalano, R.F., Fagan, A.A., Gavin, L.E., Greenberg, M.T., Irwin, C.E., Ross, D.A., & Shek, D.T.L. (2012). Worldwide application of prevention science in adolescent health. *The Lancet, 379*(9826), 1653–1664.

Creswell, J.W. (2014). *Research design: Qualitative, quantitative and mixed methods approaches* (4th ed.). Los Angeles, CA: Sage.

Durlak, J.A., Weissberg, R.P., Dymnicki, A.B., Taylor, R.D., & Schellinger, K.B. (2011). The impact of enhancing students' social and emotional learning: A meta-analysis of school-based universal interventions. *Child Development, 82*(1), 405–432.

Greene, J.C., & Caracelli, V.J. (1997). *Advances in mixed-method evaluation: The challenges and benefits of integrating diverse paradigms* (No. 74). Jossey-Bass Publishers.

Greene, J.C., Caracelli, V.J., & Graham, W.F. (1989). Toward a conceptual framework for mixed-method evaluation designs. *Educational Evaluation and Policy Analysis, 11*(3), 255–274.

Leung, J.T.Y., & Shek, D.T.L. (2011). Quantitative and qualitative approaches in the study of poverty and adolescent development: Separation or integration? *International Journal of Adolescent Medicine and Health, 23*(2), 115–121.

MacDougall, C., & Fudge, E. (2001). Planning and recruiting the sample for focus groups and in-depth interviews. *Qualitative Health Research, 11*(1), 117–126.

Miles, M.B., & Huberman, A.M. (1994). *Qualitative data analysis: An expanded sourcebook* (2nd ed.). Thousand Oaks, CA: Sage.

Morgan, D.L. (1997). *Focus groups as qualitative research* (2nd ed.). London: Sage.

Patton, M.Q. (1990). *Qualitative evaluation and research methods.* Newbury Park, CA: Sage.

Sawyer, S.M., Afifi, R.A., Bearinger, L.H., Blakemore, S.J., Dick, B., Ezeh, A.C., & Patton, G.C. (2012). Adolescence: A foundation for future health. *The Lancet, 379*(9826), 1630–1640.

Seale, C., & Charteis-Black, J. (2010). Keyword analysis: A new tool for qualitative research. In I. Bourgeault, R. Dingwall, & R. de Vries (Eds.), *The sage handbook of qualitative methods in health research* (pp. 536–555). London: Sage.

Shek, D.T.L. (2012). Qualitative evaluation of the Project P.A.T.H.S.: An integration of findings based on programme implementers. *The Scientific World Journal, 2012*, Article ID 591816, doi:10.1100/2012/591816.

Shek, D.T.L., & Lee, T.Y. (2008). Qualitative evaluation of the Project P.A.T.H.S.: Findings based on focus groups with student participants. *International Journal of Adolescent Medicine and Health, 20*(4), 449–462.

Shek, D.T.L., & Ma, C.M.S. (2012). Programme implementers' evaluation of the Project P.A.T.H.S.: Findings based on different datasets over time. *The Scientific World Journal, 2012*, Article ID 918437, doi:10.1100/2012/918437.

Shek, D.T.L., & Sun, R.C.F. (2007). Subjective outcome evaluation of the project P.A.T.H.S.: Qualitative findings based on the experiences of programme implementers. *The Scientific World Journal, 7*, 1024–1035.

Shek, D.T.L., & Sun, R.C.F. (2012). Qualitative evaluation of Project P.A.T.H.S.: An integration of findings based on programme participants. *The Scientific World Journal, 2012*, Article ID 528483, doi:10.1100/2012/528483.

Shek, D.T.L., & Sun, R.C.F. (Eds.) (2013a). *Development and evaluation of positive adolescent training through holistic social programmes (P.A.T.H.S.).* Heidelberg: Springer.

Shek, D.T.L., & Sun, R.C.F. (2013b). The Project P.A.T.H.S. in Hong Kong: Development, training, implementation, and evaluation. *Journal of Pediatric and Adolescent Gynecology, 26*(3), S2–S9.

Shek, D.T.L., & Wu, F.K.Y. (2016). The Project P.A.T.H.S. in Hong Kong: Work done and lessons learned in a decade. *Journal of Pediatric and Adolescent Gynecology, 29*(1), S3–S11.

Shek, D.T.L., Ma, H.K., & Sun, R.C.F. (2011). A brief overview of adolescent developmental problems in Hong Kong. *The Scientific World Journal, 11,* 2243–2256.

Shek, D.T.L., Tang, V.M.Y., & Han, X.Y. (2005). Evaluation of evaluation studies using qualitative research methods in the social work literature (1990–2003): Evidence that constitutes a wake-up call. *Research on Social Work Practice, 15*(3), 180–194.

Stufflebeam, D.L. (2012). The CIPP model for evaluation. In T. Kellagham, & D.L. Stufflebeam (Eds.), *International handbook of educational evaluation* (pp. 31–62). New York: Springer.

Teddlie, C., & Tashakkori, A. (2009). *Foundations of mixed methods research: Integrating quantitative and qualitative approaches in the social and behavioral sciences.* Thousand Oaks, CA: Sage.

Daniel T. L. Shek (PhD, FHKPS, BBS, SBS, JP) is Associate Vice President (Undergraduate Programme) and Chair Professor of Applied Social Sciences at The Hong Kong Polytechnic University. He is also Advisory Professor of East China Normal University and Adjunct Professor of University of Kentucky College of Medicine. He is Chief Editor of *Journal of Youth Studies* and *Applied Research in Quality of Life*, Associate Editor of *Frontier in Child Health and Human Development* and past Consulting Editor of *Journal of Clinical Psychology*. He is a Series Editor of *Quality of Life in Asia* published by Springer. He is an Editorial Advisor of *British Journal of Social Work* and an Editorial Board member of eight international journals, including *Social Indicators Research, Journal of Adolescent Health* and *Journal of Child and Family Studies*. Professor Shek has to date published 120 books, 228 book chapters and more than 500 articles in international refereed journals.

8

Focus Groups in Triangulation Contexts

Sabine Caillaud and Uwe Flick

Introduction

There are numerous ways to combine focus groups with other methods in social sciences research. Morgan (1997) proposed that focus groups can be used as a stand-alone method or in combination with other methods: as an exploratory tool or as a follow-up method. In these kinds of combinations, focus groups are conceived of as part of a sequential research design and their role is similar to their original use by Merton. Conducted ahead, focus groups permit the development of hypotheses to be tested in a survey or in an experiment (Merton 2001), or in order to find the relevant dimensions to ask for and the appropriate

---

S. Caillaud (✉)
Université Paris Descartes, Paris, France
e-mail: Sabine.Caillaud@parisdescartes.fr

U. Flick
University of Berlin, Berlin, Germany
e-mail: uwe.flick@fu-Berlin.de

wording for a questionnaire. Conducted afterwards, focus groups can help to further interpret the data as for example, understanding experimental data that do not fit with the hypotheses (Merton 2001) or interpreting survey results (Lucas and Lloyd 1999). In such research designs, focus groups provide a supplement to quantitative methods. During the 80s, focus groups were used also as a stand-alone method in social sciences.

However, 'a stand-alone method' does not mean that focus groups are necessarily used alone. In fact, focus groups as a stand-alone method can be combined with other methods, allowing for the adoption of a strong triangulation approach (Flick et al. 2012). In this chapter, we will develop this point, which, in some aspects, seems to be underdeveloped in the literature. For example, for the period between 1995 and 2015, 18,177 publications containing the word 'focus group' are indexed by the databases *Psycinfo* and *Sociological Abstracts*. But only 1% of them contain at least a reference to triangulation (and 5.74% of them contain the term 'mixed methods'). While focus groups are quite often used in combination with other methods, this is not often conceptualized as part of a triangulation strategy.

The term 'triangulation' refers, in this chapter, to the combination of different methods. The notion was first proposed by Denzin (1970) as a strategy to validate results (with the idea that results which converge across methods are right). However, this perspective was criticized and replaced by the idea that each method constitutes the phenomenon under study in a specific way and that attention should be paid to the theoretical differences between methods (Flick 1992). Thus, triangulation is perceived less as a strategy of validation than as an alternative to validation, allowing systematically for a broad and deep understanding of the phenomenon (see Denzin and Lincoln 2000; Flick 1992, 2014, 2018). In this context, divergent results are not considered as 'wrong', but should be interpreted by reference to the theoretical perspectives underpinning the use of different methods. Methods can be applied either one after the other or in parallel, but all methods should be treated on an equal footing (Flick 2014). For example, using explorative interviews in order to create a survey is not considered as triangulation, because both methods are not treated on an equal footing (Flick 2018).

Thus, in a first part, we will characterize the specific way we consider focus groups – that is, the theoretical background of this method, and consider the main differences between focus groups and individual interviewing. Then, we will provide some examples in order to illustrate how data from focus groups can enrich our understanding of the phenomenon under study, within a triangulation research design.

The aim of this chapter is to present one specific way to combine focus groups with other methods (through triangulation). This does not mean that we consider that other perspectives are not relevant; rather, in some situations, a sequential research design can be the one most appropriate to the objectives of a study.

Focus Groups as a Stand-Alone Method

Using Group Interactions for Analyzing Social Construction of Meaning

Focus groups can be considered as 'a simulation of these routine but relatively inaccessible communicative contexts that can help us discover the processes by which meaning is socially constructed' (Lunt and Livingstone 1996: 85). Defined in such a way, focus groups permit us to study how meanings, interpretations, and narratives are socially constructed during group interactions. Thus, group processes which influence the discourse are not 'biases' which should be controlled in order to capture opinions or attitudes and do not constitute a threat to the validity of data (Markova et al. 2007). In contrast to group interviews, during focus groups group interactions are explicitly viewed as research data (Kitzinger 1994). This makes them particularly relevant when it comes to studying social representations (Lunt and Livingstone 1996; Kalampalikis 2004).

Social representations can be defined both as content (images, metaphors, etc.) and as processes (elaboration, production, diffusion of shared knowledge). Social representation theory considers that groups construct their knowledge about an object during social interactions, amongst others through everyday communications (Markova et al. 2007). Focus groups are a methodological tool which provoke this specific kind of social interaction and, thus, enable the researcher to observe social interactions relating to a specific issue (the focus). Even if focus groups are not 'natural discussion', they allow social representations to be observed *in the making*, as if the researcher reproduces a 'thinking society in miniature' (Farr and Tafoya 1992). Therefore focus groups can significantly contribute to the study of social representations, as the method allows for answers with regard both to questions such as 'what' a group thinks about? And 'how' and 'why' (i.e. the processes involved) a group thinks this way? (Barbour 2007). This makes focus groups a relevant methodological tool not only for studying social representations, but, more generally, for other theoretical approaches which endorse a social constructivist approach. In her work on analyzing focus group data, Barbour (2014) highlights that is important to analyze not just for content but by also paying attention to how the conversation in these groups is organized. She refers to Halkier (2010) who advocates employing some concepts from conversation analysis for understanding what is happening during the interaction.

By considering focus groups in this manner, it becomes evident that the group dynamic is also in itself data and that focus groups can be used as a stand-alone method. For example, they can facilitate the understanding of group norms as in the study by Kitzinger where a group of mothers agreed that they have 'the right to know if another child in the play group had HIV' (1994: 110). Some assertions like 'that's right', or 'of course' underline assumptions about the existence of consent. Other group processes can be observed in focus groups (role of majority/minority, polarization, etc.) and this brings some authors to argue that focus groups can be viewed within the Lewinian tradition of group dynamics (Markova et al. 2007; Kalampalikis 2011). For example, focus groups were used in order to study how groups collectively cope with negative emotions in discussing responsibility for ecological problems (Caillaud et al. 2016). Results highlight how groups change the level of social categorization, refer to stereotypes, and maintain a high consensus in order to feel less responsible for ecological problems and how this was related to a decrease in negative emotions. Considering the group dynamic as a result in itself, rather than a 'bias' which should be controlled for, focus groups, as a stand-alone method, are well-situated to contribute to a more *social* social psychology (Greenwood 2000).

But this also implies that data from focus groups should be explored by taking into account their specificity. In fact, it would be very frustrating for a researcher who attempted to use focus groups in order to capture individual 'attitudes', because, during focus groups, participants may change their minds, transform their opinions more than once, and hold different and often contradictory points of view in the course of the discussion (Barbour 2007). Thus, the use of focus groups as a stand-alone method should be compatible with the epistemological and theoretical frame of the study.

Moreover, data obtained via focus groups are very different in nature to those obtained through individual interviews or surveys, as they are characterized by a particular group dynamic. Comparing results obtained in individual interviews and focus groups will illustrate this point and will allow us to engage in a better understanding of potential triangulation strategies.

A Specific Context of Meaning Production: Comparing Focus Groups and Individual Interviews

Focus groups are sometimes used in research designs which combine different methods (e.g. individual interviews and focus groups) without considering the particular properties of focus groups in comparison to other methods. In some cases, results from individual interviews and from focus groups may not even be differentiated: the main themes evoked by participants in both contexts may be presented together. This may be consistent with the specific aims of certain explorative studies and it may be a workable strategy for presenting results while respecting the permitted word counts of journal or report formats. However, lack of differentiation may be confusing for the reader. This is not to say that during individual interviews answers are less framed by social influence;

rather that the social context in which discourse occurs is different (Lunt and Livingstone 1996). The relationship between the interviewer and the interviewee determines the way the interviewee constructs his/her discourse and both actors contribute (of course, in different ways) to the construction of meaning (Holstein and Gubrium 1995; Haas and Masson 2006; Kvale 2007). Thus, the analysis should consider how the specific context of the interview (place, time, etc.) and the relationship between both actors have contributed to the data obtained. The same is true for focus groups (Green and Harth 1998): the analysis should take into account the context of the discussion and how the group dynamic contributes to the results. Nevertheless, the social context in which discourse is produced during individual interviews and focus groups is qualitatively different: during focus groups participants comment on each others' points of view, they may challenge themselves, manifest disagreement or ambivalence, and they debate (Kidd and Parshall 2000). In contrast, during individual interviews, the interviewee addresses his/her discourse to an interviewer who manifests empathy (Kvale 2007). The role of the moderator and interviewer is very different. In focus groups, the role of the moderator is certainly to maintain the focus of the discussion (Orfali and Markova 2002; Kitzinger et al. 2004) but also to support the exchange amongst participants, to encourage both cohesion and confrontation of opinions within the group (Acocella 2012). Thus, moderator interventions tend to be rare especially at the beginning of the discussion (Kitzinger 1994), in order to facilitate discussion and to avoid the session turning into a group interview (characterized by dialogue between the moderator and the group – Watts 1987; Acocella 2012). While, in both contexts, the meaning is co-constructed during social interaction, this is different for each method and data should not be confounded when presenting the results. Different examples can actually illustrate the ways in which focus groups and individual interviews reveal different kinds of data.

For example, Michell (1999) reported differences in the results obtained during individual interviews and focus groups with regard to young people's experiences of their social world, and – more specifically – concerning the 'pecking order' between girls, enabling the research to observe how this was expressed and maintained in the groups. However in individual interviews, the girls could report their experiences as victims of this hierarchic order and reveal their ideas about factors contributing to the status of victim in peer groups (e.g. lack of money, difficult familial relationships). Thus, the author claims that the sole use of focus groups is not adequate in all circumstances. We are tempted to add that the contrary is true too: individual interviews should not be used alone in all circumstances. During focus groups, the researcher gained insight into the social dynamic of the peer group, which the individual interviews do not permit. The comparison proposed by Michell (1999) is a qualitative one. Systematic and statistical comparisons between interview and focus groups data also support this conclusion (Kaplowitz and Hoehn 2000): data obtained are different and complementary.

Lambert and Loiselle (2008) report on their experience by using focus groups and interviews in a study about information-seeking behavior in cancer. At the beginning of the research, the methods were combined for pragmatic reasons: participants who could not participate in focus groups were invited to take part in an interview, and vice-versa. As the research proceeded, it became apparent that different types of data were generated, depending on the context of interviewing. Thus, participants in individual interviews provided more detail about the decision-making process (narration of antecedents that motivated a behaviour); whereas, during focus groups, participants described the contextual factors that might have been involved (such as the role of the oncologist). In the course of the study, the researchers decided to further exploit these differences.

Also systematic comparisons of data obtained using each method highlight the capacity of focus groups to illuminate the way in which groups, through social interactions, construct meanings. The debate, thus, is not about determining which kind of data is more valid; rather it is to understand which methods to use in which context and for which specific research aim: 'To increase the rigour of method combination, consideration should be given to the correspondence of the study aims with the data collection methods, and the epistemological assumptions of each method and their compatibility' (Lambert and Loiselle 2008: 231).

Planning Focus Groups, Analyzing and Interpreting Focus Groups Data Within Triangulation Designs

In the previously mentioned studies, individual interviews and focus groups are often planned without giving consideration to the specificity of each method. For example, the same interview guide may be used both for focus groups and individual interviews. Results are compared but the researchers do not refer to the theoretical background of each method in order to interpret the different results obtained with each method. The concept of triangulation (Flick 1992; Flick et al. 2012), supporting the reflexive development of the research design, can help in planning studies combining focus groups (as a stand-alone-method) with other methods. In order to fully appreciate the potential of each method and to obtain the full advantages afforded by the combination of methods, the strategy of triangulation offers a thought-provoking framework for planning the research design, adapting tools (e.g. the interview guide) developing analysis strategies and supporting the interpretation of data.

In the next section we will review three separate studies, which each adopted a triangulation approach, combining focus groups with other methods. All adopt the theoretical framework of social representations (Moscovici 1961). For each example, we outline the specific research aims underpinning the use of focus groups, how they were planned and analyzed in order to fulfill their aims, and, finally, how the use of focus groups within a triangulation strategy enables a ripe understanding of the object under study.

Focus Groups for Capturing the Point of View of Specific Actors

The aim of the first study (Pearce and Charman 2011) was to examine how a social psychological approach can promote the understanding of 'moral panic' concerning the issue of asylum seekers in the UK. The authors analyze the social representations of 'asylum seekers' and issues of social identity that are at play in this context in order to understand the widespread invocation of moral panic. Three methods are used in this research: a media analysis (in order to understand how the UK national press covers asylum); individual interviews with people who have sought asylum; and focus groups with members of the 'host community'. In this research, triangulation seeks to understand how the different social actors (media, members of the community, asylum seekers) approach the issue of asylum, and how they create, transform and react to the moral panic. Concerning, more specifically, the focus groups, these were used in order to explore how the community members collectively make sense of the issue of asylum. Eight focus groups were conducted with naturally occurring groups. The interview guide contains questions about participants' understanding of the term 'asylum seekers', public opinion, perceptions of media coverage, and whether asylum seekers can become 'British'. Each dataset was analyzed separately and the authors carried out a thematic analysis, comparing the results arising from the three datasets.

While core elements of social representations appeared in all data sources, some peripheral elements varied. For example, in all datasets the theme of the economic threat was present; however, the idea that asylum seekers can 'take our jobs' was found only in the focus groups. Thus, the representations originated in the media, as participants who had no direct experience with asylum seekers repeatedly call up the same representations in their discourse, but these representations are subject to transformations by the community (e.g. the theme 'economic threat' which is present in media representations is expanded in group discussions to cover the idea that 'they take our jobs'). Moreover, individual interviews furnish evidence that people who have sought asylum are aware of these negative representations and do not identify with the group of 'asylum seekers'. They adopt social mobility strategies (such as successful integration, contesting negative representations, etc.). Thus in this study, each method accesses a specific point of view on the same object (asylum). The results from the focus groups allow the researchers to understand how community members familiarize and transform representations from the media during social interactions.

Focus Groups for Capturing a Specific Dimension of Social Representations

In the first example, each method gives access to the point of view of different social actors. The second example used triangulation in order to capture the different modes in which social representations are embodied. In fact, social representations are created, circulated and transformed in different modes: habitual behaviour, individual cognition, informal and formal communication (Bauer and Gaskell 1999, 2008). Thus, we planned our research design based on triangulation in order to capture some different dimensions of social representations. This forms part of a broader study conducted in France and in Germany about social representations of ecology and ecological practices. Climate change was used as an example, as it is a typical ecological issue. Figure 8.1 illustrates the triangulation strategy developed in this research design.

Most of the time we become aware about ecological issues only indirectly – that is, through the media discourse. Thus, we analyzed how the United Nations climate conference held in Bali was presented in the main daily newspapers in both countries ($N_{articles}$ = 250) and how the media discourse (formal communication) contribute to the construction of social representations of climate change (Caillaud et al. 2012). We used it in order to access the culture-specific core of social representations, the part of 'objective culture' which circulates in each country and which should be complemented by an analysis of the 'subjective culture' (e.g. individual based data) (Sommer 1998).

Thus, episodic interviews (Flick 2014) were conducted with French respondents (N = 18) and German respondents (N = 23) in order to investigate everyday knowledge about climate change (the mode of individual cognitions). Interviewees were asked about the causes and consequences of climate change and they were invited to speculate as to how they think climate change will evolve (imagination about the future). Another part of the interview guide was specifically concerned with everyday practices (e.g. recycling, saving energy, etc.). These interviews were analyzed through a process of thematic encoding inspired by

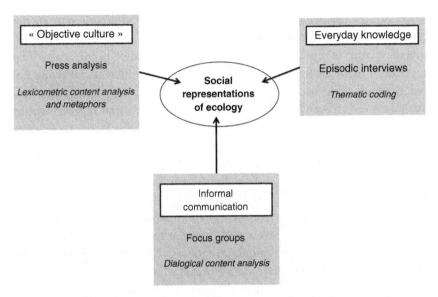

Fig. 8.1 Social representations of ecology

Strauss and Corbin (1990) and further developed by Flick (2014) for the purpose of comparative studies.

Additionally, we conducted ten focus groups (6 in Germany and 4 in France). Some of the participants had previously taken part in interviews. These focus groups were used in order to analyze how social knowledge is constructed and transformed during group interactions and informal communications. They sought to grasp social representations *in the making*. After a short discussion about images representing nature, we asked participants to comment on a world map showing the countries producing the most greenhouse gas and the evolution of this production since 1990. The moderator invited the group to discuss this map by asking *'what do you think about this map?'* Some follow-up questions were integrated into the question guide in order to encourage participants to discuss more specific issues. Thus, we asked them: *what do you feel astonished about? and why? what did you expect? In your opinion what are the reasons for the differences between countries? According to you, what are the causes of climate change?*

What are the consequences? What are the solutions? After this part of the discussion, the moderator asked the group to list their daily ecological practices and to evaluate their efficiency on a four point scale. The moderator made clear that the discussion about the efficiency of ecological practices was what was important, rather than reaching a consensus. The analysis was developed in order to understand how social representations are constructed and transformed during group interactions: thus focus group transcripts were coded using an iterative process, by combining the content of the discussion (themes) and the group dynamic (consensus, debate, laughing, etc.) into a dialogical unit in order to highlight patterns followed by the groups (Caillaud and Kalamplikis 2013).

Two main findings are relevant for the purpose of this chapter. The first one is a difference we observed between the discourse produced in focus groups and in individual interviews. During individual interviews, both French and Germans admitted that they did not know a lot about climate change and that they were not sure how to correctly explain its causes and consequences. In France, this lack of knowledge was admitted during focus group discussions and the theme was even the subject of jokes:

> FGF1 J: *there are other green-house gases but CO_2 is nearly 80%*
> Ch: *Sabine (moderator) what are the other gases?*
> J: *Sabine does not say anything, she does not help us (they are laughing) she leaves us ignorant*
> Ch: *And how, yeah she mocks us*
> S: *I wanted to revise before she arrived but I had no time (she laughs)*

Here the group dynamic underlines that this lack of knowledge recognized during individual interviews is socially accepted and something that it is possible to laugh about. In Germany, while, during individual interviews participants recognized their lack of knowledge, this ignorance was not a theme discussed during focus groups. On the contrary, participants comment on the map in a way that allowed them to claim to be 'experts':

FGG5 F: *And Brasilia should probably appear here. Because their greenhouse gas production is not very far away from France or Great-Britain.*
Ach: *it's possible yes*
F: *I don't know why they are missing right now, in regard to their greenhouse gas production, they are not very lower.*
M: *so also actually there should be an indication for South America and Africa, even if they are not on the top 10, in order to have a reference, such an information would be necessary as it is a global problem.*

This excerpt illustrates how the different participants criticized the map and positioned themselves as individuals who knew how to talk about climate change. This contradicted the findings from individual interviews. From a triangulation perspective (i.e. by referring to the theoretical backgrounds of each method), we interpret this discrepancy as signifying that, in Germany, it is not acceptable to affirm one's ignorance on this theme in front of peers, while, in France, it is acceptable to acknowledge this ignorance. This interpretation is also supported by the result of the press analysis: in Germany, climate change is presented as a moral problem for the whole of humanity (which already has consequences in Germany and, thus, concerns everybody). In France, by contrast, climate change is presented as a political and economic issue that is quite distant (consequences are presented as predominantly concerning poor countries). Also, focus groups allowed us to understand the normative function of knowledge about climate change: in Germany it is a theme you should know how to talk, but this is not the case in France. What if our research design had been based only on one method? Without individual interviews, we would have interpreted the differences between French and German discourse as signaling a better familiarization with climate change in Germany. Without focus groups, we would have simply concluded that participants from both countries acknowledge their ignorance.

The second example from this study concerns the discourse about ecological practices. Both during interviews and focus groups, participants outlined the central paradox of ecological practices: they are efficient only if everybody follows them. During individual interviews, French and German interviewees, appealed to the 'obviousness' of these practices (*'it's like doing the housework'*). When asked to narrate how they began to enact these practices, they explained that they are inherited from their parents or arise from a process of continuous reflection. These habits from the past serve to legitimate of these practices in individual interviews. During focus groups, the same practices are legitimated via a different route: when debating efficiency, participants considered that practices were efficient if the majority of the group followed them, and this became the criterion that legitimated their practices (there was no reference made to scientific arguments). Moreover, participants did not evoke habits from the past as they did during individual interviews. But their discourse constructed ecological practices as a way to act in altruistic mode (i.e. for future generations in Germany) or as a way to express one's own political values (i.e. changing the actual economic system in France). Thus, ecological practices were legitimized through different modes, depending on whether they are presented in individual interviews or in focus groups: in the context of individual interviews, ecological practices were legitimized by reference to past habits and their alleged 'obviousness'. In the context of focus groups, where participants had social support from peers, ecological practices were legitimized by reference to a social project for the future (future generations, a new society). Also, in a triangulation perspective, the different findings outlined the complex function of ecological practices which embodied both past habits and a project for the future. Focus groups, as they favour the making of social comparisons, interactions and a co-construction of meaning, allowed participants to explore a dimension absent from individual interviews, as it requires social support in order to be viewed as relevant.

Focus Groups for Feeding Back Results from Interviews

In both previous examples, focus groups were conducted in parallel with other methods. The following example involves a study of professionals' concepts of health and ageing (Flick et al. 2003). The research questions were: How is an orientation towards health and health promotion taken up in day-to-day practices of general practitioners and home care nurses, or more concretely: Which health concepts do doctors and nurses have? Which dimensions of health concepts are relevant for their professional work in health care? Which relevance do they attribute to their own subjective health concept for their own professional practices?

Here focus groups are used as in a second step, but still within a triangulation perspective. We first conducted episodic interviews with nurses and general practitioners about their experiences and practices. As the second step, we fed back selected results from the one-to-one interviews and discussed them in focus groups, consisting of participants who had already taken part in the interviews. We convened the focus groups in the two German cities where the study took place and held separate groups for physicians and nurses. A main topic was the relevance of the health concepts we found for the participants' professional practices and a discussion of the consequences that should be drawn from them on how to plan these practices. The aim is to advance a transfer of the results into the health system and its practices. For opening the discussion, we chose the barriers against prevention, health promotion and a stronger orientation towards health in the participants' own medical or nursing practice, which had been mentioned in the interviews. These had been located on the side of the patients, of the professionals (see below) and of the health system. We asked the participants to discuss the findings and then to discuss 'Do you have any suggestions for how to overcome the barriers?' At the same time we collected new data in these focus groups. In this study, we applied what Morgan (1997) sees as one central use of focus groups: 'getting participants' interpretations of results from earlier studies'.

In our focus groups, we could not feed back the whole range of our findings from the interviews due to time and capacity reasons. In order to stimulate discussion, we chose to focus on the barriers against prevention, against health promotion and against taking a stronger orientation towards health in what the participants do in their own medical or nursing practice, which had been mentioned in the interviews. In moderating the groups, we followed the following steps:

- *Stimulation.* In the beginning, the research project was briefly presented and the methods were described. Then selected results were presented that referred to the doctors' and nurses' attitudes towards prevention for older people and how to realize this.
- *Presentation of the barriers.* In the next step, we presented the barriers mentioned in the interviews from the viewpoint of patients, of professionals and those that were a product of the health system. Sometimes, for example, relatives ('interfering with care' and 'making professional care impossible') were identified as presenting problems and physical surroundings (not something anticipated) had been perceived as barriers. The following list includes a selection of barriers mentioned by patients and professionals and which were used to stimulate discussion in the focus groups:

Barriers against prevention On the patients' side	On the professionals' side
Passive consumerism	Lower income
No Interest	Lack of time
Suggestions are not followed	Lack of motivation
Resistances against suggestions	Lack of persuasion
Inconsistence in applying suggestions	Lack of qualifications
Not ready to pay for suggested activities	
Old Age and frailty	

The outcomes from these sessions are outlined with reference to the ranking exercise carried out, discussion prompts and overall results.

- *Ranking.* After answering questions for a better understanding, we asked the participants of the focus groups to rank the barriers. By nominating the three barriers they individually felt to be the most important ones using flip charts and cards, we produced a ranking for each group. This result was taken as a starting point for the following discussion of how to solve these problems.
- *Discussion.* As a stimulus for the discussion of the findings, we used the questions 'Do you find your position represented in the result? What is missing for you?' The discussion about solutions to the

problems mentioned here was initiated with the question 'Do you have any suggestions for how to overcome the barriers?'
- *Results.* At the end of the session, the main results of the discussion were noted on cards, then documented as a commonly produced result on a flip chart and finally validated with the group.

In the discussion, the general practitioners located in their client problems with regard to achieving prevention in their work, suggesting that patients come to the surgery for treatment for a disease or symptoms, rather than being open to suggestions as to how to stay healthy. General practitioners acknowledged that, as professionals, they earned their money from treating patients' diseases and not from promoting their health. They, therefore, saw their role as involving healing rather than as preventing.

A nurse mentioned that she saw age as a barrier only in connection with resistance and inconsistency, but that this was something that could be overcome:

Nurse 15: I think of course, everyone has a certain inconsistency, that is simply a human feature, that is part of us ... it is not necessarily a barrier, which can not be overcome in principle, you do two steps forward and one back, in old age, too ...

Focus groups, as an additional methodological step, allowed the participants to evaluate, comment and criticize the results from the interviews. This produced additional results at a different level – revolving around group interaction instead of single interviews. In addition to interviews and focus groups, other materials (curricula and journals) were analyzed in the study.

Conclusion

In this chapter, we have explained how focus groups, as a stand-alone method, can be articulated with other methods as part of a triangulation strategy. Thus, we argue that the theoretical background of each method has to be reflected upon, in order to meaningfully interpret divergent results. In the cited examples, focus groups were used as a methodological tool which enables the researcher to observe and analyze the social construction of meaning, referring to a Lewinian tradition of the group dynamic. In this context, social interactions are not 'biases' for which we should control; rather they are part of the results and should be analyzed too. When used in a triangulation context, focus groups can, thus, help the researcher to access a deeper understanding of the phenomenon, by furnishing results on social interactions and on the way they participate to meaning construction. This goes hand-in-hand with reflective planning and analyzing of focus groups. In fact, using the same interview guide for individual interviews and focus groups fails to recognize and take advantage of the full potential of focus groups. Rather, we have to plan for focus groups by considering their specificities and, thus, structuring the discussion and proposing methods of analysis in order to capitalize on this potential (Markova et al. 2007; Halkier 2010; Caillaud and Kalampalikis 2013; Barbour 2014) and in order to fully engage with the triangulation of methods. The example presented here illustrate how focus groups can successfully be used as part of a triangulation approach, in order to gain insights into different dimensions of the same object (e.g. social representations of ecology), in order to understand the specific role played by social actors in a phenomenon (e.g. the diffusion of moral panic) or in order to elicit participants' interpretations of results from earlier studies (e.g. the relevance of health concepts).

The examples referred to here rely on a triangulation research design using individual interviews and FG. However, it is possible to imagine other combinations. For example, in research conducted in France (in collaboration with Valérie Haas), we examined whether and how the new legal definition of disability re-organized, or impacted on the way professionals conceptualize disability and the role of the psychologist in the evaluation of disabilities. This new definition departed from the old biomedical evaluation of disability to favour a new global evaluation (including the person, the social and material environment, etc.) We conducted focus groups with multidisciplinary teams (psychologists, doctors, social worker, teachers, etc.) whose work is to propose the best care package for a person with disabilities. Participants were invited to debate about a fictitious and dilemmatic case (where medical elements contradicted psychological elements). We also conducted an online survey, which addresses similar questions and the different professionals were asked to answer individually. The interesting thing is that, during focus group discussions, the teams constructed a rather coherent representation on the role of the psychologist, in accordance with the way they represent disabilities. The different results arising from a triangulation exercise, and identified via questionnaire and focus groups are thought-provoking: while team members are able to elaborate a coherent evaluation of a specific case, but when looked at individually, they vacillate between the old and the new definitions of disability.

Finally we wish to suggest that focus groups can also be usefully combined with experimental studies and that this afford a strong triangulation research design. Mostly these methods are used in a sequential research design (e.g. Debucquet et al. 2012). A student from a seminar in Lyon proposed an experiment investigating how children (girls and boys) accept counter-stereotypical behaviours in stories depending on the way the hero is depicted (i.e. whether alone or with peers). She proposed to use focus groups in order to explore how these counter-stereotypical behaviours are accepted when children are with their peers (and not 'alone' with the experimenter). Focus groups could tap into and elucidate collective strategies elaborated by a group in relation to the depicted behaviours, allowing researchers to observe how social norms frame the discourse, how the group interactions maintain (or challenge) the stereotypes, etc. Thus, it is possible to combine qualitative and quantitative methods in a triangulation strategy (Flick et al. 2012) if we recognize that qualitative and quantitative approaches do not necessarily refer to different and incompatible epistemologies or paradigms (Kelle and Erzberger 2004; Kelle 2006; McGrath and Johnson 2003).

References

Acocella, I. (2012) 'The focus groups in social research: Advantages and disadvantages'. *Qualitative and Quantitativ*, 46: 1125–1136. doi: 10.1007/s11135-011-9600-4.

Barbour, R. (2007) *Doing focus groups*. London: Sage Publications.

Barbour, R. (2014) 'Analyzing Focus Groups', in U. Flick (ed.), *The SAGE Handbook of Qualitative Data Analysis*. London: Sage. pp. 313–327.

Bauer, M., & Gaskell, G. (1999) 'Towards a paradigm for research on social representations'. *Journal for the Theory of Social Behaviour*, 29(2): 163–186.

Bauer, M., & Gaskell, G. (2008) 'Social representations theory: A progressive research programme for social psychology'. *Journal for the Theory of Social Behaviour*, 38(4): 335–353. doi: 10.1111/j.1468-5914.2008.00374.x.

Caillaud, S., Bonnot, V., Ratiu, E., & Krauth-Gruber, S. (2016) 'How groups cope with collective responsibility for ecological problems: Symbolic coping and collective emotions'. *British Journal of Social Psychology*, 55(2): 297–317.

Caillaud, S., & Kalampalikis, N. (2013) 'Focus groups and ecological practices: A psychosocial approach'. *Qualitative Research in Psychology*, 10(4): 382–401. doi: 10.1080/14780887.2012.674176.

Caillaud, S., Kalampalikis, N., & Flick, U. (2012) 'Penser la crise écologique: Représentations et pratiques franco-allemandes'. *Cahiers Internationaux de Psychologie Sociale*, 87(3): 621–644.

Debucquet, G., Cornet, J., Adam, I., & Cardinal, M. (2012) 'Perception of oyster-based products by french consumers. The effect of processing and role of social representations'. *Appetite*, 59: 844–852. doi: 10.1016/j.appet.2012.08.020.

Denzin, N. (1970) *The research act*. Chicago: Aldine.

Denzin, N., & Lincoln, Y. (2000) 'Introduction. The discipline and practice of qualitative research', In N. Denzin & Y. Lincoln (eds.), *Handbook of Qualitative Research*. 2nd edition (8). Thousands Oaks, CA: Sage Publications, pp. 1–28.

Farr, R., & Tafoya, E. (1992) *Western and Hungarian Representations of Individualism: A Comparative Study Based on Group Discussions and Social Dilemmas* (unpublished manuscript).

Flick, U. (1992) 'Triangulation revisited: Strategy of validation or alternative?' *Journal for the Theory of Social Behaviour*, 22(2): 175–197. doi: 10.1111/j.1468-5914.1992.tb00215.x

Flick, U. (2014) *An Introduction to Qualitative Research*. 5th edition. London: Sage. (1st edn, 1998.)

Flick, U. (2018) Triangulation. In N. Denzin, & Y. Lincoln (Eds), *Handbook of Qualitative Research*. Fifth Edition. Thousands Oaks, California: Sage Publication, pp. 444–461.

Flick, U., Fischer, C., Neuber, A., Walter, U., & Schwartz F.W. (2003) 'Health in the context of being old - representations held by health professionals'. *Journal of Health Psychology*, 8(5): 539–56.

Flick, U., Garms-Homolova, V., Herrmann, W., Kuck, J., & Röhnsch, G. (2012) '"I can't prescribe something just because someone asks for it..." using mixed methods in the framework of triangulation'. *Journal of Mixed Methods Research*, 6(2): 97–110. doi: 10.1177/ 1558689812437183.

Green, J., & Hart, L. (1998) 'The impact of context on data', In R. Barbour & J. Kitzinger (eds.), *Developing Focus Groups Research. Politics, Theory and Practice*. London: Sage, pp. 21–35.

Greenwood, J. (2000) 'Individualism and the social in early american social psychology'. *Journal of the History of the Behavioral Sciences*, 36 (4): 443–455.

Haas, V., & Masson, E. (2006) 'La relation à l'autre comme condition à l'entretien'. *Les Cahiers Internationaux de Psychologie Sociale*, 71: 77–88.

Halkier, B. (2010) 'Focus groups as social enactments: integrating interaction and content in the analysis of focus group data'. *Qualitative Research*, 10(1): 71–89.

Holstein, J., & Gubrium, J. (1995) *The Active Interview*. Beverly Hills CA: Sage Publications.

Kalampalikis, N. (2004) 'Les focus groups, lieux d'ancrages'. *Bulletin de Psychologie*, 57(3): 281–289.

Kalampalikis, N. (2011) 'Um instrumento de diagnóstico das representações sociais: O grupo focal'. *Revista Diálogo Educacional*, 11 (33): 435–467.

Kaplowitz, M., & Hoehn, J. (2000) 'Do focus groups and individual interviews reveal the same information for natural resource valuation?' *Ecological Economics*, 36(2): 237–247.

Kelle, U. (2006) 'Combining qualitative and quantitative methods in research practice: purposes and advantages'. *Qualitative Research in Psychology*, 3(4): 293–311.

Kelle, U., & Erzberger, C. (2004) 'Qualitative and quantitative methods: not in opposition', In U. Flick, E Von Kardorff & I. Steinke (eds.), *A companion to qualitative research*. London: Sage Publications. pp. 172–177.

Kidd, P., & Parshall, M. (2000) 'Getting the focus and the group: Enhancing analytical rigor in focus groups research'. *Qualitative Health Research*, 10(3): 293–308.

Kitzinger, J. (1994) 'The methodology of focus groups: The importance of interaction between research participants'. *Sociology of Health and Illness*, 16(1): 103–121.

Kitzinger, J., Markova, I., & Kalampalikis, N. (2004) 'Qu'est-ce que les focus groups?' *Bulletin de Psychologie*, 57(3): 237–243.
Kvale, S. (2007) *Doing Interviews*. London: Sage Publications.
Lambert, S., & Loiselle, C. (2008) Combining individual interviews and focus groups to enhance data richness. *Journal of Advanced Nursing*, 62(2): 228–237.
Lucas, K., & Lloyd, B. (1999) 'Starting smoking: Girls' explanations of the influence of peers'. *Journal of Adolescence*, 22: 647–655.
Lunt, P., & Livingstone, S. (1996). Rethinking the focus groups in media and communications research'. *Journal of Communication*, 46(2): 79–93. doi: 10.1111/j.1460-2466.1996.tb01475.x.
Markova, I., Linell, P., Grossen, M., & Salazar Orvig, A. (2007) *Dialogue in Focus Groups: Exploring Socially Shared Knowledge*. London: Equinox Publishing.
McGrath, J. & Johnson, B. (2003) 'Methodology makes meaning: how both qualitative and quantitative paradigms shape evidence and its interpretation', In P. Camic, J. Rhodes & L. Yardleay (Eds), *Qualitative research in Psychology: Expanding perspectives in methodology and design*. Washington: American Psychological Association. pp. 31–48.
Merton, R. (2001) 'The focussed interview and focus groups. Continuities and discontinuities'. *Public Opinion Quarterly*, 51: 550–566.
Michell, L. (1999) Combining Focus Groups and interviews: telling how it is; telling how it feels. In R. Barbour & J. Kitzinger (Eds), *Developing focus groups research: Politics, theory and practice*. Sage: London. pp. 36–45.
Morgan, D. (1997) *Focus Groups as Qualitative Research*. London: Sage Publications.
Moscovici, S. (1961) *La Psychanalyse, Son Image et Son Public*. Paris: Presses Universitaires de France.
Orfali, B., & Markova, I. (2002) 'Analogies in focus groups: From the victim to the murderer and from the murderer to the victim'. *European Review of Applied Psychology*, 52(3–4): 263–271.
Pearce, J., & Charman, E. (2011) 'A social psychological approach to understanding moral panic'. *Crime, Media, Culture*, 7(3): 293–311. doi: 10.1177/1741659011417607.
Sommer, C. M. (1998). 'Social representations and media communications', In U. F. (ed.), *Psychology of the Social*. Cambridge: Cambridge University Press, pp. 186–195.

Strauss, A. L. and Corbin, J. (1990) *Basics of Qualitative Research.* London: Sage.

Watts, M. (1987) 'More than the sum of the parts: Research methods in group interviewing'. *British Educational Research Journal,* 13, 25–34.

Sabine Caillaude has a doctorate in social psychology and works at th Institute of Psychology at Université Paris Descartes. Her interests centred around collective emotions and responses to ecology, including research into representations of climate change in France and Germany. She has a commitment to qualitative methods in general, with a focus on triangulation, in particular. Her publications span social psychology and methodological journals.

Uwe Flick has degrees in psychology and in sociology and a PhD in psychology and is employed as a Professor of Qualitative Research in Social Science and Education at the Free University of Berlin, Germany. He has also been Professor of Qualitative Research at the Alice Salomon University of Applied Sciences in Berlin, Germany and the University of Vienna, in Austria. Previous appointments also include the Technical University of Berlin and the Hanover Medical School, with numerous visiting appointments. His research interests focus on everyday knowledge (subjective theories or social representations) with regard to topics such as health and illness, technological change in everyday life, and trust in helping relationships. He has published widely with regard to qualitative research methods, most recently acting as editor for the *Sage Qualitative Research Kit* of 8 volumes (with a second edition in press); *The SAGE Handbook of Qualitative Data Analysis* (2014) and *The SAGE Handbook of Qualitative Data Collection* (in press). Single authored books include *Designing Qualitative Research* (2007); *Managing Quality in Qualitative Research* (2007); *An Introduction to Qualitative Research* (5th edition 2014); and *Introducing Research Methodology – A Beginner's Guide to Doing a Research Project* (2015).

9

Hybrid Focus Groups as a Means to Investigate Practical Reasoning, Learning Processes and Indigenous Activities

Ana Prades, Josep Espluga
and Tom Horlick-Jones

Introduction

Focus groups have the potential to generate particular sorts of conversation that can reveal socially shared ways of reasoning and acting amongst groups of people with shared experiences and ways of life. This property provides a means to gain access to features of social life for which research in naturally occurring settings is difficult or unworkably expensive. In this chapter, we

---

Tom Horlick-Jones sadly died before the publication of this work was completed.

A. Prades (✉)
CISOT-CIEMAT, Barcelona, Spain
e-mail: ana.prades@ciemat.es

J. Espluga
Universitat Autònoma de Barcelona, Bellaterra (Barcelona), Spain
e-mail: joseplluis.espluga@uab.cat

T. Horlick-Jones
Cardiff University, Cardiff, UK

© The Author(s) 2017
R.S. Barbour, D.L. Morgan (eds.), *A New Era in Focus Group Research*, DOI 10.1057/978-1-137-58614-8_9

draw on almost two decades of collaborative work using focus groups. The chapter describes our itinerary in developing and experimenting with focus groups, by hybridizing the standard methodology with elements and insights coming from other techniques and research paradigms. As the chapter follows the chronological sequence of our collaborations, the detailed explanation of the methods and procedures comes at the end (before the conclusions). If the reader wants to have an overview of such methodological details in advance, he/she will find it in the section: 'The final version of our hybrid method: Details about the STAVE tool'.

Background and Rationale

In developing our research design, we were influenced by methodological developments that have begun to generate a hybridization between the use of focus groups as research methods to investigate social group norms (Barbour and Kitzinger 1999; Bloor et al. 2001), and the use of group-based techniques as part of attempts to implement processes of citizen and stakeholder engagement in policymaking and decision-making (Renn et al. 1995; Myers 2007). Such methodological hybridization reflects a well-established recent trend within social research towards the adoption of recursive instruments that provide opportunities for respondents to be more involved in the research process itself.

Amongst such recursive instruments we adopted a range of variations of the so-called reconvened focus groups (RFG). The RFG design is equivalent to a series of repeated groups (Morgan et al. 2008) where participants can bring in not only their own thinking but also the deliberations from previous group meetings, thus enriching the participants' dialogue and providing them with more control. The reflective interval periods between group meetings also allow for the creation and introduction of stimulus materials to further inspire and encourage group deliberations (Nind and Vinha 2014). The approach aims to facilitate 'deliberative, inclusive and democratic practice' (Kamberelis and Dimitriadis 2005). Thus, we tried to hybridize the RFG approach with the problem structuring methods (PSMs) approach, a class of 'low-tech' decision support methods designed to assist groups to agree the nature and boundaries of the problems they must tackle, and to secure shared commitments to action. PSMs emerged in response to a recognition of the 'wicked' nature of certain classes of management problems (e.g. Conklin 2005; Weber and Khademian 2008; Richard 2006), characterized by being ill-defined, having many stakeholders with distinctive perspectives or conflicting interests, and including intangibles and uncertainties. PSMs operate in group settings, using a participative and iterative mode of operation. It has also been argued that through their transparent tools and participative process, PSMs have the capacity to build trust and understanding between culturally diverse parties (Rosenhead and Mingers 2001). Methodologically, this approach appears to offer a powerful means to investigate the nature and variety of lay reasoning about a broad range of social issues.

Our approach is essentially concerned with understanding patterns of practical reasoning deployed by lay people to make sense of their everyday relation with these issues. Methodologically, it draws on what has been termed 'interpretative' studies of risk perception; a body of work that emerged in the mid-1990s, which has recognized the central roles of meaning and social interaction in structuring understandings of technological hazards (e.g. Zonabend 1993; Walker et al. 1998; Irwin et al. 1999; Marris et al. 2001; Timotijevic and Barnett 2006: Horlick-Jones and Prades 2009).

We have carried out collaborative work using focus groups, over almost two decades, looking for hybrid designs, and expanding its possibilities in promoting innovative forms of engagement that allow for an enhanced understanding of reasoning practices and daily behaviours. We did it mainly with the aim of supporting more efficient and meaningful communication strategies and environmental policies.

First Experiences with Reconvened Focus Groups: From the GM Debate to the Railway Safety Case Study

The public debate about genetically modified (GM) crops in the UK in 2002–2003 was the first experience (of the main author of our hybridization experiences) with reconvened discussion groups to promote familiarization with, and quasi-naturalistic deliberation about, a complex/technical issue (Horlick-Jones et al. 2007a, 2007b, Rowe et al. 2005).

A more elaborated version of the GM hybrid approach was also designed by Horlick-Jones to conduct a pilot study (Horlick-Jones 2008), in the framework of a broader stakeholder consultation programme on safety decision-making for the UK rail industry. Besides developing tools to support engagement initiatives, the study investigated everyday lay notions of what can be a 'reasonable' basis for establishing safety. The research questions dealt with the acceptability of a value for preventing a fatality (VPF); the acceptability of investing more money to reduce the risk of injury for certain types of people; and the acceptability of investing more money to reduce the risk of injury depending on the circumstances in which an accident occurs. Considering the technical complexity of the issue, the exercise presented an important methodological challenge: how to 'translate' specialized and complex economic and legal issues in a way that citizens can understand, and reason about, in an informed and considered way. Figure 9.1 shows the details of the research design.

To promote meaningful and valuable dialogues, including relevant perspectives for the discussion, two reconvened discussion groups were

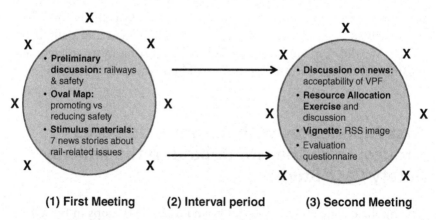

Fig. 9.1 Research design in the 'railway safety' case study

Source: Horlick-Jones 2008

run (i.e. four meetings in all) – with two 'publics': (a) frequent rail travellers (commuters and those travelling at least every week); and (b): those living close to rail lines with young families living at home. The groups were also segmented according to geographical, age and socio-economic terms. Each group included eight participants. The engagement process allowed groups of lay citizens to discuss complex issues about safety management in a considered manner—despite the inherent technical difficulty of the topic.

From a methodological point of view, the research design, although quite simple, required a well-informed approach to produce a suitable hybrid methodology, and also required skilled facilitation (social research skills in qualitative methods). This research was a first step regarding methodological challenges for focus group techniques, but it was clear that the pilot study indicated the need for further research.

Further Developments: Lay Reasoning About Fusion Energy and Communication Strategies

A comparative cross-cultural study on learning and reasoning processes concerned with fusion energy gave us an opportunity to further develop research on this methodology. In common with other new technologies, fusion is not well understood amongst the lay public and, consequently, historical associations with the fission programme have played a dominant role in shaping views towards fusion, where these exist (Prades et al. 2008). A key challenge here – and, indeed, a research problem in itself – is how to provide information in a suitably balanced way, and to promote engagement with such knowledge. This problem is not trivial at all.

Our key research questions were the following ones:

- Whether, and if so how, modes of reasoning about fusion change with increasing levels of knowledge about the technology
- The effectiveness of different informative materials in promoting understanding and engagement amongst lay public

- The role of various interpretative resources in the processes of practical reasoning: lay logical devices; pre-existing knowledge; media narratives and fantasies, etc.
- The relationship between increasing knowledge about fusion and its acceptability
- The suitability of the group-based method for generating an appropriate learning and discussion process

A research design similar to the former case (railway safety) was developed (Fig. 9.2), with some innovations.

Eight discussion groups were convened in both Spain and the UK. Each group, comprising 8–9 individuals, met for one and a half or two hours on two occasions. Participants were also invited to examine stimulus materials and to engage in information searches during the 7–10 days in between group meetings, and to keep a diary to record their findings during this period. The method used components of PSMs as facilitation devices to promote effective 'brainstorming' and to support appreciation of the relevance of everyday notions of resource allocation. We also used a vignette script (Hughes 1998), and a pack of

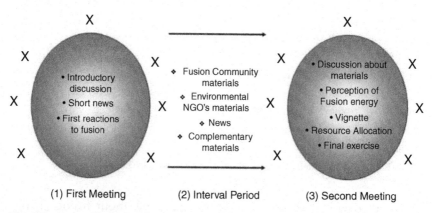

Fig. 9.2 Research design for the 'social perception on fusion energy' case study

Source: Prades et al. 2009

9 Hybrid Focus Groups as a Means to Investigate ...

written stimulus materials drawn from a range of sources: the nuclear industry, the environmentalists, and the media.

In terms of segmentation, six groups were segmented along age and socio-economic lines, with a gender balance. The views of potentially 'excluded' people (members of environmental groups and people working in the energy industry) were addressed in two subsequent groups 7 and 8. When recruited, participants were told that they were being invited to take part in discussions about 'energy issues.'

The key findings can be summarized as follows:

- **Changes in the modes of reasoning** took place as the discussion and learning process evolved and more knowledge about the technology, either technical or contextual, was acquired.
- The **effectiveness of different informative materials** in promoting understanding and engagement amongst lay publics was fully comprised
- The role of **interpretative resources** in the processes of practical reasoning was suitably acknowledged.
- **Pre-existing knowledge** and experiences were also key elements in group discussions. The main function of this knowledge is to make complex and distant issues—such as fusion energy—more familiar, or closer to daily life.
- **Narratives from the media**, such as news on technological developments or images from films (i.e. *Erin Brockovich*, *An Inconvenient Truth*, *Titanic* or *The Simpsons*) were also used by participants to make sense of fusion.
- One interesting characteristic of **reconvened focus groups** (also known as 'repeated groups') that affects the dynamics of talk is the interaction between technical knowledge provided by the researchers, background experiences, knowledge brought in by participants, and prior attitudes towards technological and environmental issues. Although participants had problems in understanding technical specifications provided by informative materials, the technical and contextual details that our participants 'learnt' form the stimulus materials played a significant role in allowing for more evidence-based discussion in the group.

Further implications of the results were that in these cases there is a need to engage with multiple sources of knowledge and uncertainty (*just good news is not good*). The key role of 'low information rationality' is also a crucial finding of relevance for future attempts at establishing a constructive dialogue with citizens. In any case, the need for engagement with lay publics and promoting two-way communication was clear, and it seemed that the methodology based on hybrid focus groups could be of interest to achieve it.

Developing a Research Tool (STAVE) for Engaging Sustainable Consumption and Environmental Policy (PACHELBEL Project)

This next step in developing the hybrid focus group methodology was a European project (Policy Addressing Climate Change and Learning about Consumer Behaviour and Everyday Life) (PACHELBEL, FP7, 2010–2012) promoted by a research consortium formed by ten institutions of six European countries. The main objective of the project was to design and change a research methodology aimed at better understanding how policymakers draw upon different sources of knowledge about human behaviour when developing policy initiatives to promote sustainable consumption. In our research, the linking process between the worlds of policymaking and everyday life was addressed through the development of a tool which we called STAVE (Systematic Tool for Behavioural Assumption Validation and Exploration), designed to support the work of policymaking for sustainability in real-world settings. With STAVE, we have attempted to provide useful knowledge about citizens' real-world sustainability-related practices. We have also attempted to reconcile the gap between citizens' actual practices (what they do) and citizens' accounts of such behaviours, as captured by conventional social research (what they say they do). All these were the research questions addressed by the project.

The STAVE tool was designed and trialled in the context of diverse live policy issues (including domestic energy use, mobility, 'smart metres', insulation of flats, and the market in new and second-hand 'white goods') across six European Union countries (France, Germany, Romania, Spain, Sweden, and the United Kingdom). Our initial motivation to address sustainable consumption and related environmental policies came with the observation from policymakers with whom we were working that it would be helpful for them, and other policymakers, to grasp something of the informal, real-world, significance of sustainability-related policy issues for target groups of consumers in specific settings. In this way, existing assumptions about likely citizen behaviours could be validated, and the prospects for new policy initiatives explored. Ideally this exploratory work would be done in a reasonably speedy and cost-effective way.

In our view this is a question of linking, and translating, research findings between the worlds of policymaking and everyday decision-making by lay citizens. Based on our recent experiments in methodological hybridization, we chose to base STAVE on the use of small groups, integrating RFGs, participant 'homework' during the periods between group meetings, and group conversations shaped by problem structuring techniques (Horlick-Jones 2008; Horlick-Jones et al. 2012).

A series of group meetings (3 in each country) (see Fig. 9.3) was designed in order to generate discussions that made visible, through a set of procedures, understandings and practices socially shared by participant citizens, the grounded and authentic accounts of citizens' actual behaviours. Group discussions and everyday life were linked by means of diaries relating to the policy issues in question (citizen engagement process). A process based on three sequential group meetings (for each group) was designed, and various stimulus materials and tasks were developed for the citizen groups that lent themselves to stimulating group discussion (i.e. cartoons, website descriptions, diary excerpts, and simulated newspaper or magazine articles). Component parts of PSM, such as oval maps and resource allocation exercises, were also used to elicit and access the shared (rather than individual and possibly idiosyncratic) reasoning of group participants. Short sustainability-related questionnaires were also used to elicit 'in principle' accounts of behaviours, which sometimes contrasted in insightful ways with the more grounded patterns of shared practical reasoning evident in the

Country	STAVE policy issue	STAVE implementations
France	Smart meters and electricity savings	STAVE 1: Nov–Dec 2011 STAVE 2–3: Jan–Feb 2012
Germany	Climate Protection Concept 2020+ (domestic energy use)	STAVE 1–2–3: July 2011
Romania	National Thermal Rehabilitation Programme	STAVE 1–2–3: June–July 2011
Spain	- Agenda 21 for Barcelona: Energy saving, waste, mobility - Participatory energy plan: Domestic energy savings with/without smart meters)	STAVE 1: June–July 2011 STAVE 2–3: Nov–Dec 2011
Sweden	Policy for climate-neutral Värmland by 2030 (mobility, consumption, electricity consumption)	STAVE 1: May–June 2011 STAVE 2: Aug–Sep 2011 STAVE 3: Sep–Oct 2011
UK	White goods, lifetime and shopping	STAVE 1: July–August 2011 STAVE 2-3: Nov–Dec 2011

Fig. 9.3 Policy issues and meetings of the whole PACHELBEL project

Source: Prades et al. 2012

group discussions and in the diaries of daily activities. A detailed description of the components of STAVE (i.e. oval maps, resource allocation exercise, short questionnaires, etc.) is provided in the last section of this chapter where we describe the final version of our hybrid method

Amongst the key findings of the project we want to highlight here the need to make everyday behaviours visible to policymakers and, in turn, make policy assumptions and needs visible to citizens.

During the group deliberations of the STAVE interventions, a large amount of qualitative data was gathered in relation to participants' reasoning about environmental issues and their everyday behaviour. Based on verbatim transcripts of the group discussions and diary data, each national team carried out a content and thematic analysis.

The project team was able to implement STAVE trials across six different European countries, at different levels in public administration, ranging from strategic to local, with a high degree of synchronization, effectiveness, and compatibility.

Studying Metaphors on Conflictive Issues (METAFPERCOM)

In illustrating our development of hybrid focus groups (by mixing them with other techniques and theoretical paradigms) the last case study we want to take into account is an on-going project related to the use of metaphors when dealing with and communicating about socially controversial issues. The project is titled 'The role of metaphor in the social definition and perception of controversial issues: Institutions, mass media and citizens' (METAFPERCOM) (funded by the Spanish Government).

The starting point relies on the fact that in every controversial social process there are different actors that compete to position their viewpoints in the public arena. Within this social dynamic, the media play an important role, since they direct political actors' views of a specific issue, which can be conflicting. Therefore, both political actors and the media struggle in order to define social issues and to influence public opinion on these topics. Discourse becomes a key element for shaping citizens' views on contested issues and metaphor reveals itself a linguistic strategy suitable for doing so. Metaphors can simplify and make political events understandable, and effective exercise of this ability can confer persuasive power on them (Mio 1997; Musolff 2004).

In this context, the METAFPERCOM project proposes a double objective:

– To analyze the discursive use of metaphors by public institutions, political organizations and the media—when they try to configure public perception of certain controversial social issues
– To capture the ways in which metaphors are understood, shared and used by lay citizens—when they make sense of such controversial questions.

To deal appropriately with this double objective, a number of topics in the public debate—covered by the media during the project's life—were analyzed in order to identify the use of metaphors by different actors. To compare contexts, a range of themes was identified and four topics were finally selected for the analysis:

- Topic 1 (Ideological- local axis): The Catalan elections and the independence process.
- Topic 2 (Ideological- global axis): The Syrian refugee crisis and the EU reaction.
- Topic 3 (Scientific- local axis): Air pollution episodes in Barcelona and Madrid.
- Topic 4 (Scientific- global axis): The Paris Climate Change 21st session of the United Nations Conference of the Parties (COP21).

For each topic, the research team analyzed the use of metaphors by the media (3 national newspapers) and by the claim makers (through their Web pages, and Twitter), and the lay discourses and reasoning practices expressed by a citizen's sample on the very same topics—both before and after receiving information from the media and the claim makers.

According to the STAVE standard protocol (as designed in the PACHELBEL project), each of the four citizen groups met on three occasions with an interval of 9–12 days between group meetings. Phone diaries and homework took place during the corresponding interval periods (Espluga et al. 2016). The implementation of the STAVE tool allowed us to address two challenges regarding citizens' perceptions: on the one hand, it sought to make visible, in an exhaustive way, the metaphors used by citizens in their everyday life when making sense of the specific topics under study. On the other, it aimed at analyzing lay understanding, interpretation and integration (or otherwise) of the metaphors used by news media and claim makers in their discourses about the selected topics. The STAVE tool has allowed us to link the media sphere (newspapers and claim makers) with the media reception sphere (citizens).

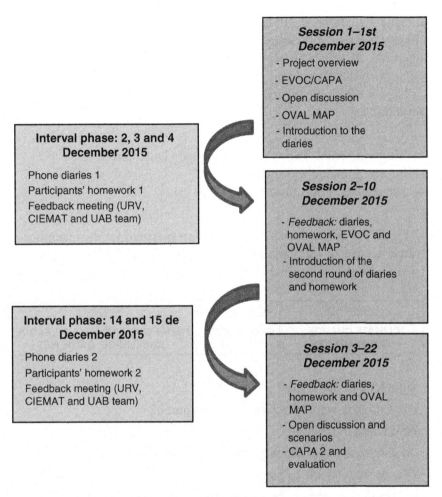

Fig. 9.4 STAVE process in Metafpercom project

Source: Authors

Figure 9.4 briefly illustrates the use of the diverse STAVE components in the METAFPERCOM project

One of the main innovations in this case is the introduction of rhetoric and narrative exercises. As mentioned earlier, the development of narratives on the metaphor was crucial to understanding the reasoning of citizens' discourses. For this reason, we developed an exercise directly focused on the interpretation of specific target domains and the development of its scenarios. We also provided a schema with some questions to help construct, in the most detailed way, the story-lines along with the central mappings.

Next we include an example used to construct the narrative corresponding to:

- Target domain: 'Paris Climate Change Conference'
- Source domain: 'sport/game'
- Metaphors: 'finish line, World Cup, game, bet...'

Figure 9.5 shows the narrative questions prepared for the metaphor of 'game' related to the Paris climate change conference that participants tried to answer collectively.

Target domain:	Source domain	Metaphors
CLIMATE CHANGE CONFERENCE	GAME/SPORT	FINISH LINE, WORLD CUP, LEAGUE, CHALLENGE, GAME, BET

What kind of game is it?
What do they want to achieve with the game?
Who starts the game?
Do someone or something provoke the situation?
Why do they decide to play?
Is someone or something helping to make the decision/s?
Who is the opponent? Why?
Who helps the opponent?
Is someone or something taking profit of the situation?
Is the action rewarded or sanctioned? By who? Why? How?

Fig. 9.5 Example of questions used to develop a 'narrative' about a socially controversial issue based on metaphors

Source: Authors

The Final Version of Our Hybrid Method: Details About the STAVE Tool

Developed in the context of the EU-funded PACHELBEL project, the STAVE tool aims to help in gaining an understanding of and providing a means of addressing citizen's daily behaviours in a range of policy contexts. The main assumption underlying the STAVE tool is that policy which seeks to address citizen behaviours will be more effective in both design and implementation if based on supportable assumptions about lay behaviour. To make this possible a knowledge brokerage system is needed to link and facilitate dialogue between two spheres that often have quite different rationalities: that of policymaking, and that of everyday lay discourses and behaviours. The hybrid focus group methodology proposed follows this direction, and its iterative nature entails using a set of procedures/methods to identify policymakers' concerns, engage citizens in reflecting about the policy area, capture the related everyday behaviours and discourses, and feed this back to the policymakers (Horlick-Jones and Prades, 2015).

A unique feature of STAVE is its reconvened and reflective character. At the citizen level, this approach entails RFGs (the very same group of citizens meeting on more than one occasion); while diary-keeping during the interval between groups session promotes reflection.

The STAVE standard protocol was based on a structured sample of citizen groups, with each group meeting on three occasions. This number seemed to offer an optimum arrangement in terms of minimizing organizational and resource demands, while offering rich insights, and also affording a degree of comparability. All citizen groups can be run in parallel or sequentially. The STAVE sequence trialled in the PACHELBEL project involved three meetings of each group of citizens, with intervening periods of 7–10 days in between, and in each of them a diary was completed by the participants.

The elements that comprise the STAVE method and its temporal sequence are shown in Fig. 9.6.

The various materials, exercises, and approaches composing STAVE are described in Konrad (2015), and Prades et al. (2016), as follows:

- **EVOC-CAPA** is a set of two short questionnaires. EVOC is a free-association exercise that asks in sum 'what does a given concept evoke for you?' This technique provides a simple way to identify the notions a given community shares (or does not share) about social issues. The CAPA instrument is designed to address the participant's personal identification with the issue (as e.g. in our case, 'sustainable consumption') including perceived capacity to act.
- **Simulated newspaper article:** Information and context were introduced in an attractive form easy to grasp by group of participants. The key issue here was to produce a narrative that a) is readily understandable for the citizens, b) links easily to everyday citizen practices in meaningful ways, c) is 'alive' in the sense that it is clearly about issues to which the citizens can relate, rather than being strictly technical, academic or abstract in nature, d) has the potential to be read in several ways through different framings.
- **Oval mapping** is a method of surfacing participants' perceptions, understandings, and ideas regarding a specific issue or question. It was developed in the context of organizational planning as a PSM

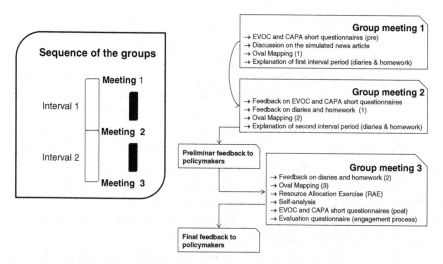

Fig. 9.6 The structure of the STAVE citizen process

(Rosenhead and Mingers 2001) (the term 'oval mapping' refers to the large oval Post-its filled up and organized by participants). Shared understandings are elicited across a continuous process of adding new and removing existing ovals which contain recorded observations, representations, and concepts. The ability to reprise or change the maps is especially convenient in the context of reconvened groups aiming to spread discussions of an issue over various sessions.

- **Diaries:** In between group sessions, participants in the STAVE process keep structured diaries for a few days on their everyday behaviour and reasoning in the research domain addressed ('consumption' in our case). These diaries are not to be confused with a personal journal people keep for recording private occurrences only for themselves. Rather, STAVE participants take notes on their everyday lives according to specifications designed by researchers, in the perspective of sharing and analyzing the collected notes in the next group discussion. Different formats can be used, including paper-based diaries, oral diaries, and electronic diaries. The diary instrument provides a means to reflexively link the group discussions with participants' everyday lives and to trigger a process of review and change of everyday practices.
- **Self-analysis exercises:** For gathering the group's autonomous feedback and shaping it in a way useable for policy feedback, a self-analysis template was created encompassing five sections: policy questions (raised by policy officials), possible answers, queries, new questions, and issues/connections.
- **Resource allocation exercise:** Group preferences are summarized and ranked on a quantitative basis. Discussion issues previously addressed (e.g. policy measures) are listed and participants evaluate and prioritize the options by distributing a fictitious amount of money (e.g. 100 M €).
- **Evaluation questionnaire:** The complete STAVE process (3 group meetings, activities, tools and exercises, diaries) was evaluated by participants from their own perspective.
- **Other stimulus material:** Cartoons, information from policy partners' Web page, real magazine articles, and descriptions of products

and policy measures were amongst other content employed to stimulate group learning and discussion (see Poumadere et al. 2015).

Information from one group session was fed back during the next session, in order to allow the participants to reflexively assess their own expressions and opinions.

Although a structured suite of methods was developed in the STAVE trials, it is not compulsory to proceed according to a fixed recipe. Rather, the idea is that the various options constitute a toolkit, from which methods can be selected for specific situations. This creates an opportunity to omit some suggested methods and to draw on others as seems appropriate. A flexible approach to the STAVE toolkit provides an opportunity to use component parts of STAVE, on their own or in combination, to generate a range of different sorts of group conversation, each with its own properties.

The STAVE tool takes into account the action of generating and providing feedback to the policymakers. As soon as the citizen group process has taken place, the STAVE operator will begin to work on translating the evidence generated by the groups into a form suitable for consideration in the policymaking context. Two stages should be highlighted.

- The first stage is called 'speedy mode'. The idea of this mode of feedback is to provide findings straight after a session or a complete STAVE intervention (three sessions). Responding in this way meets the policymakers' need for quickly available and easy to understand information. Importantly, these immediate and unrefined findings rely heavily on the materials directly produced by the citizens participating in the group(s). This is the key feedback in terms of the STAVE tool.
- At a later point, 'full feedback' will be given. This second feedback stage has a more research-oriented focus. It is based upon a thematic analysis of the group data, and provides findings to policymakers that may expand or qualify the immediate and unrefined results.

In addition, our trials suggest that providing feedback during the process is extremely useful in order, for instance, to refine the policy questions and to introduce new issues or materials in the citizen groups. This middle range feedback seems to fit best in between Meeting 2 and 3.

Conclusions

By experimenting with hybrid focus group strategies addressing different research issues, we have tried to develop a method able to generate (mainly) qualitative and (also) quantitative data revealing socially shared ways of reasoning and acting amongst groups of people with shared experiences and ways of life. As we have shown above, our methodological trials have promoted enhanced participant engagement and social accounts grounded in indigenous practices to a greater degree than with conventional focus groups. In this sense, the STAVE method can be understood as a set of tools and procedures based on focus groups strategically combined with other research techniques, with the particular characteristic of repetition over a short period of time. Some of its key features can be summarized as follows:

Reconvened & Reflexive: STAVE is essentially a 'reconvened' tool, as it entails meeting repeatedly and 'rethinking' both at the citizen and at the policy level. This iterative character of the tool engenders 'reflection', a key mechanism in successful knowledge brokering tools such as STAVE. The reconvened citizen group discussions with diaries promote reflection, while the successive interactions between the policymakers and the STAVE operator support reflection processes at the policy level. Overall, the STAVE process provides access to the reflexive (unreflective but self-referential) character of the social worlds of policymaking and everyday citizen behaviours.

The behaviour/value gap: A key benefit, as recognized by policymakers in several countries (see Prades et al. 2016), was the capacity of STAVE to shed some light on the problem we have already characterized as 'the gap between what citizens say and what they do' STAVE also has the capacity to engender a willingness by citizen participants to talk openly about their domestic and other everyday practices, giving value to their capacity to recognize, and reflect upon, the occurrence of inconsistencies between their environment-related practices and their accounts of those practices. Numerous theoretical frameworks have been developed in the literature to explain the gap between the possession of environmental knowledge and environmental awareness, and displaying pro-environmental behaviour. Although many studies have been undertaken and several sets of barriers and driving forces have been identified, no definitive explanation has yet been found. For instance, after analyzing different theoretical models, Kollmuss and Agyeman (2002) concluded that all the studied analytical frameworks have some validity in certain circumstances, and that the question of what shapes pro-environmental behaviour is such a complex one that it cannot be adequately visualized through a single framework. Although this could be true, in our view, one of the main difficulties in exploring pro-environmental knowledge, attitudes and behaviours relies on the data gathering methodology. People frequently tend to hide their true intentions and behaviours regarding domestic environmental issues, such as waste management, energy use, and others. For this reason, STAVE can be a useful methodology in investigating such research objectives, as it has been shown capable of generating a high degree of constructive engagement with groups of citizens. Such engagement is highly effective in eliciting patterns of socially shared everyday behaviours, and authentic ways of talking about such behaviours. At first, citizen participants were cautious, but as they became more involved in the process they clearly displayed a sense of freedom to explain their informal doubts and contradictions; features of their everyday experience that we suspect would be difficult to capture using more conventional social research methods.

Translation: A central challenge in the STAVE design process had been to establish translation processes in order to link the two spheres of discourse and practice. On the one hand there was a requirement to produce suitable means by which the needs of the policy community in question could be captured and translated into a form suitable for 'posing questions' to the citizen community being investigated. The second requirement was to capture the deliberations of the citizen groups, and to translate this into a form where it could be fed into the policymaking process in meaningful and constructive ways.

STAVE transforms the usual role of policymakers interested in understanding and addressing citizen daily behaviours. Typically, a policymaker wanting to learn about citizen behaviours will commission social research, in order to be a consumer of social research results. In the STAVE process, policymakers turn into producers of social research results. They work closely with the STAVE operator throughout the process in order to define and refine the research questions, and to make sense of the resulting insights about citizens' behaviours and related practical reasoning. We also found evidence that policymakers' involvement in the use of STAVE seems to have promoted an enhanced degree of reflection of the ways in which they considered policy issues, and contributed to rethink their existing knowledge and assumptions about citizen behaviours.

In substantive terms, this work has provided us with a powerful means to research on citizen reasoning about issues as diverse as railway safety and nuclear fusion power, and the ways in which that reasoning can change as people learn more about the technicalities and social context of such technologies. The methods have demonstrated their capacity to allow citizens to reason about technical and complex issues in terms familiar from their everyday lives. It has also allowed us to investigate a range of domestic and everyday consumption practices, the nature of which have important implications for environmental sustainability. In so doing, it has enabled us to address the classical gap between 'what they say' and 'what they do'—in other words, between practices and accounts of those practices. The tool's capacity to show the real-world nature of the gap between discourses and practices is perhaps one of the most significant achievements of the method. However, STAVE's limits should also be highlighted, because it is a method applicable only in certain cases. At least two conditions are required: Firstly, the policy issue at stake must be directly related to citizens' daily practices (e.g. energy use, mobility, domestic waste management, etc.). Otherwise it is not possible to apply the required degree of reflexivity to the groups and diaries. STAVE is not useful for investigating issues where people do not have direct experience. Secondly, the implementation of STAVE requires a collaborative attitude from all the partners, willing to get involved in the process. It is not a good method for cases with explicit conflict between citizens and policymakers.

Finally, it should be remarked that STAVE operates by brokering indigenous knowledge between the social worlds of policymaking and citizens' domestic and other everyday practices. In so doing, it might be regarded also as an effective means to generate capacity-building for both the policy community and the civil society.

Acknowledgements The work on which this chapter was based was part-supported by the European Commission under grant no. 244024 (FP7, 2010–2012), with the title 'Policy Addressing Climate Change and Learning about Consumer Behaviour and Everyday Life' (PACHELBEL). The authors wish to acknowledge the impulse by the late Tom Horlick-Jones of Cardiff University, and by other research partners leaders participating in the whole project: Julie Barnett, Marian Constantin, Ann Enander, Willi Konrad, Marc Poumadère, and Johnatan Rosenhead. The authors thank the citizen and policy partners in the STAVE processes conducted under project PACHELBEL. Besides, part of the presented data comes from the METAFPERCOM project, funded by the Spanish Ministry of Economy and Competitiveness (ref. CSO2013-41661-P).

References

Barbour, R., & Kitzinger, J. (eds.) (1999) *Developing Focus Group Research: Politics, Theory and Practice.* London: Sage.
Bloor, M., Frankland, J., Thomas, M., & Robson, K. (2001) *Focus Groups in Social Research.* London: Sage.
Conklin, J. (2005). *Dialogue Mapping: Building Shared Understanding of Wicked Problems.* London: John Wiley & Sons.
Espluga, J., Prades, A., & Lores, M. (2016) 'Metaphors on climate change: An exploration of their use in the press and its interpretation by citizens', Communication presented at the *Advances in Metaphor Studies Conference.* Universita degli Studi di Genova. Genova (Italy), 20–22 May.

Horlick-Jones, T. (2008). 'Reasoning about safety management policy in everyday terms: A pilot study in citizen engagement for the UK railway industry'. *Journal of Risk Research*, 11(6): 697–718.
Horlick-Jones, T., & Prades, A. (2009). 'On interpretative risk perception research: Some reflections on its origins; its nature; and its possible applications in risk communication practice'. *Health, Risk & Society*, 11(5): 409–430.
Horlick-Jones, T., & Prades, A. (2015) 'Translating between social worlds of policy and everyday life: The development of a group-based method to support policymaking by exploring behavioural aspects of sustainable consumption'. *Public Understanding of Science*, 24(7): 811–826.
Horlick-Jones, T, Walls, J., Rowe, G., Pidgeon, N., Poortinga, W., Murdock, G., & O'Riordan, T. (2007a). *The GM Debate: Risk, Politics and Public Engagement*. London: Routledge.
Horlick-Jones, T., Walls, J., & Kitzinger, J. (2007b) 'Bricolage in action: Learning about, making sense of, and discussing, issues about genetically modified crops and food'. *Health, Risk & Society*, 9(1): 83–103.
Horlick-Jones, T., Prades, A., & Espluga, J. (2012) 'Investigating the degree of 'stigma' associated with nuclear energy technologies: A cross-cultural examination of the case of fusion power'. *Public Understanding of Science*, 21(5): 514–533.
Hughes, R. (1998) 'Considering the vignette technique and its application to a study of drug injecting and HIV risk and safer behaviour'. *Sociology of Health and Illness*, 20(3): 381–400.
Irwin, A., Simmons, P., & Walker, G. (1999) 'Faulty environments and risk reasoning: The local understanding of industrial hazards'. *Environment and Planning A*, 31(7): 1311–1326.
Kamberelis, G., & Dimitriadis, G. (2005) 'Focus groups: Strategic articulations of pedagogy, politics and inquiry', In N. K. Denzin and Y. S. Lincoln (eds.) *The SAGE Handbook of Qualitative Research* (3rd ed.). Thousand Oaks, CA: Sage, pp. 887–907.
Kollmuss, A., & Agyeman, J. (2002) 'Mind the gap: Why do people act environmentally and what are the barriers to pro-environmental behaviour?' *Environmental Education Research*, 8(3): 239–260.
Konrad, W. (2015) 'La percepció del sentit de la sostenibilitat, les polítiques energètiques i els hàbits dels ciutadans pel que fa al consum domèstic de l'energia. Un estudi de cas a Alemanya'. *Papers: Revista de Sociologia*, 100(4): 453–476.

Marris, C., Wynne, B., Simmons, P., & Weldon, S., (2001) *Public Perceptions of Agricultural Biotechnologies in Europe*. Final report of the PABE research project, funded by the Commission of the European Communities, Contract number FAIR CF98-3844 (DB12SSMI).

Mio, J. S. (1997) 'Metaphor and politics'. *Metaphor and Symbol*, 12(2): 113–133.

Morgan, D., Fellows, C., & Guevara, H. (2008) 'Emergent approaches to focus group research', In N.S. Hesse-Biber and P. Leavy (eds.), *Handbook of Emergent M*ethods. New York: Guilford Press, pp. 189–205.

Musolff, A. (2004) *Metaphor and Political Discourse. Analogical Reasoning in Debates about Europe*. London: Palgrave MacMillan.

Myers, G. (2007) 'Commonplaces in risk talk: Face threats and forms of interaction'. *Journal of Risk Research*, 10(3): 285–305.

Nind, M., & Vinha, H. (2014) 'Creative interactions with data: Using visual and metaphorical devices in repeated focus groups'. *Qualitative Research*, 1–18. doi: 10.1177/1468794114557993.

Poumadère, M., Bertoldo, R., Boso, À., Espluga-Trenc, J., Mays, C., Oltra, C., & Schneider, N. (2015) 'Entre consommation durable et vie quotidienne: Les premiers balbutiements du compteur communicant en France et en Espagne', *La Sociologie de l'énergie, ed. CNRS, Collection Alpha*.

Prades, A., Horlick-Jones, T., Barnett, J., Constantin, M., Enander, A., Espluga, J., Konrad, W., Poumadère, M., & Rosenhead, J. (2016) 'Shining a light on citizens' everyday environment-related behaviours', In A. Martinuzzi & M. Sedlacko (eds.) *Knowledge Brokerage for Sustainable Development*. Saltaire (UK): Greenleaf Publishing, p. 189–207.

Prades, A., Horlick-Jones, T., Espluga, J., Oltra, C., Barnet., J., Constanti, M., Enander, A., Konrad, W., & Poumadère, M. (2012) 'Climate Change and Citizen Behaviour: a challenge for EU Environmental Policy'. *VERTICES, Revista del CIEMAT*, 7: 40–44.

Prades, A., Oltra, C., Navajas, J., Horlick-Jones, & Espluga, J. (2009) 'The social perception of nuclear fusion: investigating lay understanding and reasoning about the technology', In S. Martorell, C. Soares and J. Barnett (eds.), *Safety, Reliability and Risk Analysis: Theory, Methods and Applications*, Vol. 2. Oxford, UK: CRC Press, pp. 1371–1377.

Prades López, A. Horlick-Jones, T., Oltra, C., & Solá, R. (2008) 'Lay perceptions of nuclear fusion: Multiple modes of understanding'. *Science and Public Policy*, 35(2): 95–105.

Renn, O., Webler, T., & Wiedemann, P. (eds.) (1995) *Fairness and Competence in Citizens' Participation: Evaluating Models for Environmental Discourse.* Dordrecht: Kluwer.

Richard, J. L. (2006) 'Super wicked problems and climate change: Restraining the present to liberate the future'. *Cornell Law Review*, 94: 104–109.

Rosenhead, J., & Mingers, J. (2001) *Rational Analysis for a Problematic WorldRrevisited.* Chichester: John Wiley and Sons.

Rowe, G., Horlick-Jones, T., Walls, J., & Pidgeon, N. F. (2005) 'Difficulties in evaluating public engagement initiatives: reflections on an evaluation of the UK GM Nation public debate'. *Public Understanding of Science*, 14(4): 331–352.

Timotijevic, L., & Barnett, J. (2006) 'Managing the possible health risks of mobile telecommunications: Public understandings of precautionary action and advice'. *Health, Risk & Society*, 8(2): 143–164.

Walker, G., Simmons, P., Wynne, B., & Irwin, A. (1998). *Public Perception of Risks Associated with Major Accident Hazards.* Sudbury: HSE Books.

Weber, E. P., & Khademian, A. P. (2008). 'Wicked problems, knowledge challenges and collaborative capacity builders in network settings'. *Public Administration Review*, 68(2): 334–349.

Zonabend, F. (1993) *The Nuclear Peninsula.* Cambridge and Paris: Cambridge University Press and Editions de la Maison des Sciences de l'Homme.

Ana Prades graduated in Political Sciences and Sociology and holds a PhD. in 'Energy, Technology and Society' (Department of Sociology VI) Faculty of Information Sciences (Complutense University of Madrid). Since 1990 she has been working at the Ciemat (Research Centre on Energy, Technology and the Environment, subordinate to the Spanish Ministry of Science and Innovation). She is currently Head of the Socio-Technical Research Centre (CISOT), based in Barcelona. Her research is mainly concerned with risk perception, risk communication and public engagement, as they relate to energy technologies and climate change. She has extensive experience with qualitative and quantitative research. She was the main researcher and coordinator of the European project PACHELBEL (FP7) about developing methods to understand and promote public engagement in sustainability topics.

Josep Espluga has a PhD in Sociology, and Master in Occupational Health. He is associate professor at the Department of Sociology of the Universitat Autònoma de Barcelona, and research fellow of the Public Policies and

Government Institute (IGOP), member of the Research Group on Agriculture, Livestock and Food in Globalization (ARAG-UAB). His main interest deals with the relationships between health, work, environment and territory, with particular focus on the social perception of technological risks and socio-environmental conflicts, including public participation and engagement issues. He has extensive experience with qualitative research, with particular attention to group based research approaches.

Tom Horlick-Jones sadly died in January 2015, while this chapter was being written. He held a degree in Maths as well as a PhD in Sociology, and was Full Professor at the School of Social Sciences at Cardiff University. Before this he held academic posts at the London School of Economics and the University of Surrey. He was also a visiting scientist at CIEMAT-CISOT in Barcelona, and an honorary senior research associate in the Department of Science and Technology Studies at University College London. Professor Horlick-Jones specialized in investigating risk-related behaviour, and associated reasoning, communication and decision-making processes. He carried out important policy work and advised many organizations, and was especially known for his research and publications on the everyday negotiation of risk in practice. He produced over 100 publications throughout his career, including the books *Natural Risk and Civil Protection* (lead editor, 1995), *Social Amplification of Risk: the Media and the Public* (co-author, HSE Books, 2001) and *The GM Debate: Risk, Politics and Public Enga*gement (lead author, 2007; paperback 2009).

Section III

Innovations in Focus Group Facilitation

10

The Use of Video Recording in Longitudinal Focus Group Research

Claire Thompson, Daniel J Lewis and Stephanie J C Taylor

Overview: What Are Video Focus Group Workshops and Why Use Them?

A video focus group workshop consists of a series of linked activities, using a group discussion as a starting point, that centre around people engaging in participatory video (PV) tasks. Our research team developed these workshops in order to explore new and creative ways of addressing the challenges of conducting longitudinal research with young people on the multifaceted topic of neighbourhood regeneration.

C. Thompson (✉) · D.J. Lewis
London School of Hygiene and Tropical Medicine, London, UK
e-mail: claire.thompson@lshtm.ac.uk; daniel.lewis@lshtm.ac.uk

S.J.C. Taylor
Blizard Institute, Barrs and the London School of Medicine and Dentistry, London, UK
e-mail: s.j.c.taylor@qmul.ac.uk

© The Author(s) 2017
R.S. Barbour, D.L. Morgan (eds.), *A New Era in Focus Group Research*, DOI 10.1057/978-1-137-58614-8_10

Potential power imbalances between researcher and participant are amplified when working with children and young people, requiring an ongoing effort to develop methodologies that give 'voice' and representation to younger participants (Thomson 2009). Adopting a participatory framework is one, increasingly popular, way of countering this, especially in educational research, by recognizing young people as a group for whom greater recognition, agency, and a 'voice' are necessary (Kirby 2001). Focus group discussions are one of the most widely used methods in the participatory research toolkit and, therefore, are a logical place to start when trying to further develop participatory ethnographic methods.

The decision to introduce visual technology to the workshop format, in this case mini-camcorders, was based on both its propensity to aid longitudinal reflection and its potential appeal to younger participants. Visual approaches to qualitative research emerged as a key methodological strand in the 1990s. The visual is inextricably interwoven with personal identities, narratives, lifestyles, cultures and societies. In research contexts, images may inspire conversations and digital images can be woven into narratives. Digital images and media are increasingly used as integral elements of the work of ethnographers, so it is difficult to be a contemporary ethnographer without engaging with these media forms (Pink 2013). Our overall intention was to facilitate the generation of participant-produced digital artefacts that could then be used as prompts for comparison and critical reflection. We operationalized this by using clips of workshop footage (collected during wave one of the research) to structure a series of discussions and activities with the same participants a year later (at wave two). Traditionally, focus groups have not featured heavily in QLR methodologies and the inclusion of visual technology in our approach represented an attempt to make the format more conducive to longitudinal enquiry.

While visual methods and technologies in general have received a lot of attention (Pink 2013; Reavey 2011; Mirzoeff 2002), there has been a lot less attention paid to using visual methods with children (Yamada-Rice et al. 2015). And yet, it can be an appropriate approach, because young people have few 'official' platforms to voice their opinions and experiences. Generating research footage guided both by the intentionalities of the researcher and the participants may go some way to addressing the difficulties of capturing concerns and worldviews that are not 'adultist' (Kindon 2003). Visual research, and particularly participatory methods, offers a way to elicit perspectives and narratives from young people and serves as a way of involving them as producers of knowledge (Thomson 2009).

Planning and Conducting a Video Focus Group Workshop

Scope for Innovation in the Context of a Larger Study

The workshops were deployed as part of a larger research project and made up a comparatively small part of the overall data collection. The Olympic Regeneration in East London (ORiEL) study is a National Institute for Health Research (NIHR) funded mixed-methods prospective study exploring the health and social legacy of the London 2012 Games. The quantitative arm of the study comprised three waves of data collection in the form of both a school-based survey of adolescents (recruited from 26 East London schools) and interviews with their parents (collected through face-to-face structured interviews) (Smith et al. 2012). The qualitative arm of the study was designed specifically to explore perceptions and experiences of neighbourhood life and change during a period of Olympic-led development. Qualitative data were collected post-Games in two waves. At each wave, three data collection activities were deployed: narrative family interviews, 'go-along' interviews (Carpiano 2009) and video focus group workshops. Narrative family interviews involve as many members of the household as want to take part in a group interview (normally in the family home). We ask participants to tell us stories about their experiences in the local area and encouraged other family members present to comment on and join in with the narratives. A go-along interview is an ethnographic mixture of observation and interview, concentrated around a particular place, journey or activity (Carpiano 2009). This is a participant-led method that is intended to reveal participants' interactions with their physical and social environment and uncover how the ascribe meaning that environment. We approached those participants who had talked about particular sites in detail during the family narrative interviews and who had also expressed a willingness to take us to see these sites.

The workshops were a relatively late addition in the planning of the data collection activities and stand somewhat apart from the narrative and go-along interviews described above. They evolved out of research team discussions about interactions with adolescent participants while piloting the school-based survey, and the possibility of further exploring the more informal accounts that these revealed. Having a good working relationship with the schools participating in the study meant that we were fortunate enough to be able to augment our qualitative data collection activities with the workshops and take the opportunity to try something new to meet the challenges of conducting QLR with young people.

The sections that follow outline exactly how we went about organizing and delivering the workshops and offer some practical and theoretical reflections.

Delivering the Focus Group Video Workshop

We approached three schools participating in the quantitative study and requested of their respective gatekeepers that they each select eight students (aged 12–13 years) that they thought would be happy to take part in a half-day workshop to be held at their school and which would consist of a series of drama-like activities, including group discussions, role play and making student-videos. We also asked that the groups be as mixed as possible in terms of gender and ethnicity. Relying on school staff gatekeepers to select participants was considered a prudent move, given that the workshop format required a good deal of performativity and creativity from the participants. Teachers were in a much stronger position than the researchers, as outsiders, to gauge which students might enjoy and engage with such activities.

In line with the broader qualitative study, we conducted two waves of focus group data collection 12 months apart – returning to the same participants for the second wave. The workshops took 2.5 to 3 hours each and were organized into three main sessions:

- The focus group discussion
- Student-to-student interviews
- A prediction for the future

The Focus Group Discussion: Establishing a Participatory Framework

The room set-up and facilitation for the focus group (always on school premises) were both conventional. The participants and moderators all sat together in a circle in a private and comfortable space and the discussion followed a topic guide prepared in advance (Greenbaum 1999). The same two moderators facilitated all the workshops together. Moderator 1 led the session and Moderator 2 supervised all aspects of visual recording. Both moderators asked questions and followed up with prompts.

Two hand held mini-camcorders were brought to the workshops. For the focus group discussion, one was set up on a tripod to allow recording in the corner of the room and the other was held by Moderator 2. Moderator 2 passed the camcorder around the circle for the participants to look at and talk about at the outset of the session, which proved an effective icebreaker and allowed the participants to get comfortable with the technology. We took this opportunity to reiterate that they would be using the camcorders themselves later in the day and that one of our aims was to make a recording that we could bring back for them to watch the following year. In order to further draw the participants into the process we passed the Dictaphone around the circle and explained that we would like them to use it as a microphone, so that when one participant was speaking another would hold out the Dictaphone towards them to ensure that we produced a viable audio recording to back-up the camcorder data. The participants took to this well and quickly started to ask each other to repeat statements into the 'microphone' or to let another speaker finish. In this way, participants were taking an active – albeit relatively minor – role in facilitating the discussion and engaging with the technology from the outset. These initial additions to the traditional focus group format were intended to build rapport and help to establish a participatory research environment (Thomson 2009), thus priming the participants for subsequent and more hands-on activities as the workshop progressed.

Student-to-Student Interviews: Participatory Video

While the content of the focus group discussion was carefully planned with a topic guide, the subsequent activities were much more student-led. After the focus group we always took a short break. The moderators took this opportunity to brainstorm what we considered to be the most interesting and dominant narratives to emerge from the discussion so that we could then use them as topics for the student-to-student interviews. As is often the case in qualitative research, and particularly in group interviews, a number of themes and issues emerged that were not anticipated in the topic guide (Kitzinger 1995; Robinson 1999). Most notably, a new shopping centre in the locality featured as a very important space and symbol of development to the young people with whom we worked. Also, the proliferation and quality of 'Chicken Shops' (referring to largely independent fast food outlets that sell a variety of value meals based around fried chicken to take away and, increasingly, with eat-in facilities as well in the local area was a topic of intense interest to almost all of the participants and discussion about this subject often became quite heated. 'Chicken Shops' have become synonymous with East London and the topic of much media and public health debate. It was fascinating and unexpected to find that our participants had such considered and often conflicting views on the status of these establishments in their local area.

Before starting the practical we had a short group discussion about the key themes we identified to ensure that we had not missed anything and that the participants agreed with our interpretation. We divided the group into pairs for the activity and explained that we would like each pair to work on one of the key themes. In some cases, more than one pair wanted to work on the same theme (crime and safety was particularly popular) while other themes provoked a less enthusiastic response when offered as an interview topic. We did not challenge participants' preferences or choices in this regard and allowed then to work with the topics with which they felt most at ease.

The aim of this activity was to facilitate a participant-led exploration and debate about narratives of neighbourhood life that had emerged from the previous discussion. This left us with the challenge of providing a format and structure with which participants would feel comfortable and that would not necessitate substantial direction from the moderators. We drew upon our experiences of teaching and working in secondary schools to devise an activity similar to one that might be used in a drama workshop. We set the space up in the layout of a mock 'television studio'. At the front of the space (the 'stage') were two chairs: one for the interviewer and one for the interviewee. Facing this 'stage' area at each side of the room were the camcorders set-up on the tripods with a chair in front of each for the operators. Behind the camcorders we placed a row of chairs for the 'audience'. After working in pairs for a short time to devise their interview questions on their chosen themes, we embarked on a group performance. Each pair had a turn in front of the camera on the 'stage' performing their interview, behind the camera as 'camera men' and as members of the 'audience'. Moderator 1 led the session by ensuring turn-taking and interjecting where necessary. Moderator 2 supervised the recording and managed the 'audience'. Again, we continued to use the Dictaphone as a 'microphone'. The participants were quick to take to this activity with those behind the camera engaging in practices such as shouting '*action*' and the 'audience' responded to the interviews by clapping and, even, heckling. Group activities for video work helped to establish a shared purpose and collaboration amongst the participants (Participatory Research Group). In particular, using creative and drama-based techniques provided a means of stimulating reflection, debate, argument, dissent and consensus in order to facilitate the articulation of multiple voices and positions (Veale 2005). By role-playing the culturally familiar format of a television programme the participants could appropriate subject positions that allowed them to comfortably express these voices. The PV activity embedded in this part of the session thus provided an accessible way for participants to explore their perspectives and form a shared dialogue (Participatory Research Group 2015).

The activity facilitated a diverse array of improvizations and subject matter. In fact, one of the limitations of this approach was that it could prove very difficult to keep the activity to time and (within reason) on-topic. Additionally, on reviewing the video footage after the event, we came across numerous instances of participants pulling faces into the camcorders or deliberately disrupting the footage that had completely escaped our attention on the day. On a few occasions some of the 'camera men' were reluctant to relinquish their turn and join the 'audience'. At these times, it was necessary to briefly drop back into a more authoritative 'classroom management' stance to prevent the activity degenerating into relative chaos. Creative methodologies involve a degree of experimentation and risk-taking that can be difficult to manage, especially when working with young people (Veale 2005). Maintaining a balance between managing behaviour and allowing scope for expression and creativity was an ongoing challenge. One group both surprised and challenged us by engaging in an unexpectedly political, albeit sometimes rowdy, dialogue about the then London Mayor. The group become so agitated about pursuing this topic that we could only convince them to move on by promising them the opportunity, at the end of the session, to organize and record a short television-debate-style piece on the relative merits of the Mayor. They carried this out enthusiastically – and largely on their own – using a similar format to the one we had introduced. Although the interactions for this piece were less structured and were peppered with excited over-talking, shouting and even some running around and poor behaviour, it nonetheless generated a series of impassioned and opinionated narratives.

A Prediction for the Future

The final workshop activity, which served both as a plenary and a means of directly addressing the planned longitudinal aspects of the data collection, required a short to-camera address from each participant. We left one of the chairs on the 'stage' area and operated a hot-seat policy, where the participants again moved around, taking turns both behind and in front of the camcorders. Each participant was asked to talk to the camcorder and (a) State who (if anyone) was the most memorable or inspirational person associated with the 2012 London Games and (b) Make a prediction about something that they might do or achieve by this time next year. The participants seemed to enjoy this activity and were, by now; very familiar with operating the camcorders and the practice of turn-taking, so we found that these final sessions went quite smoothly. The predictions uttered for this last activity tended to range from the bizarre and flippant ('*I hope to get slightly better at some sports, do some hard-core studying and have punched an animal in the face. No, don't worry, I'm not gonna harm it, I just want to punch something like a badger*') to the more mundane ('*Hello, my name is Andy* and my goal for next year is to learn a bit of piano . . . and my Olympic thing is Usain Bolt*'). This is perhaps unsurprising given that this last activity, being a plenary, was facilitated in a relatively light-hearted way and intended to finish the workshop on a high-note. The overall aim was not to elicit considered speculation from the participants or further probe their perceptions of the Olympic legacy. Rather, it was produce material in a series of short clips that could serve as an introduction and icebreaker for our return visit to carry out the second wave of data collection.

On reflection, much more could have been made of this activity and it could certainly be improved upon. A more specific request than '*please make a prediction about your future for next year*' may well have generated more useful data. Notably, one participant had his own very specific interpretation of the task that could help to inform subsequent refinements of this approach. When in the hot-seat, he opened with '*Okay, hi future me, you've probably forgotten your homework, don't worry, we still have time, anyway . . .* ' As can be seen, he directly addressed his 'future' self as if he were having a conversation with this future Other. Following his logic could provide a potentially promising way of framing the task in subsequent sessions. As stated, it was our intention to bring participants into dialogue with their previous utterances, to approach data collection longitudinally by understanding the sequence and flow of utterances and how they developed (Maybin 2001). Words and utterances cannot be isolated from the sequences in which they occur and are always in dialogic relation to previous utterances and in anticipation of those yet to be voiced (Bakhtin 1981). If we had encouraged participants to record a message for their future-selves, including even a question or two that could be answered at wave two, we could have facilitated a direct dialogue in this sense. This would certainly be an avenue worth exploring in order to refine our application of the method and its longitudinal application

Using Focus Video Group Workshops for QLR

The workshop format described above could function as a stand-alone session in PV. It generated multimodal data, combining visual and verbal data, to create a rich depiction of neighbourhood perceptions and experiences. Such methods are effective because people, more especially younger people, already use multimodal forms of expressions and communication when presenting their experiences in everyday life. As people become more proficient in using new visual and multi-media technologies to convey ideas, feelings, and identities the more they readily use them in the course of social interaction (Reavey 2011). As stated from the outset, we wanted to go a step further in our application and use the workshops for longitudinal data collection. In the context of our study, the whole qualitative dataset (including workshop data) was ultimately subjected to a narrative longitudinal analysis and, in line with this, there were two broad analytically driven aims guiding all qualitative data collection:

- To identify narratives of neighbourhood perceptions and experiences
- To chart whether and how these narratives develop and change over the two waves of data collection

Data collection for the wave two workshops, therefore, had to include a substantial emphasis on revisiting wave one data. So, when we returned to our workshop participants for wave two, we needed to facilitate their reflection upon wave one narratives and give them the creative space to express new thoughts. In order to do this we also needed to create a kind of reflective dialogue with the previous wave's narratives. We wanted to retain the same overall structure of the workshops that we used in the first wave, because they worked really well and the participants enjoyed them. As stated, by the end of the first wave of workshops, they had become quite adept and comfortable with the performativity of the activities. However, we also needed to format it in a way that would facilitate reflection and longitudinal data collection in the context of a comfortable and conversational dynamic (Krueger 1994). Broadly, we approached this by showing participants a series of clips of footage from wave one to prompt discussions at wave two. Visual artefacts can disrupt narratives. When participants are faced with a representation from their past, however, they are able to imagine the emotions or their embodied states from that time. The past can, thus, enter into the present and create new narratives or more complex accounts (Reavey 2011).

The Wave Two Workshop Format

Putting this approach into practice required careful planning. Again, we allowed 2.5 to 3 hours for the workshops and they were organized into three main sessions, closely modelled on the wave one format:

- Follow-up focus group discussion
- Student to student interviews
- A message to the ORiEL team

Follow-up Focus Group Discussion: A Reflective Approach

After an initial analysis of the wave one data set and several reviews of the workshop footage, we selected the four themes we considered to be the most fruitful avenues to follow up. The relatively small proportion of overall data collection that the workshops constituted permitted us the indulgence of being able to pursue emergent areas of interest, while knowing that the original research objectives and topics were covered via the other qualitative data collection activities. Once we had agreed upon our four themes we went back to the wave one footage and compiled a short reflexive video piece (no more than 10 minutes in total) to use as a resource for the wave two workshop.

As an introduction we used the material collected for the *A prediction for the future* plenary exercise in wave one – for which each student introduced themselves, stated who their 'Olympic inspiration' was (if any) and a prediction about themselves for the year-to-come. We then selected up to three short clips of participants discussing each of the four main themes we thought particularly interesting or contentious or characterizing the tone of participant comments in general and arranged them into sequence. Lastly, we created a series of slides (see Fig. 10.1 for an example) to introduce the piece and each of the cluster of themed-clips. The intention was to show this reflexive video tool at the focus group discussion, pausing it after each theme so that the group could reflect upon the content and extend their narratives. In this way, we used the film piece to structure the focus group discussion; providing an empirical point of reflection.

In practice, structuring the focus group discussion around reflections on video clips proved to be very popular with the participants. When we returned for our second workshop, 12 months after the first, the participants were very keen to 'see' themselves and their peers on the video footage and judge how they had physically changed or grown in the intervening period. In fact, when we first showed participants the footage of themselves, as an introduction to the focus groups, the discussion rapidly went off-topic and the participants started a long conversation about their hair, voice or general appearance, which got quite loud and rowdy at times. It took some repeated efforts to bring the participants back to topic and for them to begin to discuss what was being said on the video rather than just what they could see. This was perhaps to be expected, given that the participants were of an age when changes to physical appearance brought about by the passing of

10 The Use of Video Recording in Longitudinal Focus Group Research

You in 2012	**The Games** Were you inspired? Have you been doing more sport since last year? 
Will the Olympics change Newham? Will it get better or worse? 	Is Newham a healthy place to live? What about the chicken shops? 
What is it like to live in Newham? What will it be like in the future? 	**THANK YOU !** 

Fig. 10.1 Slides from the reflexive video tool. A series of clips of participant interactions and utterances followed each of these slides. We used each of these clusters of themed clips to prompt discussion and reflection

time are still a cause of excitement and fascination. The participants were confronted with a visual representation of a less-mature version of themselves. There was a lot of laughing and some light-hearted teasing in the groups with comments such as 'Oh, don't you look cute!'. Added to which, visual selves and subjectivities are an increasingly central aspect of identity work for young people (Mirzoeff 2002). Critiquing and discussing the visual representations of themselves and their peers was a natural and comfortable activity for them.

Using video clips to structure the substantive content of the focus group discussion served as a means of almost 'picking up where we left off' the previous year. Viewing the clips vividly reminded the group of the issues and dialogue from the previous workshop, allowing participants to provide updates, corrections, critiques and reinterpretations of the narratives. Responding to visual artefacts in this way generates more complex and layered accounts, and ones that are steeped in emotional resonances and reminders (Reavey 2011). This was particularly apparent when we broached the topic of Olympic inspirations and showed participants footage of their comments about who they thought to be key figures in the Olympic spectacle and which sports (if any) they were planning to take-up as a result. The first wave of data collection was carried out a few months after the Games in 2012, when the sense of celebration and festival was widespread and palpable. When confronted after an interval with their earlier largely enthusiastic responses participants were initially taken aback. It took them a few moments to re-experience the situated tone and emotions. The juxtaposition of past and present that this method entailed was extremely useful analytically. In this particular case, it served to demonstrate the transitory aspects of neighbourhood perceptions around the Games.

Student-to-Student Interviews

We retained the same format for this part of the workshop; allowing pairs to pick from the main themes that we identified. Participants quickly slid back into the conventions of this activity and needed much less direction than was the case in the previous year. They added flourishes, such as pretending to be reporters and 'signing off' to camera after an interview. Analytically, this activity was very valuable in terms of being able to simply observe if the topics and tone of what participants chose to cover in their interviews had changed. For example, the topic of 'Chicken Shops' retained its significance for participants and their talk about it remained fairly consistent, while narratives of crime and safety became less dramatic and more nuanced. Accounts of sport and exercise were virtually absent at wave two.

By structuring the workshops in this way – using visual artefacts in the focus group discussion and deliberately retaining exactly the same format for the student-to-student interviews – we intended to both actively foster commentary on past narratives *and* allow participants to take-up and develop topics with a minimum of interference. The workshop format combines a series of activities with differing levels of participant decision-making and collaboration, giving it the scope to probe perceptions and experiences with a variety of different slants. Using a range of video production and screening activities drives an iteratively evolving process of exploration and dialogue on shared issues (Participatory Research Group 2015).

'Hello ORiEL Team': A Message for the Research Team

The last activity of the workshop was also the end of our data collection with these participants; we would not be seeing them again. As with the previous year, we finished off the session by adopting a 'hot seat' policy in the 'stage' area, with each participant taking a turn in front of the camera, behind the camera, and as an audience member. We asked the participants to each give a short to-camera address. Over the course of the two waves of data collection the participants asked us a lot of questions about the research project and demonstrated quite an interest in the use to which the results might be put. So, this time, we asked that the participants directly address the ORiEL team and record a message that we could take back to the broader research team in case there was anything we might have missed over the course of the study. In this sense, we explicitly positioned the participants as expert by asking them to talk to our research agenda in an unmediated way.

Participatory research begins with what people bring to the research endeavour in terms of everyday knowledge and intimate familiarity with their environment (Park 2006). By this point in the study the participants were familiar with what we were trying to achieve and were comfortable with the format we were using. Responses to this request tended to be quite considered and participants made an effort to try to sum-up the good and bad aspects of their Neighbourhood. The request was also treated with a little more levity than our plenary activity the previous year. The participants linked their comments to the Government and State in general and also to specific politicians. Most memorably:

> *Hi, my name's Michelle*, hello ORiEL team. I feel about the Olympics that it didn't really help Newham become anything different at all whatsoever because it has inspired me a little bit but that's because I'm obsessed with the athletes but, um, aka Tom Daley. But anyways I don't think it's helped us that much, that much because like David Cameron doesn't like, he doesn't help the public. He only thinks of like the rich people. He doesn't feel for like the working class like Margaret Thatcher, God rest her soul. But yeah, thank you.*

This felt like a wholly appropriate way to finish the workshop and the data collection, by giving the participants the last word and the opportunity to directly tell the research team what they considered to be important issues in their local area.

Conclusion

This chapter outlined the potential of visual methods workshops, based around focus group discussions, to facilitate longitudinal data collection with young people within a participatory framework. The approach emerged in the situated context of a mixed methods study addressing the complex issues of Olympic Legacy and neighbourhood perceptions. Our workshops were somewhat experimental in that they comprised a combination of activities intended to highlight the challenges of our particular project. The workshop format, as we have presented it here, is not a refined research tool; rather, it is a starting point for further development. Visual methods are not simply transferred from one project to be used again in another. Methods themselves have biographies that evolve though different projects, bringing with them and inviting and inspiring new methodologies, through their practice and findings (Pink 2013; Pink and Leder Mackley 2012). We found that using visual media to record and revisit past opinions provided a particularly vivid way of eliciting discussions about change and that embedding this in focus group discussions maintained the collaborative social setting that we strove to provide. Subsequent iterations of this approach should, hopefully, reveal further uses and applications.

References

Bakhtin, M. (1981) 'The Dialogic Imagination', *Four Essays by M.M. Bakhtin*: University of Texas Press.
Carpiano, R.M. (2009) 'Come take a walk with me: The "Go-Along" interview as a novel method for studying the implications of place for health and well-being'. *Health & Place*, 15: 263–272.
Greenbaum, T.L. (1999) *A Practical Guide for Group Facilitation*. London: Sage.
Kindon, S. (2003) 'Participatory video in geographic research: A feminist practice of looking?' *Area*, 35: 142–153.
Kirby, P. (2001) 'Involving young people in research', In B. Franklin (ed.), *Handbook of Children's Rights*. London: Routledge.
Kitzinger, J. (1995) 'Qualitative research: Introducing focus groups'. *British Medical Journal (BMJ)*, 311: 299–302.
Krueger, R.A. (1994) *Focus Groups: A Practical Guide for Applied Research*. London: Sage Publications.
Maybin, J. (2001) 'Language, struggle and voice: The Bakhtin/Volosinov writings', In M. Wetherall & S. Taylor (eds.), *Discourse Theory and Practice*. London: Sage.
Mirzoeff, N. (2002) 'The subject of visual culture', In N. Mirzoeff (ed.), *The Visual Culture Reader*. London: Psychology Press.
Park, P. (2006) 'Knowledge and Participatory Research', In P. Reason & H. Bradbury (eds.), *Handbook of Action Research: Concise Paperback Edition*. London: Sage.
Participatory Research Group. (2015) 'Participatory Research Methods' (On the *Participate* website http://participate2015.org/).
Pink, S. (2013) *Doing Visual Ethnography*. London: Sage.
Pink, S., & Leder Mackley, K. (2012) 'Video and a sense of the invisible: Approaching domestic energy consumption through the sensory home'. *Sociological Research Online*, 17(1): 3.

Reavey, P. (2011) 'The return to experience: Psychology and the visual', In P. Reavey (ed.), *Visual Methods in Psychology: Using and Interpreting Images in Qualitative Research*. London: Routledge.

Robinson, N. (1999) 'The use of focus group methodology – with selected examples from sexual health research'. *Journal of Advanced Nursing*, 29: 905–913.

Smith, N.R., Clark, C., Fahy, A.E., Tharmaratnam, V., Lewis, D.J., Thompson, C., et al. (2012) 'The Olympic Regeneration in East London (ORiEL) study: Protocol for a prospective controlled quasi-experiment to evaluate the impact of urban regeneration on young people and their families'. *BMJ Open*, 2: 11.

Thomson, P. (2009) 'Children and young people: Voices in visual research', In P. Thomson (ed.), *Doing Visual Research with Children and Young People*. London: Routledge.

Veale, A. (2005) 'Creative methodologies in participatory research with children', In S. Greene & D. Hogan (eds.), *Researching Children's Experience: Approaches and Methods*. London: Sage.

Yamada-Rice, D., Stirling, E., & Walker, K. (2015) 'Introduction', In D. Yamada-Rice & E. Stirling (eds.), *Visual Methods with Children and Young People: Academics and Visual Industries in Dialogue*. London: Palgrave Macmillan.

Claire Thompson works in the Department of Social and Environmental Health Research at the London School of Hygiene and Tropical Medicine (LSHTM). She has a BSc in Social Policy and Management, an MA in the Social Sciences, a PGCE in post compulsory education and a PhD in Human Geography. Claire is a qualitative health researcher working largely within the disciplines of sociology, geography and public health. Her research interests lie in the lived experiences of urban health inequalities and particularly around the topics of the food and alcohol environments, food poverty, and urban regeneration. In terms of methods, Claire is interested in Discourse Analysis, Qualitative Longitudinal Research (QLR) and visual methods.

Daniel Lewis is a Research Fellow in the Department of Social and Environmental Health Research at the London School of Hygiene and Tropical Medicine (LSHTM). He has a BA in Geography from LSE, and an MSc in Geographic Information Science and PhD in Geography from UCL. Daniel is a health geographer who is interested in understanding the social and spatial determinants of health, health inequalities, and the complex linkages between individuals and their environments. The approaches Daniel uses to analyze these topic areas are largely centred on geography, but increasingly integrate perspectives from public health and epidemiology. Daniel is interested in mixed methods, and how qualitative and quantitative approaches can inform research.

Stephanie J C Taylor is Professor in Public health and Primary Care at Barts and the London School of Medicine and Dentistry, Queen Mary University of London, where she is Deputy Dean for Research Impact. She also holds an Honorary Consultant position in Public Health at Barts NHS Trust and is Deputy Lead for the North Thames NIHR CLAHRC (Collaboration for Leadership in Applied Health Research and Care) theme: 'Optimising behaviour and engagement with care' and co-lead of the Asthma UK Centre for Applied Research Self-Management Support Platform. She is a recognized expert in the field of research on supporting self-management in long term conditions. Her research programme focuses on complex, adjunctive interventions for people with long term conditions with a particular emphasis on people with psychological co-morbidities or those with advanced disease and significant disability. Her interest in the childhood antecedents of long term conditions led to her longstanding collaboration with the ORIEL group.

11

Best Practices for Synchronous Online Focus Groups

Bojana Lobe

Introduction

Digital technologies are now widely used in the social sciences. With continuous technological improvements in combination with digital technologies becoming widely available in general, online data collection has become an expanding and valuable field in social sciences. Methodological innovation in the development of original or modification of conventional data collection (Jankowski 1999: 386) has taken place in both the qualitative (e.g. virtual ethnography, virtual storytelling, online focus groups, online interviews) and quantitative tradition (e.g. web surveys). Still, most online methods are facilitations of the 'traditional' methods, using infrastructure provided by the internet (Chen and Hinton 1999: 2), as used on numerous digital technologies. Consequently, the body of research work and literature on online focus groups has been steadily growing in recent years (Kenny 2005; Stewart

---

B. Lobe (✉)
University of Ljubljana (UL), Ljubljana, Slovenia
e-mail: bojana.lobe@fdv.uni-lj.si

© The Author(s) 2017
R.S. Barbour, D.L. Morgan (eds.), *A New Era in Focus Group Research*, DOI 10.1057/978-1-137-58614-8_11

and Williams 2005; Morgan and Lobe 2011, Stover and Goodman 2012; Williams and Reid 2012; Abrams et al. 2015).

Hine (2005) noted that science data collection intrinsically involves communication. When introducing a new communication medium in the process of data collection, it typically brings along a set of conceptual, practical and technological issues, as well as problems and considerations in comparison to traditional methodological approaches, which researchers practice through well-established preferred modes of communication. Online focus groups are essentially a computer mediated 'communication event' (Terrance et al. 1993: 53), which attempts to mimic a face-to-face interaction format. Although many characteristics are very similar to those of face-to-face groups, the main characteristic of online focus groups is precisely the mediated venue, through which the 'communication event' happens in the form of text, voice or video. This calls for different skills from both researcher and participants. At a minimum, both are expected to have at least some level of computer literacy (Lobe 2008) in order to establish the online interaction.

Morgan (1988: 12) emphasizes that 'the hallmark of focus groups is *the explicit use of the group interaction to produce data and insights that would be less accessible without the interaction found in a group*' (emphasis in the original). The actions and accounts made by individual participants are influenced by the social context of the group. A high quality focus group profits from good interaction amongst the members as throughout the process they 'develop an explanation or accomplish a task' (Short 2006: 108).

In this chapter, I firstly present the temporal structure and the forms of synchronous online focus groups. Then, I consider the issues in Computer Medicated Communication (CMC) interaction as the salient feature of successful online focus groups. Following this, I discuss several conceptual, practical and technological concerns, including: recruitment issues, research design issues, moderating issues and ethical issues. The present chapter draws on knowledge and insights gathered via three sets of online focus groups that I have conducted personally or in which I have been actively involved as a mentor: a set of more than 50 synchronous focus groups conducted via online messaging tools; a set of 10 audio focus groups conducted via Skype; and a set of 15 video focus groups, conducted via the ZOOM conferencing tool.

The Temporal Structure of Venues for Conducting Online Focus Groups

Data collection with online focus groups is conducted in various online venues. These venues typically differ in their temporal structure. According to the nature of computer mediated communication (CMC) there are synchronous or asynchronous (Jacobson 1999; Mann and Stewart 2000) online venues. Based on this distinction, there are two types of online focus groups: synchronous online focus groups and asynchronous online focus groups. Synchronous focus groups closely resemble 'real time' focus groups, as both researcher and respondent(s) are online simultaneously. 'Real time' interaction – if not properly moderated and addressed beforehand – can result in short and blurred answers from participants.

Synchronous CMC usually occurs via applications such as chat rooms, various instant messaging applications (Audium, MSN, AIM, Google Hangouts, Gaim, Trillian, Kadu, Pidgin, etc.) and Web Messaging facilities (e.g. Facebook Live Messenger, etc.). Further, there are various audio-visual applications (Skype, AnyMeeting, Google Hangouts, Facebook Video Chat, etc.) and web-conferencing applications (ZOOM, Meetings.io, etc.). These resources are now being used ever more frequently, since the integration of microphones and webcams into digital technologies (e.g. desktop, laptop, tablets, smartphones) has become the default practice. Most of these applications are free or easily affordable, easy to access, and many enable one-click audio-visual chat.

In contrast, asynchronous focus groups involve a certain time lag between researcher's posting the question and participants posting their answers. Asynchronous CMC, on the other hand, includes e-mail, newsgroups, mailing lists, bulletin boards, web logs (blogs), forums and other web resources (Jacobson 1999; Mann and Stewart 2000;

Ward 1999). In this chapter, the discussion is limited to synchronous online focus groups, because this format comes closest to matching traditional, face-to-face for groups. Still, it is worth knowing some of the advantages of asynchronous groups. In particular, the typing skills of a respondent are less of a constraint in asynchronous modes. In addition, the time lag between researcher's and respondent's online presence in asynchronous data collection can contributes to more exhaustive and reflective answers, as this facilitates more positive and intimacy-related exchanges (Walther 1995: 198). Further, participants can take more time to prepare their answers before entering them.

How It Is Done: Synchronous Text-Based Online Focus Groups

Text-based synchronous online focus groups are still the most commonly practiced form of online focus groups. Technologically, these are the least demanding, but at the same time the most different from face-to-face focus groups. Participants do not see or hear each other but merely establish their interaction through typing. As noted above, the typical online venue for this type of online focus groups are various instant messaging applications (Audium, MSN, AIM, Google Hangouts, etc.) and Web Messaging facilities (e.g. Facebook Live Messenger, Jive Chime, etc.).

Most of these online venues are readily available to the average computer user, and are often embedded in their computer's operating system or their web services, such as Google and Facebook services. The procedure for establishing such focus groups includes the standard procedures of locating, contacting, screening and recruiting participants (detailed discussion on this follows later in the chapter). Once the group has been composed, the participants meet at one on the instant messaging applications, as agreed upon beforehand with the moderator. Then, the groups takes the form of a classic instant messaging session, appearing within a window on each participant's screen, which allows the participant to interact, by adding their own comments to the ongoing stream that makes up the session (for an example, see Morgan and Lobe 2011: 202).

Typically, synchronous text-based online focus groups involve a high degree of responsiveness, and they are highly interactive due to the simultaneous online presence Chen and Hinton 1999). However, this can result in briefer and more superficial answers (see Mann and Stewart 2000; O'Conner and Madge 2003). This calls for an experienced moderator, as it is important to stimulate the participants to 'enter a discussion' rather than to merely 'answer the question' (Short 2006: 109). Another problem is that the classic process of turn taking can become blurred, as each person responds to whatever has appeared on their screens most recently. In this case, it helps to establish some ground rules about communication at the beginning of focus group. For example, it is important to ask the participants to enable the 'typing-in-progress indicator'. This is usually a small icon of a pencil or keyboard at the bottom of an instant messaging window, which indicates that someone is currently typing a message. We ask them to be aware of that icon when someone else is typing, so that they wait before taking their turn in the discussion. This is a rule similar to the one from face-to-face focus groups, that asks participants to only speak one person at the time, but it can be harder to implement.

Another issue in text-based groups is that typing skills can significantly influence the participation and interaction of those who type slower or faster. Hence, it is wise to make an initial screening before conducting the group and separate the slow and the fast typists into two different groups. As discussed later in the chapter, the optimal number of participants in text-based online focus groups ranges from three to four (Lobe 2008), so it is fairly easy to separate the total sample into small group according to typing skills.

A key or text-based online focus groups appears when it comes to transcriptions (which can take an enormous amount of time for face-to-face focus groups), because there is no need to transcribe the text-based sessions, (Christians and Chen 2004: 18; Oringderff 2004: 3). Also, there is no need to avoid transcription errors, as the data are recorded in the exact form that other participants saw it. This means that text-based groups produce one of the rare forms of data that are not mediated in any way by the researcher (recorded, transcribed). The output of the participants is the direct input for the analysis, and data logs gained from text-based online focus groups can be directly imported into data different types of data analysis software.

To accomplish this, it is necessary to activate the automatic-logging option in the chat application before starting the focus group. Usually, it says something like 'chat logging enabled', 'enable logging conversations', 'enable chat logging', 'log all instant messages', 'log chat', 'enable chat transcriptions' or similar. Some instant messaging applications, like Skype chat and Facebook Live Messenger, offer an opt out option, where all the logs are automatically logged if not chosen differently by the user ('delete chat history', 'delete logs', 'save chat history: never', 'disable chat logging' etc.).

In general, text-based online focus groups are easy to set up, as well as time and cost effective. Data can be collected considerably more quickly (e.g. saving time for driving to the venue of focus groups, avoiding the cost of hiring the venue, and eliminating transcription costs). But, if organizational issues are not discussed in detail with participants (e.g. how long the discussion will take; how to solve distraction issues), then text-based focus groups can last for several hours and may no longer compensate for transcription savings.

Like all forms of online focus groups, a significant feature is the absence of geographical and temporal limitations. Depending on time zones, data can be collected 24 hours a day (Christians and Chen 2004: 19; Joinson 2005: 21) from a vast population of all kinds of individuals across the globe, which can be reached more easily than ever before (Coomber 1997: 1). For example, a researcher from any country can set up an online focus groups with participants based anywhere in the world without having to consider travel costs, venue, etc. Further, digital technologies make things easier on the participants' side, as they need to allocate less time and effort to participate in online focus groups. Besides having fewer struggles with juggling schedules, chat-based focus groups minimize concerns about personal appearance (Morgan and Lobe 2011: 201). These freedoms may persuade some individuals to participate who would not normally take part in face-to-face focus groups (Oringderff 2004).

How It Is Done: Synchronous Audio and Video-Based Online Focus Groups

Synchronous audio and video-based online focus groups are technologically more demanding, as the participants need to have a digital device with functional microphone and camera. Increasingly, laptops, tablets, and mobile phones have these functionalities built in. The appropriate online venues (i.e. applications) must support real-time audio and full-motion video imaging. There are various audio-video applications (Skype, Google Hangouts, Facebook Video Chat, etc.) and web-conferencing applications (ZOOM, Meetings.io, WebEx Adobe Connect, AnyMeeting, etc.) available to the users.

Tuttas (2015) lists ten criteria, to be used in selecting an online platform that is suitable for online audio and video-based focus groups. She emphasizes the importance of choosing an application that supports meetings attended by up to ten people. Recordings of audio and video must be possible, and their access must be restricted to the research team only. Further, the applications must be easy for the participants to use, requiring no more than moderate digital competency. It is also important that participants do not need to purchase and install any software to attend the meeting. Finally, only invited participants should be able to enter the online venue.

Audio and video online focus groups are very similar to one another, the only difference being that the video is turned off when conducting audio-only focus groups. Once the participants are recruited and the online venue selected, participants can enter the discussion in two ways. First, they can be called into the group discussion by the moderator, (e.g. Skype or Google hangouts). In this case, participants need to have the latest version of the application already downloaded to their digital device. When they answer, they are a part of a group call, where they can share voice or video. Usually, the contents of a screen as well as photos can be shared in audio and video calls, if needed for the purpose of focus group. These types of audio and video applications are free of charges for the researchers and participants; however, both need to have pre-existing accounts to enter the call. These types of applications are more sensitive to the quality of internet connection, and the quality of sound and video is worse with greater numbers of participants, but they the advantage of being available on any digital device, including tablets and smartphones.

The second way that participants can join online video and audio discussions is to be invited to via various web conferencing services (ZOOM, WebEx Adobe Connect, AnyMeeting, etc.). In this case, they are initially instructed to visit the official webpage of the service and download a free plug in. This procedure is fairly easy and it takes literally only a few seconds. Usually, a researcher must have a paid account on one of these services, in order to invite participants. Once that account is activated, the researcher can easily set up the discussion by clicking on the icon, saying 'Start the video' or similar. Next, the researcher is instructed to enter the email addresses of the participants, who then receive the link to the web conference. The researcher can also copy-paste the URL for the invitation to invite participants by other means (including instant messaging, Skype, Facebook, etc.). In addition, Skype recently made a change, and is now offering a URL sharing option, where anyone can join without having a Skype application or account. However, the mainstream use of Skype. where greater quality of voice and video is assured, is still via the application.

When participants click on their invitation links, providing they downloaded the plug in beforehand, they are immediately at the meeting venue. Each participant sees a real-time, window on their own screen, where the size can be adjusted as needed. Those windows usually include options for sharing voice, video, and text. Each participant can see the video of other participants and of the researcher. The person who is speaking is usually highlighted in the main screen, while other participants and their reactions are seen in smaller screens. The moderator has the option to remove the participant, to add participants, rename them and mute them.

The services in these invitational applications are typical less sensitive to the quality of internet connection, and the quality of video is usually better with a greater number of participants. However, they are more challenging than application-based software for use on tablets and smartphones (this largely depends on the quality of a tablet or a smartphone). The optimal number of participants for audio and video online focus groups with these invitational applications is up to ten.

For both categories of application, the audio and video discussions can be recorded. Some applications need an additional plug-in to be installed (e.g. Skype), whilst other enable this by just clicking on the button 'record' (e.g. ZOOM, WebEx, AnyMeeting). The audio recordings are similar to the ones from face-to-face focus groups and can be treated in the same way. When it comes to video recording, however, there is one disadvantage in comparison to a video recorded face-to-face focus group, because the online video recording does not show the image of any other participants apart from the one that was speaking at a given time. This might pose a problem for researchers who are used to working with video recording of focus groups (Tuttas 2015).

An earlier section mentioned different typing skills as a possible obstacle in text-based focus groups. In audio and video focus groups, typing usually is not the primary source of interaction (however, participants may have the capacity write a question or a comment to the moderator. when the built-in chat is feature is activated). Instead, the quality of audio and video can be possibly problematic, depending on the different applications and services chosen. The internet connection and digital device quality issues are the most frequent problems that occur during such focus groups. It is advisable for the researcher to check the internet connection of every invited participant by setting up a short conversation with him. In doing so, the researcher gets an idea, how the connection works for that specific participant. Accordingly, the researcher can screen participants with problematic (slower) connections, and create a separate group when needed. If one or more participants experience internet connection problems, it is better to limit the interaction to audio only as the video part is often what causes technical problems.

Following the connection, it is advisable to set the basic rules about noise and disturbances before the focus groups starts. Usually prior to the focus group, we ask participants to choose a quiet room in their home, where nobody will interrupt them and the voices from their surrounding will not disturb the ongoing discussion. At the beginning of a focus group, when participants enter the application or web service, we ask them to switch off all other devices. Further, we may ask them to keep their microphone muted when they are not talking, by simply clicking the 'mute' button when they are not talking, and turning it back on when they want to enter the discussion. By doing so, none of the background noise from participants will disturb the discussion. It can take a couple of minutes for them to get used to this procedure, so the researcher should allow time for this adjustment. Even though this might look redundant to requesting a quiet setting, it can significantly improve the quality of recordings.

All the advantages of cost and time effectiveness as well as geographical coverage identified in the section about text-based online focus groups apply equally to audio and video focus groups. Despite the fact that transcriptions need to be done in the traditional way, audio and video focus groups still save time and costs by eliminating travel to the venue by researchers and participants. Greater flexibility of attendance (being able to attend from their home or wherever they have a good quality internet connection and effective digital device) can encourage a wider range of participants to attend the focus group.

Social Interaction, CMC Interaction, and Online Focus Groups

As stated above, social interaction is crucial moment for establishing a productive group dynamic in focus groups. Morgan (2010) argues that interaction in focus groups is the central concern of every focus group project. He treats this interaction as based on shared meanings that are created and negotiated by the participants in the course of their interaction. Following the classic framework of Symbolic Interactionism, all the participants in a focus group simultaneously conceive of both their own role and the roles that others play (Morgan 2012: 161). He draws upon 'Cooley's (1909) concept of the "looking-glass self," where individuals find the meanings of their own actions in the reactions of others' (Morgan 2012: 161). Therefore, social context cues are essential to establishing high quality interaction in focus groups.

Social context cues include various aspects of the physical environment such as information about the time, geographical location, along with nonverbal behaviours such as nodding approval, frowning with pleasure etc. (Sproull and Kiesler 1986: 1495). Nonverbal interaction can also be a direct source of data in video-recorded offline focus groups (Morgan and Lobe 2011: 219). Early internet behaviour studies argued that interaction in online settings was considerably divergent from equivalent behaviours in real life (Kiesler et al. 1984; Kiesler and Sproull 1986; Sproull 1986). Such behaviour divergence has mostly been attributed to the reduced availability social context cues during CMC (Kiesler et al. 1984), which would presumably make the research setting impersonal and anonymous (Kiesler and Sproull 1986: 405). From this standpoint, the lack of visual cues and nonverbal communication in CMC would weaken online interaction in comparison to the richness of real-time, face-to-face interactions (Joinson 2005: 22). This criticism was especially appropriate for early online focus groups, which were all text-based, and thus notoriously lacking visual and social context cues.

If similar limitations on interaction were universally the case with CMC, it would have serious consequences for online research methods in general and online focus groups in particular, because social context cues influence information exchange through perception, cognitive interpretation and communication behaviour (Sproull and Kiesler 1986: 1494). However, already by end of 1980s some studies on Internet behaviour (Kiesler and Sproull 1986; Martin and Nagao 1989; Sproull and Kiesler 1986) proved positive effects of CMC as a research setting, despite little social information being conveyed. Further research showed that CMC can be depicted as highly socialized, more regulated by norms and more intimate than face-to-face interaction precisely due to the lack of social context cues (Joinson 2005: 22). Joinson (2001, 2003) and Walther (1995, 1996, 2002) have contributed experimental evidence which rejects the view that the absence of nonverbal and visual cues eliminated online interaction's ability to exchange individualizing information.

For example, Walther's study on relational communication (1995: 195) provides some surprising results, showing higher immediacy/affection for CMC than for face-to-face communication. He conducted an experimental study exploring the effects of computer conferencing on the interpersonal messages that people use to define their relationships, known as relational communication. Observers then rated that relational communication from transcripts of text-based CMC conversations or from videotapes of face-to-face three-person groups, testing for intimacy-related dimensions of relational communication (Walther 1995). Walther further suggested that, being free of concerns about their appearance, people could be more focused on their inner self and thus more willing to share their personal feelings and thoughts (Walther 1996)

Similarly, Nguyen and Alexander (1996: 104) argue that due to the lack of visual cues, people can possess greater control over their self-presentation, consequently resulting in increased sociability, friendliness and openness. According to Kitchin (1998: 394), the CMC environment provides a 'disembodying experience', where people find themselves 'free of the constraints of the body'; they are accepted on the basis of their written words, not what they look or sound like (Kitchin 1998: 386–387). This disembodiment signifies that a person's online identity can be separated from their physical presence (Slater 2002: 536) – especially in text- and audio-based focus groups. For instance, if participants in an online focus group do not perceive themselves as being evaluated according to their physical characteristics, and they think they do not have to worry about their appearance, then they might have a tendency to be more open than in face-to-face focus groups.

Table 11.1 shows a comparison between face-to-face focus groups and various forms of online focus groups with respect to how social context cues are tackled.

In traditional face-to-face focus groups, moderators are able to observe directly the participation of every individual in the group. This includes non-verbal communication in the form of facial expression, eye movement, gesticulation, tone of voice, etc. The same is true of para-verbal cues such as 'um' and 'ur.' Shifting from moderating to data analysis, if face-to-face groups are only audio recorded, all non-verbal communication and visual cues will be lost. Using video cameras, both verbal and nonverbal communication can be easily documented (Mwanga et al. 1998: 708) – although it can be difficult to collect high quality non-verbal data when just one camera is used to capture an entire group. In text-based online focus groups, non-verbal communication, visual, emotional and context cues are basically non-existent, whilst para-verbal

Table 11.1 Comparison of various online groups according to social context cues

Social context cues	Face-to-face groups	Text-based online groups	Audio only online groups	Audio-visual online groups
Non-verbal communication	Easily, observed, and can be video recorded	Non-existent	Non-existent	Mostly limited to current speaker
Para-verbal communication ('um', 'er', etc.)	Easily observed, and can be audio recorded	Easily observed	Easily observed, and can be recorded	Easily observed, and can be recorded
Visual cues	Easily observed, and can be video recorded	Non-existent	Non-existent	Easily observed, and can be recorded
Emotional cues	Easily observed, and can be written in field notes	Difficult to be observed	Limited but can be written in field notes	Limited but can be written in field notes
Context cues	Easily observed, and can be written in field notes	Non-existent	Limited but can be written in field notes	Limited but can be written in field notes

communication comes in various forms, as participants write them explicitly. For example, huh, hm, uhum, ah, er, etc. are found in almost every text-based focus group transcription. In audio-only focus groups, we get the mix of face-to-face and text-only, as we are able to pick up most para-verbal communication and some degree of emotional and context cues. In video-based online focus groups, non-verbal communication is limited to the current speaker as their video image is typically enlarged; emotional and context cues are limited for the same reason.

Logistic and Organizational Issues in Face-to-Face and Online Focus Groups

Recruitment Issues

With face-to-face groups, it can be difficult to locate the participants for topics that seek specific populations. Also, recruitment is limited by geographic localities when identifying the desired participants through social network advertising and snowball sampling, so that they can convene in the same place. Therefore, it is considerably easier to locate participants who may match specialized criteria for purposive sampling through online focus groups. In particular, the means to contact participants in the recruitment process are more diverse online (e.g. not only telephone, email, but also, instant messaging, forum private messages, social media sites etc.). Plus, 'no show' participants can be easier to replace with online recruitment (Lobe 2008). Comparing the three types of online focus groups, there are no major differences in recruitment.

Research Design Issues

Comparing the research design of online and offline focus groups, Morgan and Lobe (2011) suggest looking closely at into four issues: the degree of structure of the discussion: the group composition the appropriate number of participants; and ethical issues. For the purpose of this discussion I cover the first two topics, with ethical issues addressed in a separate section. Focus groups that require a more structured approach, with carefully moderated discussion and a larger set of focused questions, are especially challenging for text-based online focus groups. The moderator's role is more effectively developed and the ability to keep a 'tight' discussion is easier in audio and video online focus groups, which makes them well-suited to both more and less structured approaches. But, the online environment, where participants are physically displaced, does create more room for disturbances at each person's site, and this poses further challenges for effective moderating. Hence, the starting instructions should be carefully considered and dealt with in online focus groups, clearly stating at minimum the key points to which participants should adhere (for instance, the posting and replying rules in text-based groups and the strategies for avoiding disturbances in audio and video groups, etc.).

The group composition issues deals with the recruitment of appropriate participants who both match the research topic and are able to generate a high quality group dynamic. For online focus groups, the researcher has a greater variety of options for composing an adequate group, as it is easier to locate specific categories of participants (see the above discussion on the recruitment and sampling). This can be quite useful for conducting projects that separate the participants into different sets of groups or 'segments,' because that strategy requires even more refined recruitment.

The number of participants in focus groups is another issue that differs greatly for the various modes of online focus groups. It also considerably depends on the personal involvement of participants with the topic. In offline focus groups, the recommended number of participants in a typical focus group with low to medium involvement is approximately 7–8 and 4–6 with high involvement (Morgan 1997). Group size is vital in online focus groups, most notably in a synchronous text-based format. For example, a discussion in a group with too many participants can move so rapidly that it can skim over complex issues that need to be addressed (Mann and Stewart 2000: 113). Further, if the discussion is held in real-time text-based chat, one can only reply as fast as one can type, which can give dominance over the discussion to those participants able to type faster. Therefore, the discussion will not be initiated or shared equally by all. As the higher number of participants in online focus groups directly contributes to increased interaction, control over the group interaction is considerably more sensitive to the number of participants than it is in offline focus groups. Therefore, groups including 3–5 participants are most appropriate for text-based online groups.

The number of participants in audio and video online focus groups is typically somewhat smaller than for face-to-face groups. In online audio groups, this is because it is more difficult to keep track of the other participants when they cannot be seen. Even when visual contact is available through online video groups, it is wise not to use too large a group, because the section of the screen showing the other participants can get crowded for those who do not have large monitors. The recommended size would thus be 4–6.

Moderation Issues

The moderating style is of crucial importance to the quality of data. Compared to text-based groups, moderation is more straightforward in audio and video online focus groups, where it is quite similar to that in face-to-face focus groups, including. However, participants are still physically displaced, which means that there is an increased possibility of disturbances and distractions but are easily detected. As noted earlier, the moderator should try to avoid this problem by introducing basic rules prior to the discussion itself (e.g. turn off mobile phones and other devised, choose a quiet room, try not have others in the room while participating, turn off other applications on the computer, etc.).

Things are more complicated in synchronous text-based focus groups. Some of the basic issues, such as asking questions, should pose no bigger problem online. However, more demanding techniques of moderation should be carefully considered in advance, such as following up on participants' responses, coping with off-topic discussion and side conversations, and managing overly active exchanges. In particular, with text-based groups, it can be difficult for the moderator to react to these issues on a timely basis. Hence, if possible, these issues should covered be during the instructions for the group.

Ethical Issues

Like any other new research method, online focus groups require a thorough consideration by scholars on how to tackle the issue of ethics. The first issue that arises is whether we need to develop a whole new set of ethical guidelines for research conducted online or whether it is sufficient to apply general research ethical guidelines to the new environment. Thomas (2004: 187) argues, there is no need for inventing 'new ethical rules for online research or try to reduce ethical behaviour in online research – or any other – to an immutable set of prescriptions and proscriptions.' What he suggests is 'an increased awareness of and commitment to' already established ethical principles that apply across traditional research methods (2004: 187). On the other hand, Hine (2005a: 5) makes a plea for a re-examination of the 'institutionalised understandings of the ethics of research' as 'online research is marked as a special category.' The specificity of online research venue is particularly emphasized by Charles Ess and the Ethics working committee of the Association of Internet Researchers (2002: 3). Ess (2004: 254) notes that the following central issues are identified by a number of ethics committees: respect for persons (as the fundamental value), privacy, confidentiality, informed consent, anonymity-pseudonymity, risk/benefits for participants, risk/benefits for the social good, public versus private space, subject compensation, justice, cross-cultural issues, special/vulnerable populations, deception, nondisclosure, conflicts of interest and research misconduct.

In spite of the fact that many of the above issues closely resemble issues central to general research ethics, there are also differences that need to be carefully considered. As explicated in the AoIR ethics report (Ess and Committee 2002: 4–6), there is a greater risk to individual privacy and confidentiality because of the enhanced accessibility to information about individuals, groups and their communication. Next, researchers could face a greater challenge in obtaining informed consent, due to the greater difficulty in ascertaining a participant's identity, due to the use of pseudonyms, multiple online identities, etc. Finally, it is more difficult to discern ethically correct approaches due to the greater diversity of online venues (emails, chat rooms, web pages, instant messaging, discussion forums etc.) and the wide reach of the media involved (people from different cultural and legal settings). Amongst these issues, concerns about informed consent and issues of confidentiality and privacy are particular relevant for online focus groups, regardless of the specific format being use.

Informed consent: Informed consent is a condition whereby research participants can be said to have given consent for participation in the research that is based upon their full appreciation and understanding of the facts surround the research, as well as any implications their participation in the research might have for them. Usually, the statement of informed consent is given in a written form that is signed by each participant. The content of the informed consent in all forms of online focus groups can be identical to those used in face-to-face focus groups; only the medium of delivery differs. If participants are willing to go by their real name, not nicknames, then the consent can be sent as an email attachment, printed, signed, scanned and sent back by each participant (or signed electronically when this is an option). Alternatively, the statement of consent can be written in the body text of an email, and participants express consent by replying to that email; in that case, the email from the participant's account suffices as a signature.

Anonymity: When people decide to participate in face-to-face focus groups offline, there is a degree of disclosure within the group. Other participants learn each other's first names, and see and hear each other, but are not necessary aware of further details, such as their surname, etc. In text-based focus groups, participants have the largest potential for full anonymity, because as little as their nick names can be revealed. However, other participants may still be able to obtain information, such as IP addresses, depending on which software the researcher uses. This means that if the researcher is promising anonymity to the participants, this will require careful investigation of any limitations in the software being used.

In video-focus groups, the anonymity can be considered in a similar way as in face-to-face focus groups. Usually, participants can be heard and seen, and their names are revealed as usually they enter the video-conferencing software. Further, some images of their surroundings may be recorded, so that other participants can see details in their homes, offices, etc. Therefore, it is useful to remind the participants in advance to use some location with a neutral background. If this is not possible, then warn participants that parts of their immediate environment will be revealed by participating in the video-based focus group, and possibly even include a statement on this issue in the informed consent forms.

Confidentiality: Confidentiality in focus groups mainly concerns what has been said and who has the access to this information. In face-to-face focus groups, the moderator records the data and the audio recording is typically destroyed shortly after the transcriptions are made. As noted earlier, text-based online focus groups, often provide an option for automatic logging of the data. As much as this can be the advantage in terms of transcription, it can also pose major threats to confidentiality for participants sharing their experiences. Therefore, it is important to remind the participants to turn their automatic logging option off, so that no one other than the researcher will have a transcription of the conversation. Of course, there is no guarantee that participants will actually disable their logging feature.

Applications for audio and video based online focus groups usually restrict recording to the person who created the discussion and not to the people who are invited to participate. Nevertheless, it is wise to remind the participants in advance not to try to record any part of the conversation in order to ensure confidentiality for everyone involved.

Privacy and security issues: In online focus groups, regardless of the format, there always be privacy and security issues that are inherent to the platforms and online services used. We know the famous saying: Once something is put online, it stays online! Therefore, it is important to investigate the privacy and data collection policies of the platforms and services we use, since these sources often collect some information. This may or may not pose an issue for our research. Some of the services may not provide the level of privacy, desired for online focus groups on sensitive issues (e.g. personal traumatic experiences, socially unacceptable practices, sensate health issues, etc.). Therefore, it is of the upmost importance to share this fact with participants, reminding them that to some degree information is going to be shared with the third party, whether it be platform or service provider. It is best to include this in the informed consent form.

Conclusions

We live in a world in which technology changes faster than most of us are able to comprehend. Therefore, it is difficult to give definitive answers and recommendations on how to how conduct online focus groups in an optimal fashion. Whatever format we choose, the platforms and means of communication are changing rapidly, at the same time that people are getting more and more skilled in the use of digital technologies. Too often, the concerns and questions we had yesterday become irrelevant tomorrow. All these factors require researchers to continuously update their technological knowledge and skills, in order to conduct as online focus groups as successfully as possible.

References

Abrams, K. M., Wang, Z., Song, Y. J., & Galindo-Gonzalez, S. (2015) 'Data Richness Trade-Offs between Face-to-Face, Online Audivisual and Online Text Only Focus Groups'. *Social Science computer review*, 33(1): 80–96.

Chen, P., & Hinton, S. M. (1999) 'Realtime interviewing using the world wide web'. *Sociological Research Online*, http://www.socresonline.org.uk/4/3/chen.html 4/3 (accessed15 January 2006): 21.

Christians, C. G., & Chen, S. S.-L. (2004) 'Introduction: Technological environments and the evolution of social research methods', In M. D. Johns, S. S.-L Chen & G.J. Hall (eds.), *Online Social Research: Methods, Issues, & Ethics*. New York/Oxford: Peter Lang, pp. 15–23.

Cooley, C. H. (1909) *Social Organization: A Study of the Larger Mind*. New York, NY: Scribner's.

Coomber, R. (1997) 'Using the internet for survey research'. *Sociological Research Online*, http://www.socresonline.org.uk/2/2.

Ess, C. (2004) 'Epilogue: Are we there yet? Emerging ethical guidelines for online research', In M. D. Johns, S. S.-L Chen & G. J. Hall (eds.), *Online Social Research: Methods, Issues, & Ethics*. New York/Oxford: Peter Lang, pp. 253–263.

Ess, C., & Committe, A. E. W. (2002) *Ethical Decision Making and Internet Research*. Association of Internet Researchers. Available at: http://www.aoir.org/reports/ethics.pdf.

Hine, C. (2005) 'Virtual methods and the sociology of Cyber-Social-Scientific knowledge', In C. Hine (ed.), *Virtual Methods*. Oxford: Berg, pp. 1–13.

Hine, C. (ed.) (2005a) *Virtual Methods: Issues in Social Research on the Internet*. Oxford: Berg.

Jacobson, D. (1999) 'Doing research in cyberspace'. *Field Methods*, 11(2): 127–145.

Jankowski, N. W. (1999) 'In search of methodological innovation in new media research'. *The European Journal of Communication Research*, 24(3): 367–374.

Joinson, A. N. (2001) 'Self-disclosure in computer-mediated communication: The role of self-awareness and visual anonymity'. *European Journal of Social Psychology*, 31: 177–192.

Joinson, A. N. (2003) *Understanding the Psychology of Internet Behaviour: Virtual Worlds, Real Lives*. Basingstoke: Palgrave Macmillan.

Joinson, A. N. (2005) 'Internet behaviour and the design of virtual methods', In C. Hine (ed.), *Virtual Methods: Issues in Social Research on the Internet*. Oxford: Berg, pp. 21–34.

Kenny, A. (2005). 'Interaction in cyberspace: An online focus group'. *Journal of Advanced Nursing*, 49(4): 414–422.

Kiesler, S., & Sproull, L. S. (1986) 'Response effects in the electronic survey'. *Public Opinion Quarterly*, 50(3): 402–413.

Kiesler, S., Siegal, J., & McGuire, T. W. (1984) 'Social psychological aspects of computer mediated communication'. *American Psychologist*, 39: 1123–1134.

Kitchin, R. M. (1998) 'Towards geographies of cyberspace'. *Progress in Human Geography*, 22(3): 385–406.

Lobe, B. (2008). *Integration of online research methods. Information technology/social/informatics collection*. Ljubljana: University of Ljubljana, Faculty of Social Sciences.

Mann, C., & Stewart, F. (2000) *Internet Communication and Qualitative Research: A Handbook*. London: Sage.
Martin, C. L., & Nagao, D. H. (1989) 'Some effects of computerized interviewing on job application responses'. *Journal of Applied Psychology*, 74: 72–80.
Morgan, D. L. (1988) *Focus Groups as Qualitative Research*. Thousand Oaks, CA: Sage.
Morgan, D. L. (1997) *Focus Groups as Qualitative Research*. Thousand Oaks/ London: Sage.
Morgan, D. L. (2010) 'Focus groups and social interaction', In J. F. Gubrium, J. A. Holstein, A. B. Marvasti & K. D. McKinney (eds.), *The SAGE Handbook of Interview Research: The Complexity of the Craft*. Thousand Oaks, CA/London: Sage Publications, pp. 161–176.
Morgan, D. L. (2012) 'Focus groups and social interaction', In J. Gubrium & J. Holstein (eds.), *The SAGE Handbook of Interview Research* (2nd ed.). Thousand Oaks, CA: Sage Publications, pp. 161–176.
Morgan, D. L., & Lobe, B. (2011) 'Online focus groups', In S. N. Hesse-Biber (ed.), *The Handbook of Emergent Technologies in Social Research*. Oxford: Oxford University Press, pp. 199–230
Mwanga, J. R., Mugasche, C. L., Magnussen, P., Gabone, R.M., & Aagaard-Hansen, J. (1998) 'Perls, Pith and Provocation: Experiences from Video-Recorded Focus Group Discussions on Schistosomiases in Magu, Tanzania'. *Qualitative Health Research*, 8(5): 707–717.
Nguyen, D. T., & Alexander, J. (1996) 'The coming of cyberspacetime and the end of polity', In R. Shields (ed.), *Cultures of Internet: Virtual Spaces, Real Histories, Living Bodies*. London: Sage, pp. 99–124.
O'Conner, H., & Madge, C. (2003) '"Focus groups in cyberspace": Using the Internet for qualitative research'. *Qualitative Market Research: An International Journal*, 6(2): 133–143.
Oringderff, J. (2004) '"My Way": Piloting an online focus group'. *International Journal of Qualitative Methods*, 3(3). Article 5. Retrieved 17/07/2016 from http://www.ualberta.ca/~iiqm/backissues/3_3/html/oringderff.html.
Short, S. E. (2006) 'Focus group interviews', In E. Perecman & S. R. Curran (eds.), *A Handbook for Social Science Field Research: Essays & Bibliographic Sources on Research Design and Methods*. London: Sage, pp. 103–115.
Slater, D. (2002) 'Social relationships and identity online and offline', In L. A. Lievrouw & S. M. Livingstone (eds.), *Handbook of New Media: Social Shaping and Consequences of ICTs*. London: Sage, pp. 533–546.

Sproull, L. S. (1986) 'Using electronic email for data collection in organizational research'. *Academy of Management Review*, 74: 159–169.

Sproull, L. S., & Kiesler, S. (1986) 'Reducing social context clues: Electronic mail in organizational communications'. *Management Science*, 32(11): 1492–1512.

Stewart, K., & Williams, M. (2005) 'Researching online populations: The use of focus groups for social research'. *Qualitative Research*, 5(4): 395–416.

Stover, C., & Goodman, L. (2012, August). 'The use of online synchronous focus groups in a sample of lesbian, gay, and bisexual college students'. *Computers, Informatics, Nursing*, 395–399.

Terrance, A. L., Johnson, G. M., & Walther, J. B. (1993) 'Understanding the communication process in focus groups', In D. L. Morgan (ed.), *Successful Focus Groups: Advancing the State of the Art*. Thousand Oaks, CA: Sage Publications, pp. 51–64.

Thomas, J. (2004) 'Re-examining the ethics of internet research: Facing the challenge of overzealous oversight', In M. D. Johns, S. S.-L. Chen & G. J. Hall (eds.), *Online Social Research: Methods, Issues, & Ethics*. New York/Oxford: Peter Lang, pp. 187–201.

Tuttas, C. A. (2015) 'Lessons learned using web conference technology for online focus group interviews'. *Qualitative Health Research*, 25(1): 122–133.

Walther, J. B. (1995) 'Relational aspects of computer-mediated communication: Experimental observations over time'. *Organizational Science*, 6(2): 402–413.

Walther, J. B. (1996) 'Computer-mediated communication: Impersonal, interpersonal, and hyperpersonal interaction'. *Communication Research*, 23(1): 3–43.

Walther, J. B., & Parks, M. R. (2002) 'Cues filtered out, cues filtered in: Computer mediated communication and relationships', In M. L. Knapp & J. A. Daly (eds.), *Handbook of Interpersonal Communication*. Thousand Oaks, CA/London: Sage Publications, pp. 529–563.

Ward, K. J. (1999) 'The cyber-ethnographic (re)construction of two feminist online communities'. *Sociological Research Online*, http://www.socresonline.org.uk/4/1.

Williams, S., & Reid, M. (2012). '"It's like there are two people in my head": A phenomenological exploration of anorexia nervosa and its relationship to the self'. *Psychology & Health*, 27(7): 798–815.

Bojana Lobe is an Assistant Professor at the Faculty of Social Sciences, University of Ljubljana (UL), where she teaches various methods courses, including Social Science Data Collection and Digital Technologies. Her research interests include online qualitative research methods, integration of qualitative and quantitative methods online, qualitative comparative analysis, researching children's experiences with mixed methods. She has authored a book Integration of Online Research Methods. She is a member of the research programme Social Science Methodology, Statistics and Informatics at UL. She is also an associate researcher at Universite Catholique de Louvain, Belgium. She is a member of Management Committee at COST Action The digital literacy and multimodal practices of young children (DigiLitEY). She has been actively involved in EU Kids Online project (www.eukidsonline.net) since 2006 and was a leading researcher in Slovenian biggest project about children's usage of internet in Slovenia since 2009 Mladi na netu (www.mladinanetu.si). She is also involved in the recent project about Young children (0–8) and digital technologies funded by JRC.

12

Performance-Based Focus Groups

Jennifer Wooten

Introduction: What Are Performance-Based Focus Groups?

Performance-based focus groups (PBFGs) in many ways resemble traditional focus groups in that the researcher-facilitator assembles a group of people with some connection to the topic to be explored. The principal difference, however, is that PBFGs include active engagement of participants' bodies as a mode of exploration. Such physical engagement may include activities resembling games, sculpting images with the body, and/or theatrical role-playing. PBFGs informed by Augusto Boal's (1979, 1992/2002, 1995) work generally involve all three and allow us to ask, 'what will we find out if we do it this way?' (Jackson 1995: xxiii).

As I argue throughout this chapter, PBFGs incorporating Boal's work are a method of possibility. In providing a space in which participants

---

J. Wooten (✉)
University of Florida, Florida, Gainesville, USA
e-mail: wooten@ufl.edu

can explore a topic in an embodied way, PBFGs make it possible for participants to analyze why they perform as they do and how they might perform differently. Performing differently, in turn, opens the possibility that participants will be changed as a result of the study. To highlight what is possible in PBFGs, in this chapter I describe: how Boal's theatrical techniques in a focus group setting allow participants' bodies to become sites of investigation, analysis, and change; why I selected PBFGs as the principal mode of data collection in a study on the linguistic and cultural identities of non-native teachers of Spanish in the US; what the PBFGs in my study looked like in practice; what data were produced; and what PBFGs potentially offer participants and researchers.

Background and Rationale: How Do Boalian Theatrical Techniques Inform PBFGs?

Boal, a Brazilian theatre director and activist, developed his theatre as a way to combat the dualisms of mind/body, verbal/physical, and spectator/actor to encourage a synthesis of the terms: 'all human beings are actors (they act!) and spectators (they observe!). They are spect-actors' (Boal 1992/2002: 15). Boal's theatre (1979), christened Theatre of the Oppressed (TO) in homage to his friend and 'theoretical father' Paolo Freire (Flores 2000: 42), aims to 'stimulate debate (in the form of action, not just words), to show alternatives, to enable people "to become protagonists of their own lives"' (Jackson 1992/2002: xxiv). It is a theatre of critique designed to move from participants' experiences to the deconstruction of the systemic forces (i.e. discourses) which shape us. TO, then, starts at the level of the local and personal in order to critique the forces that made possible such an experience and others like it, as well as to imagine how those same forces may be shifted. Boal cautions, however, 'TO [...] brings no pat answers; it poses questions' (Boal 2001: 338).

Boal privileges the body as the mode of posing questions because 'the first word of the theatrical vocabulary is the human body, the main source of sound and movement' (1979: 125). TO is founded on the following principles: our bodies 'get shaped by our respective social, cultural, political, and economic rituals' (Louis 2005: 343); theatre, that is, the act of performing physically, allows us to view and interrogate these inscriptions written on our bodies; and by changing our bodily movements, or by performing differently, we can *be* different. Performances in TO, then, are not understood in the sense of entertainment – an artistic product to be enjoyed and mused over – but, rather, as 'action, reflexivity, and dialogue' (Louis 2005: 344) that 'reaffirm, resist, transgress, "re-inscribe or passionately reinvent" repressive understandings that circulate in daily life' (Denzin 2003: 10).

Babbage (1995) explains that Boal's work has been taken up in a number of ways, with practitioners adapting TO for their own contexts. Boal advocates for such adaptation, offering TO is 'not a Bible, nor a recipe book: it is a method to be used by people, and the people are more important than the method' (Boal 1998: 120). Practitioners and researchers throughout the world have used exercises in the TO 'arsenal' (Boal 1992/2002) in various contexts, including with urban youth groups (Sanders 2004), students who are reluctant to write (Creel et al. 2000), orphans (Szeman 2005), social workers (Houston et al. 2001), the elderly (Ferrand 1995), police recruits (Telesco and Solomon 2001), maximum security prisoners (Mitchell 2001), graduate students of occupational therapy (Brown and Gillespie 1997), and dental-care professionals (Pässilä et al. 2013). Published accounts often offer anecdotal accounts of the use of TO in community and professional settings, but the context in which TO has been most widely used and empirically documented is that of teacher education (Powers and Duffy 2016; Harman and Zhang 2015; Wooten and Cahnmann-Taylor 2014; Bhukhanwala and Allexsaht-Snider 2012; Harman and McClure 2011; Souto-Manning 2011; Cahnmann-Taylor and Souto-Manning 2010; Cahnmann-Taylor et al. 2009). These studies focus on how pre-service and in-service teachers collectively critique, confront, and redress conflicts in educational spaces related to language, culture, race, ethnicity, and social and economic status via focus groups employing TO methods. By posing research questions that necessitated the presence, movement, and analysis of teacher-participants' bodies, these researchers employed what I term PBFGs (group collaborations that involve theatrical techniques) as a mode of data collection in order to make the body a site of investigation.

In the study that I share in this chapter as an illustrative example, I used PBFGs incorporating TO as a method of data collection to study the linguistic and cultural identities of nine non-native teachers of Spanish in local secondary and tertiary schools. I wanted to learn what practices or strategies participants had used and continued to use to create themselves as Spanish language users and teachers and what the goals of such self-formation in/through another language and culture(s) were. I also wanted to know what resistance or tensions (e.g. internal/ intellectual, professional, social) participants confronted in the performance of their linguistic and cultural identities and how they might challenge these. While the individual interviews I conducted with participants were well-suited to learning about individual participants' paths to becoming Spanish language users and teachers, PBFGs allowed both me, as researcher, and participants to consider, deconstruct, and reimagine the polemical moments where their linguistic and cultural identities were contested. PBFGs allowed us to consider not only the words uttered by participants during the two four-hour sessions – including what participants said, how they said it, when they said it, and to whom they said it – but also the physical bodies of participants as they engaged in performative exercises to explore and represent those identities.

Drawing on the interstices of Judith Butler's work on performativity (1990/1999, 1993, 2004) and Boal's work on performance, I believe linguistic and cultural identities are brought into being by what one repeatedly says and does – the word and the body – within the confines of discourse. For investigative coherence, my study included research methods that elicited participants' verbal and physical responses. Because 'bodies bear the marks of our culture, practices, and policies' (Pillow 2000: 214), I believed my study would be incomplete if the body were to be excluded as a space for inquiry. My previous work on creating and the creation of additional linguistic and cultural identities (Wooten 2012) indicated that a speaker's body (including physical appearance and/or gestures) is often what gives her away as not being a member of a particular language community; though one's language proficiency may be advanced, a disconnect between the linguistic and the physical often leads to a fixing question along the lines of 'Where are you from?' Though a seemingly simple question, the context in which the question is asked can make answering uncomfortable. PBFGs employing Boalian techniques in particular, then, allowed me and participants to consider in what contexts these uncomfortable moments existed, what was at the root of the discomfort, and what options existed to answer back.

What Do Performance-Based Focus Groups Look Like in Practice?

PBFGs based on Boal's work can include several types of participatory activities: games are physical interactions used to de-mechanize the body from typical movements and to create a sense of community within the group; Image Theatre involves participants using their bodies like clay to sculpt images to get at what words cannot (easily) express; and Forum Theatre invites all participants to assume the role of *spect-actor* to observe an enacted conflict generated by the group and then to jump in as an actor to propose change. Because this type of focus group looks quite different from focus groups with which participants may have already been familiar, I provided written descriptions of PBFGs, shared some exercises that I had done in previous PBFGs, and explicitly asked participants if they had questions, comments, or concerns about the PBFGs.

PBFGs using Boalian techniques generally begin with a brief introduction to the method and the session's activities by the Joker, or the facilitator of the group. More than a facilitator, however, the Joker is considered a 'difficultator' (Jackson 1995: xix) who encourages an omnipresent critical edge by problematizing the group's responses throughout the session. After this briefing, the Joker leads group members through a series of physical games to warm up, create a sense of community, and de-mechanize the body, that is, to break the body from the habitual movements it performs daily. Boal, similar to Foucault (1975/1977), stresses that our bodies are continuously disciplined through the minute organization of the everyday. For example, teachers like those in my study are regulated not only spatially (e.g. confined to classrooms, often required to be at the front of the classroom, and made to navigate through many students, their desks, and belongings), but also temporally (e.g. made to conform to a bell schedule which regulates bodily functions, such as when to eat and when use the restroom). Such regulations on the teacher body, part of what Foucault terms 'disciplinary power' (1975/1977: 156), are designed to maintain order and efficiency and become normalized to the point of invisibility.

Games

Boal's games aim to interrupt such repetitive acts. In *Games for actors and non-actors* (1992/2002), Boal describes hundreds of games to do such work, including those that challenge the space participants occupy, how they walk, how they see and mimic objects and others, and how they hear and produce sounds. Besides aiming to de-mechanize the body, these exercises are often metaphorically significant, as in 'Colombian Hypnosis' (Boal 1992/2002: 51–55) – the most ubiquitous Boalian game - and Big Chief (Boal, 1992/2002, p. 101). Colombian Hypnosis involved a leader in a pair moving her palm in different directions as the follower attempted to maintain the original position and distance between her face and the leader's palm at all times. Big Chief required participants to enact a leader's movements so well that a participant who left the room and reentered after the leader was selected could not discern who the leader in the group was.

We took our seats to debrief, and I first asked participants how they felt as they played these first two games and second how the games might metaphorically represent language learning and teaching. Lucy immediately responded that the games had an imitative quality and that they reminded her of how she tried to act like Spaniards in specific ways during her last visit. I asked her to elaborate on "acting like," and she explained that how she walked through a plaza was just one example of the numerous activities that she enacted as Lucía, her alter ego in Spanish or "the part I'm playing in the culture." Group members recounted their own imitative actions, many of which they had detailed in great length during initial interviews and which led to my selection of these two games as the first of the series. Most emphasized the need to observe very closely and then try to 'look like' and 'act like' a speaker of the studied language/culture as the first steps to be a part of the target community. Conversation moved quickly to how these games represented the inability of these language users and teachers to flawlessly imitate the 'native speaker' (which was the first time the phrase was uttered in the first PBFG). Lucy said '... there's a slight hesitation when that's not your natural movement. That hesitation may be something picked up on by people that are in the IN group.' (Capitalized words indicate when a participant heavily stressed a word in an utterance.) This delay was first viscerally felt in games and then related to some 'off' action that gives the participants away as being a part from rather than a part of the target community.

Participants' talk about performative activities allows group members to share personal experiences, that is, the experience of physically doing the activities as well as their lived experiences prior to the focus group, and their interpretations of images and theatrical interventions (to be discussed below) as a means to question the discursive conditions that enable such experiences and interpretations. In other words, participants' bodies and words are used as tools to explore how bodies and language are mutually produced. Thus, the body and language both serve as the target and the arrow.

Image Theatre

Because the native speaker/non-native speaker binary was being explicitly used by participants to describe themselves in relation to others (including the idealized native speaker), we continued into Image Theatre, where participants sculpt their bodies like clay to 'create an issue, story, or experience' that 'becomes a form of text – a weave of potential meanings' (Linds 2006: 119). The image and the multiplicity of 'potential meanings' (Linds 2006: 119) is fundamental. The construction of various images based on one word, for example, reminds us '[w]ords have a denotation which can be found in dictionaries and a connotation which can only be found in the hearts of each one of us' (Boal 1995: 174). The different images are, thus, a physical manifestation of the inability of a word to mean one thing to all people. Additionally, the possibilities that participants place on an image as they describe or title it illustrates that the interpretation of an image constructed of bodies is multiple, too. Thus, this multiplicity of the word (created by the participants who sculpt the image with their bodies) and the image (spawned by those who interpret the image) opens several sites where critique may take place, such as focusing on how various images become associated with the word and how new meanings might be constructed.

I adapted an Image Theatre exercise called 'Image of a word' (Boal 1992/2002: 176–183) in the first PBFG so participants could view and discuss how they saw themselves and others. The group collectively decided to first represent 'non-native teacher of Spanish,' and Amelia, Judith, and Lucy volunteered to show the first images of that category. Their images were evocative: Amelia placed her left hand on her hip and her right hand at her tilted forehead as if purposely hiding her face from the group; Judith had her left hand open as if balancing a book while her right hand seemed to be writing on a chalkboard; and Lucy, quizzical brow furrowed, cupped her right ear with her right hand as if straining to hear. Allison and Holly joined them to construct images, Allison pretending to type on a computer keyboard (later saying that she was searching for a translation) and Holly miming a telephone call (to a native speaker). As the second part of this activity, I asked each participant to verbalize a monologue for their image. Amelia, still covering her face, sighed, 'How do you say that again? How does that go? I can't look at them because then they'll know I don't know that word!' Judith peered down at the imaginary textbook in one hand, saying in a panicked tone, 'Let me go back to my books to research what I need to know for this class, figure out these WORDS!' The other monologues, like these two examples, solidified the link between 'non-native teacher of Spanish' and *not knowing* (i.e. being apart from) and strategies to overcome *not knowing* the embodied images had suggested. The performance of these images also overtly showed the emotions participants associated with *not knowing*, namely embarrassment, confusion, stress, and anger.

I then asked the group to consider an image for the term 'native speaker,' a purposely broader category than the first since they had to that point always referred to the other side of the binary as 'native speaker' rather than 'native speaker teacher.' Amelia gesticulated widely, as if at swatting flies, joyfully explaining in accented speech, 'Pffft, I know everything, I know all these words and don't even have to THINK about them! HAHAHA!' Holly stretched her arms out wide in front of her, offering language: 'Here it is! I know I'm right, I don't have to look anything up! Yo SÉ [I KNOW]!' Lucy's image, however, differed from Amelia's spastic portrayal and Holly's statue-like image. She stood in a very relaxed stance while holding something in her hand, later saying in an almost sleepy voice: 'I'm on a break. I get back when I get back, but right now I'm relaxed and enjoying this conversation with a friend, having a cup of coffee.' Each of the 'native speaker' images showed the native speaker being in control – having easy access to language, having the authority to use the language indisputably, and having confidence in their status as speakers.

This Image Theatre exercise illustrated how participants perceived themselves within the native/non-native binary. Whereas the native speaker was portrayed as all-knowing, they were categorized as not knowing; the native speaker was confident, yet they were insecure; and the native speaker was in control while the participants enacted haplessness. Earlier in the first PBFG, Amelia shared her goal as 'a constant race to perfection,' but the images showed that the teacher-participants believed they were losing the race. Katarina, a middle school teacher, said she felt defeated because she thought she'd 'never get there' as she pointed to the space the participants who sculpted 'native speakers' had just occupied. I asked what 'there' meant to her.

> My ultimate goal is to, you know, have a DEEEEEP understanding of the language and understand EVERYTHING. My ultimate goal is to be a native speaker, you know, somebody who is absolutely proficient in the language, someone who understands all dialects of that language, can basically talk about anything with anyone.

Katarina's concept of the native speaker – like those sculpted by other study participants moments before – is the ideal native speaker who is linguistically and culturally omniscient, the phantasm of language education who conversely has very material effects on language learners. Amelia, however, called the existence of this speaker into doubt despite having just portrayed the same figure during Image Theatre. Amelia explained that though she is a native speaker of English, she could never 'talk about ANYthing with ANYone.' Taking Katarina's mention of dialect as her starting point, she didn't believe that she would fare well 'if you were to plop me down in Shannon, Ireland.' The group agreed that language is not uniform and that no speaker could do it all. Yet, Amelia contradicted herself again in her next turn when she shared a story of having a conversation with a group of professors from Cuba:

> I've mostly been educated by Peninsular speakers and lived for a couple of years in Spain, so there were times [in the conversation] when I was just shaking my head because I could NOT, even after all of those years [of studying and teaching Spanish], you know, everything was so different to me, and I thought 'I'm never gonna be near-native, I'm never gonna get this. I'm never... I can't even follow this conversation,' it's SOOO different, you know?

While Amelia's point was to emphasize how the native speaker ideal is unrealistic because language is so diverse and dependent on so many variables, including geography in this example, she actually re-voiced Katarina's doubts about ever getting 'there,' or arriving at that desired endpoint of being able to understand and speak Spanish in every situation (that is, to embody the easy knowing portrayed in the images of 'native speaker' previously). In my role as Joker, I questioned Amelia about this contradiction. She paused for a moment, sighed heavily, and said that there is no pressure for her to perform as a native English speaker. That is, she can call on her status as a native speaker in English to soften the blow of not knowing; her competence, her identity really, is not at stake. Spanish, however, has been the focus of my study. I've dedicated my life to it. If I was to go to Cuba and not be able to communicate, that would stress me out. [...] It'd be like, 'I've studied for 20 plus years, and I still can't do this.'

Amelia's contradictory statements – which reflect the desire to be a part of and frustration being apart from – are related to her multiple identities in Spanish. As a Spanish professor, she teaches her students about linguistic variety; intellectually, she knows that the ideal native speaker doesn't exist, that communication is infinitely more than single words. Yet as a perpetual language learner invested in Spanish – evidenced by her 'constant race to perfection'– the ties to the native speaker standard are seemingly impossible to unknot.

Amelia herself noted the different goals as teacher and learner by wondering in the first PBFG if her 'constant race to perfection' was wholly personal. She explained that, when she is in the classroom, she feels very secure in her ability to lead class, relay information to students, and respond to students (i.e. she felt she had won that race). Group members (including those who had also sculpted less-than-positive images of 'non-native teacher of Spanish') overwhelmingly agreed with Amelia, several explaining their own division between their personal and professional identities in Spanish. Picking up Amelia's race metaphor, Lucy offered,

> My goal for MYSELF, the desire to be a native speaker has NOTHING to do with my classroom, it has everything to do with my perception of myself and this fantasy of not being yourself [...] I want all of it [native speakerness] and that's the part that is the race, that's probably never won, but that learning is motivated by the selfish person that wants to be native, not necessarily *(chuckles)* for the sake of the kids!

Returning to the images of 'non-native teacher of Spanish' from 'Image of a word,' however, participants represented non-native teachers as not knowing, as being oppressed by the weight of the standard of the native speaker, and having to strategize to create the illusion of knowing in class. The images that they sculpted with their bodies directly conflicted with what they said about their identities as 'non-native teachers of

Spanish.' Bodily representations yielded insights that discussion only would likely not have. When asked how they might reconcile these contradictions, teacher-participants explained that they did not always feel confident as non-native teachers but that they felt more secure in that role than as language learners chasing the all-knowing native speaker. Nonetheless, it was in their role as Spanish teachers were they said they most consistently experienced conflicts and tensions.

Forum Theatre

The most well-known element of Boal's work, Forum Theatre (FT) involves group members sharing and selecting stories of conflict to dramatize for critique and change. Though specifics of FT change according to the Joker's practice, the following model involves participants: (1) sharing and selecting a story to dramatize; (2) dividing the story into two or three scenes; (3) suggesting strategies to change the scenes by replacing the protagonist in the scenes with other spect-actors (again, the term used by Boal to acknowledge the simultaneous roles of observing and acting in TO); (4) checking for the credibility of enacted strategies; (5) changing one's actions to effect personal and societal change (Cahnmann-Taylor et al. 2009). FT is designed as a space where spect-actors can act out, meaning not only to dramatize how they are subjected but also to refuse these (subject and bodily) positions. Banks adds:

> Forum Theatre is thus, fundamentally, about troubling and dismantling fixed identities and creating paradigm shifts in the ontology of the acting subject [. . .] in and through performance, the so-called oppressed gains agency and uses the deconstruction of a narrative of oppression as an exercise in empowerment. Through the aesthetic appropriation of the image, oppression is transformed into freedom, at least in the confines of the performance space. (2006: 189)

Banks' phrase 'so-called oppressed' is instructive here. Though Boal's use of the word 'oppressed' in his 'Theatre of the Oppressed' suggests a subject who lacks power, and thus agency, Boal and Boalian scholars like Otty declare 'we are all oppressed' (1995: 87) *and* oppressors because we are always enveloped in power relations. 'Power is not something that is acquired, seized, or shared' nor is there an 'all-encompassing opposition between rulers and the ruled' (Foucault 1976: 94). Instead, power 'is the name one attributes to a complex strategical situation in a particular society' (Foucault 1976: 93). In other words, when we talk about 'oppression' in PBFGs influenced by Boal's work, we refer to a specific context in which subjects, like the Spanish teachers in my study, feel they are limited by the discursive options available to them in relation to others in the skit (especially the antagonist). This is not to say that the Spanish teachers are 'powerless' or that the antagonist is 'powerful,' but rather these circumstances are the effect of competing discourses exercised in the name of power.

In the first PBFG, I asked the teachers to consider moments when they felt tension in the performance of their second language identities. Each teacher reflected and wrote notes on provided notepads, eventually listing between six and ten tensions each. They then shared their individual lists in groups of three and decided on one theme around which to develop a two- or three-scene skit. Katarina, Allison, and Sierra created a three-scene performance later titled 'Insufficient funds' that focused on Sierra as the teacher-protagonist. The first scene, 'The job interview,' saw Sierra unable to secure employment at a private school because she was not a native speaker of Spanish. The second scene, 'Aren't you supposed to, like, speak Spanish?', focused on how the teacher felt embarrassed when she did not know a word in Spanish that one of her students had asked her. The final scene, 'Report to the office,' showed Sierra being asked by an administrator to interpret for a Spanish-speaking parent who she had difficulty understanding. In each of these scenes, the teacher-protagonist felt oppressed because she felt she was expected by others to perform as the idealized native speaker. While her personal goal (or race, remembering Amelia's metaphor), the professional expectations that she be all-knowing in Spanish expressed by administrators, parents, and students and her inability to live up to those expectations made her feel inadequate.

The participants especially identified with 'Aren't you supposed to, like, speak Spanish?' In this scene, Katarina played the part of one of Sierra's students who asked her the meaning of a word that one of Katarina's friends had used the day before. I share the trans/script, or the condensed, stylized version of the original video transcript data that acted as a mode of analysis and a means of representation (Cahnmann-Taylor et al. 2009), here to illustrate the theatricality and emotional charge of this scene in particular and the PBFGs in general:

Trans/script: Model of 'Aren't you supposed to, like, speak Spanish?'
(The bell rings, and the Spanish teacher is ready to begin her middle school class.)

TEACHER
(portrayed by Sierra): Hola clase, ¿cómo estáis? [Hello, class. How are you all?/Note that the use of the *vosotros* form of the verb *estar* indicates teacher's use of Peninsular Spanish.]

STUDENT 1
(played by Katarina): Hoooolaaaaa (pronouncing the H forcefully when it is silent in Spanish)

TEACHER: Buenos días clase, ¿qué tal? [Good morning, class. How are you?]

STUDENT 2
(performed by Allison): ¡Buenos días!

TEACHER: Buenos días, okay... *(moves to the projector by her desk to start the lesson)*

STUDENT 1: (Raises hand) Um...

TEACHER: Hoy vamos a ver *(looks up from the projector and sees Student 1's hand)* ¿Sí? [Today we're going to see... Yes?]

STUDENT 1: Yesterday, my friend Miguel who's from GuadalaJARa (pronounces 'jar' as if in English), Mexico called his brother a 'pendejo,' but I don't know what that means.

TEACHER: *(looking quizzical)* ¿Cómo? [What?]

STUDENT 1: *(slightly raising her voice)* ¡Pendejo! *(looking at the teacher with a wide-eyed expression)* What does 'pendejo' mean?

TEACHER: Mmmmmmm... *(pausing as she looks at the dictionary on the edge of her desk)*

STUDENT 2: *(having watched the teacher's gaze to the dictionary, asks in an accusatory tone)* Aren't you supposed to, like, speak Spanish?

As the Joker, I asked participants what they perceived the conflict to be in this scene. As the spect-actors interpreted it, the issue was that the teacher was put on the spot when a student asked her the meaning of a word with which she was unfamiliar. Her lack of immediate response and the subtle glance to the dictionary alerted students to the fact that she didn't know the word, causing one of them to accuse her of not speaking the language (the implication being that a speaker of a language knows all of its words, echoing Katarina's goal for herself as she described it during Image Theatre). Sierra's use of the 'vosotros' [you all, formal] form indicated her use of Peninsular Spanish, which may have explained why she was unfamiliar with the word 'pendejo,' which approximates 'idiot' or, more forcefully, 'jackass' in Mexico. Since 'pendejo' is a word that would be avoided in formal contexts like the classroom, the spect-actors also questioned the student's intent in asking for the meaning of that particular word. Did she really not know what the word meant and was curious to learn more Spanish, or did she know that it was inappropriate and hoped – along with her friend, Student #2 – to get a rise out of the teacher? Considering that the antagonists in the scene may have varied and differing motivations and experiences informing her interaction with the teacher-protagonist is an example of another Boalian technique, the Rainbow of Desire (see Boal 1995 and Wooten and Cahnmann-Taylor 2014). The spect-actors generally approached the scene keeping in mind the student-antagonists' many-hued reasons for acting as they did when they replaced Sierra as the Teacher in subsequent re-enactments of the scene.

In Forum Theatre, spect-actors who initially observe the model scene consider how they would change it for the better if they were in the protagonist's place. As the original actors begin a second run of the scene, spect-actors command them to 'Stop!' so they can assume the role of the protagonist and act out various strategies to improve the scene's outcome. Spect-actors of 'Aren't you supposed to, like, speak Spanish?' who focused on the potential disruption a word not known to the teacher might cause generally enacted classroom management strategies when acting for change (i.e. the in-control teacher took the stage). Lucy opted to leave the question unanswered while still acknowledging the possibility of learning (e.g. 'I love it when you learn new words from friends! Keep a list of those and we can all go over them later in the semester'), while Judith chose to ignore the question and focus the students' attention on the task at hand exclusively in Spanish (thus, reasserting her authority as language user and teacher). Amelia enacted an over-the-top and unrealistic (though cathartic) option to shut down Student #2's accusation by telling her, '¡Cierra el pico! [Shut your trap!]' These strategies, then, gave the teacher-protagonist options around not knowing in ways that allowed her to save face. Other spect-actors, however, looked at the scene as a potential teachable moment. Holly, for example, used the question as a way to introduce students to the concept of linguistic variety and of the impossibility of knowing it all.

Trans/script: Spect-acting strategy #5 'Teachable moment'
Student #2
(played by Allison):
Aren't you supposed to, like, speak Spanish?
Teacher
(now played by Holly):
Well, there are many different ways that Spanish is spoken. I learned Spanish in Spain, which is a little different from *(points towards Katarina)* Spanish in Guadalajara *(recasts to model the standard pronunciation of the city in Spanish)*, Mexico.
Student #1
(played by Katarina):
WHAAAA?!? *(looks around like to classmates as if to say 'No way!')* Spanish is Spanish!

Teacher:	No, it's different all over! Just like in English, there's American English, British English. Like when you were little kids in elementary school, what did you have to do when the class was going to the bathroom?
Student #1:	Line up and walk together.
Teacher:	Yeah, 'line up' here, but in Britain they say 'form a queue' *(mimes like she's writing the phrase on the board)*
Student #2:	*(surprised)* I've never seen that word in my LIFE!
Teacher:	Right, because here we say 'line.' It's just a little different!

Holly's strategy – well-received by the group – emphasized linguistic variety related to nation-states and cued students in on the Spanish she used and was teaching them. As group members discussed Holly's intervention, they recognized that their teacher stance on language conflicted with their 'personal race' to become linguistically and culturally omniscient. Lucy explained, 'we put unrealistic expectations on ourselves, like I don't need to be able to speak the Spanish of a 16 year-old Mexican boy, that will serve me NO good *(chuckling)* except when I'm interpreting for [student-parent-teacher] conferences.' Lucy, like other spect-actors, resisted what she perceived as the students' expectations in this scene – and the expectations of administrators and parents in the other two scenes of 'Insufficient funds' – that she be able to speak to anyone about anything.

When faced with expectations of native speaker-ness that they felt they could not meet, spect-actors in the scenes during Forum Theatre often moved to language teacher mode to explain linguistic variation and to position themselves as specific types of speakers (e.g. a speaker of Peninsular Spanish or of more formal, academic Spanish) that in turn allowed them to explain the communication breakdown. This move helped the teachers salvage their public reputations as language users and language teachers (doubly positioned to know and be expert) and evade being seen by others as the non-native teachers of Spanish who didn't know, had troubles, and were incomplete that they had sculpted themselves in 'Image of a word' during Image Theatre.

What Do 'Findings' in PBFGs Look Like?

In my study, participants' physical and verbal offerings throughout the two PBFGs were rife with contradictions and ambivalence, of feeling that they were both a part of and apart from the target community, of loving and hating being revealed as non-native speakers, of being validated and undermined, of feeling confident and insecure. The emphasis on multiplicity, contingency, and the constructedness of identities throughout the PBFG activities, though, served to 'troubl[e] and dismantl[e] fixed identities' (Banks 2006: 189), which in turn made agency a possibility. Spect-actors like Sierra do not have to continuously play the same role with antagonist-students (or others). They can reject the call to that subject position and answer another one instead, such as the assertive teacher who teaches her students that language is context-specific, that not knowing a word doesn't mean not being a speaker of that language, and that teachers are learners, too. Butler calls this refusal to repeat oneself as expected 'subversive repetition' (Butler 1990/1999: 42), and PBFGs based on Boal's theatrical work provide a stage for spect-actors to perform themselves differently and to imagine other possibilities for themselves and others, even if the performance isn't always 'realistic' when put to a reality check (e.g. Amelia's '¡Cierra el pico!' strategy during Forum Theatre).

The action spect-actors take outside of the performance space may or may not be to perform themselves differently; it may be a tendency to analyze situations by asking how they are acting and how they expect others to act based on discourses at work in a specific context. It may also be to question the very discourses that shape them in specific contexts. During the second PBFG as participants articulated what they were taking away from the group's collaboration, Lucy wondered, 'Maybe we're already THERE, who's to say we're not?' This question – referring to the endgame of their linguistic and cultural identities – was rhetorical; Lucy was suggesting they reconsider their own expectations of what it meant to be 'there.' It also suggests that maybe there is no *there*, that the invisible authority figures patrolling the border between native speaker/non-native speaker are no longer on the job. In follow-up interviews, four participants described themselves as feeling more positive as Spanish speakers after the group deconstructed the myth of the native speaker, two discussed considering other terms they could use to describe themselves (as opposed to non-native), one described how she was seeing examples of binaries related to language and culture in everyday life, three explained how they had enacted strategies from Forum Theatre in order to improve an interaction, and three discussed how they had used or planned to use some of the theatrical techniques in their own classrooms.

What Might Performance-Based Focus Groups Offer Researchers and Participants?

The ultimate promise of PBFGs is that they provide an aesthetic space in which participants and researchers alike can explore a topic in an embodied, experiential way. Sierra could have shared her story with everyone seated in a circle, but her frustrated reenactment of the scene with students who questioned her language proficiency packed a visceral punch that words could not have easily captured. Likewise, spect-actors that intervened in her Forum Theatre scenes judged if strategies might work or not based on if they 'felt right.' This experiential mode of investigation, however, is not without its issues. As Scott (1991) reminds us, the evidence of experience often comes to stand as uncontestable fact rather than as a point of departure to explore how one's experiences are constituted. Indeed, sometimes one person's story signals an avalanche of others who desire to share their experiences. On the one hand, such sharing during extended and/or multiple sessions (generally required in order to do a variety of activity) creates a sense of community perhaps lacking in other types of focus groups, but on the other, it also places the group's attention on personal anecdotes rather than the underlying discourses that made the experiences possible.

One of the Joker's obligations as 'difficultator' (Jackson 1995: xix) is to keep the group focused on critique rather than confession. That is, stories of personal experience are the impetus to analyze what made those personal experiences possible, how those personal experiences might be contested, and how future experiences like the personal experiences shared might be enacted differently in order to be more positive.

As I described the debriefing of two introductory games earlier in this chapter, I noted that participants quickly moved the conversation to personal anecdotes rather than engage with critical questions that I posed as the Joker ('How do you decide who to imitate? Who is worthy of imitation and why? Why imitate at all?'). Throughout the first PBFG, I consistently had to ask and re-ask such questions so that participants could deconstruct the native/non-native binary that they so often referenced in order to then rehearse how they might act differently when confronted with the oppressive standard of the idealized native speaker (be it by self-inflicted judgment – which Boal termed 'cops in the head' (1995: 8) – or by others' expectations of them). The process of sharing personal stories and sculpted images, analyzing those stories and images to see how they were created in/by discourse, and rehearsing new ways of being characterizes PBFGs that incorporate Boalian techniques, and it had two significant benefits in my study that I would like to highlight.

First, from an empirical perspective, the process generates rich and abundant data. In the case of my study, I analyzed participants' bodies individually and in collaboration to see how they moved during games, how they were sculpted to create images of various words, and how they were made to perform in scenes in Forum Theatre. Additionally, I also analyzed participants' utterances as we debriefed each activity, noting what was said, how it was said, when it was said, and to whom it was said. At times, the analyses showed contradictions – as made clear in the description of Image Theatre. These contradictions, though, fomented the notion that the creation and deployment of linguistic and cultural identities are not neat and tidy, which is a key theoretical component to my work and in-line with previous research. Indeed, the performative interventions in Forum Theatre further suggested that identities are context-specific and (especially once deconstructed) malleable since participants called on/were called to various identities in an attempt to positively change each scene.

Second, the process promotes change. While many researchers cite increased self-awareness by participants as a benefit of their studies, PBFGs that incorporate Boalian techniques quite literally help participants imagine how they can improve situations that they and their colleagues deem troubling. Forum Theatre in particular is a 'rehearsal for revolution' (Boal 1979: 122) in that it allows a space for participants to rehearse strategies – be they realistic or not – that could positively impact an interaction enacted in the group. Acting out strategies in the group and determining which strategies 'feel right' builds a new sort of muscle memory (a key tenet of Boal's work is that by changing our bodily movements, or by performing differently, we can *be* different) that can be called upon the next time the participants find themselves in a similar situation outside of the group. That is, a key goal in this work is for participants to feel more empowered. In terms of my study, all participants explained that they were thinking differently about the native/non-native binary (identified in relevant literature and in my participants' earlier anecdotes as a problem) and that they felt more positively about their linguistic and cultural identities. One participant – whose personal experiences served as the basis for the scene 'Report to the office' in which the teacher-protagonist is once again called out of class by an administrator to interpret for a Spanish-speaking parent – said that she had recently spoke with an administrator about not being the de facto interpreter for the school as a result of the interventions in that scene. While the impact that research studies have on participants is difficult to measure, my participants indicated that they began to see themselves as both English language users and Spanish language users rather than as 'failed native speakers' or 'wannabes' in Spanish. Thus, they began to focus on what they could do as opposed to what they could not do.

Conclusion

As with any method, I acknowledge that PBFGs are not appropriate for all researchers who will use focus groups in their studies. In sharing my experiences with PBFGs in the context of one particular study, I emphasize that the PBFGs in which my participants and I engaged were appropriate based on my research questions, my theoretical framework, my literature review of the native/non-native binary as a problem that could be addressed, and my personal belief that research can and should be transformative. I also acknowledge that this method, which by design 'brings no pat answers; it poses questions' (Boal 2001: 338), may frustrate some scholars who would like to find such answers. For those whose studies are a good fit, though, they will find PBFGs can be engaging for researchers and participants alike, complex in terms of data collected, and potentially empowering.

References

Babbage, F. (1995) 'Introduction to special issue: Working without Boal: Digressions and developments in the Theater of the Oppressed'. *Contemporary Theatre Review*, 3: 1–8.

Banks, D. (2006) 'Unperforming race: Strategies for reimagining identity', In J. Cohen Cruz and M. Schutzman (eds.), *A Boal Companion: Dialogues on Theatre and Cultural Politics*. London/New York: Routledge, pp. 185–198.

Bhukhanwala, F., and Allexsaht-Snider, M. (2012) 'Diverse student teachers making sense of difference through engaging in Boalian theater approaches'. *Teachers and Teaching*, 18(6): 675–691.

Boal, A. (1979) *Theatre of the Oppressed [Teatro del oprimido y otras poéticas políticas.]*. Tr. Charles A. McBride and María-Odilia Leal-McBride. New York: Urizen Books.

Boal, A. (1995) *The Rainbow of Desire: The Boal Method of Theatre and Therapy [Méthode Boal de théâtre et de thérapie.]*. Tr. Adrian Jackson. London/New York: Routledge.

Boal, A. (1998) *Legislative Theatre: Using Performance to Make Politics*. London/New York: Routledge.

Boal, A. (2001) *Hamlet and the Baker's Son: My Life in Theatre and Politics [Hamlet e ofilho do padeiro.]* Tr. Adrian Jackson and Candida Blaker. London/New York: Routledge.

Boal, A. (2002) *Games for Actors and Non-Actors*. 2nd edn. *[Jeux pour acteurs et non-acteurs.]* Tr. Adrian Jackson. London/New York: Routledge. (1st edn, 1992.)

Brown, K. H., and Gillespie, D. (1997) '"We become brave by doing brave acts': Teaching moral courage through the Theater of the Oppressed'. *Literature and Medicine*, 16(1): 108–120.

Butler, J. (1993) *Bodies that Matter: On the Discursive Limits of 'Sex'*. New York: Routledge.

Butler, J. (1999) *Gender Trouble: Feminism and the Subversion of Identity*. 2nd edn. New York: Routledge. (1st edn, 1990.)

Butler, J. (2004) *Undoing Gender*. New York: Routledge.

Cahnmann-Taylor, M., and Souto-Manning, M. (2010) *Teachers Act Up!: Creating Multicultural Learning Communities through Theatre*. New York: Teachers College Press.

Cahnmann-Taylor, M., Wooten, J., Souto-Manning, M., and Dice, J. (2009) 'The art & science of educational inquiry: Analysis of performance-based focus groups with novice bilingual teachers'. *Teachers College Record*, 111(11): 2535–2559.

Creel, G., Kuhne, M., and Riggle, M. (2000) 'See the Boal, be the Boal: Theatre of The Oppressed and composition courses'. *Teaching English in the Two-Year College*, 28(2): 141–156.

Denzin, N. K. (2003) *Performance Ethnography: Critical Pedagogy and the Politics of Culture*. Thousand Oaks, CA: Sage.

Ferrand, L. (1995) 'Forum Theater with carers: The use of Forum Theater in specific community settings'. *Contemporary Theatre Review*, 3: 23–37.

Flores, H. (2000) 'From Freire to Boal'. *Education Links*, 61/62: 41.

Foucault, M. (1975/1977) *Discipline and Punish: The Birth of the Prison*. *[Surveiller et punir: Naissance de la prison.]* Tr. Alan Sheridan. New York: Vintage Books.

Foucault, M. (1976) *The History of Sexuality: Volume 1: An Introduction. [La Volonté de savoir.]* Tr. Robert Hurley. New York: Vintage Books.

Harman, R., and McClure, G. (2011) 'All the school's a stage: Critical performative pedagogy in urban teacher education'. *Equity & Excellence in Education*, 44(3): 379–402.

Harman, R., and Zhang, X. (2015) 'Performance, performativity, and second language identities: How can we know the actor from the act?'. *Linguistics and Education*, 32: 68–81.

Houston, S., Magill, T., McCollum, M., and Spratt, T. (2001) 'Developing creative solutions to the problems of children and their families: Communicative reason and the use of Forum Theatre'. *Child & Family Social Work*, 6: 285–293.

Jackson, A. (1992/2002) 'Translator's introduction to the first edition', In *Games for Actors and Non-Actors*. London/New York: Routledge. pp. xxii–xxix.

Jackson, A. (1995) 'Translator's introduction to the first edition', In *The Rainbow of Desire: The Boal Method of Theatre and Therapy*. London/New York: Routledge. pp. xxii–xxix.

Linds, W. (2006) 'Metaxis: Dancing (in) the in-between', In Jan Cohen-Cruz and Mady Schutzman (eds.), *A Boal Companion: Dialogues on Theatre and Cultural Politics*. London/New York: Routledge, pp. 114–124.

Louis, R. (2005) 'Performing English, performing bodies: A case for critical performative language pedagogy'. *Text & Performance Quarterly*, 25(4): 334–353.

Mitchell, T. (2001) 'Notes from the inside: Forum theater in maximum security'. *Theater*, 31(3): 55–61.

Otty, N. (1995) 'Theater of the Oppressed: Cultural action for freedom: Boal, Freire, and the major pedagogy of Brecht in the context of higher education'. *Contemporary Theatre Review*, 3: 87–100.

Pässilä, A. H., Oikarinen, T., and Harmaakorpi, V. (2013) 'Collective voicing as reflective practice'. *Management Learning*, 46(1): 67–86.

Pillow, W. S. (2000) 'Exposed methodology: The body as a deconstructive practice', In E. A. St.Pierre and W.S. Pillow (eds.), *Working the Ruins: Feminist Poststructural Theory and Methods in Education*. New York: Routledge, pp. 114–124.

Powers, B., and Duffy, P.B. (2016) 'Making invisible intersectionality visible through Theater of the Oppressed in teacher education'. *Journal of Teacher Education*, 67(1): 61–73.

Sanders, M. (2004) 'Urban odyssey: Theatre of the oppressed and talented minority youth'. *Journal for the Education of the Gifted*, 28(2): 218–241.

Scott, J. (1991) 'The evidence of experience'. *Critical Inquiry*, 17: 773–797.

Souto-Manning, M. (2011) 'Playing with power and privilege: Theatre games in teacher education'. *Teaching and Teacher Education*, 27(6): 997–1007.

Szeman, I. (2005) 'Lessons for Theatre of the Oppressed from a Romanian orphanage.' *New Theatre Quarterly*, 21(4): 340–357.

Telesco, G., and Solomon, A. (2001) 'Theater of the recruits: Boal techniques in the New York police academy'. *Theater*, 31(3): 55–61.

Wooten, J. (2012) 'Confessions of a cultural drag queen, or Reflections on acting like the native speaker in foreign language education', In P. C. Miller, J. L. Watzke and M. Mantero (eds.), *Readings in Language Studies*,

Vol. 3: Language and Identity. Grandville, MI: International Society for Language Studies, pp. 114–124.

Wooten, J., and Cahnmann-Taylor, M. (2014) 'Black, white, and Rainbow [of Desire]: The color of race-talk of pre-service foreign language educators in Boalian theatre workshops'. *Pedagogies: An International Journal*, 9(3): 179–195.

Jennifer Wooten is the Director of Language Instruction and Senior Lecturer in the Department of Spanish and Portuguese Studies at the University of Florida in Gainesville, Florida. She has developed and taught courses in Spanish that focus on service-learning in local Latino communities and courses to help instructors of world languages critically consider the interstices of language, culture, and power in the language classroom, in schools, and beyond. Her research interests include non-native teacher identity, performative techniques in teacher education and in world language classrooms, and critical pedagogy. Wooten's dissertation, *Cultural Drag: Theorizing the Performances of Non-Native Spanish Teachers' Linguistic and Cultural Identities*, won the 2012 Outstanding Dissertation Award of the Second Language Research Special Interest Group of the American Educational Research Association (AERA). Her creative and scholarly publications have appeared in *Teachers College Record*, *Pedagogies*, and *Anthropology and Humanism*, amongst others.

13

Collective Production of Discourse: An Approach Based on the Qualitative School of Madrid

Jorge Ruiz Ruiz

Introduction

In recent years, social researchers who use focus groups have shown a growing interest in group discourse, recognizing that this involves much more than the simple aggregation of individual opinions or individual discourse. This has also extended to include a focus on the necessary conditions for group discourse to emerge. It seems clear that not every group technique encourages the production of group discourse to the same extent: depending on the group dynamics established in each case, more or less group discourse will be produced. This has opened a field for reflection that seeks to identify the conditions needed for the emergence of group discourse. I argue that a specific branch of discourse methodology can be particularly useful, namely the qualitative research method proposed by Jesús Ibáñez more than 30 years ago and later developed by other Spanish and Latin American social researchers of the

J.R. Ruiz (✉)
IESA-CSIC, Institute of Advanced Social Studies, Cordoba, Spain
e-mail: jruiz@iesa.csic.es

© The Author(s) 2017
R.S. Barbour, D.L. Morgan (Eds.), *A New Era in Focus Group Research*, DOI 10.1057/978-1-137-58614-8_13

so-called Qualitative School of Madrid. This paper aims to present this group technique for discourse production to a wider audience, and demonstrate that it is particularly powerful for fostering the production of group discourse.

Discussion Groups and Focus Groups: Similarities and Differences

In 1979, Jesus Ibáñez published the first edition of *Más allá de la sociología* ('Beyond Sociology') in which the author provided a methodological framework for discussion groups. This approach was the result of his research experience gained in over more than two decades of practice in the field of market research alongside Alfonso Orti, Angel de Lucas, PacoPereña and Jose Luis Zárraga, and others, who later formed the so-called Qualitative School of Madrid (Valles and Baer 2005). This theoretical framework of discussion group almost completely ignored focus group, which can result surprising because this technique had been developing at that same time.[1] Indeed, Ibañez only made two brief references to Merton's focussed interviews' as being more similar to in-depth documentary interviews with the clear intention to differentiate them from his discussion groups (Ibáñez 1979: 122, 257). In contrast, he based his discussion groups in psychoanalytic theory, especially in Bion's theories, as an interface or intersection between 'basic groups' and 'working groups' (Ibáñez 1979: 21; Dominguez and Davila 2008: 98). Later, however, other methodologies developments of this technique largely abandoned this psychoanalytic approach[2] (Martin Criado 1997; Alonso 1996; Canales

---

[1] See, for example, the paper published by Merton in 1987 in which he compared 'focussed interviews' to focus groups (Merton 1987) or the first edition of Krueger's famous handbook published in 1988 (Krueger 1988).

[2] Years later, Ibáñez also provided a foundation for discussion grou from a more constructivist perspective based on the second cybernetics (Ibáñez 1991). However, some elements of these psychoanalytic origins remain, such as the need for discussion groups to relax the censorship of inconsistencies characteristic of interviews, al least in part. In this sense, discussion groups aim to broaden the discursive field by permitting inconsistencies to a greater extent than other research situations (Callejo 2002: 97).

and Peinado 1994; Canales 2006), but neither was it based on focus groups, which were practically ignored.[3]

A similar situation has occurred amongst authors who have developed focus group methodology. In studies by these authors, no mention is made of the discussion group technique as developed by the Qualitative School of Madrid. Thus, although discussion groups have been used for a long time by Spanish and Latin American social researchers, they are virtually unknown in other countries, particularly amongst English-speaking audiences and specialists. Another example (and cause) of this separation between the methods of both techniques is the lack of papers written in English which address the technical and methodological features of discussion groups; a fact that has undoubtedly contributed to the limited international dissemination of this technique. Although numerous studies have been published that describe and explain the features of discussion groups, all have been written in Spanish (Ibáñez 1979, 1989, 1991; Ortí 1986; Martin Criado 1997; Alonso 1996; Canales and Peinado 1994; Canales 2006; Domínguez and Dávila 2008). Hence, it could be said that both techniques have followed a 'parallel' path since they rely on very different assumptions and theoretical approaches and have continued to develop in a different manner, while barely recognizing one another.

In practice, however, focus groups and discussion groups have many features in common. Based on these similarities, some authors conclude that they are actually different versions of the same technique (Valles 1997; Callejo 2001) or that the differences are more of an epistemological nature rather than a methodological one (Gutiérrez 2011). Moreover, if we consider the more inclusive (or less restrictive) definitions of focus groups, it is clear that they can also be applied to discussion groups. For example, the definition of focus groups 'as a research technique that collects data through group interaction on a

---

[3] Javier Callejo's handbook (2001) is a notable exception to this disregard forfocus groups in discussion group methodology. To a large extent, Callejo equates both techniques and makes several references to focus groups.

topic determined by the researcher' (Morgan 1996: 130) would be equally applicable to discussion groups. Or, similarly, if we consider that focus group discussion is a flexible method which permits myriad forms and can be adapted to different research purposes (Barbour 2005), discussion groups could also be considered a particular type or form of focus group.

In addition to demonstrating and highlighting these similarities, I am interested, here, in examining discussion groups in relation to the diverse forms of focus groups. This will allow us to explain in a clearer and more precise manner the specific methods and techniques of discussion groups to audiences unfamiliar with them. While it is true that discussion groups and focus groups have many similarities, some share more than others. For example, discussion groups bear a close resemblance to focus groups that emphasize the group aspect or dimension, while they differ largely from more individualized focus groups.[4] It could be said, therefore, that discussion groups are a type of focus group, but not a type of group interview (Canales and Peinado 1994: 294). In Spain and Latin America, the distinction between group interviews and discussion groups is much more marked than in English-speaking countries, where focus groups are often considered a type of group interview (Frey and Fontana 1991; Hughes and DuMont 2002; Madill 2012) that permit varying degrees of interaction between participants, a more or less structured or directive moderation, and, thus, a more or less individualized discourse.

From an individualistic point of view, interactions amongst participants – one of the principal features of focus groups – are valued in an ambivalent way. On the one hand, these interactions encourage the emergence or disclosure of the individual opinions and views of each of the participants, which, according to this approach, is the ultimate aim of the technique. However, these interactions can also be a disadvantage or drawback. Indeed, from this point of view, interactions between participants may mean that the group contaminates or biases the individual opinions of the participants. The

---

[4] For more on the differences between these two traditions and types within the focus group technique, see Smithson (2000), Wilkinson (1998), Hollander (2004), and Farnsworth and Boon (2010). A defense and summary of individualistic approaches to focus groups can be found, amongst others, in Hughes and DuMont (2002), Lezaun (2007), and Onwuegbuzie (2011).

role of the moderator is to 'structure a process of interaction conducive to the elicitation and elucidation of the most private of views, while reducing to a minimum the residuum of 'socialness' left over from the process' (Lezaun 2007: 130). From this individualistic approach, the group situation is in part an obstacle for participants to express their thoughts or individual opinions, which are regarded as the only real or authentic point of view, and hence the most interesting to collect. The group situation necessarily involves some group effects (Carey and Smith 1994). In this regard, Hollander (2004: 610) noted the pressure to conform that may lead participants to adjust their own contributions to match those of others. This phenomenon, which is known as 'groupthink', involves a 'bandwagon effect' where people endorse more extreme ideas in a group than they would express individually; and social desirability pressures that induce participants to offer information or play particular roles, either to fulfil the perceived expectations of the facilitator or other participants, or to present a favourable image of themselves. From this individualistic perspective, these group effects must be neutralized - or at least minimized - by a directive, more structured and individualizing approach to moderation.

In addition to this individualistic approach characteristic of focus groups, there is another approach that emphasizes group dimensions or aspects. According to this group-based approach, focus groups are perceived, essentially, as involving group dynamics rather than group interviews (Smithson 2008; Wilkinson 2006) in which interactions between the participants in the group are encouraged rather than interactions between the moderator and each of the participants (Parker and Tritter 2006: 26), and where moderators take on a less directive role and less structured group dynamics are used (Krueger 1991). Because the interactions between the participants and the context in which they are produced are considered fundamental to producing the focus group's results, these interactions must be taken into account when analyzing the information obtained within a constructivist perspective (Kitzinger 1994; Morgan 1996; Wilkinson 1998; Smithson 2008; Hollander 2004; Farnsworth and Boon 2010; Grønkjær et al. 2011). Last but not least, the group is considered a unit of analysis rather than the sum or aggregation of the opinions, attitudes or information of each of its participants (Wilkinson 1998; Munday 2006; Smithson 2008). In short, this conception of focus groups, which may be called collective or collaborative, fully assumes the group situation to be a characteristic of focus groups. As a result, it seeks interactions between participants to produce richer results, and these interactions are taken into account in the analysis rather than trying to eliminate or reduce their impact.

The discussion group goes further and may be considered a radical version of this type of focus group which emphasizes the group aspect. Indeed, the explicit aim of discussion groups is the collective production of a group discourse through conversation. As Alonso argued (1996: 93), 'discussion groups are essentially a socialized conversation project, in which the production of a group communication situation is useful for collecting and analyzing ideological discourse and symbolic representations associated to any social phenomenon' (translated from the Spanish). Therefore, the interest is to enhance and maximize the group dimension of the technique, that is, to encourage the flow of interactions between participants and the most intense group dynamics as possible. Thus, from the discussion group perspective, group effects no longer are viewed as a problem or an inconvenience, but can even become a source or mechanism for the production of group discourse. It is not a question of preventing or minimizing these effects through group moderation or direction; nor that these effects must be taken into account in the analysis of the data produced. According to the discussion group approach, it is precisely these 'group effects' which produce the group discourse. This proposal is more radical, as it intentionally seeks to produce and foster these effects.

Agreement as a Discursive Product Typical of Discussion Groups

Discussion groups constitute a research situation in the form of a conversation around a topic or issue proposed by the researcher to produce a shared discourse by the group, that is, the participants reach agreement on these issues. When a conversation is held in any context - not just in social research - the more or less explicit objective of the speakers is to reach agreement; a conclusion that is shared jointly or by reciprocal influence. Each participant in a conversation seeks to influence and persuade others, but may also be influenced and convinced by others in turn. Agreement can be considered the goal, or the horizon, of any conversation. In this way, the production of a shared discourse is fostered in discussion groups through the communicative exchange and interaction between participants leading to the implicit agreement in any conversation. Thus, group dynamics in discussion groups can be viewed as a process of decreased individuality, a progressive loss of individualities for the emergence of a collective discourse and a group identity (Callejo 2002).

Gadamer refers to the potential of conversation to produce a group or shared discourse – understood as an agreement amongst participants on the issues at hand – when he says that 'conversation is a process of coming to an understanding. Thus, it belongs to every true conversation that each person opens himself to the other, truly accepts his point of view as valid and transposes himself into the other to such an extent that he understands not the particular individual but what he says. What is to be grasped is the substantive rightness of his opinion, so that we can be at one with each other on the subject. Thus, we do not relate the other's opinion to him but to our own opinions and views' (2004: 387) or when he states that 'the true reality of human communication is such that a conversation does not simply carry one person's opinion through against another's, or even simply add one opinion to another. Conversation transforms the viewpoint of both' (2006: 17). The result or outcome of a conversation, to the extent that this occurs, is something other than the individual opinions of those who participated in it; it is a shared discourse. Or in the terms of Gadamer, conversation is a process that produces 'a common diction and a common dictum' (2004: 388).

However, this agreement should not be understood as absolute on each of the topics covered, at least necessarily. The degree of agreement that is reached on the various topics can be very diverse. In other words, the output of a discussion group is always a shared discourse, but the degree to which it is shared does not have to be absolute agreement. For this reason, discussion groups always allow for some degree of dissent in terms of both the group dynamics and the group output. At times, this dissent acts as a catalyst for discussion by enriching debates and bringing out important aspects that would have otherwise remained implicit. In other cases, this diversity of views is maintained until the end, meaning that the group's discursive output is only shared to some extent or with regard to some issues and not others.[5]

The goal of focus groups is not to reach consensus between participants, which is what differentiates them from other group processes such as nominal groups or the Delphi method (Krueger and Casey 2010: 381). Although agreement may be reached in focus groups, unlike nominal groups or the Delphi method, this agreement does not necessarily have to be absolute (i.e. a consensus). Thereby, the fact that full agreement is not reached does not imply that the discussion group has not achieved its goal. On the contrary: the degree of agreement reached is a feature of the discursive production of the group and, as such, a research result that must be analyzed. Discussion groups in which absolute agreement is reached on all issues are valid to the same extent as those in which there is less agreement or where major disagreements persist amongst the participants until the end. This is because the discursive product is always collective or shared insofar as it is a discourse which is produced in a collective attempt to reach agreement, to seek agreement. In sum, the discursive result of a discussion group is mutual understanding rather than consensus.

Furthermore, discussion groups, unlike nominal groups or the Delphi method, neither pressure nor push the participants to agreement. Rather, they create the conditions for conversation, and so, the agreement arises spontaneously. In no case does this agreement-based focus imply silencing or inhibiting individual or particular differences and disagreements amongst participants. On the contrary, a dynamic in which agreement is reached on the various issues in too immediate a manner and with little

---

[5] The difficulty in reaching agreement is often the cause of unease amongst participants, thus demonstrating agreement is the more or less implicit goal of the conversation. When it is not possible to reach agreement, the conversation is brought to an end, or participants change the topic of conversation. Farnsworth and Boon (2010) referred to a similar situation when they stated that 'in one group, for example, one of us found the continued splintering of discussion cognitively overwhelming. In the end, she stopped processing and went into a passive state, effectively 'shutting down'. So when it came time to introduce the next major topic she had trouble re-engaging with the focus group research agenda' (p. 615).

previous discussion is very unproductive in discursive terms, and requires more intervention by the moderator in order to reveal what lies behind this overly obvious consensus. Discrepancies are not repressed but to some extent necessary for discussion group dynamics and as such are encouraged by the moderator. Some authors argue that considering discourse as a collective or shared output implies disregarding, silencing or even stifling divergent or dissenting opinions (Onwuegbuzie et al. 2011). However, from my point of view, there is no inconsistency between shared discourse and such discrepancies. Rather, discussion groups propose reaching a shared discourse precisely through the confrontation of divergent opinions, and the kind of shared discourse that is produced in them is rarely characterized by absolute unanimity.

Moreover, discursive cleavage may occur in discussion groups, which does not necessarily mean they have not functioned well or have failed. The formation of factions within the group that engage in more or less incompatible discourses, thus making the prospect of agreement impossible, may be a plausible outcome of a discussion group, although it is not a usual one. When this is the case, it is necessary to revise the group design, as it is based on the expectation that the groups will produce a shared discourse through conversation. But in no case should this outcome be considered an error, but rather an interesting surprise, to which any type of research, and especially research based on qualitative methodology, should be open. The unexpected discursive cleavage in a group is an outcome that requires explanation, since its analysis can reveal important aspects of the social reality under investigation.

Collective or Shared Discourse Production Through Conversation

Discussion groups foster the production of a collective or shared group discourse around issues of interest to the research by setting the conditions for participants to engage in and maintain the liveliest and most intense conversation as possible. There are at least four important factors that must be taken into account to enable conversation to flow: the composition of the group or the characteristics of its members, the instructions or indications they are given to engage in the group dynamics, the nature of the discussion topic, and the type of moderation. None of these four features of discussion groups are exclusive to this technique, but each is also found in differing degrees in some versions of focus groups - especially those that maximize the group dimension or aspect. However, the specific characteristic that distinguishes discussion groups from focus groups is that all these strategies are combined, or used jointly, to ensure the optimal conditions for shared discourse to emerge through conversation.

As regards the composition of the group, the participants should be homogenous if the group is to reach some degree of consensus on the issues discussed. Group homogeneity usually refers to similarity in socio-demographic characteristics (Canales and Peinado 1994), but also to the horizontal relationships amongst participants in hierarchical or conflicting contexts (Callejo 1998). It is important to note a crucial issue here. If the aim of the group discussion is to produce a shared discourse through conversation, a necessary intermediate step for this to occur is the formation of the group in the conversation itself. For this to be possible, at least two conditions must be met: (1) that the group does not already exist, that is, that none of the participants know or have habitual or close relationships with the other members of the group[6]; and (2) that the characteristics of the participants permit a group to be formed, that is, they mutually recognize one another as being socially similar or at least close.

The homogeneity or similarity of participants has also been defended for focus groups as a way to encourage the emergence, expression or disclosure of individual views and foster a high-quality discussion about

---

[6] Of course, the artificial nature of the group is also a feature of focus groups (Morgan 1997; Hyden and Bülow 2003). However, some authors suggest the poss it can build rapport and trust amongst participants and hence the disclosure of their particular opinions or views (Barbour 2008; Kitzinger 1994). From the point of view of discussion groups, using pre-existing groups is highly problematic, if not outright unadvisable, as this prior relationship may have an adverse effect on the collaborative production of a shared discourse. The prior relationship amongst participants in a discussion group, or even mutual knowledge, is always an inconvenience because it hinders the group dynamics. Elsewhere we have defended a small group format in the form of a triangular or minimum group as the best way to ensure the production of shared discourse in these atypical or exceptional conditions (Ruiz 2012).

the topic being researched (Greenbaum 1998). The homogeneous composition of the group builds trust amongst participants who subsequently facilitate the expression of each participant's individual opinions (Morgan 1997; Hughes and DuMont 2002). However, although no doubt related to trust, the objective of this within-group homogeneity in group discussions is somewhat different. Greater trust amongst participants in group discussions is important not so much because it fosters the expression of individual opinions, but because it allows for more intense group dynamics and ensures the flow of conversation, and thus a more collective and shared discourse output. The difference may seem subtle, but it is very important to the results of the technique.

Moreover, the homogeneity requirement is relative because participants can only be homogenous to a certain degree. Thus, while homogeneity should be ensured, there should also be a certain degree of diversity in the group to allow for divergent opinions that enrich and revitalize the debates.[7] In this regard, a group that is too homogeneous may lead to dynamics that are not sufficiently intense, reaching instant consensus on the issues raised, and the discourse that is produced will be poor. Moreover, homogeneity is not an intrinsic characteristic of the group itself, but refers to the views group members have about the issue to be discussed or the topic in question. For example, while both men and women can be brought together to discuss a variety of topics, there are some topics where it is clearly advisable to separate by gender, such as contraceptive use or the division of housework. In addition, some issues that can be easily debated by both men and women in one society may be somewhat problematic in other societies. In these conditions, it is advisable to conduct discussion groups separately by gender.[8]

---

[7] This seems to be the sense of Morgan's recommendation to offset the homogeneity in the background characteristics of participants in focus groups by the greater diversity in their attitudes (Morgan 1997).

[8] In a sense, group homogeneity may be considered counterproductive with regard to the discursive production of the group, as it reduces the discrepancies amongst the participants. However, as Kitzinger (1994: 113) noted regarding natural groups, which are particularly homogeneous, when the group is properly conducted discrepancies and different opinions amongst participants emerge in all conversational contexts, even those in which unanimous agreement is initially reached.

In discussion group methodology, this within-group homogeneity is complemented by between-group heterogeneity by incorporating criteria in the research design to reflect the diversity of social discourses in a particular historical and social context. Research using discussion groups seeks to capture the diversity of social discourses by using different groups so as to cover, to the greatest possible extent, the casuistry of types of discourse found in society. Discussion group methods aim to elucidate or establish the system of social discourse around a particular issue (Conde 2009); that is, the variety of views on the matter, and the relations or interplay amongst them. Discussion group research is designed in such a way as to reach information saturation, in line with focus group research (Hennink 2007: 145). However, discussion group research is also designed to take into account the saturation of different types of existing discourses in a given social context, which involves formulating a hypothesis about discursive differences (or kinds of discourse) amongst different groups depending on their social characteristics.

Instructions for Engaging Group Dynamics

Regarding the second feature of discussion groups, it is very important that the initial instructions or indications make it very clear that the dynamics involve an exchange of views. However, these seemingly simple instructions can actually be quite difficult to put in practice. Firstly, it is very common for participants to expect the group dynamics to consist of alternating sequences of questions and answers between the moderator and the participants. In fact, these question-answer dynamics are perhaps most widely recognized as a typical social research method as, to some extent, they reproduce the logic of surveys, which is undoubtedly the most well-known social research technique. In other words, discussion group dynamics are, in a sense, strange or atypical and it is, therefore, common for these group dynamics to be hindered by such preconceptions - especially at the outset.

In order to overcome, or at least mitigate, these difficulties, the moderator can explain the group dynamics by resorting to images or concepts such as debates or conversations, which by analogy may be more familiar to the participants, for it helps them to better understand what is expected of them. It is also important that moderators specify their own role in the group and mark a distance from it. This can be done, for example, by defining their role as observers who will ask some questions during the course of the meeting. A useful indication for this purpose is to request that participants direct their contributions to all members of the group rather than to the moderator or any single participant. Doing so prevents participants' from speaking directly to the moderator and permits the debates to be carried out in an organized manner without concurrent conversations.

Nature of Discussion Topic

A third point that should be taken into account to ensure the flow of conversation amongst members of a discussion group is the importance of formulating in a suitable manner the issue to be discussed. Indeed, depending on how the issue is presented, participants may tend to express more personal or private views rather than exchanging their opinions or views with others. For example, asking participants if they are for or against contraception is different from raising the issue of the decision to have children. In the first case, the members will be prompted to take an initial position that makes subsequent conversation very difficult, while in the second case they will be encouraged to contrast and explore the different opinions. In general, it is preferable to avoid topics or issues which require an answer or taking an individual, closed position. Thus, it is preferable to raise the issues to be addressed in an indirect manner; for example, by proposing a topic that differs from the research goal but which bears a certain relationship to it and which can eventually steer the discussion to the issue that is of interest to the researcher.[9] Moreover, these indirect formulations have another advantage insofar as they foster greater spontaneity and allow for a less biased discourse.

In addition to this initial indirect approach, the moderator should take special care with regard to how the issues are raised or questions are

---

[9] Although Jesus Ibáñez recognized that the topic of discussion can be approached directly, he preferred an indirect approach due to the problems involved in a more direct approach to presenting the issues (1979: 303 ff).

asked, in order not to bias the course of the conversation or interfere negatively in the group dynamics. In this sense, it is preferable to formulate questions in such a way as to link up with what has already been said, to expand on statements, to clarify earlier responses, or to bring up a relevant issue that has not been raised in the conversation. Insofar as possible, discussion group moderators should also avoid addressing individual participants in the group but instead address the group as a whole. Thus, questions that require participants to express their individual views or opinions should be avoided, such as those directed at single participants. Obviously, individual turn-taking in answering the moderator's questions is highly unadvisable. While discussion group moderators should explore discrepancies, this should not involve individualized responses.[10] These considerations bring us to the question of non-directive moderation; the fourth characteristic that differentiates discussion groups from focus groups.

Non-directive Moderation and the Production of a Shared Discourse by the Group

The objectives of non–directive moderation are twofold: to ensure the spontaneity or natural flow of conversion in the group, without interference or bias by the moderator; and to promote and enhance group interactions. Non–directive – or less–structured – moderation is, perhaps, the most important strategy used in conducting discussion groups aimed at producing a shared group discourse. Non–directive moderation is a strategy that was developed in clinical psychology as a way to promote the so–called encounter groups, that is, groups in which participants can express or disclose their views and opinions in the freest possible way without interference or manipulation by the moderator (Rogers 1973; Gutiérrez Brito 2008). The moderator is more a facilitator than a conductor. In this setting, the moderator acts as a

---

[10] For example, with questions like 'Does everyone agree with that?'; or statements such as 'I would like to hear everyone's opinion on this issue', participants are encouraged to express differences but not individual views that hinder or close the conversation. These questions therefore contribute to building a collective discourse by contrasting different positions. Again the difference may seem subtle, but the effects on discursive output are substantial.

facilitator to elicit participants' personal views. In social research, however, non–directive moderation is somewhat different in terms of how it is presented and the objectives to be pursued. Here, non–directive moderation refers primarily to the self–containment or restraint of moderators regarding their involvement in the group, which must also be as neutral as possible.

This non-directive or less structured moderation is also found frequently in focus groups, especially those which are more group-based or collaborative (Krueger 1994; Morgan 1993; Kitzinger 1995). For example: 'typically you want a moderator to ask the question, then sit back and listen. Let the participants interact. Let them have a conversation about the question. A focus group is working well when participants begin to build each other's comments rather than continually responding directly to the moderator' (Krueger and Casey 2010: 383). Indeed, this style of moderation is characteristic of focused interviews (Merton et al. 1956), which can be considered the immediate forerunner of focus groups. In focus groups, moderators may use a non-directive style depending on their own preferences, the issue to be discussed, or the specific objectives of the research. In contrast, non-directive moderation is a central strategy in discussion groups with the aim of producing a collective and shared discourse. Thus in addition to the above objectives, the main aim of non-directive moderation in discussion groups is to establish the necessary conditions to form a group at a specific time and for a specific task.

In the initial stages, a discussion group is not really a group, but rather an artificial or contrived grouping (Lezaun 2007), a meeting or a focused gathering[11] that is artificially created by the researcher. Although this initial situation is identical to that of focus groups, focus groups allow varying degrees of grouping and various forms of group interaction (Agar and MacDonald 1995),which may oscillate between sequences similar to the dyadic interaction in ordinary interviews and a conversation (Hyden and Büllow 2003: 308). The purpose of discussion groups is to enable a group to be formed through conversation around the issue

---

[11] This is a concept formulated by Goffman and adopted by Hyden and Büllow (2003: 307) to refer to a situation in which individuals agree to sustain for a time a single focus. The point is that this concept can serve to characterize some forms of focus groups, but defines a situation that is insufficient for conducting a discussion group.

of interest to the research, so that its members can produce a collective discourse from the discourse shared by the group. Whether they are successful in achieving this aim or not will depend largely on if the moderator provides an open arena for discourse and remains neutral to allow for conversation amongst participants.[12]

To achieve this additional goal, non-directive moderation in discussion groups has some distinctive features. On the one hand, moderation is more intense. But the greater intensity of non-directive moderation cannot be understood as a difference only in terms of degree, as some authors argue (Gutiérrez Brito 2008; Valles 1997). On the contrary, as has been argued, the greater intensity of non-directive moderation seeks to encourage different group dynamics, equally intense conversation amongst participants in the group, and with it a distinctly collective or shared discursive production. On the other hand, non-directive moderation should be especially intense or even extreme in the early stages of the meeting.

Thus, in the first moments, non-directive moderation in discussion groups is practically equivalent to the moderator withdrawing from the discussion. This is because, in the beginning, the group should be established around the conversation that is based on the mutual recognition of participants as valid interlocutors in relation to the issue. The withdrawal of the moderator and the homogeneity of participants will permit the group to establish a common ground that may function as a starting point for interaction (Hyden and Büllow 2003: 311). To the extent that this common ground is established, the group will be formed to a greater or lesser extent, and the discourse will be more or less collective. 'In discussion groups, the problem arises when the moderator becomes too involved in the meeting, making it more like a group interview. This makes it difficult to talk of group discourse since what

---

[12] In this regard, discussion groups bear a close resemblance to the group discussions developed by the Institute for Social Research of Frankfurt in the 1950s (Gugglberger et al. 2013). Beyond their names, the two techniques are similar in terms of their objectives (the production of a collective discourse), and the strategies adopted to achieve them (specifically, an open and unstructured approach). However, we also found significant differences between both techniques, although this issue exceeds the scope of this work.

is shared only flows through a regulator outside the group itself (Callejo 2002: 100, translation from Spanish). Later, however, when the group has already been formed and acquires its own dynamics, usually around 30 or 40 minutes from the start, the moderator can relax this non-directive moderation and begin to intervene more directly by posing questions to the group.

A distinction should be made between dialectic and dialogic conversations. The former refers to conversations whose express aim is for partners or participants to reach agreement. In contrast, dialogic conversations are more anarchic or less formalized verbal exchanges that do not necessarily lead to agreement, but rather an increased awareness and mutual understanding of the participants' respective viewpoints. Or, in the words of Bakhtin, a 'knitted-together but divergent exchange' (Sennett 2012: 18–19). Thus, the conversation that arises in the framework of a discussion group should be more dialectic than dialogic. Dialectic conversation is more suited to the production of a collective discourse, to the extent that it implies that some type of agreement is reached amongst the participants.

Yet, this is true only in part. In the beginning, the conversations that take place in discussion groups acquire clearly dialogic characteristics: participants sound each other out, are prudent and listen, thus allowing the participants to acknowledge one another and, to some extent, identify themselves as part of a group. Only when the group has been formed through this dialogic conversation can it undertake the task of reaching agreement on the issues raised by the moderator. In this second phase, the conversation acquires more dialectic characteristics in so far as the group attempts to reach agreement and consensus and share their views, regardless of their differences. In this sense, discussion groups are formed in a dialogic manner in order to function and reach agreement dialectically. Hence, for the group to function dialectically, it must have been previously formed dialogically. The transition from one phase to another is marked by a change in how the moderator conducts the group dynamics, who may shift from an non-directive moderating style to one that is somewhat more interventionist.

Sociological Analysis of Collective or Shared Group Discourse

A collective or shared group discourse, such as that which is produced in discussion groups, is of enormous sociological value. In particular, collective discourse is a perfect means to research social representations, such as systems of norms and values, images associated with institutions, groups or objects, topics, and stereotyped discourses (Alonso 1996: 94); to explore the ideological certainties existing in a given social space (Canales and Peinado 1994: 294); or even to seek consensus in conflicting contexts (Callejo 1998). In this sense, focus groups that maximize the group aspect have also been shown to be useful in studying collective identities (Munday 2006), developing ideas collectively amongst research participants and bringing forward their own priorities and perspectives (Smithson 2008: 358), or making collective sense of personal experiences and beliefs (Wilkinson 1998). In short, the discourse that is shared and collectively produced by the group is a perfect way to gain insight into the broader social discourse.

However, in order to exploit the potential of collective discourse as empirical material, attention must be paid to the type of analysis. Indeed, collective discourse requires a sociological analysis, where the group is the unit of analysis (Kidd and Parshall 2000; Hyden and Bulow 2003). This type of analysis involves taking account of the consensus or agreements reached by the group in its conversation or discussion. But, as noted above, under no circumstances does the priority given to consensus imply a disregard for possible discrepancies or dissenting opinions within the group. This is because any agreement or consensus is relative, so that a fundamental question posed in analysis is to determine the degree of agreement or consensus reached by the group or groups on the research issues. Thus in addition to consensus, a group analysis – such as the one proposed here – should also take into account dissenting voices; issues on which agreement is weak or even nonexistent; and opinions or views that differ from those of the group. Moreover, this type of discourse analysis does not only consider the 'final' consensus reached by the group, but also the processes which have led to it, that is, the interactions amongst the participants. Hence, it is essential to pay attention to the group interactions when evaluating and interpreting the discursive output in this kind of analysis (Ruiz 2009).

Another important point is that the consensus reached by discussion groups is not always expressed or made explicit, but often takes a tacit or implicit form. Thus, for example, choosing some topics of conversation, avoiding others, or ironic and indirect ways of addressing them are important elements for the group to reach agreement or consensus. Consequently, these implicit agreements and disagreements should be considered when analyzing the discourse produced by the group (Ruiz 2014). Citing Zeldin (1998), Sennett noted that 'the good listener detects common ground more in what another person assumes than says. The listener elaborates that assumption by putting it into words. You pick up on the intention, the context, make it explicit, and talk about it'. Analysts of a discussion group resemble this good listener, but without an interlocutor standing in front of him/her; that is, when the conversation has ended.

A last feature of discussion group discourse analyses is that they are never performed in isolation, but always within the discourse system of which they are a part (Conde 2009). Thus, collective discourses produced in discussion groups must be interpreted in open contrast to other discourses that occur in the same social arena, and, which, in turn, have occurred in other discussion groups.

Conclusion: Differential Characteristics of Discussion Groups

Discussion groups and focus groups are apparently similar social research techniques, but which nevertheless seek different aims and thus give rise to very different group dynamics. Specifically, the aim of focus groups is to gather the views and opinions of participants in a context of mutual influence, while discussion groups attempt to produce a collective or shared discourse; that is, a group discourse through conversation in a group situation. While the first corresponds to a group interview situation, the second involves conversational dynamics amongst the participants.

However, new types of focus groups have recently been developed that attach greater importance and relevance to interaction amongst participants. These variants of the focus group foster conversation to a greater extent and limit individualized dynamics based on two-way interactions between the moderator and each of the participants. In this regard, these focus groups share some of the dynamics characteristic of group discussions as they explore the potential of conversation as a means to allow opinions to emerge in a group setting. Nonetheless, the difference between the two lies in the objectives of group dynamics, since these types of focus groups do not aim to produce or analyze the group discourse. Discussion groups can be considered a radical version of focus groups that place emphasis on the group, except that they pursue different objectives. Specifically, the discussion group provides concrete possibilities for social research because it is a technique aimed at producing a group discourse, understood as a collective or shared group discourse. To the extent that this is so, this is a technique similar to the focus group, which is useful when our research objectives require investigating this collective dimension of social discourse. For this reason, this chapter has tried to provide a better understanding of discussion groups for those more familiar with focus group techniques.

References

Agar, M., & MacDonald, J. (1995) 'Focus groups and ethnography'. *Human Organization*, 54: 78–86.
Alonso, L. E. (1996) 'El grupo de discusión en su práctica: Memoria social, intertextualidad y acción comunicativa'. *Revista Internacional de Sociología*,13: 5–36.
Barbour, R. (2005) 'Making sense of focus groups'. *Medical Education*, 139(7): 742–750.
Barbour, R. (2008) *Doing Focus Groups*. London, Sage.
Callejo, J. (1998) 'Articulación de perspectivas metodológicas: Posibilidades del grupo de discusión para una sociedad reflexiva'. *Papers*, 56: 31–55.
Callejo, J. (2001) *El grupo de discusión: Introducción a una práctica de investigación*. Barcelona: Ariel.
Callejo, J. (2002) 'Grupo de discusión: La apertura incoherente'. *Estudios de Sociolingüística* 3(1): 91–109.

Canales, M. (2006) 'El grupo de discusión y el grupo focal', In M. Canales (ed.), *Metodología de investigación social*. Santiago de Chile LOM, pp. 265–287.
Canales, M., & Peinado, A. (1994) 'Grupos de discusión', In J. M. Delgado & J. Gutiérrez (coord.) *Métodos y técnicas cualitativas de investigación en Ciencias Sociales*. Madrid: Síntesis, pp. 288–316.
Carey, M., & Smith, M. (1994) 'Capturing the group effect in focus group: A special concern in analysis'. *Qualitative Health Research*, 4(1): 123–127.
Conde, F. (2009) *Análisis sociológico del sistema de discursos*. Madrid: Centro de Investigaciones Sociológicas.
Domínguez, M., & Davila, A. (2008) 'La práctica conversacional del grupo de discusión: Jóvenes, ciudadanía y nuevos derechos', In A. Gordo & A. Serrano (eds.), *Estrategias y prácticas cualitativas de investigación social*. Madrid: Pearson Educación, pp. 97–125.
Farnsworth, J., & Boon, B. (2010) 'Analyzing group dynamics within the focus group'. *Qualitative Research*, 10(5): 605–624.
Frey, J., & Fontana, A. (1991) 'The group interview in social research'. *Social Science Journal*, 28: 175–187.
Gadamer, H. G., (2004). *Truth and Method* USA: Bloomsbury Publishing (translation revised by Weinsheimer, J., & Marshall, D. G.) New York: Continuum.
Gadamer, H. G. (2006) 'Language and understanding (1970)'. *Theory, Culture & Society*, 23(1): 13–27.
Greenbaum, T. L. (1998). *The Handbook for Focus Group Research*. Thousand Oaks, CA: Sage.
Grønkjær, M., Curtis, T., de Crespigny, Ch., & Delmar, Ch. (2011) 'Analyzing group interaction in focus group research: Impact on content and the role of the moderator'. *Qualitative Studies*, 2(1): 16–30.
Gugglberger, Lisa., Adamowitsch, Michaela., Teutsch, Friedrich., Felder-Puig, Rosemarie., & Dür, Wolfgang. (2013) 'The use of group discussions: A case study of learning about organizational characteristics of schools'. *International Journal of Social Research Methodology* (ahead-of-print), 1–17.
Gutierrez Brito, J. (2008) *Dinámica del Grupo de Discusión*. Madrid: CIS.
Gutierrez Brito, J. (2011) 'Grupo de discusión: ¿Prolongación, variación o ruptura con el focus group?' *Cinta de Moebio*, 41: 105–122.
Hennink, M. M. (2007) *International Focus Group Research: A Handbook for the Health and Social Sciences*. Cambridge: Cambridge University Press.
Hollander, J. A. (2004) 'The social contexts of focus groups'. *Journal of Contemporary Ethnography*, 33(5): 602–637.

Hughes, D., & DuMont, K. (2002) 'Using focus groups to facilitate culturally anchored research', In *Ecological Research to Promote Social Change*. USA: Springer, pp. 257–289.

Hyden, L. C., & Bülow, P. H. (2003) 'Who's talking?: Drawing conclusions from focus groups – some methodological considerations'. *International Journal of Social Research Methodology*, 6(4): 305–321.

Ibáñez, J. (1979). *Más allá de la Sociología. El Grupo de Discusión: Técnica y Crítica* (1986, segunda edición corregida). Madrid: Siglo XXI.

Ibáñez, J. (1989) 'Cómo se realiza una investigación mediante grupos de discusión', In M. García Ferrando, J. Ibáñez & F. Alvira (eds.), *El análisis de la realidad social. Métodos y Técnicas de* investigación. Madrid: Alianza editorial.

Ibáñez, J. (1991) 'El grupo de discusión: Fundamento metodológico y legitimación epistemológica', In M. Latiesa (ed.), *El Pluralismo Metodológico en la Investigación Social*. Granada: Universidad de Granada, pp. 53–82.

Kidd, P. S., & Parshall, M. B. (2000) 'Getting the focus and the group: Enhancing analytical rigor in focus group research'. *Qualitative Health Research*, 10(3): 293–308.

Kitzinger, J. (1994) 'The methodology of focus groups: The importance of interaction between research participants'. *Sociology of Health and Illness*, 16(1): 103–121.

Kitzinger, J. (1995) 'Introducing focus groups'. *British Medical Journal*, 311: 299–302.

Krueger, R. (1988/1994) *Focus Groups: A Practical Guide for Applied Research*. London: Sage. (Published in Spanish in 1991: *El Grupo de Discusión. Guia Práctica para la Investigación Aplicada*. Madrid: editorial Pirámide).

Krueger, R. A., & Casey, M. A. (2010) 'Focus group interviewing', In *Handbook of Practical Program Evaluation* (3rd ed.). San Francisco (CA): Jossey-Bass.

Lezaun, J. (2007) 'A market of opinions: The political epistemology of focus groups'. *Sociological Review*, 55: 130–151.

Madill, A. (2012) 'Interviews and interviewing techniques', In Harris Cooper et al. (ed.), *APA Handbook of Research Methods in Psychology*, Vol. 1. Washington, DC, USA: American Psychological Association, pp. 249–275.

Martín Criado, E. (1997) 'El grupo de discusión como situación social'. *Revista Española de Investigaciones Sociológicas* (REIS) 79: 81–112.

Merton, R. K. (1987) 'The focussed interview and focus group: Continuities and discontinuities'. *Public Opinion Quarterly*, 51: 550–566.

Merton, R. K., Fiske, M., & Kendall, P. L. (1956) *The Focused Interview*. Glencoe IL: Free Press.
Morgan, D. L. (1996) 'Focus group'. *Annual Review of Sociology*, 22: 129–152.
Morgan, D. L. (1997) *Focus Groups as Qualitative Research* (2nd ed.). Thousand Oaks, CA: Sage.
Morgan, D. L., & Krueger, R. A. (1993) 'When to use focus groups and why', In D. L. Morgan (ed.), *Successful Focus Groups: Advancing the State of the Art*. Newbury Park, CA: Sage, pp. 3–19.
Munday, J. (2006) 'Identity in focus: The use of focus groups to study the construction of collective identity'. *Sociology*, 40(1): 16, 89–105.
Onwuegbuzie, A. J., Leech, N. L., Dickinson, W. B., & Zoran, A. G. (2009) 'Toward more rigor in focus group research: A new framework for collecting and analyzing focus group data'. *International Journal of Qualitative Methods*, 8(3): 1–21. (Published in Spanish in 2011: Un marco cualitativo para la recolección y análisis de datos en la investigación basada en grupos focales. *Paradigmas*, 3(2): 127–157).
Ortí, A. (1986) 'La apertura y el enfoque cualitativo o estructural: La entrevista abierta y la discusión de grupo', In G. Ferrando, J. Ibáñez & F. Alvira (eds.), *El análisis de la realidad social. Métodos y técnicas de investigación*. Madrid: Alianza, pp. 71–204.
Parker, A., & Tritter, J. (2006) 'Focus group method and methodology: Current practice and recent debate.' *International Journal of Research and Method in Education*, 29(1): 23–37.
Rogers, C. (1970) *Encounter Groups*. London: Penguin Press, Allen Lane (Published in Spanish in 1973: *Grupos de Encuentro*. Buenos Aires: Amorrortu).
Ruiz, J. (2009) 'Sociological discourse analysis: Methods and logic'. *Forum Qualitative Sozialforschung/Forum: Qualitative Social Research*, 10(2) (online).
Ruiz, J. (2012) 'El grupo triangular: Reflexiones metodológicas en torno a dos experiencias de investigación'. *EMPIRIA. Revista de Metodología de Ciencias Sociales*, 24: 141–162.
Ruiz, J. (2014) 'El discurso implícito. Aportaciones para un análisis sociológico'. *Revista Española de Investigaciones Sociológicas (REIS)*, 146: 171–190.
Sennett, R. (2012). *Together: The Rituals, Pleasures and Politics of Cooperation*. Yale University Press.
Smithson. J. (2000) 'Using and analyzing focus groups: limitations and possibilities'. *International Journal of Social Research Methodology*, 3(2): 103–119.

Smithson. J. (2008) 'Focus groups', In P. Alasuutari, L. Bickman & J. Brannen (eds.), *The SAGE Handbook of Social Research Methods*. London: Sage, pp. 356–371.
Valles, M. S. (1997) 'Los grupos de discusión y otras técnicas afines', In M. S. Valles (ed.), *Técnicas cualitativas de investigación social. Reflexión metodológica y práctica profesional.* Madrid: Síntesis, pp. 279–335.
Valles, M. S., & Baer, A. (2005) 'Investigación Social Cualitativa en España: Presente, pasado y futuro. Unretrato'. *Forum: Qualitative Social Research (FQS)*, 6(3) (online).
Wilkinson, S. (1998) 'Focus groups in health research: Exploring the meanings of health and illness'. *Journal of Health Psychology*, 3(3): 329–348.
Wilkinson, S. (2006) 'Analyzing interaction in focus groups', In Drew, Paul, Geoffrey, Raymond & Weinberg, Darin (eds.). *Talk and interaction in social research methods*. London: Sage, pp. 50–62.
Zeldin, Th. (1998) *Conversation*. London: Harvill.

Jorge Ruiz Ruiz has a degree in Sociology from the Complutense University of Madrid (UCM) and was awarded the Complutense Prize for Research in 1992. His professional career got off to a start in 1993 with the creation of his own company for social research together other fellow students, called *Caleidoscopia Investigación Social S.L.* He later collaborated with several firms and institutions in the field of social and market research. Since 2002, Jorge Ruiz has worked at the Institute for Advanced Social Studies (IESA-CSIC), in Spain, as a specialist in qualitative research methods. His research interests have centred chiefly on the use and development of qualitative methodology and, more specifically on the Sociological Discourse Analysis and the group techniques for discursive production, which forms a significant strand in his publications.

Section IV

Theoretical Developments

14

A Kaleidoscope of Voices: Using Focus Groups in a Study of Rural Adolescent Girls

Erin E. Seaton

Introduction

When I think back on the school year I spent working with the eighteen 8th grade girls attending a small public school in rural New Hampshire, I picture our last day together at an outdoor adventure course, a kaleidoscope of voices surrounding me. The morning had swelled into an unseasonably hot and muggy afternoon, and the girls had shed their sweatshirts. Despite the heat, they stood in tangles, one cluster on the ground, heads resting against each other, another in a tight knot, arms wrapped around each other's shoulders. Since September of that school year, I had watched the girls trade clothes, share lunches, offer hugs, draw on each other's papers, and at times, even complete each other's sentences. Their alliances were not always easy and could shift on a daily basis, but despite fleeting frictions, they largely maintained a fierce sense of loyalty. For some of the

---

E.E. Seaton (✉)
Department of Education, Tufts University, Medford, USA
e-mail: ee.seaton@tufts.edu

girls, their connections to friends were the most consistent, empathetic, and enduring relationships in their lives. These knots and tangles are what I had come to learn about: the supportive relationships that sustained this group of rural girls as they forged through adolescence. As such, my research required a methodology that embodied a relational way of being, challenging the construction of narrative as an individual act.

As adolescent girls strive to create a coherent sense of identity, they face a myriad of conflicting societal messages about femininity, sexuality, and empowerment, and as a result embody these challenges to their physical and psychological well-being (AUW 1991, 1995; Bordo 1993; Brumberg 1998; Carney 2000; Driscoll 2002; Edut 1998; Fine 1988; Fine and Weis 2005; Harris 2004; Levinkron 1998; Morris 2016; Orenstein 1994, 2016; Plante 2010; Sadker and Sadker 1995; Shaw 2002; Steiner-Adair 1990, 1991; Straus 2007). However, within the literature on adolescents girls' development, rural girls' experiences of adolescence have been largely overlooked. Having lived and worked in rural communities, I wondered how the passage into adulthood differed for rural girls. If rural girls are seen or see themselves as living in the middle of *nowhere* – a place where *nothing* is happening – then how easy is it for their struggles and identity to be negated – *nobodies* in the course of human development? How difficult is it for readers and researchers to hear these stories if the significance of rural girls' very existence is consistently overlooked? And how much more problematic does this telling become when structural inequalities – such as limited access to physical and mental health services, poverty, isolation, overlapping relationships between community members, and sexual violence within their communities – make the healthy transition to adulthood even more tenuous (Brown 1998; Buckley et al.; DeYoung 1994; Kelleher et al. 1992; Petti and Levinson 1986; San Antonio 2004; Slovak and Singer 2002; Wilson et al. 1997; Wilson and Peterson 1988). While research demonstrates that supportive relationships with others and access to resources for mental health care are critical to adolescent psychological well-being (Brown and Gilligan 1992; Garmezy and Rutter 1983; Spencer 2000; Ward 2000; Werner and Smith 1982), I wondered where rural girls found support, as access to social services and supportive relationships could be far more limited than in larger communities.

Rationale and Approach

Drawing on Relational Feminist methods (Gilligan 1982; Miller 1976; Spencer 2000), I wanted to offer rural girls an opportunity to articulate their own stories in full complexity, countering the perspective that labelled rural girls as 'at-risk' that discounted rural girls' experiences as insignificant. I wanted to attend to the counter-narratives that girls provided about their identities and experiences. Relational Feminist Theory serves as a framework that attends to the voices of girls and women, reframing the way in which girls and women are understood to actively resist harmful social and cultural messages and recognizing the centrality of connections with others. Here, psychological health is defined as the ability to seek out and sustain authentic relationships with others. In opposition, psychological distress is understood to arise from repeated rejections in relationships or when one fails to find and preserve important connections with others. Attention to voice, in particular, becomes an indicator of psychological health (Brown and Gilligan 1992; Gilligan 1982, 1991, 1993, 1997; Gilligan et al. 1991). The ability to speak openly and honestly indicates a healthy ability to know, name, and hold onto one's own thoughts and feelings and sustain healthy connections with others.

For rural girls, whose lives have been predominantly silenced or ignored by the larger psychological community, both research and clinical practice, offering a space in which they can share their own stories of identity and relationships, in their own voices, presents a challenge to the narratives that have proscribed their lives. Developing a narrative of the self is an act of agency (Josselson et al. 2004; Parry 1991; White and Epston 1990; Wortham 2001). Thus, privileging the stories of rural adolescent girls becomes an act of resistance, in itself. It was my intent to provide the girls in my study the opportunity to speak out against powerful misconstructions of rural experiences and the invisibility of being white and poor. I chose to examine the girls' experiences at school because schools offer a critical site in which girls are able to test their developing sense of identity, garner support from others, and develop a sense of agency as they begin to give voice to their own experience.

The community I chose to study was located in central New Hampshire, away from the tourist areas of the lake and mountain regions that provide some communities with greater economic resources. At one time, the main source of employment in the community had come from a mill, but the mill had closed after a devastating fire. Census data from (New Hampshire Economic & Labor Market Information Bureau 2014) shows that the population of the town is close to 4,000, with approximately 13% of residents living below the federal poverty level, double the New Hampshire state average. The average household income hovers around $30,000, half the state average of $60,000. 94% of residents are Caucasian, 3% Hispanic, and the remaining 3% from Native American, Asian, and multi-racial backgrounds. While 80% of adults have a high school diploma, only 15% of adults have a bachelor's degree or higher. Despite its somewhat pastoral appearance with rolling hills and quintessential New England farms, in 2013 there were 57 sex offender registrations, 52 reported incidents of assaults, 12 reported incidents of sexual assault, and 32 incidences of children being placed in protective custody. And the girls' narratives echoed this dissonance between beauty and danger.

I had entered into the community as a teacher/researcher (Barbieri 1995; Bogdan and Biklen 2002; Burnaford et al. 2001; Ulichny and Schoener 2000). For the first half of the school year, I engaged in an intense ethnography, what Geertz calls, a 'deep hanging out' (1998). Because I believed there was a need to give back to the community, I co-taught a 12-week Language Arts on literacy and identity with the 8th grade Language Arts teacher. I modelled my instruction on the *Voices of Love and Freedom* curriculum (Snow and Selman 2001) and added the requirement of daily journal entries, writing prompts, and art activities. Outside of this program, I shadowed the students throughout their day, sitting in on the girls' other courses, going to lunch, recess, and

14 A Kaleidoscope of Voices: Using Focus Groups...   307

extracurricular activities, and attending teacher meetings. Ethnography, as Luttrell explains, offers a method for researchers to 'listen and represent those we study on and in their own terms' (2000: 499). I took daily field notes (Emerson et al. 1995), collected copies of documents such as the girls' writing and poetry, and used these to develop narrative reflections (Burnaford et al. 2001). I coded the ethnographic data by writing a second set of memos (Chambers 2000; Huberman and Miles 2002; Luttrell 2003; Mac an Ghaill 1994; Tedlock 2000) identifying narrative passages relevant to my research questions – in which students shared stories (explicitly or implicitly) about gender, identity, and psychological support within rural locations. These memos enabled me to develop a better understanding of the predominant themes within rural adolescent girls' narratives of self and relationships that strengthened and focused my interview questions. I had planned to use this data to conduct individual interviews with the girls based on a set of semi-structured questions on the girls' identities and supportive relationships that had emerged in my data analysis.

Over the first 4 months, I worked hard to gain the girls' trust, and by January, we had developed a definite rapport. The girls often confided in me when they had a disagreement with a teacher or peer. Together, we debated musical choices and fashion trends, spoke about friendships, celebrated athletic accomplishments, and strategized about how to solve conflicts. Yet, when I posted a sign-up sheet for individual interviews, not a single girl added her name. Midway through the school year, I had hit an unanticipated roadblock. I could not go forward with a narrative study if there were no interviews. I waited. A week passed and then another. Finally, I called the girls together to ask what was going on. 'I thought you wanted to be interviewed,' I said, completely perplexed. Murmurs of agreement rippled through the room. So what was it, then? What did the interviews require that was met with such resistance? 'What? What is it?' I asked. Finally, one student raised her hand. 'It's just that we don't want to be interviewed alone.'

In retrospect, I wonder how I could I have missed this? In all my research into Feminist and Relational research methods, how could I have designed a study that asked the girls to narrate stories of the self in isolation? But the individual interview is the dominant culture of narrative data collection. (Bruner 1986, 2003; Josselson et al. 2004; Riessman 1993; Spence 1982; White and Epston 1990). Even when the relational context of narrative interviewing is acknowledged–as an interaction between a speaker and listener or in the recognition of the narrator's contextual relationships–the speaker's narrative is most often portrayed as an act of individual autonomy.

Drawing on social constructionist (Geertz 1973; Gergen 1985, 1997), postmodern (Foucault 1972), hermeneutic (Habermas 1966; Ricoeur 1978; Weber 1949), and feminist (Chodorow 1978; Gilligan 1982; Tong 1998) movements in psychology, which advocate attending to the subjectivity and centrality of personal meaning-making in research, I constructed narrative a political act. For rural girls, who have been written out of studies of gender, psychology, identity, and adolescence, a narrative study offers a space in which they can build stories of their own making. Narrative (Bruchac 1997; Bruner 1986, 1987, 1990; Coles 1989; Gergen and Gergen 1986, 1988; Lieblich et al. 1998; Riessman 1993; Rosenwald and Ochberg 1992) offers the speaker a fundamental means to organize, understand and give meaning to her or his own life and relationships. In her book, *Pillar of Salt*, Janice Haaken (1998) calls this process of retelling a story of the self 'transformative remembering.' And for a rural girl, in particular, narrative becomes a form of resistance; a willingness to know and tell difficult personal truths, in the face of powerful scripts that might deny her reality. To speak about one's own life, one must come to know and understand those preexisting stories that hold power as the dominant or 'official' stories and silence alternative narratives. Psychologist Alan Parry explains,

A person's experience of the world is the most vital tool with which she has to gather information and decide for herself what it tells her. When this singular capacity is discredited, invalidated, or replaced by someone else's description, she is on the way to losing all confidence in her own judgment. (1991: 44)

In this sense, narrative is inherently a relational act; it is only through an audience that words begin to resonate (Brown and Gilligan 1992; Parry 1991; White and Epston 1990). Speaking, as Gilligan explains, 'depends on listening and being heard' (1997: 153). Novelist and essayist Dorothy Allison (1992) suggests that stories are not transcriptions of a fixed reality, but are actively crafted to persuade a listener to be moved by the 'narrative truth' (Spence 1982) within the story. Here, the dominant frame in narrative studies posits a single narrator with a listener and reifies the notion that stories are told individually.

Focus groups offer a very different way of collecting and interpreting narratives, particularly from individuals who have been marginalized or silenced. In her discussion of the focus group as a feminist practice, Madriz argues that despite the documentation of the 'collectivist nature of women's lives' (2003: 365), in Feminist research, the individual interview remains the dominant method for collection of narrative data. Here, Madriz posits that focus groups offer an opportunity for marginalized groups to develop 'collective stories and resistance narratives' (2003: 369) that challenge dominant discourses, and particularly when a researcher represents a dominant group. While this remains a persuasive argument for using the focus group as a method for work with marginalized communities, my research explores the notion that, for rural adolescent girls, the self is inextricably linked to, and defined by, connections to others, due to overlapping relationships within their close-knit community, and can only be narrated as such. While Madriz acknowledges such systems of 'multivocal conversations', her emphasis remains on the focus group as a praxis of empowerment. I argue that the context is also critical in considering whether or not to employ a methodology that includes focus groups. For some groups, focus groups serve a dual purpose, both empowering marginalized groups and serving as a means to capture a phenomenological process in which members share a common experience in which identity is collectively constructed.

The Research Approach in Practice

My first glimpse into this phenomenon of the collective construction of narratives came when I asked the 8th graders in my Language Arts class to describe a memory in response to a passage from Lois Lowry's *The*

Giver. When one student mentioned a memory of being carried outside in the night to see the spectacular fire in the mill, other students shared their own stories of the event. Students recalled the stench of smoke that lingered in the air for days. Others added that they still found scraps in the river. When word spread through the school that the 8th graders were talking about the fire, faculty members popped into the room and interrupted class to share in the community storybuilding. One teacher remembered her power going out after the fire and how she lost everything in her refrigerator. Overlapping narratives brought together stories of parents who worked in the mill with recollections of older siblings or relatives helping to battle the blaze. Everyone who was living in the community at the time of the fire had been affected directly or indirectly, and the portrait of the event that emerged was far more powerful than the single shard of a memory that the original speaker shared. Likewise, the collective retelling gave the class a sense of unity in their understanding of the fire and its impact.

Rather than a single lens, I was suddenly looking through a kaleidoscope, each individual experience refracted through multiple lenses, a co-constructed image of self, made more complex and increasingly complex and beautiful in its multiplicity. Patterns emerged not from the singular pieces of an individual story but through the designs created in community. In many narratives, one story initiated a memory or new story. At times, the girls' stories and responses challenged each other as they worked to weave together their own perspectives on an event or experience.

Such evidence challenged the construction of a narrative as an individual act. In a small, close-knit community, where both knowledge and identities were constructed in community, like a quilt, stories were also stitched together, piece by piece, to create larger, more complicated, and intersecting narratives. Narratives emerged not from a single speaker but from a symphony (sometimes cacophony) of voices. In rural contexts, overlapping relationships are common, and research on the impact of this on clinical practice is well-documented (Clopton and Knesting 2006; Erickson 2001; Gonyea, et al. 2014; Horst 1989; Owens, et al. 2013; Stockman 1990). If I accepted the premise that the girls viewed their identities as relational, asking the girls to participate in individual interviews simply did not make sense. For the girls in my study, their experiences and relationships were tightly entwined. Rarely did the girls experience a sense of privacy, even in the most intimate moments of their lives.

Five of the girls in my study had parents who worked within the community's school system, as teachers, paraprofessionals, bus drivers, or administrative assistants. The girls spoke about how quickly their parents found out when they were in trouble at school, missed a homework assignment, or failed a test. For some girls, close connections with community members offered a sense of support through 'being known.' Juliet describes friends and neighbours as 'looking out for her,' providing a sense of membership in school, in town, and at church. However, for Cassandra, whose mother and father are in prison for drug offenses, her ability to craft a sense of identity is constricted by overlapping relationships. Cassandra explains,

Teachers will talk about you, and like, Miss Jones, when she was new, she was like, 'I already heard a whole bunch of stuff about you guys.' She said that to me and Diana, I think, at the beginning of the year. I was like, you don't even know me. And like, cause, my mom – my brother and my mom, like, they're kind of like, bad, I guess, so people just assume things ... And she didn't even know me. And she's just like – she's just like, 'I – yeah – I heard something about you.'

Being known can predispose girls to prejudgements, as overlapping relationships and rumours can constrict a girl's ability to craft an independent identity for herself. For girls in a small and isolated community, others' narratives are experienced as constrictive if not inescapable.

For girls who face pre-judgements based on adults' prior relationships with or information about family members, support from peers gave the girls protection, support, and greater credibility. This was most striking in the girls' recounting of acts of sexual violence perpetrated by males in the community, as such acts not only serve to overpower and violate the female body, stripping the individual of agency (Cahill 2001; Marcus 1992). One girl, Cassandra, begins her retelling of an act of sexual violence with an invocation to her peers, asking, 'That time, about that time, remember?' She continues, describing the way in which the girls' individual voices were silenced until the group came together to demand that the police to take this accusation seriously. In her work, Madriz (2003) highlights the power of focus groups 'as a form of collective testimony.' Cassandra explains:

> Well, there's this kid, and he's a senior. He showed me and her his (pause) penis or whatever. And he showed Diana a different time. Yeah and Emily – me and Eve. Diana told. But they didn't believe her. And then like, me and Emily, and then we told. But they still didn't believe us. So, they had to tell the police. The school had to, I guess, and then the police finally believed us, because, I guess, 2 years ago he got in trouble for the same kind of thing. Yeah, and so, like, he's – he's getting married, and we're getting, like, more punished, because, like, we can't go to his – we can't go to where he works. His place. We're not allowed there because – Yeah. And he still has that privilege… And like, we're getting, and every time we see him in the hall, me and Diana get, like, scared, because we're afraid of, like – But, like, me and Diana, were kind of – and Emily – we're scared to walk by him again.

This experience of not being heard resonated across the focus groups as other girls argued, 'We tell people, but people don't believe us. Like, they'll say they'll do something and they never do. They didn't, did they?'

Strikingly, a shift occurs in these passages such that both narratives employ the collective second person plural of 'we' and 'us.' For girls who have been silenced, a collective voice seems to offer greater authority. And her lingering question, 'They didn't, did they?' draws the other girls into the discussion of how the school and community dealt with the girls' sexual harassment by another student. Describing this phenomenon in focus group interviewing, Loperfido and Ligorio (2012) explain:

> This process finely mirrors the typical interaction dynamics within focus group discussions and represents the construction of a group identity, evident in the impersonal formulation of statements and in the use of personal markers in the second person plural. A dual process therefore seems to take shape: alongside the presentation of a personal self the students try to define a 'we', an entity through which they attempt to

understand and characterize the course they have just started...The conversation is therefore structured around an increasing polyphony and interactivity that involves the gradual construction of negotiation processes amongst the participant's voices and the definition of a collective actor: the group expresses itself in parallel to the individual voices.

In the case of responding to acts of silencing, the power of the focus group serves to unite the girls in a common vision. Here, the collective voice takes precedence over the individual. For participants who have experienced a common experience or trauma, a collective story. Kai Erikson, writing about collective trauma argues that such collective narratives serve as a transformative, healing act, writing, 'It is the *community* that cushions pain, the *community* that provides a context for intimacy' (1976: 193).

Nowhere was this more evident than in Diana's story. Diana's narrative reveals not just the story of her repeated rape and the unspeakable nature of this trauma, but also the way her story is constructed communally on multiple levels. For Diana, the story of her rape was first shared with her friends and then became public knowledge in her small community, revealing how stories may be shaped by the resonances of multiple voices.

Although, from my first few days at her school, I had heard whispers about Diana's identity as a trauma survivor, the first time I heard her story narrated was during a focus group interview when I asked the girls to talk about their confiding relationships. Emily, Diana's friend, was the first person to allude to this story, when she spoke about confiding in her mother when she and her twin sister, Eve, were the first people to hear about Diana's rape. From this first reference to Diana's rape, the communal nature of this story was evident. The opening to Diana's story begins in this way, with Emily's response to my question, saying, 'One time when you told us, we told our mother and she did something about it.' To which Cassandra responded, 'Was it about Rick?' Even before Diana has time to develop her own narrative, her peers begin to narrate Diana's story.

Following Diana's choice to share the story of her rape with Eve and Emily, her narrative took on increasingly complex layers of disclosure.

The thread of Diana's story became woven into the public space of the community spinning from Diana to Eve and Emily, to their mother, to Gwen (Diana's foster mother), to the police, and further into the community, including Diana's teachers and peers, and then disclosed again within the context of this interview. With every new layer of telling, revisions and interpretations of Diana's story build with each new reconstruction of the story. The narrators, then, become agents, making decisions about their role in the story and its disclosure.

As Diana struggled to give words to her story, she asked her friend, Cassandra, to speak what she could not say. Seamlessly, Cassandra takes over the narration of the story, explaining, '[Rick] raped her,' giving birth to a communal narration of a story that no longer belongs to Diana alone. As the narrative continues, Diana becomes more active in the storytelling process, however, Eve, Emily, and Cassandra still help to provide scaffolding for the story, as in the following passage:

Erin:	When was that?
Diana:	Oh, like a year ago.
Erin:	So what happened? How did you – what did you?
Eve:	And then he did it when she was like –
Cassandra:	He's been doing it since she was, like, eight
Diana:	I didn't know what it was when I was young, you know.

It is only after Eve, Emily, and Cassandra introduce Diana's story that Diana joins in and plays a more active role in the narration.

Diana's narrative has a muddled quality about it that is not uncommon to narratives of trauma. Writing about the process of reconstructing a narrative, Breuer and Freud (1957) noted the overwhelming emotional component in retelling a story of a trauma. Both Herman (1992) and Rogers et al. (1999) alike attest to the extraordinary uses of language that narrators may employ to reconstruct such narratives, often revealing inconsistencies, gaps, and silences within their stories. Herman explains, 'Both patient and therapist must develop tolerance for some degree of uncertainty, even regarding the basic facts of the story. In the course of reconstruction, the story may change as missing pieces are recovered' (1992, 179). Herman's advice enables readers to make sense of narratives that stray from a logical and sequential path, doubling back

14 A Kaleidoscope of Voices: Using Focus Groups... 315

on themselves in revised and shifting directions. Diana's story takes on this quality in the following passage:

Erin:	Were your friends helpful to you? [to Diana]
Diana:	Oh yeah.
Erin:	Yeah?
Diana:	I was the one who told em. That's how
Eve:	Me and Emily were the first ones to know. And then we told our mother.
Diana:	Adrianne, too.
Eve:	But it must have been really hard to tell your friends.
Diana:	No.
Cassandra:	My brother.
Erin:	It wasn't hard to tell them?
Diana:	I was, like, hey this kid made me have sex with him.
Cassandra:	My brother wanted to beat him up
Eve:	You didn't really do that! You had a hard time telling us.
Diana:	She said –
Cassandra:	Yeah.
Diana:	Where were we? Weren't we inside of my room?
Emily:	Our room. Our room.
Diana:	Like, doing Truth or Dare or something, and you guys said, 'Truth. Like, have you ever done it or anything with a boy?'
Emily:	Whatever.
Eve:	No.
Cassandra:	I don't know how you told me.
Diana:	I was like
Eve:	You were crying
Diana:	Of course I was
Erin:	Of course you were!
Emily:	You were saying that, 'Please don't tell anybody.'
Eve:	Yeah. That was up in our room and you told
Diana:	I told you I tell the truth during Truth or Dare.

The flexibility of 'narrative truth' (Spence 1982) becomes a negotiated act in which the girls challenge each other's experience to create a multi-dimensional rendering of narrative, highlighting Diana's gaps and revisions in a way that I would not have been aware of, had I only heard Diana's story in isolation. Where Diana says it was easy to tell her friends about being raped, Eve and Emily remind Diana how difficult her disclosure was. Later, Diana struggles to recall where she was when she first told Eve and Emily and what the girls were doing. In fact, all three girls work together to construct the story of this revelation, challenging each other, building off of the other's comments, and revising their own versions of the narratives. Stories are not static, but alterable and shifting, revised in the processes of restoration, influenced by the limitations of the spoken word and the context in which stories are revealed.

This active process of constructing a story is heightened by way in which the girls build Diana's story as a communal narrative, revealing the many layers of their own agency, speaking, listening, telling and retelling this story within the story itself. The final few sentences of this passage mark a significant turn in the way in which a story of a trauma is presumed to be narrated. Where past and present researchers (Breuer and Freud 1957; Herman 1992; van der Kolk and van der Hart 1995; Rogers et al. 1999) argue for the necessity of reconstructing a narrative of a trauma on an individual level, Diana's story hinges on a communal storybuilding, in which 'everybody' in her small community not only knows about the trauma, but becomes part of the story itself. Communally built stories add a complexity to narratives of trauma, in particular, and in a context in which the individual is integrated so deeply into a communal context, the group bears the burden of such violence.

Implications and Applications of Communal Storytelling

Communally built stories offer both strengths and challenges. In a co-constructed narrative, speakers can challenge or validate each other, adding depth to a discussion, weaving together disparate memories and emotions, even questioning the truth of another narrator's experience. While an individual might stake a claim to a particular reality, a collaborative narrative challenges the notion that there is a singular truth to an experience. As narrators work together to tell and retell the story of an event, each voice adds a new layer, moving the narrative away from a linear storyline. Drawing on a postmodern theories of narrative (Sanders 2011) listeners see the intersections of experiences such that the narrative becomes a multidimensional, living story.

However, communal storytelling is not without its own perils. Always, the listener must be aware of the way in which particular voices and threads are valued or dismissed. While a communally built narrative may open up pathways for multiple renditions of the truth, dominant voices may also shut down or cover over other experiences and affect the control an individual has over her own construction of reality. In this sense, a researcher must be attuned to what is spoken and also what is unspoken or silenced within the group. For groups with a shared sense of identity, purpose, or experience, focus groups offer a means to better understand the way in which identities are constructed and negotiated communally rather than individually, challenging the notion that narrative identity is an independent act.

Accepting the notion that a narrative is not a fixed reality but a construction of voices built one upon another, focus groups offer researchers a way to present multiple even conflicting experiences, expose dynamics of power, and allow for participants, themselves, to negotiate the boundaries of what can be known and spoken aloud. As such, focus group interviewing offers ways to explore a range of responses to a single event or experience that might have implications for sociological, psychological, educational, and medical fields – such as children's differing reactions to a natural disaster and what mediated these emotions or the ways in which individuals with an illness may understand their diagnosis and subsequent medical treatment or discussions of stigmatized topics. This research suggests that focus group interviews can offer a meaningful methodology for researchers working with marginalized populations whose stories might, at times, confirm and disrupt dominant narratives, such that groups may be seen and heard in greater complexity. Researchers working with groups whose individual narratives conflict, particularly groups that are stereotyped, prejudged, or subjugated by dominant groups, might employ a focus group interview as a means to represent a more complex portrait. Mirrored and refracted, as the disparate pieces of a kaleidoscope, co-constructed narratives reveal a more complicated and beautiful cacophony of voices in play with each other.

References

Allison, D. (1992). *Bastard Out of Carolina*. New York, NY: Dutton.
American Association of University Women. (1991) *Shortchanging Girls, Shortchanging America*. Washington, DC: AAUW.
American Association of University Women/Wellesley College Center for Research on Women. (1995) *How Schools Shortchange Girls: The AAUW Report*. New York, NY: Marlowe & Co.
Barbieri, M. (1995) *Sounds From the Heart: Learning to Listen to Girls*. Portsmouth, NH: Heinemann.
Bogdan, R. C., and Biklen, S. K. (2002) *Qualitative Research for Education: An Introduction to Theories and Methods* (4th ed.). Boston, MA: Allyn & Bacon.
Bordo, S. (1993) *Unbearable Weight: Feminism, Western Culture and the Body*. Berkeley, CA: University of California Press.
Bruer, J., and Freud, S. (1957) *Studies on Hysteria* (J. Strachey and A. Freud, Trans.). New York, NY: BasicBooks. (Original work published 1893).
Brown, L. M. (1998) *Raising their Voices: The Politics of Girls' Anger*. Cambridge, MA: Harvard University Press.
Brown, L. M., and Gilligan, C. (1992) *Meeting at the Crossroads: Women's Psychology and Girls' Development*. Cambridge, MA: Harvard University Press.
Bruchac, J. (1997) *Tell Me a Tale*. New York, NY: Harcourt Brace & Co.
Brumberg, J. J. (1998) *The Body Project: An Intimate History of American Girls*. New York, NY: Vintage.
Bruner, J. (1986) *Actual Minds, Possible Words*. Cambridge, MA: Harvard University Press.
Bruner, J. (1987) 'Life as narrative'. *Social Research*, 54(1): 11–32.
Bruner, J. (1990) *Acts of Meaning*. Cambridge, MA: Harvard University Press.
Bruner, J. (2003) *Making Stories: Law, Literature, Life*. New York, NY: Farrar Straus & Giroux.
Burnaford, G. E., Fischer, J., and Hobson, D. (eds.) (2001) *Teachers Doing Research: The Power of Action Through Inquiry*. Mahwah, NJ: Lawrence Erlbaum.
Cahill, A. (2001) *Rethinking Rape*. Ithaca, NY: Cornell University Press.
Carney, S. (2000) 'Body work on ice: The ironies of femininity and sport', In L. Weiss and M. Fine (eds.), *Construction Sites: Excavating Race, Class and Gender Among Urban Youth*. New York, NY: Teachers' College Press, pp. 121–139.

Chambers, E. (2000) 'Applied ethnography', In N. Denzin and Y. Lincoln (eds.), *Handbook of Qualitative Research* (2nd ed.). Thousand Oaks, CA: Sage, pp.851–869.

Chodorow, N. J. (1978) *The Reproduction of Mothering: Psychoanalysis and the Sociology of Gender*. Berkeley: University of California Press.

Clopton and Knesting, (2006) 'Rural school psychology: Reopening the discussion'. *Journal of Research in Rural Education*, 21(5), 1–11.

Coles, R. (1989) *The Call of Stories: Teaching and the Moral Imagination*. Boston, MA: Houghton Mifflin.

DeYoung, A. J. (1994) 'Children at risk in America's rural schools: Economic and cultural dimensions', In R. J. Rossi (ed.), *Schools and Students at Risk*. New York, NY: Teachers' College Press, pp. 229–251.

Driscoll, C. (2002) *Girls*. New York, NY: Columbia University Press.

Edut, O. (1998) *Adiós Barbie: Young Women Write About Body Image and Identity*. Seattle, WA: Seal Press.

Emerson, R. M., Fretz, R. I., and Shaw, L. L. (1995) *Writing Ethnographic Fieldnotes*. Chicago, IL: University of Chicago Press.

Erikson, K. (1976) *Everything in Its Path: Destruction of Buffalo Creek*. NY: Simon & Schuster.

Erickson, S. H. (2001) 'Multiple relationships in rural counseling'. *The Family Journal* 9(3): 302–304.

Fine, M. (1988) 'Sexuality, schooling, and adolescent females: The missing discourse of desire'. *Harvard Educational Review*, 58(1): 29–53.

Fine, M., and Weis, L. (2005) *Beyond Silenced Voices*. Albany, NY: SUNY Press.

Foucault, Michel. (1972) *The Archeology of Knowledge*. New York: Pantheon.

Garmezy, N., and Rutter, M. (1983) *Stress, Coping, and Development in Children*. New York, NY: McGraw-Hill.

Geertz, C. (1973) *The Interpretation of Cultures*. New York: Basic Books.

Geertz, C. (1998) 'Deep hanging out', *New York Review of Books*, 22 October: 69–72.

Gergen, K. J. (1985) 'The Social Constructivist Movement in modern psychology'. *American Psychologist*, 40: 266–275.

Gergen, K. J. (1997) 'The place of the psyche in a constructed world'. *Theory & Psychology*, 7(6): 723–746.

Gergen, K. J., and Gergen, M. M. (1986) 'Narrative form and the construction of psychological science', In T. R. Sarbin (ed.), *Narrative Psychology: The Storied Nature of Human Conduct*. New York, NY: Praeger, pp. 22–44.

Gergen, K. J., and Gergen, M. M. (1988) 'Narrative and the self as relationship', In L. Berkowitz (ed.), *Advances in Experimental Social Psychology* (Vol. 21). San Diego, CA: Academic Press.

Gilligan, C. (1982) *In a Different Voice: Psychological Theory and Women's Development*. Cambridge, MA: Harvard University Press.

Gilligan, C. (1991) 'Women's psychological development: Implications for psychotherapy', In C. Gilligan, A. Rogers and D. Tolman (eds.), *Women, Girls & Psychotherapy: Reframing Resistance*. New York, NY: Harrington Park Press, pp. 5–33.

Gilligan, C. (1993) 'Letter to readers, 1993', In *A Different Voice: Psychological Theory and Women's Development* (2nd ed.). Cambridge, MA: Harvard University Press, pp. ix–xxvii.

Gilligan, C. (1997) 'Remembering Iphigenia: Voice, resonance, and the talking cure', In Shapiro, E. (ed.), *The Inner World in the Outer World: Psychoanalytic Perspectives*. New Haven: Yale University Press.

Gilligan, C., Rogers, A., and Tolman, D. (eds.). (1991) *Women, Girls & Psychotherapy: Reframing Resistance*. New York, NY: Harrington Park Press.

Gonyea, J., Wright, D., and Earl-Kulkosky, T. (2014) 'Navigating Dual Relationships in Rural Communities'. *Journal of Marital and Family Therapy*, 40(1): 125–136.

Haaken, J. (1998) *Pillar of Salt: Gender, Memory and the Perils of Looking Back*. New Brunswick, NJ: Rutgers University Press.

Habermas, J. (1966) 'Knowledge and human interest'. *Inquiry* 9: 285–300.

Harris, A. (2004) *All About the Girl*. New York, NY: Routledge.

Herman, J. (1992) *Trauma and Recovery: The Aftermath of Violence—From Domestic Abuse to Political Terror*. New York, NY: Basic Books.

Horst, E. (1989) 'Dual relationships between psychologists and clients in rural areas'. *Journal of Rural Community Psychology*, 15–24.

Huberman, M., and Miles, M. B. (2002) *The Qualitative Researcher's Companion: Classis and Contemporary Readings*. Thousand Oaks, CA: Sage.

Josselson, R., Lieblich, A., and McAdams, D. (eds.) (2004) *On Becoming the Narrator of One's Own Life*. Washington, DC: American Psychological Association.

Kelleher, K., Taylor, J., and Rickert, V. (1992) 'Mental health services of rural children and adolescents'. *Clinical Psychology Review*, 12: 841–852.

Levinkron, S. (1998) *Cutting: Understanding and Overcoming Self-Mutilation*. New York, NY: W. W. Norton.

Lieblich, A., Tuval-Mashiach, R., and Zilber, T. (1998) *Narrative Research: Reading, Analysis and Interpretation.* Thousand Oaks, CA: Sage.

Loperfido, M., and Ligorio, F. (2012) 'Chronotopes and polyphony as discursive tools to collaboratively build I-positioning', In E. Mininni and A. Manuti (eds.), *Applied Psycholinguistics: Positive Effects and Ethical Perspectives.* Milano, Italy: FrancoAngeli.

Luttrell, W. (2003) *Pregnant Bodies, Fertile Minds: Gender, Race, and the Schooling of Pregnant Teens.* New York, NY: Routledge.

Mac an Ghaill, M. (1994. *The Making of Men: Masculinities, Sexualities, and Schooling.* Berkshire, England: Open University Press.

Madriz, E. (2003) 'Focus groups in feminist research', In N. Denzin and Y. Lincoln (eds.), *Collecting and Interpreting Qualitative Materials* (2nd ed.). Thousand Oaks, CA: Sage, pp. 363–387.

Marcus, S. (1992) 'Fighting bodies, fighting words: A theory and politics of rape prevention', In J. Butler and J. Scott (eds.), *Feminist Theorize the Political.* pp. 385–404. New York, NY: Routledge.

Miller, J. B. (1976) *Toward a New Psychology of Women.* Boston, MA: Beacon Press.

Morris, M. (2016) *Pushout.* New York, NY: The New Press.

New Hampshire Economic and Labor Market Information Bureau. (2014). Community Profiles. Retreived from https://www.nhes.nh.gov/elmi/products/cp/profiles-htm/pittsfield.htm

Orenstein, P. (1994) *Schoolgirls: Young Women, Self-Esteem, and the Confidence Gap.* New York, NY: Doubleday.

Orenstein, P. (2016) *Girls and Sex.* New York, NY: HarperCollins.

Owens, J., Watabe, Y., Michael, K. (2013) 'Culturally responsive health in rural areas', In C. Clauss-Ehlers, Z. Serpell and C. M. Weist (eds.), *Handbook of Culturally Responsive School Mental Health: Advancing Research, Training, Practice, and Policy.* New York, NY: Springer, pp. 31–42.

Parry, A. (1991) 'A universe of stories'. *Family Process,* 30: 7–54.

Petti, T., and Levinson, L. (1986) 'Re-thinking rural mental health services for children and adolescents', In S. Eth and R. Pynoos (eds.), *Post-Traumatic Stress Disorder in Children.* Washington, DC: American Psychiatric Press, pp. 17–44.

Plante, L (2010) *Bleeding to Ease the Pain.* Landham, MD: Rowman & Littlefield.

Ricoeur, P. (1978) 'Metaphor and the main problem of hermeneutics', In C.E. Reagan and D. Stewart (eds.), *The Philosophy of Paul Ricoeur: An Anthology of His Work.* Boston, MA: Beacon Press, pp. 134–148.

Riessman, C. K. (1993) *Narrative Analysis*. Newbury Park, CA: Sage.
Rogers, A., Casey, M., Ekert, J., Holland, J., Nakkula, V., and Sheinberg, N. (1999) 'An interpretive poetics of the languages of the unsayable', In R. Josselson and A. Lieblich (eds.), *Making Meaning of Narratives*. London: Sage, pp. 77–106.
Rosenwald, G. C., and Ochberg, R. L. (1992) *Storied Lives: The Cultural Politics of Self Understanding*. New Haven, CT: Yale University Press.
Sadker, M., and Sadker, D. (1995) *Failing at Fairness: How our Schools Cheat Girls*. New York, NY: Simon & Schuster.
San Antonio, D. (2004) *Adolescent Lives in Transition: How Social Class Influences the Adjustment to Middle School*. Rochester, NY: State University of New York Press.
Sanders, C. (2011) 'An exploration of knowledge and power in narrative, collaborative-based, postmodern therapies: A commentary'. *The Professional Counselor*, 1(3): 201–207.
Shaw, S. (2002) *The Complexity and Paradox of Female Self-Injury: Historical Portrayals, Journeys Toward Stopping, and Contemporary Interventions*. Unpublished doctoral dissertation. Cambridge, MA: Harvard Graduate School of Education.
Slovak, K., and Singer, M. (2002) 'Children and violence: Findings and implications from a rural community'. *Child and Adolescent Social Work Journal*, 19(1): 35–56.
Snow, C., and Selman, R. (2001) *Voices of Love and Freedom*. Brookline, MA: Voices of Love and Freedom.
Spence, D. (1982) *Narrative Truth and Historical Truth: Meaning and Interpretation in Psychoanalysis*. New York, NY: W. W. Norton.
Spencer, R. (2000) 'A Comparison of Relational Psychologies', *Project Report*, No. 5. Wellesley, MA: Stone Center Working Paper Series.
Steiner-Adair, C. (1990) 'The body politic: Normal female adolescent development and the development of eating disorders', In C. Gilligan, N. P. Lyons and T. J. Hanmer (eds.), *Making Connections: The Relational Worlds of Adolescent Girls at Emma Willard School*. Cambridge, MA: Harvard University Press, pp. 162–182.
Steiner-Adair, C. (1991) 'When the body speaks: Girls, eating disorders and psychotherapy', In C. Gilligan, A. Rogers and D. Tolman (eds.), *Women, Girls & Psychotherapy: Reframing Resistance*. New York, NY: Harrington Park Press, pp. 253–266.
Stockman, A. (1990) 'Dual relationships in rural mental health practice: An ethical dilemma'. *Journal of Rural Community Psychology*, 11(2): 31–45.

Straus, M. (2007) *Adolescent Girls in Crisis.* New York, NY: Norton.
Tedlock, B. (2000) 'Ethnography and ethnographic representation', In N. Denzin and Y. Lincoln (eds.), *Handbook of Qualitative Research* (2nd ed.). Thousand Oaks, CA: Sage Publications, pp. 455–486.
Tong, R. P. (1998) *Feminist Thought* (2nd ed.). Boulder, CO: Westview Press.
Ulichny, P., and Schoener, W. (2000) 'Teacher-researcher collaboration from two perspectives', In B. Brizuela, J. P. Stewart, R. G. Carrillo and J. G. Berger (eds.), *Acts of Inquiry in Qualitative Research.*
van der Kolk, B., and van der Hart, O. (1995) 'The intrusive past: The flexibility of memory and the engraving of trauma', In C. Caruth (ed.), *Trauma: Explorations in Memory.* Baltimore, MD: The Johns Hopkins University Press.
Ward, J. V. (2000) *The skin We're In: Teaching Our Children to Be Emotionally Strong, Socially Smart, Spiritually Connected.* New York, NY: The Free Press.
Weber, M. (1949) *The Methodology of the Social Sciences.* E. Shils and H. Finch (eds. and Trans.). Glencoe, IL: Free Press.
Werner, E. E., and Smith, R. S. (1982) *Vulnerable But Invincible: A Longitudinal Study of Resilient Children and Youth.* New York, NY: McGraw-Hill.
White, M., and Epston, D. (1990) *Narrative Means to Therapeutic Ends.* New York: W. W. Norton.
Wilson, S. M., and Peterson, G. W. (1988) 'Life satisfaction among adults from rural Wortham, 2001 Wortham, Stanton. 2001. "Narrative self-construction and the nature of self"', In *Narratives in Action.* New York: Teachers College Press, pp. 136–156.
Wilson, S. M., Henry, C. S., and Peterson, G. W. (1997) 'Life satisfaction among low-income rural youth from Appalachia'. *Journal of Adolescence,* 20: 443–459.
Wortham, S. (2001). *Narratives in Action: A Strategy for Research and Analysis.* New York, NY: Teachers College Press.

Erin E. Seaton is a lecturer in the School of Arts and sciences at Tufts University, USA. She gained a Ed.M. and Ed.D. in Human Development and Psychology from Harvard University Graduate School of Education. Her subsequent research and scholarship has focused on rural and urban education, gender and development, literacy, inequalities in education, and violence prevention in schools. All of her work is underpinned by an interest in the nature and meaning of narratives, with a particular emphasis on the ways in which stories about race, class, gender, sexuality, and education shape identity formation.

15

Bringing Socio-Narratology and Visual Methods to Focus Group Research

Cassandra Phoenix, Noreen Orr and Meridith Griffin

Introduction

How to capitalize on theoretical frameworks within focus group research for the purpose of enhancing data generation and informing analysis is a topic that has received little attention within the qualitative research literature. Informed by the work of Frank (2010), in this chapter we

---

C. Phoenix (✉)
Department for Health, University of Bath, Bath, UK
e-mail: C.Phoenix@bath.ac.uk

N. Orr
PenCLARHRC Evidence Synthesis Team, Medical School, University of Exeter, Exeter, UK
e-mail: N.Orr@exeter.ac.uk

M. Griffin
Department of Health, Aging and Society, McMaster University, Hamilton, Ontario, Canada
e-mail: griffmb@mcmaster.ca

respond to this lacuna by discussing the value of approaching focus group research from a socio-narratology perspective. Additionally, and in accord with a growing awareness of visual methods within the social sciences (Pauwels 2011), we reflect briefly on the process of using research-informed film as a means of eliciting – at times new – stories in a focus group setting. We illustrate our discussion with empirical data drawn from two research projects that have used focus groups to generate insight into people's perceptions and experiences of growing older.

The first of these projects – 'Maturing Muscle' (MM)[1] – sought to understand how sharing the experiences of older adults involved in natural (i.e. 'drug free') bodybuilding might act to challenge young people's stereotypical assumptions about the ageing body and what constitutes 'appropriate behaviour' in later life (see Phoenix and Smith 2011; Phoenix and Griffin 2013). The second project – Moving Stories (MS)[2] – further developed this work by drawing on the experiences of older adults involved in a variety of physical activities. The stories of these experiences were then shared in focus group settings with young, midlife and older adults (see Phoenix and Orr 2014; Orr and Phoenix 2015). Each of these projects approached the focus group discussions as an opportunity for storytelling amongst and between participants. Moreover, the group discussions were viewed as ideal settings to trouble certain dominant storylines such as the narrative of decline (Gullette 1997). By emphasizing notions of inevitable decline and deterioration (mentally, physically and socially) in older age, this narrative can severely restrict alternative imaginings of later life.

Central to our intention of 'troubling' the dominant narrative within these focus group discussions was the use of visual media that had been created to represent our interpretations of the stories that older adults told about physicality in later life (for an example see Phoenix et al. 2012). Specifically, we used digital stories as a means of film elicitation (Meadows 2003). Banks and Zeitlyn (2015) note that, compared with photographs, film is less often used in research contexts – partly due to the logistical

---

[1] 'Understanding Experiences and Expectations of Ageing through Old and Young Bodies: A Narrative Study' was funded by the Nuffield Foundation Small Grants Scheme (Ref: SGS/36142).
[2] 'Moving Stories: Understanding the Role of Physical Activity on Experiences and Perceptions of (Self-) ageing' was funded by the Economic and Social Research Council (RES-061-25-0491).

challenges that it can pose, such as sourcing laptops, projectors, sound, power, and so forth. While we acknowledge these challenges, being able to see older bodies *being* active, while simultaneously hearing stories about the meaning of movement in later life, was paramount to our purpose of gaining insight into how people of different ages respond to these versions of ageing that seemingly countered the dominant narrative of decline.

Understanding how people listen to and respond to the stories that they hear is an important – but often ignored – component of narrative research; yet it is crucial for gaining a more nuanced comprehension of what stories can do (Smith and Sparkes 2008). This is because narratives do not only refer to past experience, but may help create experiences for their audience and move them to respond in certain ways by initiating, suggesting and even calling for, certain responses (Martin 2007). As such, and as often witnessed in focus group settings, narration is a social activity, involving other participants, who may provide storied responses to a story heard. Knowing how audiences respond to certain stories can help us to understand what it is, exactly, that stories can *do* beyond providing insight into individual experience. This way of thinking about stories and story-telling underpins Frank's (2010) notion of socio-narratology.

According to Frank (2010), socio-narratology aims to understand what the story *does*, rather than to understand the story as a portal into the mind of the storyteller. For him, the work of stories is to animate human life. Stories 'work with people, for people, and always stories work on people, affecting what people are able to see as real, as possible, and as worth doing or best avoided' (p. 3). Thus, the scope of socio-narratology is the reciprocal work of stories and humans in creating the social world. In addition, viewing stories as actors, rather than as passive accounts, enables researchers to consider what capacities enable stories to do the work that they do. After all, 'Stories do not do everything' asserts Frank. The question, therefore, is 'what do they have the capacity to do best?' (2010: 15). In what follows, we demonstrate what socio-narratology might 'look like' within a focus group discussion. We do this by paying close analytical attention to the work that the stories of physical activity in later life seemed to do with, for and on the focus group participants and the stories that they told about their own (anticipated) ageing process.

Stories of Ageing in Focus (Groups)

When discussing 'what it means to grow old' with young adults, our previous research has consistently shown that it is viewed in negative terms (see Phoenix and Sparkes 2006a, b). This finding was further supported in these more recent projects with younger participants being overwhelmingly pessimistic about ageing and growing older throughout the focus group discussion. For example, a typical response to this topic was:

> *Male 1:* Oh, it's very bleak. Um, decrepit, restricted, slow, uncomfortable. Um, dependent. Just useless, basically. That's my vision of old age.
> *Female 1:* Worried and dependent, yeah.
> *Female 2:* ...cranky, grey hair, weight gain, and ... fear.
> (MM. Group 1)

Further, when asked explicitly to describe the meaning of exercise throughout the life course, the young adults equated ageing with a slowing of the body, decreased intensity of exercise, and a shift in exercise type from that driven by notions of improvement and performance to that of lower intensity, lower impact, and with the purpose of 'socializing' and 'keeping mobile'.

Similar to the young adults responses, when midlife participants were asked what they anticipated the future to hold, they constructed their responses around a presumed inevitability of physical deterioration and resultant withdrawal from activity so as not to encounter failure, or demand too much from their imagined ageing, changing body:

> *Male 7:* ...I think as [male 5] was saying...after you get to a certain age when you're playing cricket, you become, you know, an umpire. So there's a kind of natural...progression, I guess, when it's time to stop play, you know, take the sidelines.
> *Male 2:* ...If you're doing it from a competitive perspective, if you can't be competitive anymore, then...you don't want to bring your team down, or you don't want to bring your individual achievement down...But...if you don't feel, perhaps, from a competitive perspective, that you can perform

anymore, then you're going to... say 'well I, I don't want to do that anymore'.

Male 6: ... I think a lot of the time your body... tells you to ease up on that sort of thing anyway, at whatever point it comes for the individual. When you reach a point where you just physically, your body can't take 80 minutes of... whatever.

(MS. Group 3c)

However, throughout the course of our discussions, which occured across several separate meetings with each group, it became evident that the stories told within these settings had the capacity to do things. This was particularly the case with regard to the stories shared in digital form.

What Might Stories be Doing Within a Focus Group Setting? Stories Get Under the Skin

After watching the digital story created in the Maturing Muscle project, all of the young adults involved in the focus groups responded with a declaration that they had previously lacked awareness of older adults taking part in sport or exercising 'seriously'. That is what Stebbins (1982) might refer to as a form of serious leisure, which requires considerable personal effort, knowledge and training. Viewing the digital story about the experiences of mature natural bodybuilders alerted participants to this new and – for them – novel storyline, which subsequently challenged many of their existing fixed, and rather stereotypical assumptions about what an ageing body could and could not do. For example:

Female 1: It offers more options to you, doesn't it? If you can see that there are people who are still doing bodybuilding it offers more options than just following the stereotype of, you know, just the older person who watches a lot of television and doesn't get out much ... It shows that you can have much more decision over how you live your life even when you are limited in some ways. You can still have hobbies and find a way to enjoy life.

Female 5: Yeah, I think watching the bodybuilders made me, it opened my eyes to be like, oh, you know, there are possibilities. You can do things.
(MM. Group 2b)

These comments demonstrate how the digital story worked on the young adults; educating them and expanding their frame of reference by presenting an additional route that could be imagined on their existing narrative map of ageing (see Phoenix and Sparkes, 2006a; Griffin, 2010). It is this imaginative opening that makes stories attractive and can explain why people might be willing to listen to a story and, in some instances, use it to revise the story of their own life (Frank 2010). This process was further exemplified in the focus groups within the Maturing Muscle project when the young participants shifted their discussion about other older people to one about their own ageing bodies:

Male 3: I was thinking as I was watching [the film] . . . that actually I'd quite like to look muscular and athletic even when I am that old . . . So, yeah, maybe that's me in a few years' time.
Male 2: Yeah . . . it's like he said, I wouldn't mind looking like they would on a day-to-day basis . . .
(MM. Group 2a)

Such responses illuminate how storytelling within a focus group setting has the capacity to arouse participants imaginations and, in this instance, move them to reconsider their own ageing process.

Indeed, Frank asserts that it is by attracting and holding imagination and evoking emotion that stories are able to 'ambush' people, causing listeners to become 'caught up' in the story by making 'the unseen not only visible but compelling' (2010: 41–48). Stories can resonate with those who listen to them, explaining why some people might be willing to listen to a story and find a location for it in their own 'inner library' (2010: 55). In short, Frank argues, stories can 'get under your skin'. Remaining sensitized to socio-narratology when conducting and analyzing the data constructed during our focus groups enabled us to understand more fully the manner in which the digital stories 'got under the skin' of our participants. Meeting the young people from the Maturing Muscle project for a follow-up focus group some weeks after sharing the digital story, it was notable how the interactions, on this occasion, involved participants trading examples from within their daily life where the stories heard in the previous meeting had shifted into the foreground of their thoughts. This is exemplified in the following extract:

> *Male 1*: I have thought about it a bit more, my own ageing, which I just haven't really done very much at all before...
>
> *Male 4*: I've been really attentive to other people, and watching older people, things like that. Certainly my parents, the next time I went home I was really looking at them ... I've become very sensitive to watching people and thinking about how old they look and what they do, and whether I want to be doing what they're doing when I'm that age.
> (MM. Group 3a)

These and subsequent discussions within the Maturing Muscle focus groups signalled how the digital story facilitated the process of rethinking prejudices towards being old. In this sense, the focus group meetings worked as an impetus for questions to be asked by the participants about the parameters of their socially situated beliefs concerning age appropriate behaviour, especially in relation to physical activity.

Similarly, we also witnessed (digital) stories getting under the skin of a number of the midlife participants involved in the Moving Stories project. This was especially the case when they were challenged to think about being physically active in the present in preparation for the future:

> *Female 4*: ... it does almost ... motivate you because you think in order to get to that age and be able to do that, you have to live healthily now.
>
> *Female 2*: Have you ever thought about exercising now for your future?
>
> *Female 4*: No but now I'm thinking...
>
> *Female 2*: I don't think much past a couple of years, you know.

Female 4: Yeah, it did make me think I should be more active, well, I am healthy but it does ... inspire you and you think you've got to exercise now to be able to get to that stage, to be healthy when you're older.

Female 1: It's like what we were talking about last week about role models and reference points ... I've got older people that I see, they become your reference points for what you want to be when you are older. So back to my mother-in-law going body boarding and climbing over rocks and things like that. It becomes your expectation of how you might be when you are older.

Female 3: I don't know that it's changed how I felt about being active as I get older. It's reaffirmed, I think, what I already felt about wanting to just stay active. But it was interesting, [Female 2], the question you have just asked about, do you think now about being active for your future life rather than just for now. I have to say, now I think differently about some things. I need to start incorporating into my activity things that are going to help my flexibility, which has always been there, naturally because it's only now that I've started to notice some decrease in that.

(MS. Group 3d)

For these participants, viewing the Moving Stories film opened up a reflective dialogue, an opportunity to imagine – through interaction – a different self in the future and one that had implications for the present. Seeing older adults doing physical activity and listening to their stories within a focus group setting allowed for collective discussion and reflection, thereby providing the imaginative opening for midlife participants to consider who they wanted to be over time.

Stories Connect People

In addition to 'getting under the skin', the stories told within a focus group can also connect people. For example, many of the focus group participants connected with the people in the digital story, identifying with their enjoyment of physical activity. This seemed to facilitate absorption into their story (Hinyard and Kreuter 2007), and opened up opportunities to explore together the selves that they could become in the future; referred to as 'possible selves' by Markus and Nurius (1986). For example, after viewing the Moving Stories digital story, the midlife participants described their sense of connection with those that were featured:

Male 6: I was smiling through a lot of it because you could just see that everybody in the film was really enjoying themselves. And do you want everybody to really enjoy themselves, whether you're old or young? The fact that a lot of old people don't seem to be enjoying themselves so much, maybe when you see them out in the streets, you know, or meet them in a social setting. And it's really positive seeing people who really were.

Male 3: I really enjoyed hearing everyone's motivations for what they did, because they were all completely different. So, like the guy, talking about playing badminton. He enjoyed playing a good game just for the love of the game, and not to win. And that for him was enough, and he got a kick out of it. And then the chap who just enjoyed the thrill of the ride and then the guy, you know, and the lady just dancing in the nursing home. For them, they just enjoyed the social aspect. And the lady who loved, just loved the ocean and being out. So each of these people were so different, and they had completely different backgrounds, but they knew why they were doing it, which I think is great...

Male 2: But that was interesting, you know, that all their stories were different, but there was a common theme through all of them, because actually ... there was enjoyment. It was about them feeling good about themselves, about the situation. I think one person said, 'When you're laughing, how can you be angry?' ... And it's not about being old or young, it's about, because we all, whether, you're old or young, you just want to be happy. That doesn't change, I guess, and that's what they get from it ... the point is that they were having fun. They were enjoying themselves and I hope, I hope, hope I'm like that.
(MS. Group 3c)

That the older adults were happy and having fun while being physically active challenged the audiences preconceived ideas that there may be little to enjoy in older age. Furthermore, the short discussion presented above demonstrates how the digital story worked on the focus group participants by connecting them with the storytellers (i.e. the older adults in the film) and indeed each other, through a shared realization that enjoyment of physical activity could be a common thread across the generational groups. Elements of this were also seen in the focus groups conducted with young people as part of the same study. Reflecting once again, on the digital story, one discussion went as follows:

Male 1: ...yeah I can relate to a lot of them [the participants in the digital story] really....I hadn't really considered...I think I had a lot of preconceptions about what, you know, older retired people would do, to be honest...

Male 4: Yeah, there was the one, like, people think about, it's just, like, relaxing and just chilling all day. But, that's not what they do. It was good to see that they actually carried on with things that they enjoyed.

Male 3: I think, for me, I can relate, to some extent, the enjoyment of cycling, and stuff like that. But they are at a very different stage in their life to myself. And I think, I can't relate as much to that, because, you know, they've been through an awful lot of their life. So to some extent, yes, with the activities they do and they enjoy it. But I maybe don't relate so much to where they are at in their lives.

Male 5: ...I felt a lot of connection with the woman who was swimming at the end. I, yeah, I think I share a lot of what she was saying, about her motivation to go swimming and the pleasure she gets from swimming. I felt totally in connection with her, there....and I'm not...a particular swimmer. But, it was just great the joy that she gets from it and the lust for life that she has. And the sense of adventure, I really connected with that.
(MS, Group 2c)

Similar to the previous extract, this group of young adults also spoke of relatedness and connections to the stories they had heard and, perhaps more importantly, those who had told them. They also acknowledged disruptions to their previously taken-for-granted assumptions about what (some) older bodies enjoyed doing. Of significance here, however, was what seemed to be a very clear understanding that despite examples of commonality and connectedness, their lives were undoubtedly 'different'. It was this notion of difference that provided the momentum for stories to also disconnect people.

Stories Disconnect People

The dynamic and dialogical nature of the focus group meetings enabled different responses to the digital stories. Similar to the way in which stories have the capacity to reduce a sense of 'otherness' by connecting people (Frank 2010), stories circulating within a focus group meeting can also work to disconnect and emphasize difference. This was witnessed in a focus group meeting with older adults, who expressed how disconnected they felt from one of the characters in the digital story. This particular character regularly attended a low impact exercise class and was seen in the digital story performing a series of mobility exercises including shoulder circles, arm raises, balancing on one leg and so forth:

Female 2: I found myself thinking with the lady who was moving her shoulders and, 'goodness she's only sort of, 8 years older than I am'. And I hadn't really considered that, that would be the sort of exercise I would be thinking of then, you know. I hadn't really anticipated that, that sort of, that would help me. (pause)
Female 4: No, I can't ...
Female 2: It's sober, it's sobering, isn't it?
Female 4: Yes, the horror of having to team in round a group of people, sort of doing, these, sort of exercises.
At my stage of life, I have a horror of being with a group of real oldies, doing that sort of thing. But, I think you must, I'm sure you change as the years pass and your own abilities change.
I think I felt a bit like [Female 2], I think, 'oh dear'.

Female 3:   Yes, and I think it's ... it's downhill from now on, really. If you're a young sportsperson and you have an injury ... which prevents you from doing your physical activity, the chances are that you will recover and then you can pick up where you left off. But at our age, I think you're more conscious that ... we're fighting the deterioration off. And that's part of the reason for the exercise.

Female 2:   If you don't use it, you lose it.

Female 3:   Yes, yes, yes.

Female 2:   And you ... I think that drives you on, doesn't it?

Female 1:   Depressing, really. Unless something actually drastic happens, that's us, at this limited thing and, and, whereas that you see that on television in old people's homes, isn't it? That's it, that's it, how can you prevent it really? So I try not to think about it too much, actually.
(MS. Group 5d)

This story was not one with which the participants could or wanted to self-identify. It represented something different – a 'real oldie' – from the future plotlines that they currently envisaged. As such, the story worked on disconnecting these focus group participants from the particular storyteller. Likewise, the digital story shared in the Maturing Muscle project also disconnected some of its young audience by projecting storylines about a sporting body that conflicted with those already taken-on-board as their own:

Female 1:   I think for men it's okay. The woman looked awful... Sometimes it was a bit too much. Like, why do you want your body to be on show to everyone when you're that age, happily married, or you're married with kids? You should just grow old gracefully and live a happy life. But then, why not? Why can't they do that? But, I don't know, I just don't think I like bodybuilding.

Female 6:   ... I agree with [Female 1] in the respect that I think it's okay for men, but not for women. And that's just, obviously, because of society. You don't picture women as

attractive if they have lots of muscles, they're not meant to be like that. So I think it's really good that they're keeping fit. And, you know, that they are making something with their life rather than just sitting around. But I don't really like it, if I'm honest.
(MM. Group 3b)

The ongoing struggle to resolve competing storylines about gender, age, and physicality was played out in the focus groups, as the participants worked back and forth between their own – sometimes conflicting – responses to the stories that they had heard. Indeed, as demonstrated in the example above, while the female participants generally applauded the mature natural bodybuilders' ability to challenge dominant storylines about the ageing body, some were unable to engage and thereby disconnected from the story at the point where natural bodybuilding for women was offered as an alternative way of ageing.

According to Frank 'not all stories engage all people ... any particular person will respond to the call of only some stories amongst the many that call out to people' (2010: 4). If people are not engaged or immersed in a story, they are more likely to resist it by presenting arguments that 'counter, discount or reject' its message (McQueen et al. 2011: 675). Such resistance was observed in a focus group meeting with older adults where the participants rejected the idea that physical activity in later life could be fun and enjoyable:

Female 6: I admire them [physically active older adults], but I don't particularly want to be that physically active.
Female 1: No, good for them.
Female 5: Yeah, good for them.
Female 2: It made me feel a little old, you know. And good for them if they like doing stuff like that. But, you know ...
Female 5: I don't, I don't like organized things like that. I'd rather do things with just one or two people.
Female 6: I tried squash once. Oh God, it was awful. I couldn't see the ball.

Female 4: I tried jogging and it nearly killed me. It's a bit like pounding the streets, isn't it? I can't, I can't understand anyone...
Female 6: Oh jogging, no. Oh my God, what's the fun in that?
Female 5: In what?
Female 4: Jogging.
Female 5: Oh God, no.
Female 3: Brenda always says 'they're stupid'. They'll end up having knee operations, 10 years before they need them.
Female 6: Well the bloke who invented jogging, dropped dead didn't he? And he wasn't old.
Female 5: Yes, he did.
Female 6: I can't, just can't see the point. I mean, and I'm looking at the scenery, you know ... talking to whoever you're walking with ... just heads down like that for miles.
Female 5: Most of them have music in their ears, don't they?
Female 6: And, and the really serious walkers, which is why I wouldn't join a really serious walking group, and we've got Dartmoor[3] and things like that. And it's lashing down with rain and they're all walking along with their sticks, like this. Hoods up, packs up, covered in waterproofs. And you think ... what are you doing?
(MS. Group 6d)

That these participants were not 'hailed' by the Moving Stories digital story (see Griffin 2010), may be explained by what Frank refers to as their 'narrative habitus'. This, he explains, is '... the embodied sense of attraction, indifference, or repulsion people feel in response to stories; the intuitive, usually tacit sense that some story is for us or not for us' (Frank 2010: 53). Although the participants professed admiration for the characters in the story, ultimately they dismissed both the story and its message by drawing on their own experiences and observations to contradict the notion that certain forms of physical activity could be pleasurable.

---

[3] Dartmoor is a National Park in the South West of England.

Reflective Comments

Approaching our focus groups from a socio-narratology perspective has sensitized us to the work that stories can do on, for and with people. Indeed, the data gathered in these settings – across two different projects – pointed to a number of specific capacities that stories about older physically active adults might have. Specifically, we have shown how stories can get under the skin of those who listen to them; shifting from an abstract, distant account to becoming an embodied companion for life ahead. They can also stretch and expand existing storylines; highlighting contradictions and evoking imagination (Randall and McKim 2008). In doing so, they can connect people whose storied selves may previously have developed with less awareness of other lives, or other ways of being.

Yet, conducting focus group research while being informed by a socio-narratology approach can also reveal the inherent complexities of narrating human life. Emphasizing the reciprocal work of stories and humans in creating the social world, there were instances where (pre-)existing storylines competed in such a manner that they disconnected the storylistener from the storyteller. For example, social norms surrounding what constitutes appropriate muscularity for women hindered some of the female participants' ability to engage with the Maturing Muscle digital story. In addition, for others, the notion of growing older as a burden and something which should be fought by concealing the appearance of an ageing body are dominant narratives within Western society. They are dominant because they are continuously told and retold over time by individuals and the institutions of which Western society is comprised. Generally speaking, people will always have an affinity with and a propensity to (re)tell the most dominant storyline. Our findings indicate that this likelihood is somewhat inevitable when the alternative storyline on offer fails to engage.

Importantly, as also observed during our focus group meetings, stories always do different things to different people. This characteristic speaks to Frank's (2010) assertion that stories are always out of control. Here, a number of individual responses to the digital stories illustrated how on occasions, (alternative) stories of ageing can work to reinforce existing fears about growing older. Responses of this nature illustrated how stories have the capacity to act upon listeners in ways that their tellers (and indeed re-tellers) do not anticipate (Frank 2010). Randall and Phoenix (2009) note that the capacity of stories to be out of control is inherent to every interview and focus group context. This is because neither party can possibly know beforehand the direction that their interchange will take. Within these focus groups, when participants were not inspired by the digital story to re-imagine their own narrative, their default position was to respond by using existing and dominant narratives circulating within society. In this instance, these were the oppressive and damaging narratives of anti-ageing, and old age as a burden. As such, the extent to which the digital stories worked upon the participants and evoked a sense of admiration, inspiration, fear or scepticism points to the degree of engagement that each individual had with that particular storyline and the connection that they felt with the characters.

Focus groups afford an effective means of capitalizing on the synergy arising from the interactions of the participants (Carey 2016). Approaching this synergy from a narrative perspective allows the movement and connecting / disconnecting power of stories as they work to be observed. Which outcome prevails is something that is often beyond the control of the storyteller. Indeed, what acts as a counter-story for one, may do quite the opposite for another (Phoenix and Smith 2011). Understanding what stories people are more likely to engage with is a useful first step. Being attentive to peoples' narrative habitus – their disposition to certain stories over others – is another. These challenges are important and return us to Frank's (2010; 15) overarching question imposed by socio-narratology; 'Stories do not do everything. The question is, what do they have the capacity to do best?' Further research is required if we are to address this question from a theoretically-informed methodological perspective and apply it in a useful way to focus group research.

References

Banks, M., and Zeitlyn, D. (2015) *Visual Methods in Social Research* (2nd ed.). London: Sage.

Carey, M. A. (2016) 'Focus groups – what is the same, what is new, what is next?' *Qualitative Health Research*, 26: 731–733.

Frank, A. W. (2010) *Letting Stories Breathe: A Socio-Narratology*. Chicago: The University of Chicago Press.
Griffin, M. (2010) 'Setting the scene: Hailing women into a running identity'. *Qualitative Research in Sport Exercise and Health*, 2(2): 153–174.
Gullette, M. M. (1997) *Declining to Decline: Cultural Combat and the Politics of Midlife*. Charlottesville: University of Virginia Press.
Hinyard, L. J., and Kreuter, M. W. (2007) 'Using narrative as a tool for health behaviour change: A conceptual, theoretical, and empirical overview'. *Health Education & Behavior*, 34: 777–792.
Markus, H., and Nurius, P. (1986) 'Possible selves'. *American Psychologist*, 41 (9): 954–969.
Martin, V. (2007) 'Dialogue in the narrative process'. *Medical Humanities*, 33: 49–54.
Meadows, D. (2003) 'Digital storytelling: Research-based practice in new media'. *VisualCommunication*, 2(2): 189–193.
McQueen, A., Kreuter, M. W., Kalesan, B., and Alcaraz, I. (2011) 'Understanding narrative effects: The impact of breast cancer survivor stories on message processing, attitudes, and beliefs among African American women'. *Health Psychology*, 30(6): 674–682.
Orr, N., and Phoenix, C. (2015) 'Photographing physical activity: Using visual methods to 'grasp at' the sensual experiences of the ageing body'. *Qualitative Research*, 15(4): 454–472.
Pauwels, E. (2011) 'An integrated conceptual framework for visual social research', In E. Margolis and L. Pauwels (eds.), *The SAGE Handbook of Visual Research Methods*. London: Sage, pp. 3–23.
Phoenix, C., and Griffin, M. (2013) 'Narratives at Work: What can stories of older athletes do?' *Ageing & Society*, 33(2): 243–266.
Phoenix, C., and Orr, N. (2014) 'Pleasure: A forgotten dimension of ageing and physical activity'. *Social Science and Medicine*, 115: 94–102.
Phoenix, C., and Smith, B. (2011) 'Telling a (good?) counterstory of aging?: Natural bodybuilding meets the narrative of decline'. *Journals of Gerontology: Series B. Psychological Science and Social Science*, 66B(5): 628–639.
Phoenix, C., Orr, N., and Smalley, A. (2012). Moving stories: A short film. Available to view at: https://vimeo.com/42829169 [last accessed 25 March 2016].
Phoenix, C., & Sparkes, A. C. (2006a). 'Young athletic bodies and narrative maps of aging'. *Journal of Aging Studies*, 20, 107–121.

Phoenix, C., & Sparkes, A. C. (2006b). 'Keeping it in the family: narrative maps of ageing and young athlete's perceptions of their futures'. *Ageing and Society*, 26, 631–648.

Randall, W. L., and McKim, A. E. (2008) *Reading Our Lives: The Poetics of Growing Old*. Oxford: Oxford University Press.

Randall, W. L., and Phoenix, C. (2009) 'The problem with truth in qualitative interviews: Reflections from a narrative perspective'. *Qualitative Research in Sport & Exercise*, 1(2): 125–140.

Smith, B., and Sparkes, A. C. (2008) 'Changing bodies, changing narratives and the consequences of tellability: A case study of becoming disabled through sport'. *Sociology of Health and Illness*, 30(2): 217–236.

Stebbins, R. A. (1982) 'Serious leisure. A conceptual statement'. *Pacific Sociological Review*, 25: 251–272.

Cassandra Phoenix is a Reader (Associate Professor) at the University of Bath, UK. Her research interests focus on the socio-cultural aspects of ageing, health and wellbeing. This is underpinned by an ongoing commitment to the use and development of qualitative methods to address complex health issues. Her work is published widely in gerontology, sports science, qualitative methodology, health and medical sociology journals. She is co-editor of *Physical Activity and Sport in Later Life: Critical Perspectives* (2015, Palgrave Macmillan), and co-author of *The World of Physical Culture in Sport and Exercise* (2011).

Noreen Orr is a Research Fellow in the PenCLARHRC Evidence Synthesis Team at the University of Exeter (UK) Medical School. She has a specific interest in using qualitative research methods and has led on a qualitative synthesis strand of a mixed methods review of older people and physical activity. Her work has also covered a systematic review of evidence on older people's sensory experiences of the natural environment. She has published in gerontology and sports science journals.

Meridith Griffin is an Assistant Professor in the Department of Health, Aging and Society, at McMaster University, Canada. Her research interests focus on the social-psychological aspects of ageing, health and wellbeing, disability, gender and embodiment. She is particularly interested in these issues as they play out in the social and cultural realms of leisure and physical activity. A critical qualitative researcher, she works with interpretive forms of understanding, including life history, ethnography, visual and narrative approaches. Meridith works at the intersection of the disciplines of sociology and psychology.

16

Focus Groups as Anticipatory Methodology: A Contribution from Science and Technology Studies Towards Socially Resilient Governance

Phil Macnaghten

Introduction

Focus group practitioners have tended to emphasize the capacity of the methodology for exploring how people think about topics that are familiar, that have some grounding in everyday experience, and in relation to which people develop views and opinions on a topic that is chosen by the researcher. Thus in academic projects, focus group research has explored people's views and experience on a wide variety of topics – often health related – ranging from AIDS, contraception, drink-driving, health and wellbeing, nutrition, mental illness, insomnia, fashion, to identity and numerous others. Consequently, when people are asked in focus group research to explore issues, social phenomena, services or products, the assumption is that collective small group deliberation can provide in-depth understanding on how opinions and

---

P. Macnaghten (✉)
Knowledge, Technology and Innovation Group,
Wageningen University, Wageningen, The Netherlands
e-mail: philip.macnaghten@wur.nl

© The Author(s) 2017
R.S. Barbour, D.L. Morgan (eds.), *A New Era in Focus Group Research*, DOI 10.1057/978-1-137-58614-8_16

points of view are constructed, expressed and how they are subsequently hardened into attitudes. Less articulated in the literature is the role of focus groups as an anticipatory methodology, as a tool to research public responses in-the-making, especially when confronted by unfamiliar topics, policies or social phenomena that may be of paramount interest to the researcher, but which are less obviously grounded in proximate experience. Yet, it is this anticipatory function that underpins the use of a significant body of focus group research in public policy arenas – particularly in those areas that need to claim legitimacy though the prerogative of incorporating public opinion.

In this chapter I examine the use of focus groups as an anticipatory or 'upstream' method in public perception research on new science and technology (on the idea of 'upstream' public engagement in science and technology see Wilsdon and Willis 2004). The political imperative for this research is clear-cut. In the context of widespread adverse public reaction to particular technological risk issues over the last three decades – most notably in Europe in relation to agricultural biotechnologies and their failure to command societal acceptance – policymakers have sponsored initiatives aimed at encouraging wider public engagement and societal participation in technoscientific processes, as a means of improving relations between science and society. The policy context for this kind of research involves exploring whether a deliberative form of research – in our case making use of focus groups – could lead to better representation of the potential social and ethical implications of the technology, at a stage early enough to guide (or even restrict) their further development. Indeed by the early 2000s, institutional programmes of public engagement had become constituted as an integral and strategic ingredient in the new scientific governance, whether as a route to better policy decisions, democratic renewal, citizen empowerment, or as a technique aimed at fostering greater citizen trust in governance and policy (European Commission 2002; Felt et al. 2007; Gavelin et al. 2007; Irwin 2006).

Yet, is this a possible and credible scenario? Are focus group methodologies and associated conceptual approaches up to the task? Can they plausibly give voice to the articulation of public views and opinions on topics on which participants – at least prior to the focus group intervention – have poorly formed views and attitudes?. Policy logics may demand early or upstream public engagement in the desire for robust social science and technology policy, but it is not self-evident that methodologies can be crafted that provide reliable and usable data on how people are likely to respond to a technology that remains at an early stage of development.

It is in the quest to respond to these questions that led myself and colleagues to craft an anticipatory methodology using in-depth focus groups. Rather than undertaking public engagement research after a controversial social or ethical question has arisen in relation to a new technology – as is often the case in such research (Rogers-Hayden and Pidgeon 2007) – our task was to craft an anticipatory methodology capable of articulating a contextual understanding of how people develop attitudes under conditions of unfamiliarity. Such a task is of considerable complexity – not least due to the classic Collingridge dilemma (Collingridge 1980). This states that at, an early stage of a technology's development, we are unlikely to know the social and ethical issues that will be associated with its development; whereas, once those issues are known and accessible, pathologies of lock-in, path dependency and closure may, by then, be set with public opinion already polarized.

Design Criteria

In this section I describe the design principles that have guided the development of an 'upstream' focus group methodology and how this has been applied across different research projects. These range from an early 1996/1997 project aimed at exploring public views and attitudes to agricultural biotechnology in Britain (Grove-White et al. 1997), to an ensuing 2000/2001 UK project designed to throw light on the factors likely to shape future responses to the applications of animals to biotechnology (Macnaghten 2001, 2004). A further three projects undertaken between 2004 and 2009 related to nanotechnology – one that sought to develop an 'upstream' public engagement methodology in the UK (Kearnes et al. 2006); another a cross-European project on lay ethical engagement (Davies et al. 2009); and the third project that was aimed at comparing Brazilian and UK citizen responses (Macnaghten and Guivant 2011). More recently, there was the 2011/2012 UK project providing an analysis of public discourse on climate geoengineering (Macnaghten and Szerszynski 2013), and a final 2012/2013 project on fracking technology, conducted in the north of England (Williams et al. 2015). Although these projects have covered a number of emerging technologies over a period of nearly two decades, there remain points of convergence that warrant instantiation, not least in their broad aspiration of anticipating the kinds of world – including the associated social and ethical dimensions – that novel science and technology bring into being.

Context

First, given that, by definition, people are unfamiliar with emerging technology and with the social and ethical issues it poses, the methodology has been designed to elicit a contextual understanding of how people are likely to respond and thus of the factors deemed most probable to shape future public responses. The focus on understanding context is a core element of the methodological design.

For the 1996/1997 project on agricultural technologies, for example, the key context was deemed to be everyday food practices. How people will respond to genetically modified foods, the argument went, will depend on how they think about food in general and what they consider to be the appropriate role of technology in food production (Grove-White et al. 1997). For this reason, the focus groups began with 20 minutes of discussion on what had changed in the world of food over the last 5–10 years or so, exploring with participants what had been lost and what had been gained. The discussions themselves were illuminating, as participants, in general, spoke of their ambivalence towards the use of advanced technology in food: while, on the one hand, technology had enabled people to lead more busy and convenient lives, it had, on the other hand, generated concerns about more and more food processing, the use of artificial preservatives and colouring agents and the apparent increase in food health scares. Given the proximity of the focus group discussions to the – then prominent – 'mad cow' disease controversy, participants expressed unease about the integrity and adequacy of government regulations, official 'scientific' assurances of safety, the benign intentions of food producers and processors and the increasing perceived 'unnaturalness' of food. Such early discussions provided clues to the ways in which public responses to genetically modified foods would later be configured, highlighting the salience of concepts of trust, naturalness, questions of justification and perceived agency in moderating public responses.

For the 2000/2001 project on animal biotechnology, the context was deemed to be people's wider experience of, and relationship with, animals (Macnaghten 2004). By focusing on the social practices through which people experience and reflect upon animals in their daily lives – for example, as pets, in sport, as wild animals, as prey and as subjects of animal research – it was argued that such deliberation would help illuminate the factors likely to shape future public responses to the applications of biotechnology to animals, including their sense of the continuities and discontinuities between GM animals and those determined by conventional selective breeding programmes. For this reason, the focus group started with a 60 minute discussion (out of a 3 hour focus group) deliberating on how people talk phenomenologically about, and directly experience, animals? How intelligent, how affectionate, how responsive, how like/unlike humans do participants find them to be? How do they talk about animals in relation to 'professional' or 'instrumental' uses and contexts? And how do they respond to apparent tensions, dilemmas and contradictions in their own attitudes and behaviours? While the questions were structured in a bespoke manner to the group at hand (depending on whether they were pet owners, wildlife observers, country sports enthusiasts or farmers) they, nevertheless, revealed the affective and empathetic relations in which (certain) animals were regarded in (certain aspects of) daily life and how these were collectively blanketed out in other aspects of daily life (such as in the eating of meat or the wearing of leather), as illustrated below:

Male 1: I suppose I could say I don't care about cows, pigs and sheep because I eat them.
Female 1: But do you like them in the fields?
Male 1: I like to see them in the fields but I mustn't care about them because I eat them everyday.

Male 2: You don't want to see cruelty or ...
Female 2: We're hypocrites really.
Female 3: Yes, we are.
Male 1: We're selective when we want to be.
Female 2: When it suits us.
Female 3: When you're at the supermarket you don't think about it.
Male 3: You must be able to switch off, it goes back to that point about caring doesn't it. You like them in the field but ...
Female 2: Yeah, you all go and say look at the bunnies in the field but I like rabbit pie.

(Wildlife Observers Group, North-West England, cited in Macnaghten 2004: 539).

Such contextual deliberation was instructive to the findings overall and to our argument that GM animals were likely to contribute to an issue of public controversy in so far as they symbolize and give voice to underlying tensions between 'moral' and 'instrumental' approaches to animals.

For the projects on nanotechnology, what was deemed the most relevant context was people's experience of current technologies, on how they have changed daily life (for good and ill) and how people imagined these changes would unfold in the future. Again, a lengthy discussion lasting 60 minutes was oriented towards asking participants to reflect on how different kinds of technology had impacted on everyday life (for good and ill) – both at an individual and at a societal level – before exploring questions of control and responsibility. Responding to these questions produced wide-ranging discussions on participants' experience of modern technological life and the factors that produced often contradictory and powerful pulls on hopes and desires. When, later in the focus group, the concept of nanotechnology was introduced, it became apparent that participants viewed nanotechnology broadly as an intensification of existing hopes and fears on technological modernity. Key factors which were found to mediate how people responded included whether it posed a threat to the human and to natural orders; whether it diminished or enhanced individual choice and autonomy; whether it was likely to generate more or less inequality; and whether there would be unforeseen downsides to the optimistic and seductive promises of the technology (Macnaghten et al. 2010). When this public engagement exercise was conducted later in Brazil, as a comparative study, Brazilian participants were prototypically more positive of technology and more amenable to and accepting of a standard Enlightenment master narrative, where general societal progress was conflated with technoscientific advance (Macnaghten and Guivant 2011). Such dynamics helped explain the very different structure of feeling of subsequent Brazilian responses to nanotechnology.

For the project on climate geoengineering the focus groups began with an open-ended discussion on participants' experience of the weather and the climate, designed to provide a context for future deliberations on geoengineering as a climate change modification technology (Macnaghten and Szerszynski 2013). The focus group started with a conversation on what people enjoy (and do not enjoy) about the outdoors before asking each participant to recount a story that summed up the importance of the weather. This was followed by a conversation on the climate and on the difference between the climate and the weather, designed as a way of opening up a conversation on climate change and their views on how scientists and policymakers were thinking about it. These early conversations elicited complex and nuanced responses – such as participants struggling over the difficulty of determining what is natural/cyclical about the climate and what is human-induced; of the difficulty of linking human interventions into planetary and glacial timescales; of being given mixed messages by scientists and policymakers and being unclear of their underlying motives; and of the underlying cause of climate change (often seen as being one of human greed and selfishness and in which they were implicated) – all of which proved highly significant themes in understanding subsequent responses to possible geoengineering options.

Finally, in the project on fracking, the focus groups started with a conversation on what we termed the energy and society landscape (Williams et al. 2015). This included discussion on people's perceptions of energy; on how they used energy; on prices; on the differences between different sources (both renewables and fossil fuels); and on their perceptions of current producers and regulators of energy and of their motivations. Dominant themes included the affordability of energy, as well as an all-pervading sense of mistrust in industry behaviour. Across all the groups, participants displayed a tendency to view industry actors in the energy sector as motivated by greed and profit, and the sense that these motivations and associated practices would contribute to short-termism with negative impacts on society and the environment. This contextual understanding of public perceptions of the energy industry was to prove highly influential in structuring subsequent responses to fracking, where participants questioned the trustworthiness of institutional actors, their sense of a lack of inclusive and democratic decision-making processes and their perception that we were rushed into a fracking future by policy and industry actors.

In each case the recruitment was topic-blind: indeed, the focus group participants were unaware of the particular technology under scrutiny until after these contextual factors were discussed in some detail, usually for between 40 minutes to 1 hour. This permitted analysis of how diverse contextual factors were embedded in everyday life practices and how these underpinned and framed the formation of subsequent attitudes and views on emerging technology.

Framing

The second design feature concerns framing. Given that technologies are never neutral but always framed in particular ways and for particular purposes, care needs to be exercised to ensure that the emerging technology under investigation is introduced by offering participants an inclusive range of rhetorical resources and frames, without closing down or narrowing the issue in the first place, or presuming that these align with dominant institutional frames and norms (Felt et al. 2014; Sciencewise–ERC 2010; Stirling 2008). Crucially, this involves attending to both current *and* future imagined uses of the technology: the future being a key category of emerging technologies, given their often 'promissory' character (see Adam and Grooves 2007; Brown 2000; Brown and Michael 2003; Selin 2007).

For the projects on agricultural biotechnology, for example, clear distinctions were made between current and proposed uses of techniques of genetic modification, highlighting the potential for the introjection of different genes (both plant and animal) in different contexts of application (from food production to animal rearing, to medical uses).

Exploring the salience of different frames, the focus group included a section on a simulated controversy, in the form of a short radio news commentary (put together by the researchers), in which participants were asked to respond to the discourse of different actors (in this case regulators, business and environmental groups). The project on animal biotechnology was similarly conceived, exposing people to the different kinds of application of the technology (from animal testing to livestock applications to pets to the eradication of pests to the production of drugs) and to the different frames of approaching the issue from the view point of science, commerce and animal rights activists.

For the projects on nanotechnology, different frames were introduced, ranging from dominant institutional frames that interpolated nanotechnology as a new science that would contribute to projected breakthroughs across multiple sectors and spheres of application, to other more avowedly utopian and revolutionary frames, with promises of how nanotechnology will extend and transform human sensory and physical capacities to transcend natural and physical constraint. It also covered more precautionary frames, derived from civil society actors and sceptics, that focus on the uncertain risks of the technology on human health and the environment and of wider concerns of the technology running 'out of control'. For the project on climate geoengineering, three distinct frames were introduced: one using quotes from policy institutions, reporting on the slow progress of climate mitigation (designed to provide a frame that was relatively open to geoengineering as a policy option); a second frame designed to explore civil society and oppositional perspectives on geoengineering; and a third frame setting out the geopolitical history of weather and climate modification (designed to explore the salience of alternative frames surrounding how solar radiation management techniques could be used for purposes unrelated to climate change policy). For the project on fracking, having introduced the technique of hydraulic fracturing and how it differs from conventional drilling, three frames were introduced: one a promissory account highlighting the benefits of fracking for reducing energy bills and securing energy security; the second a frame on its hazards and risks (from predominantly institutional sources); and the third a more sceptical frame of the potential of fracking including in its propensity to contribute meaningfully to climate change (from environmental and civil society actors).

Thus, in all cases, what was being presented to participants were different frames or styles of thought (Fleck 1979; Hacking 1992; Rose 2007) – not simply of what the technology is, but what it explains and what it represents. Across all the projects, these frames had been encapsulated through the use of stimulus materials, typically making use of pre-designed large A1 boards, consisting of pictures and text (all attributed) and presented to the group by the moderator to stimulate conversation.

Moderation

The third design consideration concerns the style and remit of the moderator. A senior member of the research team, usually the project PI, has, in all circumstances, conducted the focus groups, given that this role has been considered as integral to subsequent analysis and interpretation. The role of the moderator is, principally, to keep the group on topic (using a well-formulated topic guide); to raise topics; to listen empathetically and accurately to each participant's stories; to ensure a diversity of voice independent of background or experience; to probe difference and convergence between group members; to require participants not necessarily to arrive at a common output or consensus but, nevertheless, to articulate shared issue definitions (when present); and to move from one topic to the next only when the full range of arguments appears exhausted (on the role of the moderator in interaction, see Barbour 2008; Puchta and Potter 2004; Macnaghten and Myers 2004).

To help ensure that the discussions were not framed by expert discourses and norms, all of the projects have avoided the inclusion of technical experts in the focus group discussions, as previous research has indicated that the presence of experts can induce deference to prior framings amongst lay participants (Wynne 2006). Nevertheless, codified information on what the technology is, how it works and what it means, is communicated by the moderator through the use of stimulus materials, but where the practical meaning of the technology, for the participants, is derived through group discussion and deliberation. Through abiding with some general rules of good focus group moderation – that there are no right or wrong answers, that this is not a test, that all opinions matter and should be respected, that you, as the moderator, are showing due empathy to participants' views and experience (see, amongst others, Krueger 1998) – it has been surprising the extent to which participants have shown themselves able and competent to enter into the lifeworld of advanced technoscience – whether this be animal and plant biotechnologies, nanotechnologies or climate geoengineering.

Moderating is, nevertheless, a practical skill and, over the years, the author has given postgraduate courses (both in the UK, in mainland Europe and in Brazil) on such themes as: how to translate a research question into a topic guide; how to ask non-leading questions; how to summarize a conversation; how to listen accurately and empathetically to people's stories; how to be genuinely interested in what people are saying as a slice of social life; how to probe, use pauses and deal with talkative and shy participants. Indeed, the trick is not simply to understand *what* people are saying but to understand *why* people are saying what they are saying and only then to move from one topic to the next.

Sampling

The fourth design feature concerns sampling and group design. Across all projects we have developed sampling strategies that have been designed to be both broad and deep. Each project typically has involved between six and eight groups, each group meeting for between 2 and 3 hours, sometimes reconvened. The groups have been made up of between six and eight participants, according to standard focus group norms, and have been professionally recruited to cover a diverse variety of backgrounds, localities and demographics (age, gender, socio-economic class) but with topic specific or theoretically informed variants (for an explanation of the idea of the theoretical sample, see Glaser and Strauss 1967; see also Miller et al. 1998; Gobo 2005).

For example, for the project on agricultural biotechnology, two groups were put together to include those who commonly read labels on packaging, taken as a proxy for a particular proximal relationship to food, while for the project on animal biotechnology groups were selected on account of their having particular relationships with animals: specifically, groups of pet owners, wildlife enthusiasts, hunters and shooters and farmers. For the nanotechnology projects, groups were convened with people who had shared life histories or work experience on issues that were seen as potentially relevant to the framing of response to nanotechnology, such as sharing interests in technology or politics. For the project on climate geoengineering, groups were selected of people who had a practical interest in the climate: specifically, a group of gardeners, another of outdoor manual workers and another of outdoor enthusiasts. For the project on fracking, three groups shared a strong relationship with 'the earth' and practical interest in 'the environment' (allotment holders, ex-miners and associates and employees of a Wildlife Trust), with the remaining three groups sharing a relevant positionality in relation to fracking as constituting a form of 'progress', through a strong relationship with time and the future (mothers with young children, members of local industrial history societies and parents of university students).

The decision to bring participants together on the basis of shared experience is a design feature aimed at fostering a favourable setting for the collective discussion of an unfamiliar topic (see Macnaghten and Myers 2004; Morgan 1988). The decision to involve uninformed participants, who have no particular a priori stake or position in the debate, and who do not know each other prior to the group, is a technique designed explicitly to produce an open-ended sociality, where people can develop opinions and attitudes through structured interactive conversation in a safe and empowering space. In this way, the 'upstream' focus group methodology can be considered as helping foster the creation of (albeit temporarily) 'technoscientific citizens' who have been became authorized to develop opinions on the social and ethical dimensions of emerging technology and whose (local) opinion formation can be seen as a technique for opening up new ways of thinking about emerging technology. The methodology thus contributes to a tradition of policy-oriented research that uses small groups as a deliberative space, where lay publics can share their experience and develop positions, and where social scientists can bring recognition of such local knowledge, in the hope of making decision-making more socially robust (see also Burgess 2005; Burgess et al. 1988a, b).

Analysis and Interpretation

Fifth, there is the matter of analysis and interpretation. Again, of course, there are multiple styles and approaches to the analysis of focus group transcripts that depend, not least, on what the analysis is seeking to do. Macnaghten and Myers (2004) distinguish between two broad styles of analysis: between styles that converge on *how* people talk in focus group settings (often inspired by conversation analytical traditions; see also Myers 2004) and those that focus on the content of *what* people say and where the role of the analyst is to interpret its meaning (often inspired by narrative or discourse theoretical traditions). Our approach is firmly in the latter camp, where the role of the analyst is, first and most importantly, to become acquainted with the raw data (a standard procedure of one of the authors is to listen to the tape recordings continuously on long car journeys), to organize key rhetorical arguments into themes or discourses through the use of codes, to articulate the interplay between thematic concerns and wider social discourses and narratives, and to interpret this meaning within a framework of theoretical and policy concerns.

For these reasons the focus of the analyst is often to look for convergences, between and across groups, and to see how these differ – or not – from extant policy or academic understandings. For the 1996/1997 project on agricultural biotechnology, for example, it had been assumed (within then dominant scientific and policy narratives) that GM foods were no different in kind from non-GM foods; that current forms of regulation and oversight – that assume that the technology can be managed on a case-by-case basis on independent scientific risk assessments – were sufficient to assure safety and, thus, by implication, public acceptability; and that public resistance would best be countered through official reassurance and the provision of quality information (Grove-White et al. 1997, 2000). Against such assumptions the focus group data provided convergent findings to the contrary: that GM technologies presented distinctive patterns of ambivalence and concern compared to non-GM food production; that participants expressed mixed feelings about the integrity and adequacy of present patterns of government regulation and, in particular, about official 'scientific' assurances of safety; and that, in many ways, public concerns had a latent rather than an explicit quality that reflected wider issues of trust in UK political institutions. Choosing to report on such findings, we often used iconic examples such as the ones below, that illustrate one of the central dynamics at play in the focus group discussions: namely, that the more people reflected upon the technology and its application in real world circumstances, the more concerned they became:

Female 1: I started out not too bad when I had the discussion, I thought I'd have an open mind about it, but I've changed my mind as soon as I saw that [one] about the human gene, it really... suddenly the enormity of it made me feel really awful. I got an awful feeling about it, because I thought it was something that, I think we're touching things that we don't realize and I think we're taking things out of the earth and we're now trying to correct it by using things like genetic engineering because the mistakes were made. And I feel that time's just ticking by and we don't realize what's going to happen in the future. I think something terrible could happen; it's given me a bad feeling really.

Moderator: So [you are saying] it's as if we're trying to fix something which...?

Female 1: Yes, because the earth hasn't got what it used to have. We feel we have to put something back into the food to make it better, and maybe we're correcting things in the wrong way. I don't know...

Female 2: It's a frightening thought to think that time's ticking away though...

Female 1: Yes. It's something that I'd like to put at the back of my mind now. I wouldn't like to think about it again. I probably wouldn't – but when we talk about it, it does bring it to your mind. But then I'll probably put it to the back of my mind now...

(Lancashire Working Women's group, cited in Grove-White et al. 1997: 20).

In the Uncertain World report (Grove-White 1997) we suggested that this sequence reflected the sense of open-ended uncertainty evoked by discussion of the technology in several of the groups, and the strong feelings of impotence and fatalism this seemed to engender. In such circumstances, unambiguous unilateral assertions by industry and government spokesmen that the technology can and should be managed safely on a 'case-by-case' basis was presented as likely to have the effect of compounding, rather than assuaging, the mistrust felt by individuals across all population groups. Thus, notwithstanding the subtle differences in participants' responses within and across the focus groups, it was the convergences in public talk and their contrast with official discourses and understandings that drove the analysis of the data and their interpretation. Indeed, when the GM food and crop controversy unfolded in the UK and Europe in 1998/1999, and when the then UK chief scientific officer was exposed to the Uncertain World study, he responded in a personal communication as follows, thus speaking to the potential political salience of this anticipatory mode of focus group research:

> 'I now have had a chance to read "Uncertain World", which I wish I had indeed read earlier. It is in many ways a remarkably prescient document. (May 1999)

While not as politically opportune as in the Uncertain World GMO study, nevertheless, each of our focus group projects has sought to reconfigure a dominant policy and/or academic perspective through close reading and interpretation of public views. Thus, in the project on GM animals, we highlighted the salience of the category of 'naturalness' as a *bona fide* category for policy deliberation (Macnaghten 2001, 2004). In our projects on nanotechnology, we highlighted the prevalent tragic quality of participants' responses and how these ran counter to the Enlightenment master narrative, typically shared by policy actors, that assume implicitly that advanced (nano)science and innovation under current conditions of regulation and oversight would generate societal progress and environmental betterment. Finding this narrative not to be prevalent in structuring participants' responses, we argued the need for policy responses to identify and engage with the counter narratives that were actually structuring public responses (Macnaghten 2010; Macnaghten et al. 2010; Macnaghten et al. 2015). In the project on climate geoengineering, we highlighted the conditionality of public acceptability and the perceived implausibility of these conditions being realized in practice, thus posing a governance challenge which hitherto had been poorly diagnosed (Macnaghten and Szerszynski 2013). While, in the fracking project, we diagnosed the likely failure of the current institutional attempts at public engagement as framed within a restrictive risk and safety framework, that we saw to be poorly aligned with participants' responses, as reflected in their expressed wariness over promised benefits; their scepticism over the possible capture of decision-making by powerful incumbent interests; and their sensed lack of representation in decision-making processes.

Conclusion

This chapter has sought to articulate the role of focus groups as an anticipatory methodology in relation to matters of public concern. Located within the field of science and technology studies, focus groups have been presented as offering a partial and powerful response to a policy prerogative – one explicitly shared by the author – of the need to articulate in advance the social and ethical dimensions of a technology, such that these factors can be integrated into the development of that science or technology. The argument is one associated with democratic governance and has become a staple of the science policy narrative of responsible innovation (EPSRC 2013; Owen et al. 2013; Stilgoe et al. 2013). Unless science and innovation processes are embedded in societal values, the argument goes, the alternative approach, implicitly embedded in neoliberal styles of technological appraisal, is one where the articulation of the good – or what Rene von Schomberg describes as the 'right impacts' of science and innovation – is delegated to the market (von Schomberg 2013).

Within this formulation, focus groups are presented as offering potential in opening up social imaginaries (Taylor 2004) of the different kinds of futures enabled by (advanced) science and technology, including their societal and ethical dimensions, as a means of injecting social agency in technological appraisal. This mode of public engagement thus proceeds with the simple idea that 'the future could be otherwise' (Irwin 2016), and that these conversations have a role in 'helping society to get better at the conversation between today and tomorrow' (Macnaghten 2016).

Naturally, such a formulation brings to bear particular responsibilities for the focus group practitioner. In this chapter, I have sought to articulate the systematic thinking that underpins how the methodology has been put to use by the author and colleagues. I hope this is the start of a new range of conversations that aim to test the validity, reliability, cultural contingency and context dependencies of the approaches adopted, so as further develop the robustness of the methodology and its application in practice. Given our collective need to produce models of anticipatory governance in line with societal values, and as a counter-weight to market-inspired models of technological governance, I suggest this is a task worth pursuing.

Acknowledgements I would like to thank my collaborators for the many conversations that contributed to my thinking on focus groups and to their various application in science and technology governance. Particular thanks are extended to: Sarah Banks, Sarah Davies, Robin Grove-White, Julia Guivant, Alan Irwin, Matt Kearnes, Greg Myers, Richard Owen, John Scott, Jack Stilgoe, Bron Szerszynski, Laurence Williams, James Wilsdon and Brian Wynne. Finally, and most importantly, I would like to thank all of our focus group participants for their remarkable contributions on the most challenging of topics. Any errors or inconsistencies or misrepresentations remain my full responsibility.

References

Adam, B. and Groves, C. (2007) *Future Matters: Action, Knowledge, Ethics.* Boston, MA: Brill.
Barbour, R. (2008) *Doing Focus Groups.* London: Sage.
Brown, N. (2000) 'Organizing/disorganizing the breakthrough motif: Dolly the cloned ewe meets Astrid the hybrid pig', In N. Brown, B. Rappert and A. Webster. (eds.) *Contested Futures: A Sociology of Prospective Technoscience.* Aldershot, Hants: Ashgate, pp. 87–110.

Brown, N. and Michael, M. (2003) 'A sociology of expectations: Retrospecting prospects and prospecting retrospects', *Technology Analysis and Strategic Management* 15(1): 3–18.

Burgess, J., Limb, M. and Harrison, C. (1988a) 'Exploring environmental values through the medium of small groups. Part one: Theory and practice', *Environment & Planning* A 20(3): 309–326.

Burgess, J., Limb, M. and Harrison, C. (1988b) 'Exploring environmental values through the medium of small groups. Part two: Illustrations of a group at work', *Environment & Planning* A 20(4): 457–476.

Burgess, J. (2005) 'Follow the argument where it leads: Some personal reflections on "policy-relevant" research', *Transactions of the Institute of British Geographers* 30(3): 273–281.

Collingridge, D., 1980. *The Social Control of Technology*. Open University Press, Milton Keynes, UK.

Davies, S., Macnaghten, P. and Kearnes, M. (eds.) (2009) *Reconfiguring Responsibility: Deepening Debate on Nanotechnology*. Durham: Durham University.

Engineering and Physical Science Research Council [EPSRC] (2013) Framework for Responsible Innovation. https://www.epsrc.ac.uk/research/framework/(Accessed 13 July 2016).

European Commission (2002) *Science and Society: Action Plan*. Luxembourg: Commission of the European Communities.

Felt, U., Wynne, B., Callon, M., Gonçalves, M., Jasanoff, S., Jepsen, M., ... Tallacchine, M. (2007) *Taking European Knowledge Seriously* (Report of the expert group on science and governance to the science, Economy and Society Directorate, EUR 2 (2700). Directorate-General for Research). Luxembourg: Office for Official Publications of the European Commission.

Felt, U., Schumann, S., Schwarz, C. and Strassnig, M. (2014) 'Technology of imagination. A card-based public engagement method for debating emerging technologies', *Qualitative Research* 14(2): 233–251.

Fleck, L. (1979) *Genesis and Development of a Scientific Fact*. Chicago, IL: University of Chicago Press.

Gavelin, K., Wilson, R. and Doubleday, R. (2007) *Democratic Technologies? The Final Report of the Nanotechnology Engagement Group (NEG)*. London: Involve.

Glaser, B. and Strauss, A. (1967) *The Discovery of Grounded Theory*. Chicago, IL: Aldine Press.

Gobo, G. (2005) 'Sampling, representativeness and generalizability', In G. Gobo, J. Gubrium, C. Seale and D. Silverman (eds.), *Qualitative Research Practice* (pp. 65–79). London: Sage.

Grove-White, R., Macnaghten, P., Mayer, S. and Wynne, B. (1997) *Uncertain World: GMOs, Food and Public Attitudes in Britain*. Lancaster: CSEC and Unilever.

Grove-White, R., Macnaghten, P. and Wynne, B. (2000) *Wising Up: The Public and New Technologies*. Lancaster: CSEC and Unilever.

Hacking, I. (1992) '"Style" for historians and philosophers', *Studies in the History and Philosophy of Science* 23(1): 1–20.

Irwin, A. (2006) 'The politics of talk: Coming to terms with the "new" scientific governance', *Social Studies of Science* 36(2): 299–330.

Irwin, A. (2016) 'On the local constitution of global futures', *Nordic Journal of Science and Technology Studies* 3(2): 24–33.

Kearnes, M., Macnaghten, P. and Wilsdon, J. (2006) *Governing at the Nanoscale: People, Policies and Emerging Technologies*. London: Demos.

Krueger, R. (1998) *Moderating Focus Groups: Focus Group Kit 4*. London: Sage.

Macnaghten, P. (2001) *Animal Futures: Public Attitudes and Sensibilities Towards Animals and Biotechnology in Contemporary Britain*. Lancaster: IEPPP and AEBC.

Macnaghten, P. (2004) 'Animals in their nature: A case study of public attitudes on animals, genetic modification and "nature"', *Sociology* 38(3): 533–551.

Macnaghten, P. (2010) 'Researching technoscientific concerns in the making: narrative structures, public responses and emerging nanotechnologies', *Environment & Planning* A. 41: 23–37.

Macnaghten, P. (2016) *The Metis of Responsible Innovation: Helping Society to Get Better at the Conversation Between Today and Tomorrow*. Inaugural Lecture, Wageningen University, Wageningen (NL), 12 July 2016.

Macnaghten, P. and Guivant, J. (2011) 'Converging citizens? Nanotechnology and the political imaginary of public engagement in Brazil and the UK', *Public Understanding of Science*, 20(2): 207–220.

Macnaghten, P. and Myers, G. (2004) 'Focus groups: The moderator's view and the analyst's view', In G. Gobo, J. Gubrium, C. Seale and D. Silverman (eds.), *Qualitative Research Practice*. London: Sage, pp. 65–79.

'Macnaghten, P. and Szerszynski, B. (2013) 'Living the Global Social Experiment: An analysis of public discourse on geoengineering and its implications for governance', *Global Environmental Change* 23(2): 465–474.

Macnaghten, P., Davies, S. and Kearnes, M. (2010) 'Narrative and Public Engagement: Some findings from the DEEPEN project', In R. Von Schomberg and S. Davies (eds.), *Understanding Public Debate on Nanotechnologies: Options for Framing Public Policy*. Luxembourg: Publications Office of the European Union, pp. 11–29.

Macnaghten, P., Davies, S. and Kearnes, M. (2015) 'Understanding public responses to emerging technologies: a narrative approach', *Journal of Environmental Planning and Policy*. http://goo.gl/7mOfDv.

May, R. (1999) *Personal Communication to Robin Grove-White*. Unpublished manuscript.

Miller, D., Kitzinger, J., Williams, K. and Beharrel, P. (1998) *The Circuit of Mass Communication*. London: Sage.

Morgan, D. (1988) *Focus Groups as Qualitative Research*. London: Sage.

Myers, M. (2004) *Matters of Opinion: Dynamics of Talk about Public Issues*. Cambridge: Cambridge University Press.

Owen, R., Bessant, J. and Heintz, M. (eds.) (2013) *Responsible Innovation: Managing the Responsible Emergence of Science and Innovation in Society*. London: Wiley, pp. 51–74.

Puchta, C. and Potter, J. (2004) *Focus Group Practice*. London: Sage.

Rogers-Hayden, T. and Pidgeon, N. (2007) 'Moving engagement "upstream"? Nanotechnologies and the Royal Society and Royal Academy of Engineering inquiry', *Public Understanding of Science* 16(3): 346–364.

Rose, N. (2007) *The Politics of Life Itself: Biomedicine, Power, and Subjectivity in the Twenty First Century*. Princeton, NJ: Princeton University Press

Sciencewise-ERC (2010) *Guiding Principles for Public Dialogue on Science and Technology-Related Issues*. http://www.sciencewise-erc.org.uk/cms/guiding-principles/ (Accessed 13 July 2016).

Selin, C. (2007) 'Expectations and the emergence of nanotechnology', *Science, Technology & Human Values* 32(2): 196–220.

Stilgoe, J., Owen, R. and Macnaghten, P. (2013) 'Developing a framework of responsible innovation', *Research Policy* 42(9): 1568–1580.

Stirling, A. (2008) '"Opening up" and "closing down": Power, participation, and pluralism in the social appraisal of technology', *Science Technology & Human Values*, 33(2): 262–294.

Taylor, C. (2004) *Modern Social Imaginaries*. Durham, NC: Duke University Press.

von Schomberg, R. (2013) 'A vision of responsible research and innovation', In R. Owen, J. Bessant and M. Heintz (eds.), *Responsible Innovation: Managing the Responsible Emergence of Science and Innovation in Society*. London: Wiley, pp. 51–74.

Williams, L., Macnaghten, P., Davies, R. and Curtis, S. (2015) 'Framing fracking: Exploring public responses to hydraulic fracturing in the UK', *Public Understanding of Science* (Published online on 13 July 2015).

Wilsdon, J. and Willis, B. (2004) *See-Through-Science: Why Public Engagement Needs to Move Upstream*. London: Demos.

Wynne, B. (2006) 'Public engagement as a means of restoring public trust in science: Hitting the notes, but missing the music?' *Community Genetics* 9(3) 211–220.

Phil Macnaghten has worked in the science and society field since the mid-1990s on a series of science and technology controversies, notably: GM food and crops, transgenic animals, nanotechnologies, synthetic biology, geoengineering and fracking. He has developed in-depth qualitative methodologies for researching controversial technologies which, in turn, have informed policy approaches to dialogue and public engagement. More recently this approach has contributed to the development of the 'anticipation-inclusion-reflexivity-responsiveness' (AIRR) Owen/ Macnaghten/ Stilgoe Responsible Innovation framework which is being adopted by UK research councils and implemented across the portfolio of EPSRC-funded research. Currently working at Wageningen University in the Knowledge, Technology and Innovation Group as Personal Professor, Phil was previously an honorary professor at the University of Campinas (Brazil) (2012–2015) and Professor of Geography at Durham University (UK) (2006–2015). His recent book (edited, with Susana Carro-Ripaldo) is *Governing Agricultural Biotechnology: Global Lessons from GM Crops* (Routledge 2016).

17

Using Focus Groups to Study the Process of (de)Politicization

Sophie Duchesne

Introduction

The growing distance that seems to characterize the relationship that citizens entertain with politics – in Western democracies, in particular – is a matter for concern. How to make democracy work when those who are supposed to be the source of legitimate power don't bother to engage? (Hay 2009; Stoker 2009) Although the causes of citizens' de-politicization are most probably largely external to them – as, for instance, the disappearance of social capital, the role of modern media, globalization and the blurring of political accountability, neoliberalism and the individualization of social relations (Zürn 2016) – their effects should also be analyzed, observed and interpreted. Interrogating such effects is all the more important, if we hope to find triggers that would help in reversing the trend of de-politicization.

S. Duchesne (✉)
CNRS (National Centre for Scientific Research), Centre Emile Durkheim, Sciences Po Bordeaux, Domaine universitaire, Cedex, France
e-mail: s.duchesne@sciencespobordeaux.fr

Focus groups might prove useful for studying (de)politicization – provided that they are designed appropriately. I did have experience of this in a study dedicated to attitudes towards European integration (Duchesne et al. 2013).[1] The original project aimed to analyze a more specific process, conflictualization, that is, how people accept or avoid conflict in public discussion. We first conducted an experimental series of three groups on delinquency which yielded promising insights (Duchesne and Haegel 2010, 2004). We decided to replicate the study in a broader setting, in order to compare the French dynamic we had already observed with other national contexts. We looked for funding and, for different reasons, ended up with a project where European integration became the topic to be discussed. We ran the series of groups, about thirty collective interviews in three cities, and contrary to our previous study, hardly got conflictive discussions, even in the French groups. We first tended to consider that our design had gone wrong – mostly because of the topic[2]: the European Union was clearly not something to which people could relate directly[3] and participants recurrently indicated that they consider it a political issue; the kind of issue they would never discuss spontaneously. They thus found it difficult to adjust to a situation that was obviously quite strange to them. We looked closer into this and concluded that the situation we had created in these focus groups was indeed a 'test of politicization': that is, a situation where participants were directly and inadvertently confronted with politics.[4] My objective in this chapter is to follow up on this serendipitous

---

[1] This chapter draws on work that I did a couple of years ago with Florence Haegel. See the many references to our common publications in the text.

[2] There were three main differences between the experimental study and this one, on top of the comparison and the number of groups: the topic then – Europe instead of delinquency; the location – the French groups were convened in rooms where Sciences Po, a French elite school for higher education, was highly visible which was not the case for the preliminary study; and the recruitment: the first time, we recruited them though a job centre while the second time, we advertised widely and looked for them directly.

[3] The groups were convened in 2006. A couple of qualitative studies at the time showed how remote the EU was for people. P. Lehingue even suggested that producing opinions on European questions requires a specific political sophistication, a squared one (Gaxie et al. 2011: ch.8).

[4] In reference to Haskier's chapter in this book, what happened in these groups is probably not recognisable to participants' everyday contexts. On the contrary, the situational context of these focus groups is meant to activate the processes that prevent politicization to happen in everyday contexts.

finding and to underline crucial issues one should address in designing focus groups as test of politicization. One justification for this is also that a large part of the methodological literature regarding focus groups is written by scholars specialized in health sciences (Barbour 2007). Mainstream sociology and political science are still a bit late in this regard, although the method has, more recently, become quite fashionable in these disciplines (See e.g. Dervin 2015; Garcia and Haegel 2011; Guillemette et al. 2010a, b).

In the first section of this chapter, I will return briefly to what politicization means and underline the reasons why focus groups need to be designed in specific ways in order to address this topic. In the second section, I will put forward three points that seem to me particularly important here: recruiting purely lay citizens; combining homogeneity and heterogeneity in the sampling; and moderating in a non-directive way. In the last section, I will discuss how to analyze this data.

Politicization and Focus Groups: Elective Affinities

In political theoretical terms, politicization means that we should address issues as objects of collectively binding decision-making (de Wilde et al. 2016) – that is, through considering problems as collectively shared and as a matter of agency (White 2010). Yet, from a sociohistorical and sociological point of view, politics is a specific and, even, specialized field, whose (relative) autonomy can be traced back historically in societies. Politicization, thus, can be understood as a process involving infringement of the borders of this specific field (Lagroye 2003). This happens, on the one hand, when any kind of issue becomes a matter of political debate; on the other hand, when lay citizens become involved in political affairs. At the individual level, this infringement requires some degree of political sophistication, in combination with some conscience of it.[5] Alternatively, politicization proceeds from

---

[5] What is referred to in French as objective and subjective competence, the first (equivalent to political sophistication) being mostly knowledge and understanding of political actors, institutions, rules, issues, etc. and the second, confidence in her/his own authority and capacity to have a say (Bourdieu 1977; Gaxie 1978).

citizens' ability to adapt to the political order by 'translating' into political categories, ways of thinking and arguing learned and experienced in other social circumstances (Déloye 2007).

In particular, when lay citizens 'talk politics',[6] they rephrase or reinterpret political categories into categories with which they are familiar: that is, they rely on experiences and meanings taken from their ordinary lives to make sense of political questions, issues or events under discussion. This process is, thus, to be studied as a heuristic object, allowing for the empirical analysis of the cognitive (and yet socially and politically determined) discrepancies between the political field and other fields familiar to lay citizens.

The borders and possible translations between the political field and other ones vary in time and space. However, as an infringement that requires knowledge and/or abilities, politicization is necessarily limited and representative democracy is actually based on this limitation.[7] Mass citizenship, based on universal suffrage, maintains the idea of universal access to politics. Citizens are somehow aware of the fact that this is theory[8] – not to say myth – and generally speaking, they defend themselves from it – notably by resisting even the idea of discussing politics (Conover and Searing 2005) – whereas this is usually considered the very first step in political commitment.[9] How then can we design ways to observe and understand how lay citizens get involved in political discussion and engage with politicization if they don't want to?

Here, clearly, surveys hardly help as what we aim to analyze is the very process of translation of ordinary categories into political categories and

---

[6] In reference to William Gamson's book who contributed to (re)introduce focus groups in sociology and political science (Gamson 1992).

[7] The advantages of passive citizenship, that might also be considered a sign of satisfaction on the part of citizens, have long been debated. Representation makes democracy work with limited citizens' involvement. See for instance earlier work of Dahl (Dahl 2006; Dahl 1989)

[8] As confirmed by the discrepancy between the recurrent support for democracy expressed in survey and the not less recurrent and even growing disgust for politics (Hay 2009).

[9] I writing these lines when France experiences a version of the Occupy movement, the *Nuits debouts*, which illustrates dramatically how political engagement begins with learning (and here possibly reinventing) political discussion. http://www.theguardian.com/world/2016/apr/08/nuit-debout-protesters-occupy-french-cities-in-a-revolutionary-call-for-change.

17 Using Focus Groups to Study the Process of (de)Politicization

vice and versa.[10] The most obvious strategy is ethnography. Eliasoph, Hamidi and Cramer Walsh spent years observing people discussing political issues in civic groups involving either parents, neighbours and members of environmental or leisure associations (Eliasoph 1998; Hamidi 2010) or in informal groups (Cramer Walsh 2004). Eliasoph and Hamidi show how people tend to avoid discussion of politics in public settings, even when they have concerns regarding political issues that they express in face-to-face conversations with the researcher. Cramer Walsh confirms that groups of acquainted people rarely address what happens in the political sphere, even if what matters to them might be considered by observers as political. All of these authors, then, actually end up studying de-politicization.

Gamson, on the contrary, choose to organize focus groups and confront lay citizens – and more specifically, working class people – with political issues (Gamson 1992), in order to show that they have their own ways of discussing these issues which are not reducible to media influence. His influential book shows that ethnography might not be the only – and possibly not the most efficient – way, to access and observe political discussion. In this case though, focus-groups convened pre-acquainted people in the hope of reproducing or generating naturalistic discussion amongst friends and relatives. One might want to go a step further and assume a more experimental approach. Indeed, focus groups, as a method for social scientists, have different origins: field and research action that value more contextualized ways of collecting data; also behavioural sciences that rely overtly on experimental methods (Morgan 1996).

Moreover, feminists have largely supported the use of focus groups in social sciences. In a recent review article about focus group research, Kamberelis and Dimitriadis underline that the method, despite its apparent descent from media and marketing research, was widely used by research projects with explicitly political aims. A main argument here is that the group empowers interviewees and gives them the strength to resist the framework of interrogation and rephrase it in their own terms.

---

[10] Although some experimental survey design could help (Sniderman and Grob 1996).

Of course, using a method for politically oriented action research or for political science research is not the same thing, but these authors also state: 'In fact, focus groups are spaces where the personal can (and often does) become political.' (Kamberelis and Dimitriadis 2014: 335).

Focus groups, if designed accordingly, allow discussions to evolve in unpredicted ways. They offer participants a space to take hold of the questions offered as stimulus and follow their own avenues as they help each other to express their mind. This makes them very useful to study politicization.

Generally speaking, at the individual level, we can distinguish between three kinds of information that might be collected or constructed within interviews, notably with lay citizens. First, factual data – let's call this information – regarding what happens or happened for them and their circumstances. Second, representations, that is, insights into the way interviewees see, understand or interpret what happens or happened to them or around them. Third, some sorts of competence that are involved in the way interviewees confront themselves with the discursive situation that the interview constitutes. These competences refer partly to (general) social and cognitive skills related to language and sociability. They also put at stake more specific abilities referring to the topic under discussion. Here, the relationship – be it distant or close – that interviewees entertain with politics is being tested, as it influences their ability to decipher other people's political opinion or ideology, to make alliances and/or take a stand. It might also have consequences on their capacity to assume ambivalence and contradiction and, more importantly, to identify interests, including their own.

In-depth qualitative research on politicization allows for a focus mainly on this third kind of data: the competences lay citizens exert when they are confronted with a political topic. This can be done with face to face interviews but the relationship between a politically unsophisticated interviewee and an interviewer, who is, by construction, more knowledgeable in this matter, is unbalanced (Duchesne and Haegel 2001). It does not leave much room for the former to 'translate' the question into his/her own categories of experience. As a result, face-to-face interviews with lay citizens hardly confirm more than the distance between partners in this encounter and serve to underline citizens' negative feelings towards politics. It does not provide a window for understanding how they can engage with political issues – as everybody does at some point, even fleetingly. In focus groups, the relationships between participants might create the room that is needed to explore construction of meanings, provided that they have been designed in an appropriate way.

How to Design Focus Groups as Test of Politicization?

As Morgan stated, the first lesson in order to avoid focus groups going wrong is to keep 'looking at the project as a whole' (Morgan 1995: 523) and thus make the decisions regarding design while keeping in mind what we are looking for. Following Morgan,[11] I shall address the ways focus groups should be designed in a study on politicization according to three headings: recruiting, sampling, developing questions and moderating. Analysis will be dealt with in the next section.

Recruiting Purely Lay Citizens

When health sociologists run focus groups, they recruit patients, GPs, nurses, or patients' family members through relevant medical institutions or associations. When political sociologists try to study citizens or public opinion, they do not have access to such channels to reach them through providing a ready-made sampling pool. They could potentially interview anyone; but tend actually to interview people who are over-politicized. It is well-documented that the more remote people feel from the political field, the less likely they are to accept to participate in interviews, in general, and, in particular, in interviews on political topics (Gaxie 1978). If we do want to understand the roots of de-politicization, it is of paramount importance to recruit lay citizens who reflect the

---

[11] The points I shall make in this section indeed follows most of Morgan suggestions made in this 1995 article. This is no wonder as we made intensive use of this paper when we designed our focus groups.

diversity of the population both socially (not only in terms of social class but also ethnic, gender, generation, and more importantly, education wise) and politically. This is true for surveys and individual interviews; this is even truer for focus groups. Taking part in focus groups is more demanding, both because the meeting cannot be arranged at the time and place requested by the potential interviewee and because the idea of having to expose their own thoughts to others might be stressful. Researchers then tend to leave recruitment to public opinion research firms (for instance Baglioni and Hurrelmann 2016; Stoker et al. 2016; when they do not interview students as e.g. Bruter 2005). These firms maintain panels and can provide – for a price – participants selected according to researchers' criteria. But these panel members are not lay citizens with regard to their ability to discuss afresh any issue, including political ones: they are used to it, they have developed the skills for that. In this respect, they are not representative anymore of their fellow citizens, even when, on paper, they meet the sampling criteria.

It is, thus, particularly important for this kind of project to control the recruitment, as costly as it can be, in time and resources. The recruiting team has to make sure that the participants do not choose to participate because they are specifically interested in politics[12]; that is, no more so than an 'average' citizen, which sets the bar quite low, in particular for less-educated people. In this case, in order to encourage participation, rewarding participants seems to be difficult to avoid. Moreover, special efforts have to be made in order to locate people in diverse and socially contrasted environments: one has to access them where they live, where they work, where they go shopping, where they spend free time, instead of waiting for them to volunteer.

This can be all the more difficult if the team decides to recruit participants who don't know each other. Whether this is preferable to using pre-acquainted groups, however, is debatable. Observing how groups of relatives and/or friends react and discuss when they are confronted with political issues is just as interesting as observing a

---

[12] Nor because they take a special interest in social science, as this would not make then representative either of the 'average' citizens.

group of strangers doing the same – it is simply different and affords different insights. Gathering a group of acquainted people seems easier as you have 'only' to convince one person to invite people s/he knows at his/her place, instead of convincing every single participant to come to an unknown location. On the other hand, when interviewing a group of relatives, you largely lose control of recruitment.[13] Moreover, in this kind of design, participants tend to know about each other's general political opinions. It means that we don't get to see if and how people identify other people's positions; furthermore, it raises difficulties for understanding the grounds of their agreements and disagreements as they won't necessarily make explicit what they've already shared[14] (Leask et al. 2001; Vicsek 2007). It thus makes sense to go for unacquainted groups. It makes then the 'test' more challenging as we know that people avoid discussing politics even more when they don't already know the people with who they are speaking (Mutz 2006)

When advertising for focus groups to investigate de-politicization, it is essential not to disclose the real purpose of the discussion. First because advertising a discussion as political would reinforce the political selective process and prevent many people from volunteering; second because participants would tend to prepare. We had the occasion to confirm these expectations during our last project. The topic was on Europe and most participants to this series of groups, who were recruited to discuss 'social issues', made it clear that they actually thought it was not a social but a political issue. One of our Oxford groups had to stop after about an hour of discussion, due to unforeseen circumstances. It was meant to reconvene two weeks later. Although participants knew they would be rewarded again, had agreed to come back and had confirmed their participation, two participants out of five did not show up. A third one turned up but he had clearly prepared. This young Muslim man explicitly changed his mind between the two sessions, from expressing quite a

---

[13] That was Gamson's strategy and he notes that interviewees tend to invite those who they reckon would be most competent and who happened to be the most educated and/or belong to the highest social groups in their acquaintance.

[14] A similar experience than interviewing people you know (Bourdieu 1993).

positive and open attitude towards European integration to expressing a strong opinion against it, based on a firm position against secularization. In the second session, the discussion became almost impossible as this participant came along with the express purpose of stating his position, making it clear that he would not change his opinion, nor even listen to alternative views. This feature – advertising interviews without being clear about the topic and the aim of the research project – might be considered ethically problematic.[15] In this case, it seems scientifically necessary. We thought it was acceptable: first, because what is political or not is however matter of discussion. Second, on no occasion, did we force or even solicit verbal contributions from individuals. In the case mentioned above, when three of the five original participants came back for a second try, one of them, the only woman, clearly struck by the harsh conflictive tone of the discussion, did not say a word and we let her remain silent. Lastly, we always kept some time at the end of the session for informal talk and some kind of debriefing. We tried to make sure all participants would go back home feeling comfortable.[16]

Sampling: Mixing Social Homogeneity and Political Heterogeneity

Our project drew on a few decades of survey research in European studies. It had consistently been demonstrated that national and social belonging are the first two properties that influence individual attitudes towards European integration. But the reasons for that either remained largely to be explained (national) or were debated (social). We thus decided to sample our groups according to a

---

[15] Let's note that ethical issue are generally speaking less considered in France that in the UK or the US, which might explain that we decided to go that way. It seems however to be the right decision for our purpose.

[16] In the Oxford case, we had to get participants to read and fill forms that acknowledge that the discussion could become harsh and where they confirm they would ask for help if they feel disturbed by it. This was neither required in Paris nor in Brussels.

17 Using Focus Groups to Study the Process of (de)Politicization

double segmentation: national (France, UK and French-speaking Belgium) and social (working class, employees and executives). We also convened a fourth series of groups in each country with activists that we recruited *via* local branches of the main political parties in each country. They were meant to help with identifying the ideological arguments developed by parties, but, as we became aware of the 'test of politicization', we came to use it as a sort of control group: the comparison between the ways activists played the game and how others behave confirms the specific competences of the former and, by contrast, helps in identifying which competences lay non-activists citizens resort to in handling the discussion.[17]

Sampling by segmentation allows participants to find common ground in the discussion and spares some of them from being too heavily dominated by others; here, it seems all the more appropriate that politicization often involves disagreement and taking a stand. For the sake of the test, I would also recommend trying to mix social homogeneity with political heterogeneity. The recruitment involves asking questions of people who volunteer for the discussions, in order to ascertain their social characteristics. A few political questions may be introduced, in limited number, without disclosing what the discussion is about. For the same reason, it might be better to ask general value questions which are known as structuring political opinion – like attitudes towards the welfare state, immigration, authority, equality and order – rather than asking about electoral choices or positions on the left-right continuum. Adding political criteria into social sampling sometimes seems like squaring the circle when it comes to forming the groups, but it adds a lot to the efficiency of the test of politicization.

---

[17] We followed Morgan's advice and run two groups of each. This turned out particularly useful for the comparison. Because of the many accidents that characterize recruitment – notably people who happen to be really different from what they look on paper on the one hand and those who don't show up on the day of the event on the other hand –, we ended up with working class, employees and executive of different sorts. Once we had completed the series, we organized our groups in two sets: in the first one, we put the twelve groups that distributed the more evenly in the three countries along the social spectrum (Garcia and Van Ingelgom 2010) – and the political spectrum for militants. National comparison relies on this first series only.

Developing Questions and Moderating: Adapting the Nondirective Approach to Focus Groups

Focus groups, unless they are employed in order to interview more people in less time, are usually moderated in quite open ways. At least this is what is recommended by many experienced users. But the discussion is organized around the experience they share – be it a kind of illness and treatment, of violence or bad treatment, of practice or situation, etc. In political science, and in particular for our purpose, studying (de)politicization, the discussions are organized around topic(s) rather than common experience. That explains why we prefer to speak of the 'collective interview' (Duchesne and Haegel 2009). The specific dynamic of focus groups, which relies on people adding up their narratives related to the same experience, does not work as such. We need other ways to fuel discussions in order to take full advantage of its potential, especially when the topic seems a little remote from personal experience; and preferably ways that would not put the moderator in the front stage. A possible source of inspiration is the nondirective interview.

The nondirective approach refers to a mix of Rogers' proposal to translate counseling ways of listening to a patient into research interviewing, on the one hand, and methodological advices taken from the research program conducted in the 30's at the Western Electric company by Roethlisberger and Dickson, on the other hand. In France, this approach was supported by Michelat, a sociologist, trained as a psychologist, who worked in one of the leading political science research centre (Michelat 1975; Roethlisberger and Dickson 1975; Rogers 1945). The main principle is to look for questions instead of answers: that is, to help interviewees formulate their own questions in relation to the topic under investigation. Here, for focus groups conceived as a test of politicization, it was, indeed, paramount not only to let participants behave in their own way, but also to induce them to express their doubts and questions. In a face-to-face nondirective interview, the interviewer has to refrain him/herself from asking questions other than the introductory one and has to accommodate the interviewee by listening (and notably accepting silences needed for the interviewee to think), repeating, rephrasing what s/he says. We adapted the nondirective approach to collective interviewing with the following features:

First, we opted for small groups. We invited six to seven participants, but were satisfied when four turned up. With such numbers, participants are in position to really talk to each other. It also gives everyone a chance to secure the floor without us having to ask them directly (unless we noticed that someone was trying in vain to have a say). In the larger groups (6 to 7 participants), there were always a couple of them who remained silent most of the time.

Second, we employed a moderation technique used in consultancy in a way different from its original intention (which was solving problems in an organization). The technique consists of the moderator writing on cards what participants say as the discussion proceeds and pinning them up from time to time, using them to stimulate discussion when exchanges peter out. In doing so, the moderator gives back to the group the main points it is raising in a way that approximates what a nondirective interviewer does when s/he rephrases what the interviewee has already said in order to rekindle his/her discourse. Moreover, it provides the moderator with a task that induces him/her to stick to the participants' words and also prevents him/her from intervening. Lastly, as participants are all positioned to face the board, it is easy to set up a video-recording. The camera reinforces the public character of the discussion, which was part of the test.

Thirdly, we asked a limited number of questions: five for three hours of discussion. The project was also dedicated, and funded as such, to the study of attitudes towards European integration. This topic remains – or remained, in 2006 – very unfamiliar for most people, thus we did not dare ask only one question, as we reckoned participants would have changed the topic quite quickly.[18] Indeed, this is what they did – French and British working class people and employees in particular. These five questions worked as reminder of what they were expected to discuss. It allowed us to avoid refocusing the discussion; a task that some

---

[18] We did some tests groups in the three countries beforehand that confirmed than more than one question was needed and helped phrasing them.

participants actually assumed. However, we had plenty of time to keep the discussion going and let the participants take it where they wanted. We also took time for a break, with drinks and a snack, so that participants could talk informally and get to know each other a little bit.

This set up – few participants, limited number of questions, no refocusing from the moderator, no prompting either, even to participants who remained largely silent and the writing up of the points or arguments on the board – gave a kind of nondirective tone to the moderation, made all the more evident in that we also facilitated the expression of disagreement. In a face-to-face nondirective interview, as the interviewee explores the topic, his/her thoughts evolve and s/he comes to contradict most of the time or at least, to formulate some very ambivalent views. In a collective discussion, ambivalence and contradiction are also the rule – in particular, with regard to remote and imposing objects, such as political ones. But public contradiction amongst strangers is seldom considered normal social behavior. In this case, our original focus on conflictualization helped out. The series of questions was indeed elaborated, as said before, in order to facilitate conflict. Moreover, we used what was called 'the flash rule'[19] to make clear that expressing disagreement with something that had been said was perfectly acceptable and even appreciated. Participants made very different use of it, from asking for clarification to strongly disagreeing. Notably, they used it to challenge both the questions we asked them and conventional representations of the EU.

Altogether, our design did produce a kind of situation where participants successfully managed to discuss together a topic that they explicitly declared political – in particular, during the moment of informal talk; that is during the break and after the session. They managed it in different ways, both individually and collectively.

---

[19] Participants were told from the beginning that if they did not agree with what someone was saying, instead of interrupting, they could let the moderator know. She would then draw a 'flash' on the card and come back to it later. The first time a participant asked for a flash, the moderator thanked her/him, indicated that she was in pleased. This indeed helped making disagreement known.

Analyzing: Looking at Alliances

In the last decade, the literature on how to analyze focus groups and, in particular, how to take advantage of interaction amongst participants, has multiplied. Each author suggests his/her way to deal with this and report it. As Morgan notices, this is particularly the case for academic research users while more applied researchers are more 'substantively' oriented (Morgan 2010): the former pay more attention to the way things are said and the latter to what is said. Using focus groups to set up a test of politicization clearly points in the first direction. Politicization, understood as a process of adaptation to a special field – the one of government and power -, is performed with varied types of behavior, skills and knowledge. Those are what we aim to analyze. This does not mean that the topic itself – here Europe – is not part of the test for politicization; nor that the topic itself does not interest us as researchers.[20] Discussion is facilitated by topics that are closer to daily experience and for which partisan repertoires are clearer and more readily available to lay citizens; moreover how things were said constitute the core of the analysis of the process of politicization.

Following Hay, I do not consider that political discourse analysis should be viewed as a specific kind of analysis (Hay 2013). Politics is about power, from agency to domination. Moreover, here we are looking for translation and adaptation from social fields to the political. When it comes to lay people, power refers frequently to collective actors and empowerment to belonging. In addition, political opinions are by nature controversial: they refer to alternative ways to distribute wealth amongst people – politics being 'who gets what, when and how' (Lasswell 1950) – and/or to partisan or politicians' manifestos in competition.

Here again, focus groups are very appropriate for observing and understanding how people interact together in order to deal with the incitement to talk politics. Basically, they have to make alliances in the

---

[20] Indeed, most of the publications that resulted from our focus groups analysis address the topic itself (Duchesne et al. 2000; Duchesne et al. 2013; Van Ingelgom 2014).

group in order to formulate views or take a stand in front of the others – or altogether, as a group, in opposition to an external other. In our specific case, as participants were chosen because they had, at least on paper, opposing political views, we could expect the discussions to get polarized; but this does not always happen: the groups also tend to look for and develop a common ground against a more or less defined other, which is sometimes embodied in the research team.

The way to analyze the discussions does not differ from reports from other focus groups users interested in interactions (Belzile and Öberg 2012; Duggleby 2005; Lehoux et al. 2006; Stevens 1996). We developed our own way drawing on Billig and Kitzinger and Farquhar (Billig 1992; Billig 1991; Kitzinger and Farquhar 1999). We produced an interpretative narrative account for each discussion, based on video recording, field notes and questionnaires, looking at what happened between participants (Our template is detailed in Duchesne et al. 2013: 190–192). We interpreted what was said as chain reactions depending from what the speaker had heard and understood (or might have) from what had been said before, rather than an expression of his/her pre-existing opinions. These accounts were discussed by the research team. In a way, they constitute the data as much as do the transcripts themselves. Our first results are indeed a comparison of these narratives (Duchesne et al. 2000), according to our double segmentation, national and social. Content analysis came second, along with more specific discourse analyses. Here, the video recording was a decisive element. We could never have produced these interpretative accounts without looking at the ways participants behaved, who they were looking at and paying attention to, and how. Body language was an intrinsic part of the play. When looking at the recordings, it is impossible to deny that discourse is action (Potter and Wetherell 1994).

The comparison between the narratives shows that participants performed the test of politicization in very different ways. In a nutshell, regarding the location, Belgian groups are more sophisticated and deliberative, the French more conflictual and the British quite obsessed with knowledge. Regarding social belonging, we see how executives rely on personal/individual resources, while working class groups struggle to find common ground despite their differences. Attachment to the Welfare

State seems to constitute one of the most powerful sources for this. Following Hydén and Bülow who suggest looking for who is talking in the groups (Hydén and Bülow 2003), we notice also that these groups – executive compared with working class ones – do not address their fellow participants by putting forward the same aspects of their identity. Executives mainly speak as professionals and cultural-nationals (or cosmopolitans) while working class participants refer to their experience as governed people.

There is one dimension that we did not take into account when recruiting participants – as the 'test of politicization' was not foreseen – and which happens to be very important: the participants' degree of political interest. In groups where one (or more) of them happens to be an activist, s/he strongly influences the discussion, leading others to adapt to the situation. The comparison with activist groups here is very heuristic and reinforces the experimental aspect of our design. They clearly feel comfortable with the topic and the situation and play their parts according to their political affiliation. They easily identify others participant's political belonging and challenge them accordingly. They make fun of conflict and competition. They don't need allies in the group to take a stand: their party provides them with permanent allies and allows them to speak for a collective even when they are isolated in the focus group. These features, characteristic of the activists groups, can then be observed in the other groups where they are only residual and could not easily be identified without knowing the whole picture.

Conclusion

In this chapter, I tried to draw lessons from a focus group study, originally designed to analyze attitudes towards European integration and conflictualization, but which turned out to function for participants as a 'test of politicization'. In the current and growing context of disaffection towards politics, what can we learn from it in this respect?

First, our study confirms what is already well documented about people's distrust towards politicians and disaffection regarding politics. In these discussions, participants rarely mention parties and political actors, and, when they do, they associate them either with the media and show-business, or with corruption and selfishness.

Second, it demonstrates that disaffection is not a question of incompetence or carelessness. While they might sometimes be mistaken, participants report lots of information about the state of the world. They clearly seek to keep themselves informed. The ways in which they understand what is going on with globalization certainly cannot be viewed as being stupid. In this respect, it helps in explaining the puzzling relationship between the population's growing educational level and their growing disaffection for politics.

More importantly, these data provide an unparalleled resource for studying collective belongings or identifications and their transformation. As Tilly said, identities 'play an indispensable role in the sealing of agreements and the coordination of social interaction' (Tilly 2003: 608). As a consequence, they are indispensable for political agency. In these groups, when interacting with each other in order to find a common way to talk politics, participants disclosed much of the parts of their identities that can generate a common ground. Amongst these, being governed, being subjected to the same rules and the same policies, appears to be particularly important – at least for working class groups; more important, indeed, than being fellow citizens (understood here as being 'the sovereign people', the voters) (Dupuy and Duchesne 2017).

The richness of this data is the consequence of a series of decisions we made when we designed the discussions, and then tried to apply in a systematic way. Recruitment was a big deal. We chose to select our participants one by one and arranged our groups carefully in order to maximize social homogeneity and political heterogeneity. We assumed the experimental dimension of our design in a scientific context that tends to prefer observation in real life. We adapted a moderation technique used by consultancy in order to create the conditions for collective non-directive interviewing. We asked a limited number of questions and made sure participants would have the time to get used to the situation and find their ways to deal with it. Before any kind of content analysis, we went through an interpretative stage where we paid full attention to the way the relationship between the participants – and us – evolved. Lastly, we took our time before reaching our conclusions. Indeed, we are still analyzing this data. We ran these groups in 2006, two books have already been published using this data and yet we continue working on it. Focus groups might sometimes be used in applied research for quick answers; but they do provide researchers with very rich qualitative data for which there is, apparently, 'never the last word' (Andrews 2008).

Acknowledgements I'm very much indebted to Florence Haegel, with whom I worked for many years and with whom I experimented with regard to this focus group design; as well as Elizabeth Frazer and Virginie Van Ingelgom, co-authors of the book *Citizens reactions to European integration compared: Overlooking Europe*. I'm also grateful to Claire Dupuy, with whom I continue to revisit this data. Special thanks to Virginie who commented on the first version of this chapter, as well as this' volume editors, and more particularly Rose Barbour who turned it into readable English.

References

Andrews, M. (2008) 'Never the last word: Revisiting data', In M. Andrews, C. Squire and M. Tamboukou (eds.), *Doing Narrative Research*. London: SAGE Publications. pp. 87–101.
Baglioni, S. and Hurrelmann, A. (2016) 'The eurozone crisis and citizen engagement in EU affairs', *West European Politics*, 39(1): 104–124.
Barbour, R. (2007) *Doing Focus Groups*. London: SAGE.
Belzile, J.A. and Öberg, G. (2012) 'Where to begin? Grappling with how to use participant interaction in focus group design', *Qualitative Research*, 12(4): 459–472.
Billig, M. (1991) *Ideology and Opinions: Studies in Rhetorical Psychology*. London: SAGE.
Billig, M. (1992) *Talking of the Royal Family*. London: Routledge.
Bourdieu, P. (1977) 'Questions de Politique', *Actes de La Recherche En Sciences Sociales*, 16(1): 55–89.

Bourdieu, P. (1993) « Comprendre », In P. Bourdieu (ed.), *La Misère Du Monde*. Paris: Le Seuil. pp. 903–925.
Bruter, M. (2005) *Citizens of Europe? The Emergence of a Mass European Identity*. New York: Palgrave Macmillan.
Conover, P.J. and Searing, D.D. (2005) 'Studying "everyday political talk" in the deliberative system', *Acta Politica*, 40(3): 269–283.
Cramer Walsh, K. (2004) *Talking about Politics: Informal Groups and Social Identity in American Life*. Chicago: The University of Chicago Press.
Dahl, R.A. (1989) *Who Governs? Democracy and Power in an American City*. New Haven: Yale University Press.
Dahl, R.A. (2006) *A Preface to Democratic Theory*. Expanded ed. Chicago: University of Chicago Press.
Déloye, Y. (2007) 'Pour une sociologie historique de la compétence à opiner « politiquement »: Quelques hypothèses de travail à partir de l'histoire électorale française', *Revue française de science politique*, 57(6): 775–798.
Dervin, F. (2015) *Analyser l'identité: les apports des focus groups*. Paris: L'Harmattan.
de Wilde, P., Leupold, A. and Schmidtke, H. (2016) 'Introduction: The differentiated politicisation of European governance', *West European Politics*, 39(1): 3–22.
Duchesne, S. and Haegel, F. (2001) 'Entretiens dans la cité. Ou comment la parole se politise', *EspacesTempsLesCahiers*, (76–77): 95–109.
Duchesne, S. and Haegel, F. (2004) 'La politisation des discussions, au croisement des logiques de spécialisation et de conflictualisation', *Revue Française de Science Politique*, 54(6): 877–909.
Duchesne, S. and Haegel, F. (2009) *L'enquête et ses méthodes: l'entretien collectif*. Paris: A. Colin.
Duchesne, S. and Haegel, F. (2010) 'What political discussion means and how do the French and (French speaking) Belgians deal with it?' In M.R. Wolf, L. Morales and K. Ikeda (eds), *Political Discussion in Modern Democracies in a Comparative Perspective*. London: Routledge, pp. 44–61.
Duchesne, S., Haegel, F., Frazer, E. et al. (2000) 'Europe between integration and globalization. Social differences and national frames in the analysis of focus groups Conducted in France, Francophone Belgium and the UK', *Politique Européenne*, (30): 67–106.
Duchesne, S., Frazer, E., Haegel, F. and van Ingelgom, V. (2013) *Citizens' Reactions to European Integration Compared: Overlooking Europe*. Houndmills: Palgrave Macmillan.

Duggleby, W. (2005) 'What about focus group interaction data?', *Qualitative Health Research*, 15(6): 832–840.

Dupuy, C. and Duchesne, S. (2017) 'La réanalyse au service de l'interdisciplinarité ?' Recherches Qualitatives Hors Série, 21, art.4.

Eliasoph, N. (1998) *Avoiding Politics: How Americans Produce Apathy in Everyday Life*. Cambridge: Cambridge University Press.

Gamson, W.A. (1992) *Talking Politics*. Cambridge: Cambridge University Press.

Garcia, G. and Haegel, F. (eds.) (2011) 'Entretiens collectifs: nouveaux usages?' *Revue française de science politique*, 61(3).

Gaxie, D. (1978) *Le Cens Caché: Inégalités Culturelles et Ségrégation Politique*. Paris: Le Seuil.

Gaxie, D., Hubé, N. and Rowell, J. (eds.) (2011) *Perceptions of Europe: A Comparative Sociology of European Attitudes*. Colchester: ECPR Press.

Guillaume Garcia et Virginie Van Ingelgom, «Étudier les rapports des citoyens à l'Europe à partir d'entretiens collectifs: Une illustration des problèmes de la comparaison internationale en méthodologie qualitative», Revue internationale de politique comparée, 2010, vol. 17, no 1, p. 131–163.

Guillemette, F., Luckerhoff, J. and Baribeau, C. (2010a) 'Entretiens de groupe: Concepts, usages et ancrages vol.1', *Recherches Qualitatives*, 29(1).

Guillemette, F., Luckerhoff, J. and Baribeau, C. (2010b) 'Entretiens de groupe: Concepts, usages et ancrages vol.2', *Recherches Qualitatives*, 29(3).

Hamidi, C. (2010) *La Société civile dans les cités: engagement associatif et politisation dans des associations de quartier*. Paris: Economica.

Hay, Colin (2009) 'Disenchanted with democracy, pissed off with politics', *British Politics*, 4(1): 92–99.

Hay, C. (2013) 'Political discourse analysis: The dangers of methodological absolutism', *Political Studies Review*, 11(3): 321–327.

Hydén, L-C. and Bülow, P.H. (2003) 'Who's talking: Drawing conclusions from focus groups—some methodological considerations', *International Journal of Social Research Methodology*, 6(4): 305–321.

Kamberelis, G. and Dimitriadis, G. (2014) 'Focus group research: Retrospect and prospect', In P. Leavy (ed.) *The Oxford Handbook of Qualitative Research*. Oxford: Oxford University Press. Ch.16.

Kitzinger, J. and Farquhar, C. (1999) 'The analytical potential of "sensitive moments" in focus group discussions', In R. Barbour and J. Kitzinger (eds.), *Developing Focus Group Research: Politics, Theory and Practice*. London: Sage, pp. 156–172.

Lagroye, J. (ed.) (2003) *La Politisation*. Paris: Belin.
Lasswell, H.D. (1950) *Politics: Who Gets What, When, How*. New York: P. Smith.
Leask, J., Hawe, P. and Chapman, S. (2001) 'Focus group composition: A comparison between natural and constructed groups', *Australian and New Zealand Journal of Public Health*, 25(2): 152–154.
Lehoux, P., Poland, B. and Daudelin, G. (2006) 'Focus group research and "the patient's view."' *Social Science & Medicine*, 63(8): 2091–2104.
Michelat, G. (1975) 'Sur l'utilisation de l'entretien non directif en sociologie', *Revue Française de Sociologie*: 229–247.
Morgan, D.L. (1995) 'Why things (sometimes) go wrong in focus groups', *Qualitative Health Research*, 5(4): 516–523.
Morgan, D.L. (1996) *Focus Groups as Qualitative Research*. Thousand Oaks, Calif: Sage Publications.
Morgan, D.L. (2010) 'Reconsidering the role of interaction in analyzing and reporting focus groups', *Qualitative Health Research*, 20(5): 718–722.
Mutz, D.C. (2006) *Hearing the Other Side: Deliberative versus Participatory Democracy*. Cambridge: Cambridge University Press.
Potter, J. and Wetherell, M. (1994) 'Analyzing discourse', In A. Bryman and R. Burgess (eds.) *Analyzing Qualitative Data*. London and New York: Routledge, pp. 47–66.
Roethlisberger, F.J. and Dickson, W.J. (1975) *Management and the Worker: An Account of a Research Program Conducted by the Western Electric Company, Hawthorne Works, Chicago*. Cambridge, Mass.: Harvard Univ. Press. (1st edition 1939)
Rogers, C.R. (1945) 'The Nondirective Method as a technique for social research', *American Journal of Sociology*, 50(4): 279–283.
Sniderman, P.M. and Grob, D.B. (1996) 'Innovations in experimental design in attitude surveys', *Annual Review of Sociology*, 22: 377–399.
Stevens, P.E. (1996) 'Focus groups', *Public Health Nursing*, 13(3): 170–176.
Stoker, G. (2009) 'What's wrong with our political culture and what, if anything, can we do to improve it? Reflections on Colin Hay's "Why We Hate Politics"', *British Politics*, 4(1): 83–91.
Stoker, G., Hay, C. and Barr, M. (2016) 'Fast thinking: Implications for democratic politics', *European Journal of Political Research*, 55(1): 3–21.
Tilly, C. (2003) 'Political identities in changing polities', *Social Research*, 70(2): 605–620.

Van Ingelgom, V. (2014) *Integrating Indifference. A Comparative, Qualitative and Quantitative Approach to the Legitimacy of European Integration.* Colchester: ECPR Press.

Vicsek, L. (2007) 'A scheme for analyzing the results of focus groups', *International Journal of Qualitative Methods,* 6(4): 20–34.

White, J. (2010) 'European integration by daylight', *Comparative European Politics,* 8(1): 55–73.

Zürn, M. (2016) 'Opening up Europe: Next steps in politicisation research', *West European Politics,* 39(1): 164–182.

Sophie Duchesne is CNRS senior researcher and member of Centre Emile Durkheim at Sciences Po Bordeaux. She is a political sociological and is specialized in the analysis of political identities, notably national identities, and qualitative research methods. She coordinated the CITAE project (Citizens talking about Europe), a joint qualitative and comparative project research between Sciences Po, the University of Oxford and the Catholic University of Louvain la Neuve, on attitudes toward European integration, using focus groups. She is the (co)author of *Citizens' Reactions to European Integration: Overlooking Europe,* with E. Frazer, F. Haegel & V. van Ingelgom, Palgrave MacMillan, 2013 and wrote together with F. Haegel the first textbook on focus groups published in France (*L'Enquête et ses Méthodes: Les Entretiens Collectifs,* Nathan, collection 128, juin 2004). She is the former President of the French social sciences and humanities research council.

18

Practice Theoretically Inspired Focus Groups: Socially Recognizable Performativity?

Bente Halkier

Introduction

It is a well-established argument in qualitative methods, that methodological assumptions and the operative uses of the methods in question should be coherent with the theoretical perspective underpinning the empirical research (e.g. Blaikie 2007; Silverman 2006). This argument is also explicit in influential texts about focus groups (e.g. Barbour 2007: 37–40; Stewart et al. 2007: 8). Focus groups as a methodological approach have been conceptualized and used empirically along a continuum of relatively diverse theoretical positions, ranging from different types of scientific realism (e.g Fern 2001) and critical realism (e.g. Stewart et al. 2007) to various types of social constructivism (e.g. Barbour 2007). One of the methodological themes where realist, critical realist and social constructivist inspired focus groups differ in practice concerns the understanding of the relations between the content of

B. Halkier (✉)
Department of Sociology, University of Copenhagen, Copenhagen, Denmark
e-mail: beh@soc.ku.dk

expressions in the focus group and the social dynamics of group interactions (e.g. Morgan 2010).

The methodological literature on focus groups has seen a growth in contributions which address the relations between the content of what focus group participants discuss and the forms of the focus group interaction and the interpersonal communication in relation to all aspects of the analytical design, from sampling, through to moderator-strategies and to analysis (Barbour 2007: 129–36; Belzile and Öberg 2012; Duggleby 2005; Farnsworth and Boon 2010; Grønkjær et al. 2011; Halkier 2010; Morgan 2010; Puchta and Potter 2005; Warr 2005; Wibeck et al. 2007). Across otherwise different perspectives, the social interaction dimension of focus groups is typically used to argue for the specific methodological capacities of the method in producing qualitative data.

The differences in theoretical perspective, however, come to the fore when the specific implications for various elements in research designs involving focus groups are discussed. The article by Morgan (2010) on the role of interaction in focus groups illustrates the diversity in implications drawn. In the article, he argues the important point that ' . . . saying that the interaction in focus groups produces the data is not the same as saying that the interaction itself is data' (Morgan 2010: 718). Morgan juxtaposes the knowledge interests of researchers who primarily analyze the substantive content of focus group data with the knowledge interests of researchers who primarily analyze the interaction and interpersonal communication in focus groups. His main argument seems to be that we, as researchers using focus groups, ought to display more analytical flexibility as to how much and how the social interaction is explicitly a part of the analysis and reporting of focus group data, because different knowledge interests (and I would add different theoretical perspectives) are, in principle, equally legitimate – as long as a scientific argument can be presented. Thus, there is considerable diversity regarding which specific methodological implications are drawn from the importance of the social interaction dimension of focus groups.

In this chapter, I want to draw attention to one of the issues in the discussions about the implications of the importance of the social interaction in focus groups. The issue is how culturally and socially recognizable are the patterns of expression in focus group interactions to participant everyday life contexts; or how uniquely situational to the focus group itself are these patterns. By cultural and social recognizability, I mean the extent to which social actors have already been in contact in their own contexts with the kind of practices, interactions and discourses which are being talked about and perhaps enacted in the focus groups.

The chapter consists of the following parts. First, I will address how recognizability is discussed in the existing methodological focus group literature. Second, I will suggest that a practice theoretical perspective (Warde 2005) on focus group use enables the researcher to occupy a middle position regarding recognizability and situationalism: that is, to be able to shed light both upon patterns of everyday activities across contexts as well as situational negotiations of these patterns in their making and re-making. Third, I will discuss how recognizability can be produced in focus groups employing various methodological strategies, such as network groups and media representations. I will provide empirical examples from research using focus groups on contested food habits, drawing upon communication research as well as the sociology of consumption.

Recognizability and Focus Group Literature

Setting up the discussion of the existing literature between assumptions about social recognizability and assumptions about the situational uniqueness of focus group exchanges, of course, involves a simplification. First, several usages of focus group data seem to fall in between the two types of assumptions, or are not necessarily explicitly clear on this particular issue; although they address some analytical implications of taking seriously the importance of the interaction. Second, the issue of social recognizability of focus groups often seems to blend two distinct, but closely linked methodological discussions. One discussion is about the character of the focus group data. Can the data be seen as a result of 'naturalistic interaction' or as 'socially recognizable interaction'? The other discussion is about the generalizability of the analytical inferences made on the basis of focus group data. Can the analytical inferences be seen as culturally transferable to focus group participants' contexts via a theoretical framework, or are the analytical inferences largely unique results of particular situational formations and processes of the specific group of participants?

Keeping these distinctions in mind, existing methods discussions on the implications of the importance of the interaction dimension of focus groups appear to fall into three groups in relation to the issue of recognizability, emphasizing either the cultural transferability of inferences; the social recognizability between focus groups and everyday exchanges; or the situational character of focus group interaction.

Putting Differing Approaches to Recognizability into Context

Amongst the group of contributions that focuses on the *cultural transferability* of focus group data inferences, there are some discussants who also assume that focus group data can be seen as coming close to somewhat naturalistic expressions and exchanges (e.g. Belzile and Öberg 2012; Fern 2001; Franklin and Lowry 2001; Kidd and Parshall 2000; Stewart et al. 2007). In an article about computer-mediated focus groups, Franklin and Lowry (2001: 170), for example, argue that focus group data are generalizable in the same manner as other types of qualitative data – namely,to the theoretical framework – and they position themselves as researchers using a naturalistic approach to inquiry, based on phenomenology and ethnography, and an assumption about the existence of (and need to understand) multiple realities (ibid: 171). Likewise, in their textbook on focus groups, Stewart et al. (2007: 165) conclude that focus group data and findings can be generalized beyond the group itself, although not in a representative manner. Their main theoretical argument is that, in order to learn from existing knowledge on small group dynamics, researchers should take into consideration both individual, interpersonal and environmental dynamics in the focus group interaction (ibid: 35). In this group of contributions, the social recognizability of what goes on in focus groups is not explicitly addressed, but perhaps, implicitly views focus group data as naturalistic and/or focus group data inferences as generalizable.

Another group of commentators argue explicitly in favour of seeing focus group data as expressions and negotiations that are *socially recognizable*, so that the focus groups provide a window onto the everyday contexts of the participants (e.g. Barbour 2007; Bloor et at. 2001; Brannen and Pattman 2005; Demant 2006; Farnsworth and Boon 2010; Peek and Fothergill 2009; Warr 2005). One variety of this argument that views focus group data as socially recognizable is based on understanding the expressions, exchanges and negotiations in the focus groups as enacting or re-enacting existing meanings and relations in the social networks and contexts of the participants. In an article about analyzing group dynamics in focus groups on the experiences of poverty and social exclusion, Farnworth and Boon (2010: 619–20) conclude that the social dynamics not only shaped the explicit narratives in the focus groups, but also supported participants' more tacit performances of their experiential background. Proponents of this approach often use focus groups based on existing social networks in their empirical research. Another strand of the argument for focus group data to be seen as socially recognizable is based on understanding the expressions, exchanges and negotiations in focus groups as being in accordance with – or even representing collective or public discourses in society. In an article on sociable interaction in focus groups, building upon focus group research about romantic relationships, Warr (2005: 202) argues that focus group discussions involve the intermingling of personal and public frames of meaning. In a methodology text-book contribution, Demant (2006: 142) even categorizes focus group data as 'discourse fragments'. Thus, overall, explicit arguments are advanced for the social recognizability of focus group exchanges, and the dynamics of recognizability are described, mainly as reflecting either social network relations or public discourses.

The third group of commentators tends to understand focus group data as largely *situational*, where researchers must be careful not to under-estimate the specific constellation, expressions of content and processes that come together in constructing focus group interactions as data (e.g. Freeman 2006; Grønkjær et al. 2011; Jakobsen 2012; Wibeck et al. 2007). In an article about dialogue and deliberative capacities of focus groups, Freeman (2006: 91) argues that the social and cultural knowledge expressed in focus groups is co-constructed in the realm of the groups, and that it is, thus, dependent upon the formation and articulation of communicative processes, which are specific for each focus group. Although much less particularistic in their approach, Wibeck et al (2007: 263) also conclude that focus group data consist of knowledge that is 'elaborated and co-constructed in focus groups'.

I tend to find myself assuming a middle position, where I view focus group data as socially recognizable, as well as also relatively situational. In the next section, I will outline how a practice theoretical perspective might be used to sustain such a methodological middle position regarding focus group data.

Theoretical Inspiration On Recognizability in Focus Groups

Most versions of practice theories have in common that they revolve around the concept of social practices. The social practices themselves are the analytical unit, and empirical research based on practice theories focuses on the details and patterns of how ordinary activities are carried out and carried through, embedded in contextual potentials and conditions (Halkier et al. 2011). The theoretical root that inspires practice theories comes from a reading of the theoretical elements about social action processes in, amongst others, Pierre Bourdieu's (1990) early concepts of habitus, field and practical sense, Judith Butlers (1990) understanding of performance, Anthony Giddens' (1984) structuration theory, and Michel Foucault's (1978) later thinking about social regulation of bodies through discourses and technologies.

This type of theoretical perspective has been re-visited over the last 15 years, thanks to several influential works of conceptual synthesis published in this period (e.g. Reckwitz 2002; Schatzki 2002; Shove et al.

2012; Warde 2005). The contributions of these conceptual developments have been debated and used in empirical research across a number of social scientific research fields – such as consumption, environmental change, family life, media use, and organizations. These current practice theoretical syntheses aim to understand the complexities of mundane performativity: that is, the patterns in how activities are done, re-done and done in a slightly different way. Practice theoretical syntheses in current usage share a number of main assumptions, and in the following I am listing four of them, relevant to the discussion about the social recognizability of focus groups. First, mundane performativity is organized through multiple collectively shared practices, such as eating, transporting, working and parenting. Thus, practices in everyday life are social, and they are central to the organization and ongoing flow of action. Second, the activities of each practice cover both routinized embodied processes and discursive sense-making processes. Hence, what is being done in everyday life is understood as always being a mixture of tacit and explicit elements, in equal interdependence with each other. Third, the individual is seen as a carrier of practices and a meeting place for the intersection of the many different overlapping practices of each context. Accordingly, what is being done in everyday life is nearly never only one kind of practice. Consider the practice of eating, which typically overlaps with cooking, shopping, cleaning, everyday logistics, transporting, parenting, partnering etc. Fourth, ways of performing different activities in and across practices consist of processes of dynamic accomplishments of anticipated and acceptable conduct. In other words, to practice something in everyday life involves normative negotiation of what one can be expected and accepted to do – for example, how to eat and how to do parenting.

Such a practice theoretical perspective entails a number of methodological implications, and I will mention the two most relevant ones in the context of this chapter on focus groups. These are to avoid methodological individualism, and to understand all types of qualitative data as 'enactments'.

The first methodological implication is to avoid working on the basis of methodological individualism (Jepperson and Meyer 2011) when designing empirical qualitative research and when analyzing and making inferences from empirical qualitative datasets. This implication comes from the assumption of working with shared practices and social varieties of carrying out practices as the analytical unit, rather than the individual. The second methodological implication is that of understanding both individual interview data, focus group data and participant observational data as practitioners' 'enactments' or performances – albeit in different social contexts. This implication comes from the core understanding of a practice theoretical perspective regarding the performativity of everyday life: to say something is also to do something and vice versa. Thus, I use the term 'enactments' for all qualitative datatypes, because it resonates with the ongoing discussions about sophisticating the traditionally firm and hierarchical distinction between participant observational data, which are seen as generally more valid data about everyday practices, while interview data is seen as being less valid (see e.g. Atkinson and Coffey 2003).

When discussing whether and how focus group data can be socially recognizable, the two methodological implications above from a practice theoretical perspective come centrally into play. If the unit of analysis in focus group data is not individuals but, rather, social practices or elements thereof, then it follows that whether the individual participants in focus groups would conduct themselves in the very same manner in their life contexts as in the focus groups is not necessarily relevant as a criterion for judging the validity of data interpretation. When mothers in a focus group discuss which kind of meals are considered good food, they express and negotiate the social norms relating to family cooking, and the researcher gets to know about the collective elements in what is expected, accepted and not accepted. In this connection, it is less important whether and how much each individual mother conducts herself in accordance with her expressions. This suggests a disagreement with the argument in the focus group literature that favours a view of expressions and negotiations as naturalistic and therefore generalizable (e.g. Franklin and Lowry 2001).

If focus group data are understood as enactments or performances, it is relevant to use social recognizability as a criterion for the validity of interpretations of focus group data (e.g. Warr 2005). It is precisely the enactments and re-enactments of parts of practices in social interaction that is a precondition for social practitioners to recognize and know what makes up different practices and variations of doing them (Warde 2005: 133–35). Practices – such as cooking – come into being in the process of activities being regularly carried out in front of, together with, and in relation to others. Thus, the elements and expressions of, for example, cooking conduct will become recognizable to other practitioners by being shown and shared. Parts of such enactments and re-enactments also take place in focus group interactions, much in line with the argument put forward by Farnworth and Boon (2010). When mothers in focus groups negotiate which kinds of cakes are appropriate to bring to a school party, it would be difficult for them to do so, if not at least part of such an activity and such categories of appropriate and inappropriate guest food were socially recognizable to them.

However, the situationalism argument in the focus group literature (e.g. Wibeck et al. 2007) can also resonate with a practice theoretical perspective. When ways of performing different activities consist of processes of continuously accomplishing conduct socially, activities and interaction about activities will potentially be done, re-done and done slightly differently by way of little adaptations, improvisations, negotiations and experiments. In the focus group literature, Jakobsen (2012: 113) argues in favour of seeing expressions in focus group data as socially performed, rather than individually pre-formed. At the same time, this makes it possible to see each focus group as rather unique and the focus group discussions as primarily situationally formed, which can be seen as an argument against understanding these data as socially recognizable. In one focus group with mothers, negotiations about proper meals might focus on health; in another they might focus on convenience products – according to the concrete processes and trajectories of the conversations.

Instead of seeing the situationalist and the recognizability arguments as mutually exclusive, it might be possible, instead, to see focus group data as characterized by different levels and degrees of recognizability and situatedness and, thus, to argue that the degree of social recognizability can vary between different types of research projects applying focus groups. In the more general discussions about analytical generalization, it is argued that it is possible to generalize on the basis of qualitative data no matter how unique they may seem, because of the 'doubleness of the situation' (Delmar 2010: 121–22). This means that every situation or situated dataset always contains both unique elements and, at the same time, elements that are recognizable or typical across situations (Halkier 2011: 788).

Thus, when combining the 'doubleness of the situation' understanding with a practice theoretical perspective, I will suggest that a double or middle position is possible: focus group data can be used to investigate certain patterns of everyday activities across contexts, as well as being used to show how these patterns become situationally negotiated.

Methodological Strategies in Producing Recognizability

In this section, I present three methodological strategies which have worked in terms of helping to produce some social recognizability in the focus groups I have conducted in my practice theoretically inspired empirical research about contested food habits. The strategies are only examples, and there are many others (see e.g. Colucci 2007, although the argument is not explicitly about recognizability), due to the different research fields in which focus groups are used. But the three strategies I present here are methodological choices which have worked well empirically in my experience. Also, the strategies relate closely to the types of argument presented in the focus group literature about what the dynamics of social recognizability might consist of, as described earlier in the chapter. The three strategies are, respectively, network groups, food items as input, and media representations as input.

The first methodological strategy consists in carrying out focus groups, based on *existing social network groups*. Choosing to sample for focus groups participants who already know each other is part of an old discussion in the focus group literature. There used to be a widely circulated assumption that focus groups with people who did not know each other was the most valid sampling choice, partly due to the dominance of business studies/marketing research in using focus groups

(Morgan and Krueger 1993: 6). But as focus groups have become a growing part of the methodological repertoires of other parts of the social sciences, network focus groups have also become a valid sampling choice (Barbour 2007: 66–68; Bloor et al. 2001: 22–24; Hansen et al. 1998: 265–68; Morgan 1997: 37–38) – depending, of course, upon research questions and theoretical approach.

The social recognizability in network based focus groups comes from the participants already having relations and shared experiences regarding the themes of the focus group. This means that they know something about each other's different practices and ways of doing and saying things, and they are somewhat familiar with interacting and communicating with each other.

One example of using this strategy in my own empirical research comes from a research project on how parents with pre-school children handle potential food risks, such as salmonella bacteria in chicken, pesticide residues in fruits and vegetables, and artificial additives in manufactured goods (Halkier 2001). The methodological design involved a combination of six focus groups with parents and text-analysis of different genres of public texts about food risks. The focus groups varied according to gender inside the groups, mainly because of most parents participating as couples, and they varied according to educational level and habitat between the groups. Across these varieties, the participants in each focus group explicitly addressed each other's enactments on food risk handling in everyday life and often referred to their existing knowledge about each other's lives and existing discussions and social norms in their network. Here is a concrete extract from one of the focus groups with parents, where they are negotiating how to deal with the hygiene around raw eggs and the risk from salmonella bacteria:

Marie: 'But it's not different than...we made lemon mousse[1] for- ...how many people [Sara: "Uh!"] on New Year's Eve, what was it, sixty people?'

---

[1] Lemon mousse is a classic Danish dessert that mainly contains sugar, lemon juice and lemon peel, and raw egg whites that are whipped stiff.

Melissa: 'Yes, it was.'
Kristian: 'It was all right.'
Sara: 'With organic or non-organic eggs?'
Kristian: 'With eggs.' [laughter]
Sara: 'With eggs???'
Marie: 'Come on, didn't they boil for a second?'
Kristian: 'We usually boil the shells.'
Jan: 'No-o-o, we didn't get around to that.'
Sara: 'Well, you just talked about it???'
Melissa: 'We don't know if they're alive! [laughter]. But we haven't heard any rumours.'

The negotiations take their starting-point in a concrete event shared by some of the participants (Kristian, Marie, Jan and Melissa), and Sara who did not take part in the specific event questions explicitly what went on with the eggs and the dessert, thereby pushing the others to participate in reconstructing and legitimating their procedures in relation to potentially risky food.

Another concrete example comes from a research project on how female readers of a lifestyle magazine (which endorses cooking from scratch) cook and handle the normativity around home-made meals (Halkier 2009). The methodological design was a combination of repeated individual interviewing with female readers, and three focus groups varying across age groups (20s, 30s and 40s) with one of the readers and some of her female friends. Also in this study, the participants in the focus groups drew upon their existing relations and experiences together in their negotiations, exploring consensus and disagreements about how to relate to a normative demand of cooking from scratch. The following exchange comes from a consensus building process in the focus group with female readers in their 40s, discussing the appropriateness of take-away pizza:

Dorte: 'But at a pinch, you know...a fresh pizza and a round of salad...and then it's one of those days...'
Birgit: 'Yeah, but there I would rather choose to say, all right, don't we have some fish we can just chuck on the frying pan or...some other easy things, and then some vegetables, because often when

you order from such a place, right, but then I order some salad to go with it, but the rest of the family they DON'T... [pause]... Then you sit there and eat French fries together with those pizzas, then I don't think it's good food any more...'

Karen: 'Mmm' [in affirmative tone of voice].
Sonja: 'Mmm-mm' [in affirmative tone of voice].
Dorte: 'No all right, that's bloody true.'

This consensus about take-away pizza not being an appropriate meal comes after a longer negotiation – only a part of which is shown here – and Dorte, Karen and Sonja finally agree with Birgit, apparently on the basis of their experiences with take-away meal examples such as the one Birgit highlights. Also, none of them in the end questions Birgit's enactment of how she deals with 'easy' meals in her family, reflecting some experiential knowledge through their network with how Birgit provides meals.

The second methodological strategy consists of using *ordinary food items as input* to the focus group discussions. It is often highlighted in the focus group literature how stimulus material can form a valuable role with regard to starting-questions, moderation and exercises in focus groups (e.g. Barbour 2007: 84–90; Colucci 2007; Stewart et al. 2007: 92). The main argument is that questions, talk and discursive exercises do not, in themselves, necessarily spur sufficient, sufficiently concrete and sufficiently varied discussions and negotiations. Thus, relevant concrete types of input can make the participants relate to more embodied and material dimensions of their enactments. In my own research, the choice of the food items as input works in this manner, and, at the same time, the food items are everyday items which potentially connect with experiences in the daily life of the participants with the enactments and interaction in the focus group, thus, adding to the social recognizability. The relevant concrete material input will, of course, differ between research projects within different research fields, and, in my research on contested food, it is central to include the concrete food itself.

One example of using this strategy comes from the previously described research project on parents with pre-school children and food risk. A pile of ordinary foodstuff accompanied the third starting-question in these focus groups, which was about whether the participants connected the discussions they had had hitherto about food risks with environmental questions. The concrete selection of food items was characterized by being, on the one hand, ordinary types of food you could find in almost any Danish kitchen, and, at the same time, food that lent itself to being paired to represent environmental issues and contradictions. An example of one of these paired food items was conventionally but locally grown red peppers and organically grown red peppers from the other end of Europe.

In the following exchange from one of the focus groups with the parents about food risk, it is clear how they use the concrete food items on the table to enact, discuss and relate to their daily lives with shopping, cooking and eating:

Katrine: 'And I MUST admit, with cucumbers and such things, there I look for you know... or with most vegetables I have begun to see whether they're Danish. I don't know if they are less sprayed [Caroline: "No, no."] or what they are, but...'

Caroline: 'But at least they are not artificially grown such as the apples we now hear about that lie around for a whole year before we get them, right. Typically, that's not how it is if it's season's fruit, right, that is from our home country, then it's grown here and now.'

Jes: 'Then you also have to pay a bit more, right? You know, I will rather... if for example you have to buy a bag of apples or something... I buy these apples that are slightly more expensive, you get a little less, if I can see that... it's proper apples, not so polished or how to put it.'

The 'not-so-polished' reference to risky food occurred several times in the negotiations, and one of the concrete food items was a package of 'glossy' apples.

Another example of the strategy with using food items as input to help producing social recognizability comes from the research project with female readers of a particular lifestyle magazine. Here, the foodstuff was used directly as part of an exercise, which consisted of asking the participants to sort a pile of ordinary foodstuff into two piles. One pile should be with the kind of food they would serve for guests/use in guest meals, and one pile should be with the kind of food they would absolutely not serve for guests. Furthermore, they had to try to agree as a group upon which food items to put in which pile. This exercise elicited much detailed negotiation about normatively acceptable food conduct which could have been difficult to produce without the material foodstuff and which could have consisted in interaction with much less connection to the normativities in the daily lives of the participants. Here is an example from the focus group with female readers in their 20s, where they are in the middle of sorting the pile of foodstuff and have arrived at the honey cake slices:

Paula:	'Honey cake slices, I also don't fancy that.'
Susy:	'Honey cake slices, they're absolutely fine.'
Paula:	'No, no, no, no, no, no!'
Susy:	'Yes.'
Paula:	'No, no, no girls... cake, you make that yourself.'
Susy:	'Yeah, but I could... [Paula: [interrupts] "Even if it's Amo[2] "...]... put them on a plate and serve them for guests, honestly really Paula, you could do that too.'
Paula:	'No, no.'
Anna:	'There are different guests.'
Susy:	'Yep.'
Paula:	'I could never... [pause] [laughter, everybody talks at the same time]... serve honey cake slices...'
Susy:	'No, honey cake slices, they are good.'
Anna [he, he]:	'They are good.'
Paula:	'IF I should serve something ready-made, then it had to be, you know, cookies, REAL cookies, not clammy Karen Wolff[3] cookies, but... [Anna [interrupts]: "I have never tasted those"...]... such cookies that have been treated and... such luxury stuff.'

---

[2] Amo refers to a brand of flour and other baking products, including ready-made cake powders and bread mixtures.

[3] Karen Wolff is the most common Danish brand of cheap ready-made biscuits and cookies, which you can get in every store.

The participants use the food items to negotiate their normative enactments, and in doing this, they use the food to refer to activities known and recognizable from their partly shared everyday life, such as what conduct can normally be expected from each other regarding guests and food.

The third and last methodological strategy I will address for accessing social recognizability in focus groups is to use *media representations as stimulus material*. This strategy has much in common with the second one about food items in that it also involves relevant concrete input. The only difference is that media representations perhaps tend to be associated with less material and more interpretative and discursive dimensions of socially recognizable elements of everyday life. The use of media materials in focus groups as input to discussions and exercises has been a widely acclaimed and used strategy in the focus group literature, not only in communication- and media studies (Hansen et al. 1998: 274–76; Jensen 2012: 271-72), but has also been used more broadly in the social sciences (Barbour 2007: 84–90; Demant 2006; Warr 2005: 205–06). Media texts often represent public and social network discussions about the various issues of interest for researchers who use focus groups. The argument for using media clips for stimulus material is thus related to the previously mentioned understanding of focus group data as 'discourse fragments' (Demant 2006: 142), that the discussions in focus groups draw upon fragments or parts of already existing discourses. The present media saturation of everyday life (Couldry 2004) makes it both easier and more difficult to use media representations as part of focus groups. It is perhaps easier to use media clips, because there are so many relevant ones to choose from in all sorts of formats and genres, and because it can be assumed that most citizens are in contact with a variety of such media representations. It is perhaps also more difficult to use media clips, because few concrete media representations become shared by everybody, also due to the media development with much more 'pull-media' where citizens pull media discourses towards them according to their own criteria for relevance and interest (Bjur et al. 2013).

One concrete example of the use of media representations in my own research using focus groups comes from the study on female readers of a particular lifestyle magazine. In these focus groups, I presented the participants for physical copies of the lifestyle magazine in question, 'Isabellas. Enthusiastic about everyday', since not all the participants were readers (as were those individually interviewed), and they were also presented with clips from the website and web shop connected with the magazine. The accompanying starting-question was 'What kind of story do you feel this magazine tells you about cooking?' Across the age-group differences in the three focus groups, two different understandings of expected and acceptable cooking were enacted in direct relation to the media representations. On the one hand, the representations in the magazine and website were associated with a discourse on 'good cooking' as involving cooking meals from scratch, and on the other hand, the representations were associated with a discourse on cooking from scratch as 'unrealistic cooking'. Both discourses were embedded in enactments in the focus groups where the women referred to their knowledge of each other's everyday life as well as connections with more widely circulated discourses on 'proper family food'. In the following excerpt, the participants in the focus group (with readers in their 30s) negotiate the two different discourses and normative expectations against each other with concrete reference to a picture of homemade buns in the magazine:

Britta: 'Hmm, it's a bit like this, you could dream yourself away, imagine if I made it, how delicious wouldn't that be...but there is a 1:8 change of that happening...'
Connie: 'But you would make these, wouldn't you? You would make these buns where there is a little...'
Britta: '...ribbon round the middle with name on...'
Anja: '...in a good year, yes! (laughs)'

The second concrete example comes from a presently ongoing study on young people and their relationship with convenience food. The methodological design involves a combination of individual interviews with 12 young people, aged 20–25 years, and four network-based focus groups, where four of the individually interviewed sampled a group from their close social network, and varying between the groups according to gender and level of education. In the following extract, the young people discuss different media-clips about food, including an example of a posting on

Facebook, which produces this exchange where they refer explicitly to their own recognizable experiences with this type of media-use:

Nanna:	'Because the other day, where Maria wrote that she was not at all in x-mas mood because she hadn't had "æbleskiver" and "gløgg",[4] then I don't think "Argh, how irritating! Something about food." I also commented upon it, and I think that's nice, I think it is...'
Helle:	'It's more this, "Oh, I've lived on veggie-sticks for a whole week" or... [Nanna: "Yeah!"], you know, as if I care, right?'
Nanna:	'Yeah, they only want to be confirmed in how good it is, that they are so great, but you can read between the lines that they think it's a hell, and I think 'Just don't then', you can find a middle way.'
Ingrid:	'You know, I really don't think...'
Helle (interrupts):	'And then they only post photos that look good. We all know that they are standing in the kitchen afterwards, eating everything they shouldn't, but they don't make photos of that, do they?'

The participants use the Facebook posting in the media clips to discuss what acceptable displays and uses of food in social media might involve, which they then compare with their own experiences.

Conclusion

Qualitative data generated via focus groups are characterized by being produced on the basis of social interaction and interpersonal communication in groups. One of the discussions in the focus group literature about the possible analytical implications of the importance of social interaction for data has to do with whether, how much and how the patterns of expression in focus groups are culturally and socially

---

[4] Æbleskiver is a smaller Nordic version of doughnuts and are traditionally served at nearly all x-mas gatherings in Denmark, together with 'gløgg' which is warm spicy wine.

recognizable with regard to participants' everyday contexts, or whether, how much and how these patterns are situational and, therefore, unique to the focus group setting itself.

In this chapter, I argue that it is possible to work with a middle position regarding focus group data: focus group data can be seen as producing knowledge about socially recognizable patterns of everyday activities across contexts, as well as furnishing knowledge about situational negotiations of these patterns in their concrete making and re-making. My argument is based on a practice theoretical perspective on focus groups, and, in this chapter, I outline three methodological strategies for helping to produce social recognizability in focus groups; network groups, food as input and media representations as input (and illustrate with empirical examples from my own research on how people handle normatively contested food in everyday life).

In order to come back to the question of the social recognizability of focus groups, one could perhaps ask whether these three methodological strategies tip the balance too much towards socially recognizable performance in focus group interaction at the expense of the situational uniqueness? First, I have never conducted focus groups or seen focus group data from other research projects that did not clearly also reflect the situational specifics of, for example, the composition of the group, the turn-taking throughout the interpersonal communication, and the content of the issues addressed and enacted in the conversational processes. Second, one way forward to cater for both social recognizability and relevant situational specifics of focus group data might be simply to recognize that focus groups are applied differently in different kinds of research projects with different types knowledge interests. Thus, focus group data will be characterized by different levels of and different degrees of both social recognizability and situatedness.

References

Atkinson, P. and Coffey, A. (2003). Revisiting the relationship between participant observation and interviewing. In J.F. Gubrium and J.A. Holstein (eds.), *Postmodern Interviewing*. London: Sage.

Barbour, R (2007). *Doing Focus Groups*. London: Sage.
Belzile, J.A. and Öberg, G. (2012). Where to begin? Grappling with how to use the participant interaction in focus group design. *Qualitative Research*, 12, 459–72.
Bjur, J., Schrøder, K.C., Hasebrink, U., Courtois, C., Adoni, H. and Nossek, H. (2013). Cross-media use. Unfolding complexities in contemporary audiencehood. In N. Carpentier and K.C. Schrøder (eds.), *Audience Transformations*. London: Routledge.
Blaikie, N. (2007). *Approaches to Social Enquiry* (2nd ed.). Cambridge: Polity Press.
Bloor, M., Frankland, J., Thoms, M. and Robson, K. (2001). *Focus Groups in Social Research*. London: Sage.
Bourdieu, P. (1990). *The Logic of Practice*. Cambridge: Polity.
Brannen, J. and Pattman, R. (2005). Work-family matters in the workplace: The use of focus groups in a study of a UK social services department. *Qualitative Research*, 5, 523–42.
Butler, J. (1990). *Gender Trouble: Feminism and the Subversion of Identity*. New York: Routledge.
Colucci, E. (2007). 'Focus groups can be fun': The use of activity-oriented questions in focus group discussions. *Qualitative Health Research*, 17, 1422–33.
Couldry, N. (2004). Theorising media as practice. *Social Semiotics*, 14, 115–32.
Delmar, C. (2010). 'Generalizability' as recognition: Reflections on a foundational problem in qualitative research. *Qualitative Studies*, 1, 115–28.
Demant, J. (2006). Fokusgruppen – spørgsmål til fænomener i nuet [The focus group – questions for phenomena in the present]. In O. Bjerg and K. Villadsen (eds.), *Sociologiske Metoder. Fra teori til Analyse i Kvantitative og Kvalitative Studier* [Sociological methods. From theory to analysis in quantitative and qualitative studies]. København: Forlaget Samfundslitteratur.
Duggleby, W. (2005). What about focus group interaction data? *Qualitative Health Research*, 15(6): 832–40.
Farnsworth, J. and Boon, B. (2010). Analyzing group dynamics within the focus group. *Qualitative Research*, 10, 605–24.
Fern, E.F. (2001). *Advanced Focus Group Research*. London: Sage.
Foucault, M. (1978). *The History of Sexuality*. Vol.1. Harmondsworth: Penguin.
Franklin, K.K. and Lowry, C. (2001). Computer-mediated focus group sessions: Naturalistic inquiry in a networked environment. *Qualitative Research*, 1, 169–84.

Freeman, M. (2006). Nurturing dialogic hermeneutics and the deliberative capacities of communities in focus groups. *Qualitative Inquiry*, 12, 81–95.

Giddens, A. (1984). *The Constitution of Society*. Cambridge: Polity Press.

Grønkjær, M., Curtis, T., Crespigny, C. and Delmar, C. (2011). Analysing group interaction in focus group research: Impact on content and the role of the moderator. *Qualitative Studies*, 2, 16–30.

Halkier, B. (2001). Consuming ambivalences. Consumer handling of environmentally related risks in Food. *Journal of Consumer Culture*, 1, 205–24.

Halkier, B. (2009). Suitable Cooking? Performances and positions in cooking practices among Danish women. *Food, Culture and Society*, 12, 357–77.

Halkier, B. (2010). Focus groups as social enactments: Integrating interaction and content in the analysis of focus group data. *Qualitative Research*, 10, 71–89.

Halkier, B. (2011). Methodological practicalities in analytical generalization. *Qualitative Inquiry*, 17, 787–797.

Halkier, B., Katz-Gerro, T. and Martens, L. (2011). Applying practice theory to the study of consumption: Theoretical and methodological considerations. Editorial article. Special issue of *Journal of Consumer Culture*, 11, 3–13.

Hansen, A., Cottle, S., Negrine, R. and Newbold, C. (1998). *Mass Communication Research Methods*. London: Macmillan.

Jakobsen, H. (2012). Focus groups and methodological rigour outside the minority world: Making the method work to its strengths in Tanzania. *Qualitative Research*, 12, 111–30.

Jensen, K.B. (2012). *A Handbook of Media and Communication Research* (2nd ed.). London: Routledge.

Jepperson, R. and Meyer, J.W. (2011). Multiple levels of analysis and the limitations of methodological individualism. *Sociological Theory*, 29, 54–73.

Kidd, P.S. and Parshall, M.B. (2000). Getting the focus and the group: Enhancing analytical rigour in focus group research. *Qualitative Health Research*, 10, 293–308.

Morgan, D.L. (1997). *Focus Groups as Qualitative Research*. London: Sage.

Morgan, D.L. (2010). Reconsidering the role of interaction in analyzing and reporting focus groups. *Qualitative Health Research*, 20, 718–22.

Morgan, D.L. and Krueger, R.A. (1993). When to use focus groups and why. In D.L. Morgan (ed.), *Successful Focus Groups*. London: Sage.

Peek, L. and Fothergill, A. (2009). Using focus groups: Lessons from studying daycare centers, 9/11, and Hurricane Katrina. *Qualitative Research*, 9, 31–59.

Puchta, C. and Potter, J. (2005). *Focus Group Practice*. London: Sage.
Reckwitz, A. (2002). Toward a theory of social practices. A development in culturalist theorizing. *European Journal of Social Theory*, 5, 243–63.
Schatzki, T. (2002). *The Site of the Social. A Philosophical Account of the Constitution of Social Life and Change*. Pennsylvania: Pennsylvania State University Press.
Shove, E., Pantzar, M. and Watson, M. (2012). *The Dynamics of Social Practices. Everyday Life and How it Changes*. London: Sage.
Silverman, D. (2006). Interpreting qualitative data. London: Sage.
Stewart, D.W., Shamdasani, P.N. and Rook, D.W. (2007). *Focus Groups. Theory and Practice* (2nd ed.). London: Sage.
Warde, A. (2005). Consumption and theories of practice. *Journal of Consumer Culture*, 5(2): 131–53.
Warr, D.J. (2005). 'It was fun... but we don't usually talk about these things': Analyzing sociable interaction in focus groups. *Qualitative Inquiry*, 11(2): 200–225.
Wibeck, V. et al. (2007). Learning in focus groups. *Qualitative Research*, 7(2): 249–67.

Bente Halkier has recently taken up appointment as Professor of Sociology at the University of Copenhagen. Prior to this she was a Professor in the Department of Communication and Arts at Roskilde University. She holds degrees in political science and sociology, with a PhD in social science from Roskilde University. Her current research interest include civic engagement, contested food and mothering. She has extensive experience from large-scale European research projects and has served on the Danish Social Science Research Council. With a particular interest in qualitative methods, she has written about the potential of hybrid approaches, combining insights from discursive psychology with conversation analysis and positioning theory.

19

Conclusions: A Call for Further Innovations in Focus Groups

David L. Morgan

Introduction

As **Rose Barbour's** introduction noted, our goals for this collection of articles included both highlighting current best practices and presenting more novel approaches to focus groups. In this concluding chapter, I want to concentrate on the new ideas within the preceding chapters, and to think about other areas that are ripe for development. My purpose in doing so is to encourage an agenda of self-conscious methodological innovation in our field.

Starting with the original work of Merton (Merton and Kendall 1946; Merton et al. 1956), and continuing with the re-introduction of focus groups into the social sciences (e.g., Krueger 1988; Morgan 1988), the main theme within focus group research has been to summarizing 'what works.' In those days, focusing on this theme was a sensible approach for convincing a potentially sceptical audience to pay attention to what was

D.L. Morgan (✉)
Portland State University, Portland, USA
e-mail: morgand@pdx.edu

then an unproven method. Now, with the widespread adoption of focus groups, the situation is radically different. Yet, the field as a whole has not moved very far from the tried and true strategies that were already apparent 30 years ago. The creative aspects of this book present an excellent opportunity to call for more imagination in how we do focus groups in the future.

Current Accomplishments: Creating More Innovative Forms of Interaction

One of the main themes that I detect in the preceding chapters is the goal of creating forms of group interaction that are equally interesting to both the researchers and the participants. This goal is fundamental to successful focus groups, because our data depends on a lively and well-focused discussion amongst the participants. Hence, there is particular value to techniques that create engaging interaction. Fortunately, the authors of these chapters have made strong contributions to our toolkit in this regard.

Some of these contributions consist of broad justifications for research approaches that rely on the participants' perspectives, such as the more theoretical portions of the chapters by **Duchesne** (Chapter 17) and **Ruiz** (Chapter 13). Others provide very specific procedures for engaging participants, such as video (**Phoenix et al.**, Chapter 15, and **Thompson et al.**, Chapter 10) and performance (**Wooten**, Chapter 12). Still others provide detailed agendas for encouraging participants to interact around potentially unfamiliar topics (**Macnagthen**, Chapter 16 and **Prades et al.**, Chapter 9) Taken together, these chapters should provide useful food for thought as future researchers consider techniques for promoting active exchanges amongst participants.

Current Accomplishments: Repeated and Reconvened Groups as an Option

An interesting but unanticipated aspect of the preceding chapters is that at least five of them describe focus groups that met for more than one session. All of the authors of these chapters use the terminology of

19 Conclusions: A Call for Further Innovations in Focus Groups

'reconvened' focus groups, while in my own work I have referred to this strategy as 'repeated' focus groups (Morgan et al. 2008). My co-authors and I distinguished between two types of repeated groups. In the first instance, the same set of participants is brought together for a further section; for example, if there were seven participants in a group, the hope would be that all of them would return. In the second instance, the broader set of people who participated in the earlier groups could be used as a recruitment pool for drawing the participants for the later groups; for example, if there were five groups in the first wave of interviews, these groups might provide the basis for creating three groups at the next wave.

Since all of the chapters in this collection have used 'reconvened' to mean bringing the same set of participants together for a second time, it seems wise to rely on that vocabulary – and possibly to speak of the second format described above as 'returning' participants. Aside from whether the participants are interacting with the same people twice, the biggest difference between the two strategies is in the difficulty of recruitment. This difficulty is illustrated by one of **Duchesne**'s groups, to which only three of the original five participants returned. This suggests the importance of recontacting the participants in reconvened groups to ensure they come back Alternatively, drawing returning participants from a larger pool makes more people available.

There is considerable diversity in how much the current authors say about their reasons for conducting reconvened groups. **Duchesne** and **Macnaghten** simply mention that some of the groups were reconvened. In contrast, both **Thompson et al.** and **Wooten** designed their projects with a repetition of the groups. For Thomson et al., this meant bringing their original participants back a year later to view and respond to videos that they had recorded at the initial sessions. For **Wooten** it meant having participants create performances in two consecutive sessions so that the earlier preliminary work allowed for more complex presentations in the second session. This idea of either reacting to or building on the content of the first set of focus groups is certainly a sensible motivation for reconvening groups.

Prades et al. (Chapter 9) give the most detailed description of their reasons for reconvening groups. In particular, given the complexity of the issues in their research, the first set of groups helped sensitize participants to the general content of the topic. This created the chance to see how participants' reasoning changed as they became more engaged with the topics. For example, the researchers introduced pre-prepared stimulus materials in the earlier groups, in order to increase the participants' knowledge about and awareness of the topics. This material also had a continuing influence on the participants' thinking, which could be observed in the later groups. In addition, these researchers used the time gap between the two sessions to assign 'homework' such as diary keeping, which served as a further basis for the second round of discussion.

The complexity of the research topics in **Prades et al.** came from the technological nature of those topics, but I believe that reconvening groups or using returning participants could be useful in any area where the participants are relatively new to the topic. Often, we work with participants whose experiences have already given them strong opinions about the subject matter of the research. But several of the authors in this volume have worked with topics to which the participants either had little exposure to or were unlikely to have thought about in a self-conscious manner (e.g., **Halkier,** Chapter 18). When this is the case, there may well be value in bringing participants back for a second round of discussions.

Further Opportunities for Innovation: Group Size

My own efforts to develop new ways of doing focus groups have concentrated on very small groups. In particular, I have been exploring the issues involved in doing dyadic interviews where there are only two participants (Morgan 2015; Morgan et al. 2013; and Morgan et al. 2016). This approach has been widely used in the family literature (e.g., with spouse partners), but the current effort is to create a new alternative, which,

19 Conclusions: A Call for Further Innovations in Focus Groups

like individual and group interviews, can serve as a general method for collecting qualitative data. Of course, this effort only works if dyadic interviews generate the same kind of data-rich interaction that is characteristic of focus groups, and experience in the work cited above definitely indicates that this is the case. In addition, systematic coding to the interaction in dyadic interviews and focus groups indicates that there are more commonalities than differences (Morgan and Hoffman 2016).

One of the key advantages of dyadic interviews is that they allow more time per participant, making it possible to obtain more depth and detail on each person. For example, if there are six participants in a 90-minute focus group, each participant has 15 minutes, but even a 60-minute dyadic interview doubles that amount of time. Another advantage of the dyadic format is that it naturally matches some existing conversational formats, such as telephone calls, so that the participants can respond to the moderator's questions by simply talking back and forth. Our work in Morgan et al. (2016) illustrates this through dyadic interviews with pairs of rural physicians. Given the participants' relative isolation, focus groups would have been impractical; as an alternative, the telephone conversations produced a lively exchange of experiences and options.

At the other end of the size spectrum, there is clearly room for innovation with very large groups. Although the two participants in a dyadic interview clearly represent a minimum size for focus groups, the upper end of the size spectrum remains open. One potential model for further work in this area comes from meetings known as World Cafes or Knowledge Cafes (e.g., Brown and Isaacs 2001). These meetings typically involve 25 participants who are split into smaller groups of five or so. There are often two sections to the overall session, with participants moving to new groups to share the content of their earlier discussion. This is just one possible approach to larger focus groups, but it does demonstrate the potential for further experimentation at this level. For example, if an initial round of small groups each had a moderator, then the initial round could be followed by a group consisting of a senior researcher leading a discussion amongst the moderators. This approach could have the advantage of summarizing a rather larger volume of data in a relatively rapid period of time.

Further Opportunities for Innovation: Heterogeneity in Group Composition

One area that has long been open for more inventive work is heterogeneity in group composition. This is a good example of a research design that may well get over-used because it works so well. The more participants share a similar background and outlook with regard to the topic, the easier it is for them to generate a free-flowing discussion. Because the quality of data from a focus group depends on the quality of the interaction amongst the participants, anything that facilitates that interaction has obvious value, and homogeneity has a powerful influence in this direction.

Aside from simply having more familiarity with homogeneous groups, I suspect that one of the reasons for the lack of heterogeneous groups in focus group research is the potential for conflict. In general, focus groups attempt to avoid conflict amongst participants, and one good way to accomplish that is to bring together participants who share similar experiences and perspectives. But pursuing this strategy to the point of limiting heterogeneity may be taking things too far. The concept of 'common ground' is useful in this context (Hyden and Bulow 2003; Lehoux et al. 2006; Moen et al. 2010). Common ground emphasizes a mutual understanding of the issues involved in the topic, so that each participant can be reasonably sure that the others will be able to relate to what they say. Even when there is considerable room for disagreement within the group, there can still be enough common ground to carry on a respectful discussion.

The most serious barrier to doing more with heterogeneous groups is undoubtedly a lack of knowledge about implementing them. Without enough security about *how* to make heterogeneous groups work, there is little reason to think about *when* to use them. I believe that thinking in terms of common ground can also help in this regard, because anything that gives the participants a sense of common ground will help them engage with each other. As an example, I had a colleague who conducted a programme evaluation for a project that occurred at multiple units within an organization. The evaluation plan called for bringing together representatives of the different units to compare their experiences, even though their jobs had very little to do with each other and most had not met previously. The solution my colleague found was to have them each talk about their history with the programme on their unit: How did they first hear about the programme? How well did their first encounters with the programme go? And so on. The participants very quickly realized that one thing they all had in common was their experience with the programme, and they easily developed a group dynamic around the reasons why the programme did or did not work well in their particular units. The result was a deeper understanding of not just what the barriers and facilitators were for this programme but also how those factors operated across a wide set of circumstances.

This example suggests a general strategy for dealing with heterogeneous groups, starting with descriptions of common ground in the instructions, and following through with questions that allow the participants to use their shared vocabulary and discover their mutual interests. The first or 'discussion starter' question is particularly important in this regard, because it is the point when the participants begin to learn about each other and the ways in which they relate to the research topic. Of course, building on the earlier instructions and paying careful attention to the discussion starter question are both tactics that apply to focus groups in general, but this also indicates that working with heterogeneous groups may require little more than thoughtful adaptations of the procedures we already use.

Further Opportunities for Innovation: Emergent Approaches to Research Design

One of the things that the chapters of this book share with the existing literature on focus groups is a strong tendency toward linear research design, which begins with a pre-determined research design followed by data collection, and completed by a separate data analysis phase. This format is rather ironic, given the frequent advice in qualitative research that our research should evolve and emerge during data collection. Our choices about both which people to interview and what questions to ask them should be open to change once we encounter issues that go beyond what we anticipated in our early thinking. The initial research design is a best guess based on our assumptions before we encounter any real data.

Letting the research design emerge during data collection does not require stopping after each group to reconsider how to do the next group. Instead, I have argued (Morgan et al. 2008) that there are a number of ways to 'plan for emergence.' One option mimics the classic three sections of a funnel format in interviewing, except that rather than applying the funnel within each interview, the same structure is used for three sets of interviews. This means that the first set of interviews will be largely exploratory and use a few broad questions to explore the participants' perspectives. Based on a preliminary analysis of what is learned in those groups, the next set would pursue a narrower, more researcher-driven agenda. Finally, a set of 'wrap-up' groups would target specific issues or subpopulations that would provide closure for the project as a whole.

This three-part structure is only one example of how a project could be self-consciously separated into smaller subsets. Consider the following possibilities for two-part designs. One option would be to stop at the midpoint and reassess the initial decisions about group composition and interview questions. Another option would allow for more extensive pre-testing than usual, by setting aside a smaller set of more exploratory groups at the beginning, followed by setting the design for the bulk of the groups. A final option would be to conduct the majority of the groups according to a pre-determined design, and then allow for a smaller set of follow-up groups that addressed concerns that were discovered during those earlier groups. As these examples illustrate, there are many alternatives that fall between a linear approach that adheres to a fixed research design and an anything goes approach that allows for a completely emergent research design.

Conclusions

In the end, the point of being more inventive in doing focus groups is not innovation for innovation's sake; instead, the goal is to expand the range of possibilities for future research. The process of designing any set of focus groups consists of a number of different decisions: who the participants should be, what questions to ask, how to moderate the groups, etc. In making those decisions, we need to consider the best available models. Often, this decision-making has an 'if ... then' character, such as 'if you are in this situation, then consider these options.' But in order to pursue this kind of reasoning, we have to know both what our options are and how to evaluate those options. That is the point behind the approaches to focus groups presented throughout this volume:, to demonstrate both best practices in current research and new ideas for future research.

References

Brown, J. and Isaacs, D. (2001) 'The world cafes: Living knowledge through conversations that matter'. *The Systems Thinker*, 12: 1–5

Hyden, L. and Bulow P. (2003) 'Who's talking: Drawing conclusions from focus groups'. *International Journal of Social Research Methodology*, 6: 305–321

Krueger, R. (1988) *Focus Groups: A Practical Guide for Applied Research*. Thousand Oaks, CA: Sage.

Lehoux, P., Poland, B. and Daudelin, G. (2006) 'Focus group research and "the patient's view"'. *Social Science and Medicine*, 63: 2091–2104.

Merton, R. and Kendall, P. (1946) 'The focused interview'. *American Journal of Sociology*, 51: 541–557.

Merton R., Fiske, M., and Kendall, P. (1956). *The Focused Interview: A Manual of Problems and Procedures*. New York: Free Press

Moen, J., Antonov, K., Nilson, L. and Ring, L. (2010) 'Interaction between participants in focus groups with older patients and general practitioners'. *Qualitative Health Research*, 20: 607–617

Morgan, D. (1988) *Focus Groups as Qualitative Research*. Thousand Oaks, CA: Sage.

Morgan, D. (2015) *Dyadic Interviews*. London: Routledge

Morgan, D. and Hoffman, K. (2016) 'A System for Coding the Interaction in Focus Groups and Dyadic Interviews', Paper presented at the *Fifteenth Qualitative Methods Conference*, Glasgow, UK.

Morgan, D., Fellows, C. and Guevara, H. (2008) 'Emergent approaches to focus groups research', In S. Hesse-Biber and P. Leavy (eds.), *Handbook of Emergent Methods*. New York, NY: Guilford Press, pp. 189–206.

Morgan, D., Ataie, J., Carder, P. and Hoffman, K. (2013) 'Introducing dyadic interviews as a method for collecting qualitative data'. *Qualitative Health Research*, 23(9): 1276–1284.

Morgan, D., Eliot, S., Lowe, R. and Gorman, P. (2016) 'Dyadic interviews as a tool for qualitative evaluation'. *American Journal of Evaluation*, 37: 109–117.

David L. Morgan is a professor of sociology at Portland State University. He is a sociological social psychologist, who is widely known for his work on focus groups, including his book, *Focus Groups as Qualitative Research*, and as co-author of *The Focus Group Kit*. In addition, he has worked extensively on mixed methods, including a book *Integrating Qualitative and Quantitative Methods*. Most recently, he has published *Essentials of Dyadic Interviewing*.

Index

A

Absence of geographical and temporal limitations, 232
Academic and non-academic research teams, 36
Access, 4, 7, 18–21, 47, 50, 65, 71, 84, 89, 94, 100, 163, 164, 172, 179, 187, 229, 233, 245, 259, 304, 305, 345, 368, 369, 371, 372
Adolescent psychological well-being, 304
Advertising interviews without being clear about the topic and the aim of the research project, 374
Agency, 4, 55, 208, 263, 268, 305, 306, 311, 316, 347, 367, 379, 382
Agreement, 9, 26, 91, 98, 282–285, 293, 294, 295, 307, 373, 375, 378, 382, 396, 400, 416

Agricultural biotechnology, 10, 344, 345, 350, 353, 355
Analysis, 10, 36, 46, 47–48, 53–55, 117, 131, 133, 135, 140, 160, 164, 166, 167, 172, 190, 252, 253, 264, 281, 282, 285, 294–295, 325, 346, 350, 352, 355–358, 371, 379
Analysis and interpretation, 352, 355–358
Analysis and reporting skills, 36, 47–48
Analyzing, 2, 4, 5, 9, 11, 36, 47, 53, 150, 157–159, 162, 172, 190, 195, 198, 270, 281, 282, 295, 330, 379–381, 383, 393
Anonymity, 18, 23, 243, 244, 245
Anticipatory or 'upstream' method, 10, 21, 343–359
Apply content analysis, 89
Approach, 2, 277–295

Asynchronous CMC, 229
Asynchronous online focus groups, 8, 229
Attitudes towards European integration, 366, 374, 377
Audio-video applications/Audio-visual applications, 229, 233
Automatic-logging option, 232

B

Back-translated/back-translation, 77, 88
Basic rules, 235, 242
Benefits, 2, 21, 27, 28, 68, 91, 93, 97, 98, 114, 115, 120, 132, 135, 141, 148, 243, 270, 351, 358
Benefits of focus groups, 97
Bi-lingual community members, 67
Bi-lingual moderator, 74
Blurred the focus, 11
Brainstorm/ Brainstorming, 117, 184, 212

C

Card exercise, 11
Cards, 99, 170, 171, 377
Chat rooms, 229, 244
Citizen and stakeholder engagement, 180
Climate change, 2, 7, 164–167, 186, 190, 192, 349, 351, 352
Climate change modification technology, 349
Climate geoengineering, 10, 346, 349, 351, 353, 354, 358

Closed social world, 3, 19, 20, 30, 32
Co-construction of meaning, 4, 19, 25, 168
Coded, 141, 166, 307
Code/coding, 89, 117, 141
Collaboration, 5, 48, 92
Collaborative production of discourse, 10
Collective identities, 294
Collective narrative, 62
Collective production of discourse, 2, 9, 277–295
Colloquial language, 67
Combining homogeneity and heterogeneity in the sampling, 367
Combining quantitative and qualitative data, 141
Commissioning, 4, 36, 37, 48, 54, 116, 199, 200, 344
Communal narratives, 9, 316
Communal Storytelling, 316–317
Community, 5, 10, 44, 61, 62, 65–68, 71, 72, 75, 77, 86, 89, 92, 94, 110, 163, 194, 198, 200, 253–255, 268, 269, 304–306, 310, 313, 314
Community-based organizations, 5, 86
Community-based process, 94
Community partnerships, 92
Community storybuilding, 310
Comparing focus groups and individual interviews, 159–161
Comparison(s), 11, 39, 43–45, 51, 54, 55, 112, 159, 161, 168, 208, 228, 235, 237, 238, 375, 380, 381

Competing storylines, 337
Complex health-related behaviour change interventions, 6, 109, 111
Complexities of mundane performativity, 395
Composition of the group/ the characteristics of its members, 22, 94, 286, 287, 407
Computer literacy, 228
Computer Medicated Communication (CMC), 228
Concerns about personal appearance, 232
Confidentiality, 24, 25, 30, 71, 86, 94, 243–245
Conflictualization, 366, 378, 380
Consensus, 2, 9, 89, 158, 166, 214, 284–287, 293–295, 352, 401, 402
Constant comparative approach, 117
The content of data, 11
Context, 129–151, 155–173
Conversation analytical traditions, 355
Cost, 36, 39, 45, 98, 100, 115, 232, 236, 372
Counter-narratives, 10, 305
Counting, 141
Criteria, to be used in selecting an online platform that is suitable for online audio and video-based focus groups, 38, 39, 87, 233, 240, 288, 345–346, 372, 375, 402
Cross-cultural comparisons, 10, 183

Cross-cultural focus group discussions, 59–79
Cross-cultural issues, 90–93, 243
Cross-cultural research, 4, 59, 60–64, 65, 66, 68, 69, 72, 73, 76, 77, 78
Cultural appropriateness, 65, 66
Cultural background, 60, 65
Cultural brokers, 61, 65, 70
Cultural dynamics, 87
Cultural and ethnic diversity, 116
Cultural familiarity, 86
Cultural knowledge, 60, 71, 72, 394
Culturally, 11, 60, 61, 65–68, 74, 181, 214, 260, 267, 390, 392
 On culturally appropriate strategies, 61, 65
Culturally relevant, 61, 66, 67, 68
Cultural norms, 5, 59, 60, 62, 65, 74, 87
Cultural sensitivity, 4, 59, 60, 63, 65, 66
Cultural transferability of focus group data inferences, 392
Culture other than one's own, 86
Culture-specific, 164

D
Data Analysis, 2, 44, 60, 63, 64, 66, 69, 76–79, 89–90, 116, 232, 238, 307, 417
Deadlines, 36, 39, 47, 50–51
Debriefing, 40, 92, 94, 270, 374
Decisions relating to health care and health insurance, 35
Delphi method, 284

De-politicization, 11, 365, 369, 371, 373
Descriptors, 135, 140–141, 148, 150–151
Developing questions and moderating, 371, 376–378
Development, 6
 framework, 111, 115, 122
 model, 115, 116
 phase, 6, 111
 process, 110, 112–113
Dialectic conversation, 293
Diaries/diary, 52, 120, 184, 187, 188, 190, 193, 195, 414
Digital stories as a means of film elicitation, 326
Disciplinary advantages, 19, 29–30
Disciplines, 2, 17, 62, 255, 367
Disclosure of potentially sensitive, or controversial, matters, 23
Discourses, 10, 277–295
Discussion guide, 65–67, 69
Dissent, 214, 283–285, 294
Diversity in the group, 287
Dominant narrative, 212, 317, 326, 327, 339, 340
Dyadic interviews, 414, 415

E

Ecological practices, 7, 164, 166–168
Eliciting data, 19, 21–28
Emergent research design, 418
Empathetic approach, 30
Empowering, 9, 272, 309, 354
'Enactments', 265, 395–397, 399, 401, 404, 405

Environmental issues, 2, 8, 68, 185, 188, 198, 402
Environmental policies, 181, 186–189
Episodic interviews, 164, 169
Ethical, 8, 10, 20, 65, 67, 68, 72, 78, 90, 93, 96, 228, 240, 241, 243–246, 344–346, 354, 374, 374n15
Ethical approval, 65, 68
Ethical concern, 96
Ethical conduct of research, 93
Ethical issues, 8, 68, 228, 240, 241, 243–246, 345, 346, 374n15
Ethical responsibility, 78
Ethical training, 72, 94
Ethnography, 227, 306, 307, 369, 392
Evaluation, 6, 49, 109–111, 114, 122, 129–151, 195, 416
Evaluation questionnaire, 195
Everyday life, 11, 26, 117, 186, 187, 190, 200, 216, 269, 348, 350, 391, 395–396, 399, 404, 405, 407
Exert when they are confronted with a political topic. This can be done with face, 370
Existing social network groups, 398
Experimental approach, 130, 369
Expert knowledge, 45, 55
Exploratory qualitative research, 61, 85
Exploratory tool, 155

F

Face-to-face, 8, 69, 86, 228, 230–232, 235, 237, 238, 240, 242, 244, 245, 369, 376, 378
  communication, 237
  focus groups, 230–232, 235, 238, 242, 244, 245
  groups, 228, 238, 240, 242
Facial expression, 238
Facilitator(s), 9, 23, 40, 69, 70, 78, 79, 88, 92, 93, 95, 96, 97, 111, 118, 122, 251, 255, 281, 290, 291, 417
Facilitators, skills, 5, 9, 92
Feasibility, Feasibility testing, 6, 37, 111
Feeding back results, 168–171
Feminist(s), 87, 305, 307–309, 369
Field Training, 67, 72–73, 78
First or "discussion starter" question, 417
The flash rule, 378
Flexibility, 4, 12, 52, 56, 59, 60, 62–64, 69, 74, 117, 131, 236, 315, 390
Flexibility of "narrative truth", 315
Focus group
  as an anticipatory methodology, 343–359
  facilitation, 8–9, 69, 74–75
Follow-up method, 155
Formative
  focus groups, 75, 114, 118, 120
  phase of intervention development, 118
  research, 110, 111, 113–115, 116–118
Forum Theatre, 255, 262, 266–271

Foster commentary on past narratives, 221
Fracking, 10, 346, 349–351, 354, 358
Framing, 194, 216, 305, 350–352, 354
Funding body/bodies, 1, 3, 5, 53, 57
Funding, funding climate, 2, 4, 6

G

Games, 8, 24, 26, 27, 99, 192, 209, 215, 220, 251, 255, 256–257, 268, 270, 375
Gatekeepers, 20, 21, 23, 210
Generalizability/generalizable/ generalize, 11, 93, 130, 136, 391–393, 396, 397
Go-along' interviews, 209
Grant reviewers, 85–87
Ground rules about communication, 231
Group, 4, 183
  composition, 69, 70, 116, 240, 241, 416–417, 418
  confidentiality, 24, 25
  context of data collection, 61
  discourse, 9, 277, 278, 282, 285, 290, 292, 294–295
  dynamic(s), 70, 72, 74, 98, 158–160, 166, 172, 236, 241, 277, 281–283, 285, 286, 286n6, 287, 288–289, 290, 292, 293, 392, 393, 417
  homogeneity, 286, 287, 287n8, 288
  processes, 157, 158, 284
  size, 70, 241, 414–415

Between-group
  heterogeneity, 288
Within-group homogeneity,
  287, 288
Group is the unit of analysis, 294
Group size and composition, 70
Groups with ongoing relationships
  among participants, 97
Groups of strangers, 97
Groupthink, 281

H

Hard-to-reach, 5, 31, 93
Hard-to-reach' participants, 5
Heterogeneity, 12, 288,
  367, 374–375,
  382, 416–417
Heterogeneity in group
  composition, 416–417
Heterosexist bias, 93
Hierarchies, 20, 29, 87,
  94, 161, 286, 396
Homogeneous and
  heterogeneous focus
  group composition,
  12, 22, 116
Homogenous, 22, 286, 287
How to provide information in a
  suitably balanced way, 183
Human Immunodeficiency Virus
  (HIV), 5, 83–102, 115, 158
Hybrid focus groups, 179–200
Hybridization, 180, 181, 187
Hypotheses, 43, 55, 98, 155, 156
Hypothetical questions or
  scenarios, 67

I

Identity, 9, 10, 22, 88, 89, 92, 93,
  98, 163, 220, 238, 244, 260,
  283, 304–309, 311–313, 317,
  343, 381
Image Theatre, 255, 257–262, 265,
  268, 270
Implementation, 6, 37, 90, 92,
  110–112, 122, 133, 135, 136,
  190, 193, 200
Implications for participants, 28–29
Indirect formulations, 289
The individual interview, 161, 254,
  307, 309
Information searches, 184
Informed consent, 68, 243–246
Initial screening, 231
Innovations, 2, 3, 8–9, 12, 184, 191,
  209, 227, 357, 411–419
Insiders, 5, 18, 20, 21, 71, 75, 92
Instant messaging, 229–232, 234,
  240, 244
Instructions, 241, 243, 286,
  288–289, 306, 417
Instrument design and
  translation, 66
Interaction and interpersonal
  communication, 390
Inter-disciplinary collaborations, 2, 3
Interpretation(s), 48, 66, 71, 73, 76,
  77, 79, 92, 93, 141, 157, 162,
  167, 169, 172, 190, 192, 213,
  215, 220, 237, 257, 258, 314,
  326, 352, 355–358, 396
Interpretative studies of risk
  perception, 181
Interpreter, 74, 271
Interpretive paradigm, 63, 64

Interview guide, 46, 162–164, 172
Invitation, 234–235
Iterative process, 70, 88, 111, 113, 166

K

Keyword analyses approach, 150

L

Language, 36, 44–45, 54, 60–62, 65, 66–78, 88, 89, 92, 97, 98, 100, 119, 122, 253, 254, 256, 257, 259–263, 265–269, 271, 306, 309, 314, 370, 380
Large group, 415
Lay citizens, 7, 183, 187, 189, 367–372, 379
Lay ethical engagement, 10, 345
Levels and degrees of recognizability and situatedness, 397
Linguistic background, 60
Linguistic and cultural identities, 252, 254, 270, 271
Linguistic skills, 44
Logistical challenges, 4, 23
Longitudinal, 6, 8, 132, 133, 207–223
Longitudinal design, 8
Longitudinal Focus Group, 207–223
Longitudinal mixed-methods design, 132

M

Macro and micro approaches, 2
Manage group dynamics, 70, 74
Marginalized communities, 309
Marginalized populations, 93, 95, 317
Matching of moderators, 71

Materials, 7, 10, 12, 53, 54, 97, 112, 120, 171, 172, 180, 183, 184, 185, 187, 193, 195, 196, 197, 215, 218, 260, 294, 352, 401, 403, 404, 414
Media representations, 12, 163, 391, 398, 404, 405, 407
Metaphors, 6, 135, 140–141, 148, 150, 151, 157, 189–192, 256, 261, 263
Methodological principles, 60
Methodological rigour, 59, 63
Methodological skills, 4, 46, 55, 65
Mhealth, 6, 109–124
Mixed methods, 2, 3, 5–7, 61, 85, 88, 90, 97, 98–100, 131, 132, 133, 150, 156, 209
  design, 2, 3, 85, 132
  research, 6, 61, 98–100
Moderating, 169, 228, 238, 241, 242, 293, 347, 353, 367, 371, 376–378
Moderating in a non-directive way, 367
Moderation, 46, 55, 62, 70, 72, 74, 75, 242–243, 280–282, 286, 290–293, 352–353, 377, 378, 382, 401
  issues, 242–243
  techniques, 70, 377
Moderator, 8, 12, 23, 64, 69, 71, 74, 75, 114, 118, 160, 165, 166, 211–213, 230, 231, 233–235, 238, 241, 242, 245, 281, 285, 288–293, 296, 352, 353, 376–378, 378n19, 390, 415
Multi-disciplinary composition of the team, 38

Multi-disciplinary teams, 6
Multifaceted stigma, 93
Multilingual, 36
Multiple languages, 74

N

Nanotechnology, 345, 348, 349, 351, 354, 357
Narrative, 8–10, 61, 62, 76, 94, 95, 131, 141, 150, 157, 184, 185, 191, 192, 194, 208–210, 212–214, 216–218, 220, 221, 262, 304–317, 326, 326n1, 327, 330, 338–340, 349, 355, 357, 358, 376, 380, 393
Narrative or discourse theoretical traditions, 355
Narratives from the media, 185
Naturally-occurring groups, 163
Naturally-occurring settings, 179
Nature of the discussion topic, 286
Negotiating access, 19–21
Network focus groups, 399
Networks, 12, 19, 27, 39, 43, 47, 53, 240, 391, 393, 398, 399, 401, 404, 405, 407
Nominal groups, 284
Nondirective approach, 376–378
Non-directive interviewing, 11, 382
Non-directive moderation, 290–293
Non-verbal communication, 238, 240
Nonverbal interaction, 237
"No show" participants, 240
Not to disclose the central topic, 11
Number of participants, 231, 234, 235, 240–242

O

One-to-one interviews, 7, 169
Online focus groups, 8, 227–246
Online venues, 229, 230, 233, 244
Online video, 8, 234, 235, 242
Open and non-leading questions, 66
Optimal number of participants, 231, 235
Oral consent, 68
Oral mapping exercise, 7
Outsider(s), 17–32, 60, 61, 71, 75, 79, 92, 93, 211
Outsourcing qualitative data collection, 37
Oval mapping, 194–195
Overdisclosure, 96, 97

P

Panel members, 372
Para-verbal cues, 238
Participant
  eligibility criteria, 87
  'homework', 187
Participatory, 2, 8, 207–209, 211–214, 221, 255
Participatory framework, 8, 208, 211–212, 222
Participatory research, 208, 212, 214, 221
Particular proximal relationship, 353
Patterns, 7, 11, 19, 89, 166, 181, 187, 198, 310, 355, 391, 394, 395, 398
Patterns in the data, 89
Patterns of practical reasoning, 7, 181

Perceptions and experiences of growing older, 326
Perform, 97, 252, 255, 260, 263, 268, 270
Performance-Based Focus Groups (PBFGs), 8, 9, 251–272
Performative exercises, 254
Performativity, 8, 11, 210, 217, 254, 257, 270, 389–397
Physical setting, 22
Piloting, implementation and evaluation, 122
Piloting phase, 122
Policy makers, 7, 35, 37, 53, 130, 132, 186–188, 193, 196, 199, 200, 344, 349
Policy-making and decision-making, 180
Policy-oriented research in health care, 36
Political discourse analysis, 379
Political heterogeneity, 374–375, 382
Postmodern theories of narrative, 316
Potential for conflict, 416
Potentially "excluded" people, 185
Power
  dynamics, 87, 88, 94
  imbalances, 208
  relationships, 4
Practical interest, 10, 354
Practical reasoning, 7, 179–200
Practice theoretical perspective, 11, 391, 394–398, 407
Practice theoretical syntheses, 395
Pre-acquainted groups, 372
Pre-established relationships, 28

Pre-existing, 4, 24, 44, 47, 184, 185, 233, 286n6, 380
Pre-existing groups, 24, 286n6
Pre-existing knowledge, 184, 185
Pre-existing panels, 47
Pre-testing, 110, 111, 117, 118–122
Privacy, 24, 86, 94, 96, 243–245, 311
Privacy and security issues, 245
Probe(s), 66, 69, 72, 74, 79, 88, 89, 114, 215, 221, 352, 353
Problem structuring methods (PSMs) approach, 180, 181, 184, 187, 194
Problem structuring techniques, 187
Programme
  evaluation, 6, 129–151, 416
  implementers, 6, 133–136, 148
  participants, 130, 131, 135, 148, 151
  recipients, 6
Promote discussion, 66, 70
Public
  opinion, 2, 163, 189, 344, 345, 371, 372
  policy, 10, 344
  vs. private space, 243
Publications, 19, 38, 52, 53, 122, 156, 366n1, 379n20
Public engagement in science and technology, 344
'Publics', 46, 183, 185, 186, 354
Purposive recruitment, 70
Purposive sampling, 135, 136, 240

Q
Qualitative Longitudinal Research (QLR), 208, 210, 216–217

Index

Qualitative School of Madrid, 9, 277–296
Quality of internet connection, 234
Quality of sound and video, 234
Question guide, 165
Question(s), 9, 11, 18–20, 25, 26, 29, 36, 37, 39, 48, 53, 66, 67, 72, 78, 84, 86, 88, 89, 94, 95, 100, 113, 130, 132, 136, 140, 158, 163, 165, 168, 170–172, 182, 183, 186–189, 192, 194, 195, 197–199, 211, 213, 216, 221, 229, 231, 235, 241, 242, 252, 253, 255, 257, 260, 265, 266, 268–270, 282, 287–291, 293, 294, 307, 312, 313, 316, 327, 340, 345, 347, 348, 350, 353, 368, 370, 371, 375, 376–378, 382, 389, 399–402, 405, 407, 415, 417, 418
Questioning, 9, 26, 29, 66, 67, 316
Questionnaire(s), 19, 23, 89, 98, 131, 156, 173, 182, 187, 188, 194, 195, 380
Quotations, 76, 78, 115

R

Random sampling, 6, 135
Random selection, 133, 136
Range of participants, 236
Range of topics, 22, 24
Ranking, 170
Rapport, 67, 68, 70, 71, 72, 74, 75, 114, 117, 212, 286n6, 307
Recognizability, 391–406
Recommendation, 10, 35, 40, 43, 53, 55–57, 110, 287n7
Reconvened, 12, 180, 181–183, 185, 193, 195, 353, 412–414
Reconvened discussion groups, 181, 182
Reconvened focus groups, 7, 12, 180, 181–183, 185, 413
Recruiting purely lay citizens, 367, 371–374
Recruitment, 46, 93
  issues, 228, 240
  strategy, 98
Recruitment was topic-blind, 350
Recruit participants, 36, 46, 69, 75, 372
Reflective interval periods, 180
Reflexive, 2, 7, 10, 97, 162, 195, 196, 218
Reflexive approach, 7
Reflexivity, 64, 70, 73, 74, 77, 199, 253
Relational Feminist methods, 305
Relational Feminist Theory, 305
Relational framework, 10, 91
Relational way of being, 304
Relationship with time and the future, 354
A relevant positionality, 354
Reliability, 130, 141–147, 150, 359
'Repeated' focus groups, 413
Repeated groups, 180, 185, 413
Repeated and Reconvened Groups as an Option, 412–414
Research design, 5, 7, 12, 90, 131, 132, 155–157, 159, 162, 164, 167, 172, 173, 180, 182–184, 228, 240–242, 288, 390, 416, 417–418
Research design issues, 228, 240–242

Index 431

Research ethics boards, 86, 94
Resource allocation exercise, 187, 188, 195
Responsive materials, 7, 10
Rhetoric and narrative exercises, 191
Rigour, 4, 43, 59, 63, 161
Risk/benefits for participants, 243
Role of the facilitator, 9
Role of the moderator, 160, 281, 352

S
Sample
   selection, 8
   size, 64, 70
Sample/sampling, 6, 8, 10, 11, 19, 22, 30, 43, 47, 54, 55, 64, 70, 88, 89, 93, 98, 115, 135, 136, 190, 193, 231, 240, 241, 353–354, 367, 371, 372, 374–375, 390, 398, 399, 405
Sampling: mixing social homogeneity and political heterogeneity, 374–375
Sampling pool, 47, 371
Sampling by segmentation, 375
Saturation, 64, 70, 288, 404
Science and technology studies, 343–359
Scientific realism, 389
Section on a simulated controversy, 351
Segmentation, 185, 375, 380
Segmented, 88, 183, 185
Segmented focus groups by age, 88
Segments, 241
Selection of study participants, 64
Self-analysis exercises, 195
Self-presentation, 238

Semi-structured topic guide, 88
Sensitive, 5, 23–25, 29, 30, 71, 75, 78, 79, 83–102, 115, 234, 242, 245
Sensitive topic, 5, 24, 30, 78, 79, 90, 93–98, 115
Sex, 5, 83–102, 306
Sexual Minority, 83, 93
Sexual orientation and gender identity, 93
Shared dialogue, 214
Shared life histories or work experience, 354
Silencing, 284, 285, 313
Similarities and differences, 26, 148, 278–282
Simulated newspaper article, 7, 194
Situational, 11, 366n4, 391–394, 397, 398, 407
Situationalism argument, 397
Situationally negotiated, 11, 398
Skilled focus group facilitators, 95
Skills, 4, 5, 8, 9, 36, 38, 40, 44, 46, 47, 50, 54, 72, 74, 78, 92, 183, 228, 230, 231, 235, 370, 372, 379
Small groups, 11, 27, 187, 231, 286n6, 343, 354, 377, 392, 414, 415
Social constructionist/constructivism, 131, 157–159, 172, 308, 389
Social constructivist approach, 158
Social context cues, 8, 236–238
Social dynamics of group interactions, 390
Social group norms, 180

Social homogeneity, 374–375, 382
Socially recognizable, 11, 389–407
Social norms, 61, 62, 173, 339, 396, 399
Social psychological approach, 162
Social representations, 157, 158, 162, 163, 164–168, 172, 294
Social-structural context(s), 93, 94
Social-structural factors, 85
Socio-narrative/socio-narratology, 10, 325, 327
Special/vulnerable populations, 243
Sports science, 2, 3, 17
Stakeholders, 36, 47, 53, 112, 135, 140, 141, 148, 180–182
Stand-alone focus group, 2
Stand-alone method, 155–159, 162
Stereotypical assumptions, 326, 329
Stimulate discussion, 169, 170, 377
Stimulation, 170
Stimulus materials, 12, 180, 184, 185, 195, 352, 401, 404, 414
Stories, 10, 131, 173, 209, 262, 270, 304, 305, 307–310, 313, 314, 316, 317, 326, 327, 328–340, 352–354
Structural inequalities, 304
Structured approach, 241, 292n12
Study design, 60, 63–66, 76
Subjective/subjectivity, 64, 73, 77, 95, 97, 130, 133, 164, 169, 219, 308, 367n5
Substantive content, 220, 390
Survey, 5, 61, 85, 98–100, 155, 156, 159, 172, 209, 210, 227, 288, 368, 368n8, 372, 374
Sustainability, 2, 186, 187, 199
Symbolic Interactionism, 236
Synchronous audio and video-based online focus groups, 233–236
Synchronous online focus groups, 8, 227–246
Synchronous text-based online focus groups, 230–232
Systematic comparisons, 161

T

Taken-for-granted assumptions, 335
Techniques of moderation, 242
Technological and environmental issues, 185
Tender/tendering, 36, 38–40, 43, 45, 54, 56
Terminology, 61, 85, 93, 111, 115, 412
Thematic analysis, 89, 163, 188, 196
Themes, 89, 98, 116, 117, 119, 132, 141, 159, 166, 190, 212, 213, 217, 218, 220, 307, 349, 353, 355, 389, 399, 412
Theoretical background, 157, 162, 167
Theoretical developments, 3, 9–12
Theoretically-focused applications, 2
Theoretically-informed focus group, 9
Theoretical perspectives, 11, 156, 389–391, 394–398, 407
Theoretical principles, 4, 63
Time and Budget, 65, 68–69
Timeframe, 46
Toolkit, 196, 208, 412
Topic areas, 2, 3
Topic guide, 88, 116, 211, 212, 352, 353

Training, skills, language and identity, 92
Transcribing, 73
Transcript(s)/transcriptions, 45, 70, 71, 73, 74, 76–78, 89, 166, 188, 231, 232, 236, 238, 240, 245, 264, 309, 355, 380
Transdisciplinary collaboration, 85, 92
Translated transcripts, 71, 73, 76, 77
Translate/translating, 6, 7, 66–78, 88, 89, 92, 111, 182, 187, 196, 198, 199, 258, 282, 293, 353, 368, 370, 376, 379
Translating qualitative data, 6
Transparency, 77
Travel, 45, 49, 183, 232, 236
Triangulated/Triangulation, 7, 90, 132, 133, 135, 140, 148, 150, 151, 155–173
Trust, 5, 69, 74, 92, 94, 132, 181, 286n6, 287, 307, 344, 347, 354, 356
Type of moderation, 286
Typing skills, 230, 231, 235

U

'Upstream public engagement,' 11, 344, 345
Use media representations as stimulus material, 404
User-centred approach, 111
Using ordinary food items as input, 401

Using quotes from policy institutions, 351
Utilizing existing social networks, 12

V

Validation, 50, 156, 186
Validity, 61, 67, 77, 90, 130, 157, 198, 359, 396
Verbatim transcripts, 188
Vernacular, 92, 93, 97, 100
Very large focus groups, 12
Very small, 12, 414
Video focus group workshops, 207–210
Video-recorded/recording, 11, 207, 237, 377
Vignette script, 184
Visual approaches, 208
Visual artefacts, 217, 220, 221
Visual methods, 8, 10, 208, 325–340
Voluntary participation, 94

W

Web-conferencing applications, 229, 233
Web Messaging facilities, 229, 230
Working with children and young people, 208
Work spaces, 32

Y

Youth development, 6, 130, 132, 133

CPSIA information can be obtained
at www.ICGtesting.com
Printed in the USA
LVOW13*1559081017
551580LV00011BA/336/P